# LIBERALISM, ANTI-SEMITISM, AND DEMOCRACY

Peter Pulzer
*(by kind permission of Jane Bown and Christ Church, Oxford)*

# Liberalism, Anti-Semitism, and Democracy

## Essays in Honour of Peter Pulzer

edited by

HENNING TEWES

and

JONATHAN WRIGHT

OXFORD

UNIVERSITY PRESS

# OXFORD
UNIVERSITY PRESS

Great Clarendon Street, Oxford OX2 6DP
Oxford University Press is a department of the University of Oxford.
It furthers the University's objective of excellence in research, scholarship,
and education by publishing worldwide in

Oxford New York

Athens Auckland Bangkok Bogotá Buenos Aires
Cape Town Chennai Dar es Salaam Delhi Florence Hong Kong Istanbul
Karachi Kolkata Kuala Lumpur Madrid Melbourne Mexico City Mumbai
Nairobi Paris São Paulo Shanghai Singapore Taipei Tokyo Toronto Warsaw
with associated companies in Berlin Ibadan

Oxford is a registered trade mark of Oxford University Press
in the UK and in certain other countries

Published in the United States
by Oxford University Press Inc., New York

British Library Cataloguing in Publication Data
Data available

Library of Congress Cataloging in Publication Data

Liberalism, anti-semitism, and democracy: essays in honour of Peter Pulzer/edited by
Jonathan Wright, Henning Tewes.
p. cm.
Includes bibliographical references.
1. Antisemitism—Germany. 2. Antisemitism—Austria.
3. Jews—Germany—History—1800–1933. 4. Liberalism—Germany—History.
5. Jews—Germany—Intellectual life. 6. Germany—Ethnic relations. 7. Pulzer, Peter G.J.
I. Wright, Jonathan. II. Tewes, Henning.
DS147.G4 L52 2001    320.51′0943—dc21    2001021212

ISBN 0-19-829723-8

1 3 5 7 9 10 8 6 4 2

Typeset by J&L Composition Ltd, Filey, North Yorkshire
Printed in Great Britain
on acid-free paper by
Biddles Ltd.,
Guildford & King's Lynn

# PREFACE

This is a collection of essays in honour of Peter Pulzer, Gladstone Professor Emeritus of Politics and Public Administration at All Souls College, Oxford. Contributions focus on some of the central themes in Pulzer's scholarship: the failed emancipation of Jews in Germany and Austria and the rise of political anti-Semitism, as well as the democratization and political stabilization of Germany and Austria after 1945. Common to all the essays is a concern with liberalism and the fate of liberal democracy in twentieth-century Europe.

In British academia the practice of honouring the achievements of a particular scholar by means of a *Festschrift* is less frequent than in Germany and Austria. Hence a few words about the history of this volume. Some of the contributors are Peter Pulzer's contemporaries and colleagues, others are former students. They have written from universities and other institutions in Britain, the United States, Germany, Austria, and Poland. For the editors it was particularly encouraging to encounter the immediate enthusiasm of those approached about the idea. The reason, we are certain, is not only Peter's academic distinction, but also his popularity as a person. What this *Festschrift* celebrates, in other words, is not only the scholar, but also the man.

H.T., J.W.
*Warsaw and Oxford,*
*March 2000*

# ACKNOWLEDGEMENTS

The editors would like to record their thanks to the following people and institutions: Angela Davies from the German Historical Institute in London translated Fritz Stern's text which appeared originally in German in his 'Das feine Schweigen. Historische Essays'. (München, C.H. Beck, 1999). I.B. Tauris granted permission to reprint Peter Pulzer's essay 'From Danube to Isis: A Career in Two Cultures', which appeared originally in Peter Alter (ed.) *Out of the Third Reich: Refugee Historians in Post-War Britain* (London: I.B. Tauris, 1998). Dominic Byatt and Amanda Watkins from Oxford University Press provided kind and professional editorial help from the very beginning of this project.

# CONTENTS

## III Citizenship and Human Rights

## IV Responsible Governments and Stable Coalitions?

## V A Celebration of Genius

# LIST OF FIGURES

# LIST OF TABLES

# LIST OF CONTRIBUTORS

SUDHIR HAZAREESINGH is a Fellow of Balliol College and a University Lecturer in Politics, University of Oxford

DAVID HINE is an Official Student (Tutorial Fellow) at Christ Church and a University Lecturer in Politics, University of Oxford

MAX KAASE is Professor of Political Science and Comparative Social Research as well as Dean of Humanities and Social Sciences at the International University Bremen.

ANDREI S. MARKOVITS is Professor of Politics in the Department of Germanic Languages and Literatures and Adjunct Professor of Political Science and Sociology at the University of Michigan, Ann Arbor

JAN W. MÜLLER is a Fellow at All Souls College, Oxford

WOLFGANG C. MÜLLER is Professor of Government at the University of Vienna

JAN PALMOWSKI is a Lecturer in European Studies and Director of the Centre for Twentieth-Century Cultural Studies, King's College, University of London

WILLIAM E. PATERSON is Professor of Politics and Director at the Institute for German Studies at the University of Birmingham

ANTON PELINKA is Professor of Political Science at the University of Innsbruck

DAVID SCHOENBAUM is Professor of History at the University of Iowa

DAVID SOUTHERN is a Barrister and visiting Professor of Law at Queen Mary and Westfield College, University of London

FRITZ STERN is University Professor Emeritus, Columbia University

HENNING TEWES is the Director of the Konrad-Adenauer-Foundation in Poland

JONATHAN WRIGHT is an Official Student (Tutorial Fellow) at Christ Church and a University Lecturer in Politics, University of Oxford

# 1

# Subtle Silence and its Consequences

## *Fritz Stern*

I am delighted to join colleagues in celebrating Peter Pulzer's achievements in age and work. What follows is a translation of a lecture I gave at the University of Munich in November 1998 under the title 'The Subtle Silence: Steps toward Criminality'. I hope this will go some way toward expressing my admiration for Peter's work, so deep and so wonderfully varied. I have always seen him as one of those rare colleagues of outstanding quiet courage, a model from which we can all learn and a happy antithetical example to those I discuss below

The phrase 'subtle silence' comes not from me, but from Friedrich Nietzsche. In *Beyond Good and Evil*, Nietzsche, that apprehensive analyst of modern Germany, wrote about the 'profundity' attributed to the Germans, and asked himself what Goethe had actually thought about them. 'But', Nietzsche went on, 'he never pronounced clearly on many things around him, and all his life he was good at maintaining a subtle silence; he probably had good reasons.'[1]

This deliberate, refined, purposeful silence characterizes an attitude with its own history. It also had harmful consequences, and in order to address the contradictions in German history straight away, I should like to quote from a letter which Lise Meitner, the great German–Austrian physicist of Jewish descent, wrote to a Dutch friend in October 1945: 'You ask about my attitude to Germany. I can express it best metaphorically: I feel like a mother who sees that her favourite child has gone hopelessly astray.'[2] Perhaps only a natural scientist could express so much about the German–Jewish relationship so succinctly: the favourite child who has gone hopelessly astray.

But in order to prevent misunderstanding, I must start with a historical observation. When I speak of 'preliminary steps' of the crime, this is not intended to create the impression that I believe in anything like a foreordained 'staircase' of history, an absolutely inevitable procession of events. On the contrary: the historian should always be conscious that history is not predictable or predetermined and that the present always contains many possible futures.

The triumph of National Socialism was not the fulfilment or crowning of German history—that was the legend propagated by the Nazis. Nor was it an accident nor a coincidence. It was avoidable and there were brave opponents. But there was also much in German history and in the life of that time that favoured it including, among other elements—and I do not want to put it more strongly—a certain tradition of 'subtle silence'.

Subtle silence, refined silence, silence to preserve one's own human decency; it may not be far from a pernicious silence or concealment. Certainly, there is a 'noble' or heroic silence, silence that prevents betrayal. In our century, thousands upon thousands of people have been tortured to degrade them into betraying other human beings. As Ernst Reuter wrote: 'Just as I will never cease to hear the screams of those beaten at night, so I could never forget how those comrades of mine stood upright and unbroken before their tormentors and, though defenceless, still commanded their respect.'[3]

But regarding that other silence, I tend to agree with Natasha Mandelstam, who wrote in her memoirs of the time of the Soviet terror: 'Silence is a real crime against humanity'.[4] This cruel century could be given the motto: we did not see the evil, we did not want to see it, we did not want to believe the atrocities—and in this way the silence began. For looking away and remaining silent are closely connected. And yet there is the old promise, the ancient human longing to bear witness, to wrest a memory from misfortune, 'to live in the truth' (Václav Havel) even with oneself.

My concern here is with silence in the political and social realm. Silence and concealment are related in that most individuals and peoples tend to cling to 'pleasing illusions' (as Edmund Burke put it) to spare themselves, their family and community and their nation. This thought is contained in the archetypically German word *Vaterland*, fatherland, which covers so much—the love due, the obligation—and it may especially promote the tendency towards maintaining pleasing illusions. Only at rare historical and psychological moments do individuals and peoples tend to subject themselves to critical scrutiny and shed their pleasing illusions.

It is never easy for a society or nation to achieve an understanding of self. In the nineteenth century the novel made an enormous contribution towards this sort of self-discovery. I am thinking here of Balzac or Dickens and many others, who in their novels subjected their own country and its classes to withering criticism. Dickens's books, for example, are one great indictment of the rapacious inhumanity of a society wallowing in prosperity. And this confrontation, which one finds in English and French poetry and literature, is in every way more muted among German nineteenth-century authors—up to, let us say, Friedrich Spielhagen who was hardly read, or Theodor Fontane who was not read until late in the century and who reacted against the widespread tendency to prettify reality.

Much was passed over in silence, even concealed, in middle-class German society. I say this although I come from a country which at the moment could do with a little more silence about the private sphere. In the German Kaiserreich, however, silence had its unintended consequences—after all, it also invited public exposure, often in a satirical fashion. The master of caustic-affectionate truth was Heine, and his fate among the German public is well-known.

I must limit myself to a brief sketch of silence, which, of course, risks the danger of falsification. I just want to indicate that there was a connection between this silence and later political misjudgements and crimes. In the Kaiserreich, riddled with contradictions as it was, silence was concentrated on private and delicate matters, on money and sexual morality. Its translation into politics began with the falsification of the German victory of 1871. German triumphalism after 1871 has often been documented and described—just think of Nietzsche's warnings. But for all the chauvinism, there was also patriotic criticism, especially after 1890. To name just one example: Max Weber was a patriot and a nationalist, and in passionate analyses he exposed Germany's political inadequacies, the weakness of German politics and political culture, and argued for giving a higher value to parliamentarism as a school for the nation and as a recruiting ground for politicians.

There were a number of critics associated with each other—I am thinking of Max Weber and Ernst Troeltsch, of Hans Delbrück and Walther Rathenau—who turned against the cartel of anxiety (to borrow an expression from Ralf Dahrendorf) and who hoped that a Germany in need of reform would not exhaust itself in dogged class warfare. These men, however, were more the exception than the rule and among the historical profession in particular there were scarcely any critical voices. The profession was loyal to the state. Many of them wrote in the spirit of the Prussian flag: in black and white. What was missing then, and has unfortunately often been missing in German and European history, was true conservatism as Edmund Burke defined it: 'A state without the means of some change is without the means of its conservation.'[5] Too many subscribed only to the principle of conservation in the midst of a society undergoing dynamic transformation.

Silence only became of great political importance, however, with Germany's politicization in the First World War. Truth, we know, is the first victim of war, and in this war the public lie was elevated into a weapon. Censorship was ubiquitous: at the first press conference held by the German General Staff on 3 August 1914, the spokesman said: 'We will not always be able to tell you everything but what we shall tell you is true.'[6] Only the first part of this statement was taken to heart. The longer the appalling war lasted, the more the truth was disguised. Eventually the people were lied to in order not to discourage them. This too is a common experience: the English style of dramatizing danger did not suit the German leaders; they did not trust their own people. Military defeat came as an unanticipated disaster—and at the same moment it was reinterpreted to make the cause of the catastrophe not the superior power of the Allies but enemies at home who had attacked the brave army from the rear. The stab-in-the-back legend was the German triumphalism of 1871 in reverse.

What does this have to do with 'subtle silence'? I am thinking of the many people who were aware of the true situation, who talked about it in private, but who mostly avoided explaining it in public. For example, Bethmann Hollweg, Germany's Chancellor until 1917, published his memoirs in 1921. He knew better than anyone with what disastrous narrow-minded arrogance the military had demanded and been given political responsibility, only to make all the wrong decisions for the sake of a victorious peace (*Siegfrieden*). He, a victim of the High Command, who as early as 1914 had recognized Tirpitz's fatal role as the 'father of the lie', expressed only very mild criticism of Tirpitz and Ludendorff in his memoirs, although Ludendorff had often publicly attacked him. More than thirty years ago I spent some time studying Bethmann, trying to understand the tragedy of this decent man. I came to the following conclusion: 'Perhaps Bethmann's most culpable act was to have seen and understood so much and to have said so little. His semi-silence, though understandable, facilitated the second and worse triumph of the very passions he deplored.'[7]

Some patriotic scholars—if only the difference between patriotism and nationalism had been understood at that time!—made clear statements about the end of the war. Thus Friedrich Meinecke in October 1918: 'A dreadful, gloomy existence awaits us in any circumstances. Although my hatred of the enemy's predatory nature continues to smoulder, my anger and disgust at the German politicians who relied on force is equally intense. Their arrogance and stupidity plunged us into this abyss.'[8] Ernst Troeltsch, the great liberal theologian, wrote on the day of the armistice: 'At least, the killing has stopped, the illusion is dispelled, the system has collapsed under the weight of its sins.'[9] These honest insights were rarely made public, partly because it was feared correctly that any accusations against the old regime would feed the greed of the Allies. The concern for one's own country and the desire not to harm it is absolutely understandable from the perspective of the time, but it too had consequences. And it too belongs to a certain German tendency—and one which has survived almost to the end of the twentieth century—to regard criticism as fouling one's own nest. And those who were keenest on nest hygiene were for the most part those who did their country great harm.

However, at the time of the revolution in November 1918—modest as it was, it still aroused the deepest anxiety—a debate took place, and indeed had to take place, about whether the Kaiser's regime should be publicly scrutinized and exposed and, if so, how. In Munich, Kurt Eisner, Independent Socialist and Bavarian Minister-President, published documents from Munich archives about the outbreak of the war. These documents demonstrated the degree of responsibility of Germany's pre-war policy, the policy of July 1914, for what had happened. There were strong differences of opinion within the German cabinet in March and April 1919: should the documents about the prehistory of the war be published or not? One member of the Reich government, Eduard David, argued that the rest of the world already knew a great deal and the only thing that would help now was 'complete openness and truth'. The present government, having been unaware of this material, should emphasize 'that Germany had completely done away with the old system'.[10] Even Reich President Friedrich Ebert, the reluctant revolutionary, advocated 'the severest condemnation of the sins of the old government'.[11] The cabinet decided to postpone the issue.

The Allied accusation of war guilt followed later, giving the German people a moral basis for its hatred of Versailles. Concealment, encouraged and directed by the German Foreign Ministry, strengthened the hands of Weimar's enemies at home—a sign of the continuity of attitudes among the ruling classes. With few exceptions, German historians contributed to this obfuscation. Although they did thorough work, no real revision of the record of the Kaiserreich was undertaken. There was no intellectual armistice, either within the nation or among nations. However, Fritz Hartung's judgement, expressed in 1946, that German historiography was responsible for the fact 'that the German people learned nothing from the collapse of 1918' may be too harsh.[12]

There were magnificent exceptions, people who worked to achieve clarity and truth. To mention only a few: the often forgotten jurist, Gustav Radbruch, and also Thomas Mann's speech in 1922, *Von deutscher Republik*—an extraordinary declaration of faith by someone who had felt and therefore knew the temptations of the dark depths of German *Innerlichkeit*. And finally there was Ernst Troeltsch, one of the most impressive thinkers of the early post-war period, a Protestant theologian and historian at a time when the Protestant churches were mourning the Kaiserreich and expressing their contempt for the Weimar Republic. On 7 July 1922, after Rathenau's murder, Troeltsch wrote:

Despite all the revolution the old officials are still in power, the courts judge in the spirit of the old regime, the representatives of the left are murdered, while those on the right escape unscathed. The murderers can always disappear with the help of widespread and wealthy organizations, their accomplices are favoured by the law and acquitted . . . Rathenau fell at the front, causing all his friends the most painful anguish. His death is a catastrophe for the fatherland and incomprehensible to the rest of the world, and new evidence of the barbarism of the German ruling classes, which foreigners can use to revive anew the dogma of war guilt.[13]

Troeltsch cannot have found it easy to use the word 'barbarism'. Published in the *Kunstwart*, his views evoked little response. He died seven months later at a relatively young age, a great loss for the non-silent moderates.

It is obvious that there was a dialectical relationship between silence and concealment on the one hand, and revelation and polemical exposure on the other. Even at that time, the drawings of George Grosz and the satires of Kurt Tucholsky were more effective than the complicated truths of Troeltsch or Thomas Mann. Left-wing polemic was so mercilessly accurate that it struck at the heart of what the right held dear. It violated everything they thought holy.

Even Troeltsch could not have imagined the rise of a much crueller form of barbarism. The spiritual confusion of Germany in the final phase of the Weimar Republic is still a shockingly dark chapter. National Socialism managed to combine German idealism with absolute nihilism. To mention just one example of the extreme confusion: in March 1931 the church newspaper with the largest circulation, the *Evangelisch-Lutherische Kirchenzeitung*, described National Socialism as 'the rebellion of a young German Volk that feels deeply the humiliation of the Fatherland, hates and abhors the poisoning of German thought by foreign influences and has inscribed upon its banner the old virtues of truthfulness, honour and loyalty'.[14]

Hitler made no secret of his intentions. Although he could dissemble—both before and after 1933—his murderous hatred of enemies, Jews and Marxists, was unmistakable. The fact that he supported murderers, and supported them without qualification after the murder in Potempa in August 1932, did not diminish the enthusiasm for and the faith in the 'Führer'. In July 1932, 37 per cent voted for him; in June 1940 the percentage would probably have been much higher. I have described National Socialism as a temptation—and it was that—but it was also recognized as such.[15] Many voices were raised in warning but many of them were tied to a political party. Thus Kurt Schumacher in February 1932: 'The whole of National Socialist propaganda is a ceaseless appeal to the filthy beast in man.'[16] Fundamentally, however, the power of National Socialism, its pseudo-religious character, was not understood. Too often, it was interpreted from a Marxist point of view, that is one focused on particular material interests, while not taking seriously enough the widespread faith in salvation, faith in the power of this common man, Hitler, to redeem his country—much of this faith born of resentment.

Much has been written about the failure of the German élites, that is, of those who insisted on a particular moral claim to spiritual leadership. What they had to accept in 1933 in order to be able to believe in a national rising comparable to that of August 1914! The street battles of 1932 and 1933 were over (I can still remember them), but the period of terror in the SA cellars, in Prinz-Albrecht-Straße in Berlin and everywhere else had begun. What followed, blow by blow, was the repudiation of human rights, the dismantling of the rule of law and of the basic civil rights of the constitution—not as an abstract proposition but as an everyday occurrence: 'protective custody' meant the loss of liberty with no right to a judicial defence. Political enemies were condemned to terror, torture, beatings and humiliation: nevertheless, the silence was not broken. Then Jewish and politically 'unreliable' colleagues began to be dismissed from universities, hospitals and all public positions—and this too raised very few protests. The psychologist, Wolfgang Köhler, protested in public and nothing happened to him. If twenty people had done the same, things would have turned out differently, he wrote to an American friend in 1934.[17] Otto Hahn wanted to organize a protest but Max Planck warned him that if thirty protested today, there would be 150 ready to take their positions tomorrow.[18] The dismissals were not simply an attack on science but also on the much-vaunted autonomy of the universities. Then came the burning of books, an explosion of German resentment against the Enlightenment which had already been diagnosed by Friedrich Nietzsche. Without the co-operation of the élites, the rapid implementation of the dictatorship would have been impossible (as Hans Mommsen has demonstrated for the civil service[19]). Subtle silence shifted to cowardly silence and with it came mass conformity and enthusiastic support. One could complement this by a brief mention of the reaction abroad. The Concordat with the Vatican in the summer of 1933, to take one example, was only the beginning of a widespread process of accommodation and sympathy, especially on the right.

Even at this moment, however, and literally in the first hour there were exceptions—Dietrich Bonhoeffer in a radio broadcast on 1 February 1933 warned against a state which made total claims on the lives of its citizens.[20] In Munich it is enough to mention Karl Huber and the Scholls whose courage and decency cost them their lives. Thinking of such people I can only repeat the words of Wolfgang Kunkel, who said here in Munich University: 'Those who nevertheless decided to act and risked their lives deserve our gratitude all the more.'[21]

Was this admiration and gratitude sufficiently felt and expressed after the war? Has the heritage of resistance to two German dictatorships been adequately cherished? We should think not only of resistance. Even active decency on the part of their fellow citizens made a real difference to the lives of the oppressed. We should remember those who behaved well spontaneously because they could not do otherwise, who visited the persecuted and the outcast and helped them. The importance of what the English poet, William Wordsworth, called 'little, nameless, unremembered acts, I Of kindness and of love'[22] should also be acknowledged. The lesson to be drawn from this is that the inviolability of basic human rights must be defended immediately. Martyrdom cannot be expected or demanded but preventive civil courage (*Zivilcourage*) can be learnt and practised.

In the early post-war years, the temptation to maintain a 'subtle silence' was great. In saying this, I do not underestimate the difficulty of arriving at an understanding of the past. But the feelings that Siegfried Kaehler, a German historian who had always kept his distance from National Socialism, expressed to his son in May 1945 may have been shared by many of his colleagues: 'If universities are to continue to exist, we will have the task of preserving the tradition of the real and true Germany and defending it both against the slander already being put about by democratic Jewish propaganda and against Anglo-Saxon self-righteousness.'[23] Only Fritz Fischer's *Griff nach der Weltmacht* ('Germany's bid for world power'—the English edition has the bland title, *Germany's War Aims in the First World War*, which loses the bite of the original) sparked off the first great argument among German historians at the beginning of the 1960s. It was no coincidence that the point at issue was the question of war guilt, something which had always been controversial.

The victims too kept silent for a long time. They felt shame; the memory of humiliation and inhumanity was seldom expressed—in many families it remained unspoken. Only the second generation, the grandchildren, felt constrained to confess and to bear witness. Of course there were exceptions, such as Primo Levi for example, who wrote in order to bear witness, so that memory could arm against recurrence.

It is not surprising that most Germans remained silent after 1945. They were aware of their own sacrifices, but they did not think of the millions of others whose lives had been destroyed, of the murder of six million Jews and the deaths of three and a half million Russian prisoners or of the almost six million in forced labour. Eventually the cruel truth did break through and I should like here to mention Martin Broszat and the Munich Institute for Contemporary History as representative of many other researchers and people who have done so much in recent decades to reveal the past in all its horror.[24] In February 1998, Hubert Markl, the President of the Max-Planck-Gesellschaft gave an admirable speech to mark its fiftieth anniversary:

Those who think that fifty years after the end of the war and total collapse the time for such introspection has passed, are in my opinion deeply misguided. On the contrary, all that has passed is the time for silence born of shame and suppression without remorse, for keeping quiet so as not to wound, and the will to forget of the immediate post-war period.[25]

The past still has many dark places, which must be investigated in this spirit.

Our voices, the voices of scholars are today easily drowned out by the propagandists, who remind us of Jacob Burckhardt's warning against the 'terribles simplificateurs'. Even more dangerous are the media, who play with the horrors of the past and trivialize evil. The trivialization of the Holocaust—especially in the media or in literary form—demeans the memory of the victims. We know that images on television or film convey impressions that are much more immediate than our words and that in the conscious memory of today's world the historical context is often completely forgotten. Such an enormously complicated past demands exacting research, and represents a rare, perhaps unprecedented challenge to scholarship and literature. I believe that we historians bear a special responsibility here.

In conclusion, I should like to reaffirm my sense that 'subtle silence' has done Germany much harm. Silence too has its context; it can be pure gold or common coin. I should like to quote again the people I mentioned at the beginning. Lisa Meitner wrote in the autumn of 1945 to her friend: 'The tragedy is that even people such as Laue or Otto Hahn did not understand the fate to which their passivity consigned their own country.'[26] The passivity and silence of decent people was at least as important for the success of National Socialism as the roar of the enthusiasts. To understand everything that has happened is not easy for any person or any country. As Nietzsche, the most profound of all German psychologists, wrote: 'The allure of knowledge would be small if there were not so much shame to be overcome on the way . . . 'I have done that' says my memory. 'I cannot have done that' says my pride, and remains inexorable. Eventually memory yields.'[27] Must it be so? Could not a modest pride come to the aid of memory and give it fortitude?

# Notes

The translation was undertaken by Angela Davies, German Historical Institute, London. This essay first appeared in German in Fritz Stern, *Das feine Schweigen: Historische Essays* (Munich: Verlag C.H. Beck, 1999).

1. Friedrich Nietzsche, *Sämtliche Werke: Kritische Neuausgabe*, ed. Giorgi Colli and Mazzino Montinari, v (Munich: Mouton de Gruyter, 1980), 184–5.
2. Letter to Dirk Coster, 15 Oct. 1945; Meitner Collection, Churchill College Archives Centre, Cambridge. Cf. Ruth Lewin Sime, *Lisa Meitner: A Life in Physics* (Berkeley, Calif.: University of California Press, 1996), 311.
3. Letter to Victor Gollancz, Ankara, 18 July 1945; Ernst Reuter, *Schriften: Reden*, ed. Hans J. Reichhardt, ii (Berlin: Propyläen Verlag, 1973), 588.
4. Nadezhda Mandelstam, *Hope Against Hope: A Memoir*, tr. Max Hayward (London: Collins Havvill, 1989), 43.
5. *Edmund Burke, Reflections on the Revolution in France*, ed. L. G. Mitchell (Oxford: Oxford University Press, 1999), 21.
6. *NS-Presseanweisungen der Vorkriegszeit: Edition und Dokumentation*, i. *1933*, ed. Hans Bohrmann (Munich: K. G. Saur, 1984), 30–1.
7. Fritz Stern, 'Bethmann Hollweg and the War: The Bounds of Responsibility', in Stern, *The Failure of Illiberalism* (London: Allen & Unwin, 1972), 118.
8. Quoted from Hans-Georg Drescher, *Ernst Troeltsch: Leben und Werk* (Göttingen: Vandenhoeck & Ruprecht, 1991), 453 n.107.
9. Drescher, *Ernst Troeltsch*, 453.
10. *Das Kabinett Scheidemann: 13. Februar bis 20. Juni 1919*, ed. Hagen Schulze (Boppard am Rhein: Harald Boldt, 1971), 147.

11. Ibid. 88.
12. Winfried Schulze, Der Neubeginn der deutschen Geschichtswissenschaft nach 1945. Einsichten und Absichtserklärungen der Historiker nach der Katastrophe, in Ernst Schulin (ed.), *Deutsche Geschichtswissenschaft nach dem Zweiten Weltkrieg (1945–1965)* (Munich: Oldenbourg, 1989), 24.
13. Ernst Troeltsch, 'Gefährlichste Zeiten: Berliner Brief', *Kunstwart und Kulturwart*, 35/11 (1921/2), 293, 296. Id., *Spektator-Briefe: Aufsätze über die deutsche Revolution und die Weltpolitik, 1918/1922* (Tübingen: Mohr, 1924), 281–8.
14. Klaus Scholder, *The Churches and the Third Reich*, i. *Preliminary History and the Time of Illusions 1918–1934* (Engl. edn., London: SCM Press, 1987), 137–8.
15. Fritz Stern, *Dreams and Delusions: The Drama of German History* (London: Weidenfeld & Nicolson, 1987), 147–91.
16. Klaus Schönhoven and Hans-Jochen Vogel (eds.), *Frühe Warnungen vor dem Nationalsozialismus. Ein historisches Lesebuch* (Bonn: Dietz, 1998), 246.
17. Mary Henle, 'One Man Against the Nazis—Wolfgang Köhler', *American Psychologist*, 33/10 (Oct. 1978), 942.
18. Otto Hahn, *Mein Leben* (Munich: Bruckmann, 1968), 145.
19. Hans Mommsen, *Beamtentum im Dritten Reich: Mit ausgewählten Quellen zur nationalsozialistischen Beamtenpolitik* (Stuttgart: Deutsche Verlags-Anstalt, 1966).
20. Dietrich Bonhoeffer, 'Wandlungen des Führerbegriffs in der jungen Generation'; expanded version published as 'Der Führer und der Einzelne in der jungen Generation', in *Dietrich Bonhoeffer Werke*, ed. Carsten Nicolaisen and Ernst-Albert Scharffenorth, xii. *Berlin 1932–1933* (Munich: Christian Kaiser Verlag, 1997), 242–60.
21. Wolfgang Kunkel, 'Der Professor im Dritten Reich', in *Die deutsche Universität im Dritten Reich: Eine Vortragsreihe der Universität München* (Munich: Piper, 1966), 133.
22. 'Lines composed a few miles above Tintern Abbey' (1798), *William Wordsworth, Poems*, ed. John O. Hayden, i. (Harmondsworth: Penguin, 1982), 358.
23. Letter to Martin Kähler, Göttingen, 19 May 1945; *Siegfried A. Kaehler, Briefe 1900–1963*, ed. Walter Bußmann and Günther Grünthal (Boppard am Rhein: Harald Boldt, 1993), 300.
24. Klaus-Dietmar Henke and Claudio Natoli (eds.), *Mit dem Pathos der Nüchternheit. Martin Broszat, das Institut für Zeitgeschichte und die Erforschung des Nationalsozialismus* (Frankfurt-am-Main and New York: Campus, 1991). Of particular relevance, Ernestine Schlant, *The Language of Silence: West German Literature and the Holocaust* (New York and London: Routledge, 1999).
25. Hubert Markl, 'Blick zurück, Blick voraus', in *Forschung an den Grenzen des Wissens. 50 Jahre Max-Planck-Gesellschaft 1948–1998* (Göttingen: Vandenhoeck & Ruprecht, 1998), 13.
26. Letter to Dirk Coster, 15 Oct. 1945 (see n. 2 above).
27. Friedrich Nietzsche, *Jenseits von Gut und Böse, Sämtliche Werke*, v. 85, 86.

# I

Peter Pulzer and his Work

# 2

# From Danube to Isis:
# A Career in Two Cultures

## *Peter Pulzer*

Most historical writing—at any rate writing on modern history—is also autobiography. Often this works indirectly. The writing may be entirely impersonal and drily objective, with no visible connection to the author's life-story. The details may be derived from archives, newspapers, or interviews, and therefore not part of the author's own experience. But what about the choice of subject itself, the agenda, the questions to be addressed, and the conclusions to be formulated? Are they chosen at random? Do they derive from some purely external stimulus? Or do they come from inside the scholar, because something that once happened to him goes on growing inside, because the world as he has experienced it has features that cry out for an explanation?

No doubt no two historians are alike. The ambition to write the definitive work on medieval China or Renaissance Mantua may have no connection with the author's own life. But more often than not, when the subject is the nineteenth or twentieth century, there is a link between person and subject, though here, too, it is safe to say that no two links are alike. In my own case there are certainly links, though not all of them are the obvious ones. Indeed, the request to write this chapter has encouraged me to explore them a little more thoroughly than I have so far bothered to do in the course of a rather busy professional career.

I was born in Vienna in 1929 at the beginning of the world economic crisis. My parents were secularized, non-observant Jews of the professional middle class, not particularly affluent, but devoted to the life of the mind and the arts. Politically they belonged to the Social Democratic Party, but were not, as far as I can remember, particularly active in it. However, it was difficult not to become aware of political and public events during the 1930s, even if these did not affect one directly and if, as a child, one could see little or no connection between them. I remember, in chronological order, the brief civil war in

Vienna in February 1934, when there was some shooting in the inner court-yard of the block of flats in which we lived and I could watch smoke rising from the Karl-Marx-Hof in the distance; the assassination—or rather, the funeral—of Chancellor Dollfuß, murdered by Nazis in June of that year; the abdication crisis in Britain, the topic of a number of disrespectful jokes; and the Spanish Civil War and the Sino-Japanese War, both recorded in the news-reels that I saw on my occasional visits to the cinema. These events evidently made an impression on me, but I connected them with an external world that made no difference to my own life.

All of this changed abruptly in March 1938, though even then the impact came by stages. I am pretty certain that I was unaware of the existence of Adolf Hitler until the day of the *Anschluß*. I did know of 'Nazis' in the preceding weeks, since the newspapers, the radio news and family conversation were full of little else, as Austrian Nazis, though banned, became bolder and more vio-lent, flaunting swastika armbands and flags in public. The *Anschluß* itself I experienced in peculiar circumstances. I was in bed with flu, puzzled by the constant drone of aircraft and heavier-than-usual traffic in the street. My mother explained that Austria had ceased to be an independent state, that the Nazis were now in control, that as a consequence life would become difficult for Jews and that I was to watch what I said to anyone, since no one could now be trusted. The illusion that public events affected only others was over. So was the assumption that being Jewish, of which I was only dimly aware, was marginal to one's existence.

In part my early distance from Judaism was due to my parents' secularism, in part a consequence of where we lived. Our house was some way from the main concentration of the Jewish population of Vienna. There were only a handful of other Jewish boys at my elementary school. All that distinguished me from the other pupils was that I did not attend religious instruction on the grounds that I was 'konfessionslos'. Along with the few Protestant boys I was classified as non-Catholic. It was only after the *Anschluß* that I learnt how superficial our family's dissociation from organized Jewish life was. Most of our closer friends and acquaintances turned out to be Jews, as did the family doctor and the kindergarten I had attended. These links were not religious. They were social and ethno-cultural. In this way I learnt (though not in so many words) how archaic forms of affinity and ascription could survive—or revive—in an allegedly modern society.

Step by step we were resegregated. My father, a design engineer with a civil engineering firm, lost his job, but was fortunately able to freelance for them. Then I was obliged to change to a Jews-only school, which was a long way from home, but academically highly acceptable. Violence hit us at the time of *Kristallnacht*, when our flat was ransacked by the SA and my father and grand-father were—fortunately briefly—dragged off. After that we were evicted from our flat, because a local Nazi big-wig had his eye on it. Gradually I learnt that the world was full, if not of enemies, then at least of potential enemies. Resegregation took other forms. My father reregistered with the Israelitische Kultusgemeinde, much against the grain, given his anticlerical outlook. A friend of the family, greatly distressed at my lack of a Jewish upbringing, took me to the Great Synagogue in the Tempelgasse on Yom Kippur, my first visit to this or any other place of worship. At the age of 9½ I learnt what the *torah* was. He also taught me Hebrew, which my parents accepted, since Palestine (as it then was) was a possible destination for our emigration. Preparations for emigration now dominated our lives. Our preference was for an English-speaking country a safe distance from the continent of Europe: Britain, Australia, or the United States. But we were not choosy. On his application form my father filled the destination space with the words, 'die ganze Welt'.

In the end we left for Britain in February 1939, having been sponsored by the family of a retired Anglican clergyman in Hertfordshire. They quite literally saved our lives and I am happy to say that we have maintained contact with their children and grand-children. For my parents the move to Britain was an upheaval, even a trauma, facing my father with the challenge of finding a job in a country he did not know and of whose language he had only a smattering. For me it was an adventure. I did not join my family in Hertfordshire, but spent the first few months in a small boarding school—or rather an intimate residential home—for a crash course in English. My father succeeded in finding a job within a few weeks and we moved to New Malden in south London, near his place of work. This move to a large extent determined the way I was to grow up with one foot in the culture we had left behind and the other in that of our new host society—biculturally, as I like to call it.

The aims of this biculturalism were not necessarily easily reconciled. On the one hand there was a consensus within our family that we had left Central Europe for good. Too much had happened, too much that did not bear dwelling on, for the migration to be reversed. We might, if the political climate changed, resume contact with acquaintances or visit relatives, but as a place in which to settle, as a place of permanent residence, Central Europe was out of the question. That meant that the first priority was to learn English, to acculturate to our new environment, to integrate into British society. For my father English was a professional necessity, for my mother an everyday social necessity. For me and for my younger sister learning the language was an educational necessity. Fortunately my crash course had stood me in good stead and in the spring of 1940 I gained a place at the local grammar school. More by accident than by design we had settled in a part of London where there were very few refugees. While we established contact with those that lived in our neighbourhood, we lacked the support network that we would have benefited from in north-west London, in Swiss Cottage, or Golders Green. At both the schools I went to I was the only refugee pupil. What was initially a deprivation became a challenge: we were forced to adapt in a way that we might not have done had we been protected by the comfort of an immigrant ghetto. Thus the omens favoured relatively quick acculturation.

But what we were to do about the culture we had brought with us? Desirable as it was that I should command perfect English as soon as possible, it was equally desirable that I should not forget my German. What, therefore, was the family lingua franca to be? The answer was a compromise, which ensured that all of us remained bilingual. That meant not only that we occasionally conversed in German, but that one continued to read German books, of which we had managed to bring out quite a few. Given that at the age of 10 I had hardly begun to read any German literature, I therefore received at least some of the literary education that would have been mine had I grown up in Vienna.

This might be a point at which to digress from the autobiographical chronology and anticipate answers to the question how much of my cultural persona is attributable to my early history? How much of my literary and artistic tastes have their roots in German-speaking Central Europe? In music I lean heavily towards the Austro-German classics. But these are the mainstay of concert programmes and record collections everywhere, so perhaps that proves nothing. I love to hear Brendel play Schubert or Elisabeth Schwarzkopf sing Richard Strauss, but the same goes for millions of people who have never set foot in Vienna. I did acquire an early appreciation of Mahler, well before he achieved the popularity he now enjoys; that may be the only significant exception in my otherwise rather conventional tastes. But I also have a special love for the English Tudor and Jacobean polyphonists and this I owe to a phase in my life I shall come to later. What goes for music, goes for literature. When I find myself in a German city with a good theatre I try to go to performances of the great classics, which are not often played in Britain. But equally I try to see Racine or Molière when I am in Paris. So here again, not too much should be read into my theatre-going habits, especially since I do not exactly ignore Shakespeare or Restoration comedy or modern British playwrights. However, when it comes to twentieth-century literature that specializes in the Viennese Jewish love–hate relationship with the rest of the human race—reaching its acme in Schnitzler and Karl Kraus—I do feel a special resonance. No doubt the refugee emigration helped to popularize aspects of Central European creativity that had been previously neglected in Britain and America. But here, too, the impact should not be exaggerated. The greatest British advocate of Freud in Britain was Ernest Jones, of Bertolt Brecht it was Kenneth Tynan, of Elias Canetti it is Iris Murdoch, of Karl Kraus it is Edward Timms. There is no one-to-one correlation here. In any case, the purpose of this digression is to make a point to which I shall return, namely that it is very difficult to disentangle the formative influences one has undergone.

I attended my grammar school until 1947: my days there covered the whole of the war. While its course was of universal interest, at school and outside it, my family had, of course, a special stake in its outcome. We shared with every-one the German air raids of 1940 and 1941, as well as the assaults with 'V' weapons in the summer of 1944, but we also knew that a successful German invasion of Britain would have more drastic consequences for us than for our neighbours, and that the elation we would feel at the defeat of Hitler would be more intense. Once more public events impacted on personal fate. My school presented, as I have indicated, an entirely English environment. The syllabus was rather narrow: it included Latin and French, but not (in contrast to my sister's school) German. To my astonishment and embarrassment, I was regarded as an expert on all things to do with Nazi Germany. Where would Hitler attack next? How good was the German army? Above all, the constantly nagging question: how could the German people support someone as mani-festly mad and wicked as Hitler? Why did they not rise in revolt against him? I coped with these questions as well as a teenager could. Perhaps my attempts in this respect served as an apprenticeship for my later career in punditry.

In 1947 I left school and went to King's College, Cambridge, to read history. After taking my BA in 1950 I did my military service in the Royal Air Force and then returned to Cambridge for graduate work. At this stage of my edu-cation the influences on my later career became much clearer. The Cambridge history syllabus was wide and covered everything from ancient history and the medieval European economy to modern times. I took a fair spread of sub-jects, but concentrated as far as possible on the period that interested me most, the nineteenth and twentieth centuries. My special subject was the Third French Republic from Boulanger to Dreyfus, which involved an in-depth study of those twenty-odd years with documentation and primary sources. I read, among others, the works of Edouard Drumont, Maurice Barrès, Charles Péguy, and Léon Blum. This was the first time that I had had to come to grips at an academic level with a phenomenon that I had witnessed often enough at a personal level: the European radical right. I had to write essays, and pass an examination, that required me to understand and explain integral nationalism, religious and racial prejudice, blood-and-soil mystique, and anti-Semitism. Above all, it confronted me with a paradox that it has taken me the best part of a lifetime to try to resolve: Why was it that the cen-tury that I had always associated with the expansion of liberty, with reason, progress, and respect for human dignity, with a repudiation of traditional authoritarianism and ancient prejudices, spawned, in its last decades, those irrationalities and superstitions that have haunted my century? Quite a lot of what I have written and lectured on in the past forty years constitutes an attempt to come to terms with that conundrum. My answers, like everyone else's, have been tentative, but I hope I have made my contribution.

So much for one part of my education and one part of my academic agenda, the part that can be traced most directly to my own life-history. There were, however, others. Cambridge broadened my mind, as it is bound to do, and helped me to understand my own times better than I should otherwise have understood them. But it was also a further stage in my anglicization, as school had been before. In contrast with my school, King's and other colleges had undergraduates with backgrounds similar to mine and this was naturally a bond between us. But the majority of my contemporaries and friends, including those with whom I have maintained lifelong contact, were British and, for the most part, not Jewish. Perhaps some of them found my company interesting and worthwhile because I was slightly different from them; if so, I hope I was able to reciprocate. As with my fellow students, so with those who taught me, the influence was overwhelmingly British. Of those whose lectures I attended, only two had a Central European background: Nikolaus Pevsner and Eric Hobsbawm. Those who taught me in college were English to their marrows. Like the best Oxford and Cambridge tutors they treated me as an individual, but without flattery and without concessions. The two who influenced me most, Christopher Morris (now dead) and Noël Annan (still alive and vigorous), both imbued me with the gift of scepticism, a respect for empiricism, and, more than anything else, the necessity of writing good, plain English. Both taught me, in a very English way, not to be solemn about my work. Their advice to me was full of common sense that disguised professionalism of a high order. When I asked Noël Annan what book would most help me to a better understanding of Victorian England, he replied, *Middlemarch*. When Christopher Morris thought that I was overdoing the revision for my Part II Tripos, he firmly ordered me to the university cricket ground, where the West Indies were playing on their first post-war tour with such giants as Worrell, Walcott, and Weekes. Relaxation, I learnt, was the key—or at any rate a key—to academic success. My six years in Cambridge undoubtedly formed me more strongly than any other period in my life. Sometimes when I listen to myself lecturing I think I can hear echoes of those who lectured to me.

My life at Cambridge was not exclusively academic. There was music (though I was never a performer). The services at King's College Chapel, which were attended mainly by non-believers, and the recitals by the University Madrigal Society opened the world of Tallis, Gibbons, and Byrd to me, to take their place beside Haydn, Mozart, and Schubert. There was also politics. For the reasons I have given, it was impossible for an adolescent of my circumstances to ignore politics, but until I went to university I had not been a participant. Now I joined the Labour Club and the debates of the Union Society. Though I never achieved high office, this heightened my interest in British politics, which also played a part in my academic career.

During my undergraduate years I had no clear notion of my professional future and certainly no well-formed ambition for a university career. This became probable only when I got a First in both parts of the Historical Tripos and the College encouraged me to think I should get financial support if I wanted to return as a research student. Even that, however, provided no guarantee; not every author of a successful doctoral thesis climbs the academic ladder. Moreover, my time in the RAF would give me time to reflect further and to formulate my topic. When I did return to Cambridge in 1954 my plans had matured and clarified. I would once more take up the challenge posed by the Dreyfus affair: the apparent paradox of illiberalism in an age of liberalism, of persecution and discrimination in an age of emancipation. This time, however, I should tackle the question comparatively. I knew, or thought I knew, the background of the affair and the extent to which the literature of ideological anti-Semitism had flourished in nineteenth-century France—not only Drumont and Barrès, but before them the Chevalier Gougenot des Mousseaux, Alphonse Toussenel, and Pierre-Joseph Fourier. I was aware, as who could not be, of the stages by which the Nazis' racial fantasies had led to marginalization of Jews, then their deportation and finally mass murder. As for Austria, I had witnessed with my own eyes what Karl Kraus had, in a different context, called the Austrian laboratory of the end of the world and I knew enough Austrian history to have heard of Karl Lueger and Georg von Schönerer. What remained to be done? Quite simply, to synthesize the phenomenon of European anti-Semitism in the late nineteenth and early twentieth centuries and to provide an historical explanation of the disasters that had befallen my family, my generation, Europe, and the world. Three years, I thought, would be adequate to the task.

My doctoral supervisor was Hugh Seton-Watson of the University of London, who combined no-nonsense Scottish scholarship with a deep, family-based understanding of Central and Eastern Europe. He was the ideal guide for my purposes. He introduced me to the existing literature, suggested lines of approach, let me get on with it and drew thick lines through all the passages in my draft chapters that he thought were rubbish. He was totally intolerant of any pretentiousness and superfluous theorizing, of any conclusions not supported by the evidence. He cured me of any lingering tendency to use long, empty words, completing the purge begun by my undergraduate tutors. I spent six months in the archives and libraries of Vienna and three months in Berlin. Other than for brief tourist visits, these were my first extended stays in either country since 1939. I met fellow students and younger historians, who were nevertheless still of a generation to have remembered the Third Reich and the war. Sometimes there were problems of communication. More than once, after I had explained to an archivist or librarian what materials I wanted, I would get the response, 'Ah, yes, you are interested in the Jewish Questions'. 'No, no', I would reply, 'the anti-Semitic question'. Puzzlement sat on their brows.

Though the purpose of my stay was research, its effect was also a reimmersion in the culture of my parents and grandparents. Given the rate of exchange in the 1950s, Austria and the Federal Republic were cheap for anyone coming from Britain. I exhausted the concert, opera, and theatre repertoires of both cities, which gave me my first taste of Schiller, Goethe, Lessing, Grillparzer, Schnitzler, and Nestroy on German-speaking stages. My only previous exposure to German theatre of that quality had been during the Berliner Ensemble's memorable visit to Britain in 1956. I also spent my time doing what I most like doing, that is, wandering around, discovering—or in the case of Vienna, renewing my acquaintance with—not only the baroque of Schönbrunn and Charlottenburg, but the more characteristic townscapes of Otto Wagner and Friedrich Schinkel some decades before they became as popular as they are now. Even as a child I had admired the *Jugendstil* of the Viennese metropolitan railway that Wagner designed, though without knowing the name of the architect or anything about *fin de siècle* style. All these meanderings were a source of great pleasure, but they brought something else home to me. Though I think I understood what I saw better than if I had found myself in, say, Chicago or Leningrad, I did not feel at home in either Vienna or Berlin. I was a visitor—a visitor, no doubt, with special associations—but still someone whose real home was somewhere else. I had spent too long in Britain, undergone too many formative experiences, had become too accustomed to English as the language of daily use, to re-acclimatize myself to places in which I almost certainly did not want to be at home. Vienna, I realized, though the place of my birth, was not my *Heimatstadt*.

I also made the discovery, in the course of my researches, that all thesis-writers make, namely that I had bitten off more than I could chew. I was collecting so much material on Germany and Austria before 1918 that any thought of including France soon turned out to be unrealistic; in any case, restricting the thesis to Germany and Austria made additional sense. I felt more confident in my judgement on them, even though my starting-point had been the Dreyfus affair, and the interaction between developments in the German-speaking areas was much clearer and much more in need of demonstration. I completed my thesis in 1960. It was published in 1964, translated into German in 1966, reissued in 1988, and is still in print. I suppose that whatever professional reputation I have is based on it more than on anything else that I have written.

In choosing my research topic I had set myself a specific aim: to try to solve a problem that certainly related to my own life, but that I hoped was also of more general interest and concern. The book was reasonably well received and quite widely adopted as a course text in the United States. On the other hand it was not my intention to devote my life's work to this topic. I did not want to become a one-trick circus dog. By the time I finished my thesis, I had been appointed to a lectureship in politics at Oxford; by the time my book was published, I had become an Official Student (that is, a Tutorial Fellow, a tenured position) at Christ Church, Oxford, in politics and modern history. The syllabus that I was required to teach did not have all that much to do with my research preoccupations. Modern German history came into it, as did twentieth-century political movements. No one at this stage wanted to write any theses that I would have been qualified to supervise on anti-Semitism, or modern Jewish political history, or even theories of nationalism. The subjects I mainly taught were comparative government, international relations, and British government.

This change of tack did not disturb me. I had, after all, applied for these jobs knowing what they would entail, and the responsibilities that went with them fitted some of my other interests. Growing up when I did, I had acquired a general interest in—one might almost say, obsession with—politics. This was strengthened during my time at Cambridge, but did not originate there. I was particularly fascinated by the 1945 general election in Britain, which resulted in the defeat of Churchill and the election of the Labour government. It was the first free election I had experienced. I kept a voluminous file of newspaper clippings on the campaign and its outcome, which I still have. When, in 1995, the Fabian Society decided to organize a meeting and an exhibition on the fiftieth anniversary of this event, I was able to supply some material for it from this collection.

The early 1960s saw a sudden boom in the scientific study of electoral behaviour, which had originated in the United States and then spread first to Britain and then to Germany and elsewhere in continental Europe. Given my obsessions and my presence in Oxford, where David Butler of Nuffield College was the pioneer of the new science, I was well placed to take advantage of this boom. Over the next twenty years I wrote for various British newspapers on aspects of electoral analysis, as well as commenting on campaigns and popular votes for British and foreign broadcasting media. In 1967 I published a text book, *Political Representation and Elections in Britain,* which went through three editions and sold more copies than any of my other books. At the same time, given my continued interest in German politics, I also began to follow current West German party and electoral developments more closely. I took part in the first academic election study in the Federal Republic, organized by the Sociology Department of the University of Cologne in 1961. In fact, my first publications, which appeared before my book on anti-Semitism, were on West German party politics. Later in the 1960s I participated in a comparative study, initiated by Political and Economic Planning (PEP) of London, of West European party systems, contributing the section on Austria.

I hope that by now the nature of my bi-culturalism and its influence on my scholarly interests have become clearer. I had the major advantage of being bilingual and of being able to maintain an interest in German and Austrian affairs at least as great as that in British politics. On the one hand Britain was my home and I was a politically active citizen there. Much of my teaching related to current British issues and in so far as I was known to the British public at all it was in connection with my contribution to domestic topics.

Similarly, what I wrote on post-1945 German and Austrian politics fell largely under the heading of my appointment as a lecturer in politics, informed though it was by my own historically determined insights. It is fair to say that in the ten years after the publication of my book on anti-Semitism, my interest in German-related subjects took a subordinate place. After my 1961 election study I did not revisit the Federal Republic until 1969, again for an election study. I went to Vienna briefly in 1967 in connection with the PEP project, but that was my only visit to Austria between 1958 and 1984. My main foreign engagements were a series of visiting professorships in the USA, first at the University of Wisconsin, then at the Johns Hopkins Graduate School in Washington, DC, and at the University of California in Los Angeles. In each case I taught in the political science department. I seemed to have attained one of my ambitions, that of not being a one-trick circus dog.

One's first trick, however, is never entirely forgotten. I had published my book on anti-Semitism at a low point of interest in that subject. Though I was asked to write a few reviews and give the odd lecture on related topics, there was not much demand for a follow-up. By the 1970s the situation began to change. Interest in German-Jewish history had revived and the subject was beginning to flourish. In part that was undoubtedly due to the pioneering work of the Leo Baeck Institute, founded in Jerusalem in 1955, and its increasingly scholarly and influential *Year Book*. In part it was also due to the broadening range of interest on the part of the German—and, somewhat later, Austrian—historical profession, which was a general phenomenon of the 1960s. The session on German-Jewish history at the *Historikertag* in Braunschweig in 1974, the first of its kind, was a significant symptom of this increased interest. This had two consequences. Though the lingua franca of German-Jewish studies continued to be English, since most of its practitioners were domiciled in English-speaking countries and the Leo Baeck Institute's *Year Book* was published in English, innovative works were once more appearing in German. In part the authors were German-born scholars living in the United States, Britain, or Israel, like Ernest Hamburger, Hans Liebeschütz, and Jacob Toury. The even more significant second consequence was that a generation of West German historians was emerging who devoted themselves to researching and popularizing the social, cultural, and political history of the Jews of Germany. They, in turn, have cultivated a successor generation of doctoral students and young academics, so that German-Jewish studies are now part of the mainstream of German historiography. This welcome development provided my own work with a new environment and I was gradually drawn back to my original interest, first in Britain, then in the USA, then in Germany and Austria.

Let me mention a few instances of this development, in order to illustrate both the range of activities that arose out of this new level of interest and the way I was able to become involved in some of it. My entry into structured and

organized German-Jewish history came, as for so many in both the English-
and German-speaking worlds, through the Leo Baeck Institute, in my case
that in London. The first invitation came in the 1960s, with a request to contribute an essay on anti-Semitism in the Weimar Republic to the first of the
Institute's now celebrated *Sammelbände, Entscheidungsjahr 1932*. Unfortunately I could not accept that—I had too many other commitments—but I
was able to participate in the third *Sammelband, Juden im wilhelminischen
Deutschland*, which came out in 1976. My essay in that dealt with the role of
Jews in public life during the Kaiserreich. Originally that chapter was to have
been written by Ernest Hamburger, the author of the standard classic work,
*Juden im öffentlichen Leben Deutschlands*, but he was beginning to feel too old
for this project, especially as he was also working on a sequel to his first volume to cover the Weimar Republic, a sequel that he was unfortunately unable
to complete. This did mean, however, that I was able to seek his advice and
draw on his unique store of personal knowledge and mature judgement. One
could not have wished for a better apprenticeship.

There was another respect in which this particular approach suited me. I
think of myself primarily as a historian of modern Germany and Austria. I
have never been a specialist on the internal life of Jewish communities, on
Jewish thought, or on Jewish doctrinal or organizational controversies. Given
my secular upbringing and my broad interests in political history, I approach
German-Jewish topics under two headings: to consider the German-Jewish
experience as part of German (or Austrian) history, and the political developments of those two countries in their impact on modern Jewish history. It is
the interaction that fascinates me, not the treatment of hermetically isolated
topics. In this way I follow the tradition founded by Ernest Hamburger, and
by Jacob Toury in Israel, with his *Die politischen Orientierungen der Juden in
Deutschland*. Later works, like Werner Mosse's two volumes on the German-
Jewish economic élite, follow a similar method. Looked at in this way, the
study of anti-Semitism, and of Jewish and gentile reactions to it, fits into a
general consideration of modern mass movements and of nationalism, xenophobia, and ethnic exclusiveness. The study of Jewish participation in business, politics, or the media fits into a general consideration of the openness of
particular societies and of the social mobility and career patterns that they
permit. The study of Jewish family structures, fertility, and marital stability
can shed light on overall discussion of these subjects and of the degree to
which particular moral traditions can survive in societies in which there is a
general trend towards homogenized secularism. In this way the study of
Jewish themes adds a dimension to the study of our own times and our forefathers'; it also makes it accessible and attractive to those who have no personal links with Jewish life.

I have no means of knowing whether I contributed, through my early writings, to the present level of interest in German- and Austrian-Jewish history.

There is, however, no doubt that the growth of interest has brought me back to that subject more than would otherwise have been the case. In the last twenty years I have written ten papers on various aspects of it, published one major book, *Jews and the German State* (1992) and contributed to the four-volume *History of the Jews in German-Speaking Central Europe since the Seventeenth Century*, edited by Michael A. Meyer of Hebrew Union College, Cincinatti, which is being published in English, German, and Hebrew. I have lost count of the number of conferences that I have attended and at which I either read papers or acted as discussant. Most of these papers have been demand-led, that is, they were a response to requests from academic bodies in Britain, the USA, Germany, Austria, and Italy. No doubt I should have continued to work on this and related topics in any case, but almost certainly not on this escalating and sometimes hectic scale.

The growth in demand has been gratifying in a number of ways. It is a recognition that my original choice of research, and the questions and answers it entailed, had some justification. It has enabled me to make contacts with a growing number of scholars in three continents, whose agenda coincides, or at least overlaps, with mine. Lastly, some of the occasions at which I have been present have given me particular satisfaction. The first conference of the Leo Baeck Institute on German soil took place in Berlin in 1985; the Institute's fortieth birthday was celebrated not only in London, New York, and Jerusalem, the sites of the original centres, but in Bonn, where a public meeting attracted a large number of people who would otherwise not have given as much thought to the subject or heard of the organizations involved. It certainly gave me a feeling of something achieved that I was able to be present at both, and to act as something of a missionary for German-Jewish studies, given that these studies have a didactic as well as a purely scholarly aspect in the German-Austrian context. But the sweetest of all experiences occurred in Vienna in 1984. I was invited on the occasion of the magnificent exhibition 'Traum und Wirklichkeit' (Dream and Reality) that dealt with *fin de siècle* Vienna. I not only took part in a long discussion on the Austrian-Jewish identity on the television talk-show *Club 2*, but was asked to lecture on the history of Austrian anti-Semitism in Karl Lueger's very own City Hall. That gave me quite a thrill.

In spite of these increasing demands, which will no doubt continue, I remain committed to having more than one trick in my repertoire. Though I have supervised a number of doctoral theses on modern Jewish topics, generally, though not always, with a German context, most of my teaching has been in comparative politics, with a German and occasionally Austrian bias. My most recent two books, *German Politics 1945–95* and *Germany 1871–1945*, published by the Oxford University Press in 1995 and 1997, are the outcome of this teaching and my next book will, if my plans materialize, also be on general German political history.

How, then, to answer the question of the influence of my personal background on my scholarly interests? The first thing to say is that I have two backgrounds, one Central European, the other English. Though born in Vienna, I have spent seven-eighths of my life in Britain. I have been a British citizen since 1947. My main language is English; it is the language in which I prefer to speak, teach, and write and in which I communicate with my family. Though I have Central Europeans, or their descendants, among my close acquaintances, the vast majority of my social or intellectual circle is British. In so far as I have been politically active, that has been in Britain and in a British context. I suspect that my predominantly empirical ways of thought owe a great deal more to my English education then to any other factor. It may even be—and others can judge this better than I can—that the way I think and write about German-Jewish topics has been influenced by my English education and environment and by the model of Jewish–gentile coexistence that I grew up with in Britain. If I were asked to place myself socially—in itself no doubt a British preoccupation—it would be in the English professional middle class, which has shown itself accommodating and welcoming to many people like me. I move with ease in continental Europe and the fall of the Iron Curtain has enabled me to extend my repertoire. I can now go, with a minimum of bureaucratic hassle, to those parts of Central Europe that share a Habsburg or German heritage, but were until recently closed off. I can relish the baroque, neo-classicism, and art nouveau of Prague and Budapest, Riga and Cracow, even Lviv and Tchernivsty (Czernowitz to my readers), as I have long relished them in Vienna, Munich, and Berlin. But could I *live* in any of these cities?

I could if I had to. The practicalities would pose no problems. I speak the language, I know where to get a reasonably priced schnitzel and which tram to catch to which theatre. But I would not feel totally comfortable. There are too many ghosts. If I had to live outside Oxford and outside Britain, I might be better off somewhere totally neutral, like Zürich or Grenoble or Boston. I shall continue to write about modern Jewish history and the German-Jewish and Austrian-Jewish experience; they are part of my life, but not the whole of my life. I shall continue to observe and write about the politics of Germany and Central Europe. But I shall prefer to do so from the comfort and safety of this side of the Channel. I know where my roots are, but I also know where my home is. I do not want to change either of them.

# 3

## The Committed Observer of a Janus-Faced Century: Peter Pulzer on Liberalism, Anti-Semitism, and Democracy

### *Henning Tewes*

Valedictory lectures are rare occasions.[1] Most academics give inaugural lectures when they take up a professorial chair, and leave quietly when the time has come. The idea of a scholar reflecting back on his or her career and life, however, is in many respects an appealing one. This is especially true if the professional career is as distinguished and the personal history as unusual as they are in the case of Peter Pulzer. Pulzer had not given an inaugural lecture when he was appointed to the Gladstone Chair at All Souls College, Oxford, in 1984. It was thus customary that he should speak to the University before his departure from the chair, imparting, among other things, a view on how his subject should be taught. This he did in May 1996. There was a danger, Pulzer argued at the end of the lecture, in the academic becoming closely involved in politics: too many great scholars in the twentieth century had ended up 'defending the indefensible, and excusing the inexcusable'. He himself, he said, had pursued knowledge in the spirit of Dr Bernard Rieux, the protagonist and narrator of Albert Camus's *La Peste*. Like Rieux, Pulzer said, he had tried to be *un observateur engagé*, a committed observer, a witness, in other words, of events that had had a direct impact on his personal life and that had cried out for an explanation.

One might add that, as so often with Peter Pulzer, the mentioning of Dr Rieux served as a subtle hint at a more central message, namely at Rieux's closing sentences at the end of *La Peste*:

Hearing the cries of elation rising from the town, Rieux remembered that this elation was always threatened. For he knew what this joyous crowd was unaware of and what one can read in books, that the bacillus of the plague never dies nor disappears, that it can stay dormant for years in furniture and linen, that it waits patiently in rooms, cellars, trunks, handkerchiefs and papers, and that, perhaps, the day might come when for the misery of man, the plague would wake its rats again and send them to die in a happy town.[2]

The Gladstone Chair of Government and Public Administration at All Souls is one of the most prestigious chairs of political science in Britain. Pulzer's immediate predecessors, Samuel Finer and Max Beloff, became household names in British political science. This is not the case for Pulzer, partly because he originally made his academic name in the then rather marginal study of political anti-Semitism, and partly, one might suggest, because his publishing career was an unusual one, even by the standards of an Oxford don. After *The Rise of Political Anti-Semitism in Germany and Austria*, Pulzer published *Political Representation and Elections in Britain* in 1967, which featured the quotation most widely cited in connection with his name: 'Class is the basis of British party politics; all else is embellishment and detail.'[3] When he took up the Gladstone chair, Peter Pulzer had not written a book for seventeen years.[4]

It is difficult of course to speculate about the reasons for this. The teaching load of an Oxford don is a heavy one, which is why most Oxford academics publish less than their colleagues at other universities. Also, the mad run on publishing is a rather new feature of (British) academic life, and, one might add, not one widely seen as a blessing. More specifically, Pulzer is quite simply not a person who likes other people to determine his agenda. One may doubt that he would have engaged in a flurry of publishing even if this had been fashionable at the time. The hierarchy of his personal priorities is largely impenetrable to outside influences. This seems to be a personal observation, ill-placed in an appreciation of Pulzer's scholarship. We will see in the following pages, however, that this particular trait of character had a profound effect on Pulzer's writing, not only in terms of the topics he chose, but also in terms of his approach to them, the approach, that is, of the committed observer.

Finally, quantity is not to be confused with quality. Pulzer's articles of the 1970s and 1980s were substantial and appeared in the best journals. They formed the heart of his reputation in political science when he left Christ Church for the Gladstone chair. If by the mid-1990s he had become the doyen of German political studies in Britain, these articles were the reason. What is more, they have not lost any of their relevance. If the following remarks, or this Festschrift as a whole, induced readers to dig out the odd dusty volume of the *Political Quarterly* or *Political Studies* of the 1960s and 1970s, they would have fulfilled their most important aim.

Peter Pulzer, David Sorkin observed, is a 'historian of fate'.[5] Like Fritz Stern and George Mosse, he combines the intellectual traditions of his adopted homeland with a profound insight into German, and Austrian, politics and culture. His scholarship is deeply touched by the experience of National Socialism, trying to come to terms with the large questions of this century's political history, which had, after all, had an immediate, tangible impact on his own life. At first sight, one might be tempted to argue that Pulzer's writings can be separated into two seemingly divergent strands. These are on the one hand the inquiry into Jewish-German history, the rise of political anti-Semitism, and the failure of emancipation before 1933, and on the other hand the analysis of elections, political parties, and party systems in Germany and Austria after 1945. Although it might appear as though the geographical focus on Germany and Austria was the tie holding these divergent academic interests together, one can, at a closer look, also identify a common theme. This is the concern with the fate of liberal democracy at large. In the Janus-faced twentieth century, the committed observer was concerned with the consequences of liberal failure, and with the conditions for liberal success.

Thus, Pulzer's enquiries into German-Jewish history can be seen as a concern with the question of what happens if liberalism fails. Discrimination against Jews in the state administration, in the public debate, and in political parties—the consequence of unsuccessful emancipation—says much about the general level of political development in a given country, and in particular about the extent to which liberal concepts have found expression in constitutional arrangements and everyday political practice. Equally—against the background of a concern with liberalism—the analysis of elections and political parties in Germany and Austria after 1945 can be interpreted as a concern with the conditions of democratic consolidation. Political parties, in Pulzer's analysis, were of critical importance for this process, both in West Germany or in Austria (though the concomitant degree of domestic liberalization in Austria was smaller). One may put the common theme of Pulzer's work more poignantly and argue that the flourishing of political anti-Semitism is intimately related to the weakness of liberalism, while in turn liberalism can only survive in a democracy where political parties combine representation with effective government. This thematic nexus of Pulzer's scholarship is at the heart of the different contributions to this volume.

## *Jewish-German History*

If one speaks of the 'historian of fate', one should be cautious. Biography only goes so far. In a sense, every historian and political scientist is concerned with democracy and totalitarianism, since these were the two forms of government that dominated the twentieth century. Moreover, many scholars of anti-Semitism are no 'historians of fate', and many people who suffered from anti-Semitism in their personal lives were not prompted to study it academ-

ically. Although it is true that in Pulzer's case we have to do with biographi-
cally induced interests, the conclusions drawn belong above all to the realm of
the mind. This is especially true for his writing on Jewish-German history,
where the experiences of the man could have affected—or even clouded—the
conclusions of the scholar. Camus's committed observer is also a *témoin objec-
tif*, an objective witness, who, in Pulzer's case, writes on Jewish-German history not in order to denounce, but in order to understand.

The aspect of Jewish-German history that originally aroused Pulzer's interest was the rise of political anti-Semitism in Germany and Austria from the
1860s to the First World War. Since anti-Semitism is a phenomenon that exists
in relation to Jews but is at the same time quite independent of their particular characteristics, Pulzer's study of political anti-Semitism focused primarily
on gentiles. With *Jews and the German State*, he later added the specifically
Jewish contribution to the building of a German state and a German nation.
Both of his major works on Jewish-German history therefore overcome the
divide between Jews and gentiles. The Jewish aspect is only one, even though
a particularly important, aspect of German political history. It hints at many
of the themes that have become accepted as the defining features of this history, in particular at the discrepancy between dynamic socio-economic
change and the conversely growing immobilism of political structures
between 1871 and 1918. On the politics of Germany's and Austria's Jewish
communities, on the peculiarities of Jewish life and Jewish consciousness in
the Empire, Pulzer writes less, and if so, only in relation to the broader question of emancipation. Since Jews were an integral part of the society around
them, their omission from the study of this society, in Pulzer's view, would be
inaccurate. If others had imposed an artificial distinction between Jews and
gentiles, so be it. The worst one could do was to accept this division and repeat
it by studying Germany's Jews in isolation. Pulzer was never prepared to let
others dominate his agenda. If Hitler had wanted to make Vienna 'judenrein',
one had all the more reason for going back. If the Nazis had set Jews and gentiles against one another, there was an even greater incentive to study what
they had in common. If a reaction against anti-Semitism triggered strong
mechanisms of self-defence in many Jews, especially after the Holocaust,
Pulzer was all the more determined not to have his judgement clouded.

In *The Rise of Political Anti-Semitism* Pulzer argues that modern, political
anti-Semitism constitutes something different from earlier forms of Jew-baiting. Its preconditions were industrialization and the reaction against it, partial
(and incomplete) liberalism, partial (and incomplete) assimilation, and the
attempts of a pseudo-scientific movement to make anti-Semitism part of a
coherent set of ideas. This means that if we want to understand National
Socialism and the Holocaust, we have to turn to the decades that preceded the
First World War, for 'during it the movements and ideologies developed which
matured after 1918'.[6]

One of Pulzer's central arguments consists of the conceptual distinction between Christian-conservative and racialist anti-Semitism. Christian-conservative anti-Semitism was propagated by more traditional conservative forces, including the churches, and rested on the dual pillars of *prejudice* and *coexistence*. It was conservative-feudal in the sense that it maintained or established social boundaries that could not be crossed: the type of coexistence between Jews and Gentiles it favoured was thus a discriminating one, but it was coexistence nevertheless. It follows that the violence of Christian-conservative anti-Semitism was epidemic, that is, that after occasional outbursts of violence, life would return to 'normal'. This points to the differences from racialist anti-Semitism, which relied on science in order to justify its claims and motivate its followers, and which developed a logic that entirely denied the Jews their place in society. Racialist anti-Semites thus contradicted the assumption of *prejudice* and *coexistence*, since they saw the difference between Jews and gentiles as one of blood, not of faith or cultural habits. As a consequence, they did not accept baptism, which to many Jews had been a necessary response to Christian-conservative anti-Semitism, as well as to liberal demands of acculturation.

In order to clarify his conceptual distinction, Pulzer describes Christian-conservative anti-Semitism as *pre-liberal*, racialist anti-Semitism as *post-liberal*. This hints at the central significance of liberalism in Pulzer's thought. Christian-conservative anti-Semitism was pre-liberal, because it granted everyone a place in society without guaranteeing that this place be based on equality. It was primarily an expression of regret for a world untouched by industrialization and urbanization, with fixed moral standards and rigid social hierarchies. It was, in Pulzer's words, a 'rearguard action fought by a generation which had lost the battle'. Racialist anti-Semitism, on the other hand, was decidedly post-liberal. It had accepted the liberal challenge to religion and relied on the liberal concepts of science and rationalism, while denying the liberal concept of individual rights and the rule of law. Its anti-Semitism was an end in itself. Unbound by the traditional standards of Western morality, it stood for 'tribal purification through a perpetual cathartic riot of intolerance'.[7]

This, however, only concerns the ideological thrust of the two ideal-types of anti-Semitism. What Pulzer also emphasizes is that the rise of political anti-Semitism in the last decades of the nineteenth century was a political as well as an ideological novelty, because it participated in the mobilization of classes that had hitherto been politically passive. Anti-Semitism as a permanent political feature needed party organization, constant campaigning, and masses that followed it. In this respect, it was inherently post-liberal, because it relied on the prior effects of industrialization and urbanization. What Pulzer perhaps underemphasized is that pre-liberal or post-liberal ideological components could combine with post-liberal political practices in different constellations.

Karl Lueger, for instance, the mayor of Vienna between 1897 and 1910, propounded an anti-Semitism that was ideologically pre-liberal. That his political temperament, in contrast, was decidedly post-liberal can be seen from the fact that he instrumentalized anti-Semitism partly in response to popular demand. Like Adolf Stoecker, the Protestant clergyman in Berlin in the 1880s, Lueger found that his public appearances were more successful if larded with anti-Semitic agitation. By and large, then, Christian-conservative anti-Semitism combined traditional Jew-baiting with new forms of political mobilization. In contrast, racialist anti-Semitism was not only an organizational but also an ideological novelty. An example was Georg von Schönerer, Lueger's rival in Austria, who combined racialist anti-Semitism with mass campaigning, even though he never emulated Lueger's electoral success in Vienna. What was really new about the rise of political anti-Semitism, then, was that (1) political parties used it as a central part of their electoral appeal and strategy, and that they did so with methods that could only work in a post-liberal society, and that (2) some of these parties propagated an anti-Semitic ideology that denied the Jews their place in society.

While Christian-conservative and racialist anti-Semitism can be distinguished conceptually, however, their effect in practice was similar. Pulzer maintains that anti-Semitism was a largely 'spontaneous' sentiment, which existed independently of political leadership, and which actually tempted politicians to adopt anti-Semitic programmes in the pursuit of electoral success. Moreover, in effect the two types of anti-Semitism worked hand in hand. This becomes even clearer in Pulzer's own later writings, where he stresses the effect of the churches in preparing the ground that racialist anti-Semitism later took over.[8] With hindsight we can understand, Pulzer states, that 'the relative smoothness with which Jews were eased out of one profession or economic sector after another after 1933, the lack of protest against the principle of discrimination, as opposed to specific instances of it', suggests that there existed a 'pervasive non acceptance, within significant sectors of German society, of the Jew as a truly equal fellow-citizen'.[9] Having said this, Pulzer's argument on the 'spontaneity' of anti-Semitism is more cautious and more finely tuned than more recent variants of the 'spontaneity' thesis.[10] Even after 1933, when the rule of law had been superseded by the rule of terror, spontaneous violence by gentiles against Jews was rare, if it existed at all.[11] What Fritz Stern identifies as a 'subtle silence' and Pulzer as the 'pervasive non-acceptance' was a question of permissive weakness, conformism, and cowardice, rather than one of eliminationist aggression. There is a difference between a society of psychopaths and a society that permits psychopaths to commit their crimes.

From the perspective of 1914, political anti-Semitism had by no means turned out to be a success story. Its direct political influence was small. Legal equality, which had been established by the so-called Emancipation Law of

3 July 1869, had not been renounced. Despite the Lueger phenomenon in Vienna, anti-Semitic parties had enjoyed only occasional electoral success, and to the extent that they had enjoyed success (for example, gaining twelve seats in the Reichstag elections of 1898), it had largely evaporated after the turn of the century.[12] Anti-Semitism was decidedly more effective in cultural terms, through youth movements (like the *Wandervogel* and the *Deutsche Turnerschaft)* and the student organizations, than in direct political terms. Above all, however, it was dormant for twenty years before the radicalization of the First World War, economic upheaval, and the divisions of German society established the conditions under which it could flourish.

When *The Rise of Political Anti-Semitism* was conceived and written in the 1950s, the study of political anti-Semitism was by no means a fashionable field. Its reprinting in 1988 reflected the argument's continued relevance, but also the growing interest in the field in the 1980s and 1990s. It is a short and accessible book, with a clear argument and an elegance of style that is typical of its author. As Andrei Markovits recalls in his moving account, it had a considerable effect on those who tried to come to terms with the Holocaust, especially at a time when there was little literature on the topic. Markovits's observation, however, also prompts a further question. If there was so little literature that could guide Pulzer the graduate student, what did he make of those books that were available? What guided him through a desert in which he was, to all intents and purposes, a pioneer?

One book that must have made an impression on Pulzer was Hannah Arendt's *The Origins of Totalitarianism,* published first in 1951 and including a long first part on anti-Semitism. We do not know, of course, what Pulzer thought when he read *The Origins,* and to what extent precisely he had by then already developed his own ideas. As a speculative intellectual exercise, however, it might be enlightening to compare and contrast Arendt and Pulzer on anti-Semitism. Above all, one is struck by a similarity of biography (although Arendt was a generation older), by the attempt to explain the twentieth century as the outcome of the nineteenth, and by the common commitment to write in order to explain, rather than to accuse. If Karl Jaspers wrote about Arendt that she was oblivious to the sentence *So musste es kommen* (it had to happen), one may also apply this to Pulzer: German history was no one-way street to Auschwitz.[13] A reluctance to accept facile *post-hoc* explanations while at the same time trying to understand why the Holocaust happened in Germany, rather than anywhere else, is a common element. Both, in addition, link the rise of anti-Semitism to the rise of nationalism, in particular in Austria.

This is where commonality ends. Arendt produced a grand sweep of an argument; the merit of her book lies in its contribution to political thought rather than to good historical writing. Pulzer, on the other hand, uses the meticulous tools of history and political science. His central argument is not all-encompassing, but he is conscientious in proposing only arguments supported by empirical evidence. Moreover, while Arendt interprets the rise of anti-Semitism *as a reaction to Jewish assimilation,* which, in her argument, prompted the respective host societies to resent the Jews even more, for Pulzer anti-Semitism occurs *despite* assimilation, since racialist anti-Semitism, as a new phenomenon, could not be quenched by the change of cultural habits or religious practices. This hints at a second conceptual difference. While Arendt and Pulzer agree that anti-Semitism was a historically new phenomenon in the last decades of the nineteenth century, they disagree on its origins. In Arendt's argument the crucial link lies in the relationship between Jews and the nation-state. While the aristocratic élite of the old nation-states had granted a minimum of legal protection and considerable clandestine influence to its Jewish bankers, these in turn had helped to finance the old order, state formation, and war. This came to an end as nationalism undermined the *raison d'être* of the nation-state by generating, amongst others, imperialist aspirations, which in the particularly intolerant Central European variant of pan-Germanism, threatened not only the Other outside the boundaries of the nation-state, but also the Other within it.

In contrast to Arendt, Pulzer plays on the link not between the Jews and the nation-state, but between Jews and liberalism. He does not emphasize the large bankers, the Rothschilds, Warburgs, Bleichröders, and their political aspirations, but the Jewish middle class, the lawyers, doctors, and small businessmen, the journalists and intellectuals committed to the creation of a society without hereditary privileges of class or religion, where careers would be built on talent, not on prerogative. The society they strove for would guarantee freedom of speech and association, and equality before the law, as well as a market economy. In other words, while Arendt is concerned with the small group of Jews who had enjoyed a privileged status in the old order, Pulzer identifies the agenda of the far greater number of Jews who saw their political and economic interests best protected by an order that was new, and essentially liberal.

Again, Pulzer's concern with Jewish-German history points us to a larger concern with the fate of liberalism. The emancipation of Jews in Germany had to be unsuccessful as long as liberalism, which had made inroads into German political culture in the 1840s, and then again in the 1860s and 1870s, failed to become the dominant theme in constitutional arrangements and political practice. In part this had little to do with Jewish emancipation. The continued discrimination of the Prussian electoral law, the aristocratic influences of the Bundesrat, the unaccountability of the Reich government to the Reichstag, all were examples of a political system that was, at best, semi-democratic. The clampdown against the Catholic Church between 1871 and 1880, and against the Social Democrats between 1878 and 1890, illustrated that Jews were not the only group in the Empire that suffered from discrimination. Yet while the

1869 law had established Jews and gentiles as equal before the law, differences in the practices of individual states, in particular in university and
judicial appointments, turned discrimination into a fact of everyday life. In
addition, Pulzer argues, the existence of the question of Jewish emancipation
throughout the nineteenth century lent it a perpetual, notorious character. It
came to be seen as a constant part of the public debate, which could never
be resolved.[14] In contrast to France, where, as Sudhir Hazareesingh illustrates
in Chapter 9, a widespread consensus on the meaning of citizenship had
already emerged in the Second Republic, citizenship in Germany continued
to be contentious.

This meant that life for the Jews in the Empire was difficult but not
unbearable. Though in politics and the public administration Jews continued to endure discrimination, they flourished in other areas, especially in
business, journalism, and, as David Schoenbaum illustrates in Chapter 15,
the arts. In addition, one could find consolation in the fact that discrimination was a widespread phenomenon and that one could channel one's political energies into the establishment of a society in which Jews could prosper.
After 1848 Jews became increasingly involved in the liberal cause, not, as
Pulzer emphasizes, in order to represent narrowly defined Jewish interests
but because the liberal agenda linked Jews most easily to their gentile com-
patriots. It did so because the conservative and later national-imperialist
causes, while appealing to certain Jews' orthodox morality, did not endorse
their commitment to the abolition of feudal privileges, while socialism, in
sharing the commitment to equality before the law and thus attracting a
number of prominent Jewish intellectuals, did not win the hearts of the
larger number of Jews, because it challenged their economic status. Not all
liberals were free of anti-Semitism, to be sure, and it would be facile to
equate liberalism with the Jewish cause. Yet those Jews involved in the building of the German nation from the 1850s to the Weimar Republic overwhelmingly pursued liberal politics, and did so in the spirit of responsibility
for the nation as a whole. Ludwig Bamberger, whose sheer persistence had in
1876 led to the establishment of the Reichsbank, said at the graveside of
another German nation-builder of Jewish origin, Eduard Lasker, who had
striven for a single legal code for the Empire: 'Not he, but the majority of the
German nation spoke through his mouth for more than ten years.'[15]

Though Bamberger's words may have reflected aspiration rather than reality, they point to the intimate connection between liberalism and Jewish
emancipation. As a consequence we can follow Pulzer's argument that the
fate of the Jews was a matter over which the Jews themselves had little control. It was a *dependent variable*.[16] The critical junctures in the history of
failed Jewish emancipation in Germany were the moments when liberalism
fell short of establishing itself as the dominant theme in German politics:
in the aborted revolution of 1848–9, the incomplete democratization at

the inception of the Empire in 1871, and perhaps most importantly in Bismarck's turn towards iron and rye in 1878–9. This, in conjunction with the peculiarities of German nationalism, which had been conceived in the Napoleonic Wars as specifically directed against the enlightened rationalism of the French Revolution, and which had sacrificed the goal of liberal democracy to that of national unity after 1849, set the tone of German politics in the Empire. Even though, as David Southern points out in Chapter 10, the liberal agenda of individual rights became increasingly accepted over the following fifty years, its progress was never sufficient. The victory of 1871 signified not only the victory of Prussia over France, but, Pulzer argues, 'of dynasty over parliament, autocracy over democracy, the army over the middle class'. This was the *explanatory variable*: as German politics before 1918 was not dominated by the middle classes, the Jewish 'desire to assimilate was bound to meet with frustration'.[17] The prejudices and resentments against the Jews had found their humus, where they slumbered, and from where they could flourish when the First World War and economic crisis led to the radicalization of German society that served as the ultimate trigger for later tragedies. As Jan Palmowski illustrates in Chapter 6, even a traditionally liberal city like Frankfurt am Main could not resist the trend of national politics after the turmoil of war and defeat.

The link between the fate of liberalism and the fate of Jewish emancipation does, however, raise a number of questions. One is about the nature of German liberalism: was it benign, innocent, and ultimately unsuccessful against a political culture that acted as a *force majeure*? Or did it fail because of its own faults? As Jan Müller emphasizes in Chapter 8, even the liberalism of the Weimar Republic was all too often an acceptance of the necessary rather than a positive embracing of a just form of government. Thomas Mann, one of the few intellectuals who came out in favour of the Weimar Republic, did so not because it was the natural consequence of the striving for freedom, rationalism, and the rule of law, but because he had convinced himself that it would offer the best conditions for the flourishing of German *Kultur*.[18]

Pulzer does hint at the shortcomings. Liberalism, he argues, was slow 'to recognize that anti-Semitism flourished through its own failure to respond to human needs'.[19] This phrase is so cautious, however, that one wonders what it actually means. What failure? What human needs? When were the mistakes made and by whom? One such failure lay with the gentile liberals' often ambiguous view of Jewish emancipation, which Jonathan Wright illustrates in Chapter 7 in the case of Gustav Stresemann. Another failure—and this is a more general observation—was a general élitism on the part of liberal politicians, which prevented the spread of liberal principles beyond the circles of the liberal *Honoratioren* (notables). Democracy and liberalism do not have to go hand in hand. Just as we can follow the Tocquevillian argument that democracy is above all a matter of mobilization and participation (of which Karl

Lueger was a master), which is only rendered benign by liberal principles (like the protection of the individual, the rule of law, an economy of market rules), liberal aspirations can be élitist and highly sceptical towards the spread of popular participation. Many scholars have argued that German liberalism was dominated for too long by notables and bourgeois élitism sceptical about the lower orders and that the incorporation of new interests and aspirations was the last thing on its agenda.[20] Liberals in Germany not only made the mistake of underestimating the power of anti-Semitism, but also failed to broaden their popular backing and electoral base.[21] This made them, and ultimately Germany's Jews, so vulnerable.

Secondly, German liberals were satisfied too early and with disastrous consequences with their role in parliament, as opposed to a role in government. Pulzer does emphasize this in his scholarship on German political parties, but it is a point that can also be made in the context of Jewish-German history. Since liberals did not aim for power with sufficient vigour at the national level and did not organize their parties in order to exercise governmental functions, they contributed to the low esteem in which parliamentarianism and political parties were held in Germany. The political culture that emerged in Bismarck's Empire was one in which, because of constitutional provisions, executive power was not accountable to the Reichstag, since ministers were directly appointed by the Kaiser and only responsible to him. The lure of treating parliament as a talking shop was one liberal politicians gave in to too quickly. They thus had a share in the undermining of the institutions of democratic representation, if not during the Empire, than at least in the Weimar Republic. If parliamentarians are perceived as irresponsible windbags, oblivious to the realities of power, the call for a strong leader becomes more vociferous.

## Democracy and Party Politics

The German politician who was able to combine the adherence to liberal democracy with strong leadership more effectively than anyone before him was Konrad Adenauer. Even though politicians with impeccable democratic credentials, like Ebert and Stresemann, had exerted leadership before, the conditions in which they acted were less favourable. As a rule of thumb, strong leadership in German politics had often not coincided with the adherence to liberal democratic principles. This illustrates that one can gain insights by tracing the development of German political parties and systems of government over time, and indeed, this historical approach is characteristic of Pulzer's writing on post-1945 German politics. While many a German analysis of government and politics in the Federal Republic begins in 1949, Pulzer in his *German Politics* starts in 1945, and devotes a whole chapter to the period between the collapse of Nazi Germany and the inception of the Federal Republic.[22] There was no clean break, no *Stunde Null* (zero hour) as many in West Germany sought to suggest. Yet despite his pointing to the obvious continuities, Pulzer recognizes the significance of the historical break: out of all the ruptures of German history between 1806 and 1990, the one between 1945 and 1949 was the most important. How, then, he asks, did the Germans, and the Austrians, get from there to here?[23]

It is significant, especially against the background of the failures of political parties in the Weimar Republic, that in Pulzer's view the reasons for the successful establishment of parliamentary democracy in West Germany and Austria after the war ought to be sought not in constitutional provisions but in the role of political parties. In the case of the Federal Republic, this argument can be subsumed under the term 'responsible party government'; in the case of Austria, under the term 'stable coalition'. Let us consider these in turn.

Responsible party government is about the link between electoral choice and government formation. The term *responsible* signifies the government's responsibility to the electorate, that is, the extent to which voters can hold those who are in power responsible for the affairs of the country. For this, they need two instruments. First, voters must be able to identify easily where responsibility lies. Secondly, they must be able to confirm or reject those who are in office at the polls. In the ideal (Westminster) type of responsible party government, the identification of political responsibility is facilitated by a uni-cameral legislature and a centralized system of government, both of which prevent the dispersion of power.[24] The confirmation or rejection of the government of the day is facilitated by a two-party system, which establishes clear alternatives, and which means that electoral choice has a direct and measurable impact on government formation. Elections in the Westminster model are about the rejection or confirmation of government. In many other democracies they are not.

When the Federal Republic was established in 1949, little in its constitutional provisions seemed to point to the establishment of responsible party government. It was not only a federal state, in which the central level of government played no legislative and only a small administrative role in large areas of politics; its federalism was also one in which the *Länder* governments, through the Bundesrat, participated in certain areas of policy-making at the central level. In addition, the first elections in 1949 sent nine parties to the Bundestag, and the establishment of a two-party system therefore seemed far off. What government would be formed was not the outcome of electoral choice but of post-election negotiations in parliament. With the majority being narrow, it was by no means evident that the first Adenauer government would last until the elections in 1953, rather than suffering premature dissolution, the fate of so many of its predecessors in the Weimar Republic. Finally, the Chancellor and the government were mentioned in the constitution as constitutional organs like the Bundestag. Neither the Chancellor nor the ministers have to be members of parliament; it is sufficient that the Chancellor has the confidence of the Bundestag. This means that the Basic Law does not establish an overlap between executive and legislative functions that is so typical for the Westminster model. The line of division it establishes runs not between governmental majority and oppositional minority, but between legislative and executive, as had been the case in the Empire and in the Weimar Republic.

It was thus by no means clear that responsible party government would become a feature of German politics. If the Federal Republic developed towards it nevertheless, this was a question of default rather than design. One reason lay in the rise of the CDU, which had benefited electorally by not having to compete in the Russian zone of occupation, where it would have been weak, and thus established itself first as a strong (30 per cent) and then as the dominant party of the Federal Republic. This had a number of effects on the political system as a whole. First, the CDU unified the forces of the centre-right, which had been highly divergent in the Weimar Republic, especially because of its bi-confessionalism and its subsumption of liberal and conservative forces. Secondly, even though the CDU was a highly heterogeneous party, it managed to reduce social tensions before they hit the electoral arena and thus prevented some of the social fragmentation from which Weimar politics had suffered. Thirdly, the CDU's dominance established the principle of a Chancellor democracy in which the Chancellor played the dominant role in his party and presented himself and his government to the voters at elections. This went some way to linking electoral choice with government formation.

A second reason lay in the behaviour of the SPD, which in reaction to Adenauer's prominence nominated a Chancellor candidate, and thus presented the electorate with an even clearer choice. That the SPD moved into the political centre by abandoning Marxism at the Bad Godesberg conference in 1959 only supported this process. From the 1960s onwards, it became a credible alternative. A third reason, following from this, was the shift of the FDP, which in many respects had been to the right of the CDU in the 1950s, and which in the mid-1960s changed course and established itself as a pivotal party between CDU and SPD. While Bad Godesberg had liberated the SPD from its '30 per cent ghetto' (in which it had been caught in the Weimar Republic), the shift of the FDP to the centre offered it a strategic partner. The possibility of achieving a majority without the CDU suddenly became a real one. In addition, the introduction of the 5 per cent hurdle in 1953, together with the polarization of cold war politics, led to a reduction in the number of parties represented in the Bundestag from nine to three. The icing on the cake came with the federal election in 1972, prior to which SPD and FDP had asserted their willingness to continue in coalition if mathematically possible. For the first time, then, West German voters could choose not only between political parties and party leaders, but also between government and opposition. Despite the diluting effects of federalism and constitutional review, West German politics in the 1970s had moved a long way towards the establishment of responsible party government.

Put differently, responsible party government in West Germany made liberal democracy work. Political parties were the key agent of West German democratization. This point can be illustrated by a comparison with other countries. As David Hine observes in Chapter 12, political parties in postwar Italy were far more effective in self-maintenance and clientele politics than in effective, liberal-democratic government. Because of the stand-off between Christian Democrats and Communists, Italy did not experience a consensus on the formal rules of government, on the main lines of economic policy, or on foreign policy orientation. In contrast, German political parties did manage to establish a consensus on the formal procedures of government (as early as the 1950s) and operated in a consensus-oriented arena from then on, especially in terms of foreign and economic policy. One may also suggest that German political parties were capable of large-scale consensus because they underwent a long-term liberalization in their ideological make-up.

If the key to West German democratization was responsible party government, for Austria it was 'stable coalition'. After the Second World War Austria became an example of political stability and successful democratization, yet the political and party systems implanted in it in 1945 were the same as those of the inter-war years. The reason for this, Pulzer proposes, was the acclimatization of political culture. In the inter-war years the *basic consensus*, the basis of any democracy, had been lacking. As Anton Pelinka illustrates in Chapter 5, the *Lager* had emerged in the first hours of Austrian political culture at the turn of the century and remained one of its most defining elements. The profound conflicts that riddled Austrian society were thus translated into politics and the rigidity of the different *Lager* was a mechanism that formalized social tension. After the war, politics mediated social tension, and the *Lager* pacified where before they had exacerbated social conflicts. Pulzer identifies a number of reasons for this turn-around. He mentions the occupation statute, which functioned as an external political stabilizer, and the general prosperity of the 1950s and 1960s, which functioned as an external economic stabilizer. In addition, the practice of *Proporz*, by which state enterprises and political offices were distributed strictly according to the proportional claims of the *Lager*, solved the crisis of distribution, which had crippled Austrian society in the inter-war years. At this juncture it is very useful to add Wolfgang Müller's analysis (in Chapter 11) of the conditions of consociationalism, and explain that Austrian party leaders were more capable of commanding their grass roots after the war, which helped them in operating the consociational system. Finally, the decline of political ideology eased tension in the party system, and reduced the polarity between the Christian-conservative and social-democratic poles. In other words, the parties were crucial to the stabilization of Austrian democracy because they operated, in concert, the institutions they had called into being, and thus legitimated them.

The arguments of 'responsible party government' in West Germany, and of 'stable coalition' in Austria were essentially in place in the late 1960s and early 1970s. While they have stood the test of time well, it would be peculiar if the last thirty years had not shed new light on them. Throughout the 1990s political commentary on Austria was concerned with the electoral impact of the *Freedom Party* (FPÖ) under Jörg Haider, especially after its success in the 1999 general election led to its participating in a government led by the Austrian People's Party (ÖVP). Within the context of diplomatic sanctions by the EU against Austria as a reaction to the new ÖVP/FPÖ government, many commentators were tempted to conclude that Haider was a ghost from the past. Especially because of his anti-foreigner rhetoric and his sympathetic comments on the Third Reich, it was argued that Austria had never faced up to its part in National Socialism, and had not changed since the Second World War. The years of 'stable coalition', in this argument, were only a mask; the real character of Austrian politics had survived underneath.

Not least against the background of Pulzer's scholarship, this seems an oversimplification. Regardless of the prejudices and resentments that might have survived in Austrian society, one is tempted to point out that right-wing populist extremism is also a prominent phenomenon in countries that had, in the 1930s and 1940s, succumbed far less to fascism than Austria. There had to be something else involved other than the reawakening of old ghosts. In addition to the argument that the *Freedom Party* is the expression of ancient sentiments that had survived the liberalization of the Second Republic, one may therefore also want to describe it as the Second Republic's own child. The Haider phenomenon represents the resentment against a political class which functioned as a 'cartel that, at times, has been not only corrupt, but corrupt with impunity'.[25] More importantly, it is also a function of 'stable coalition', since the coalition between the Austrian Social Democratic and People's Parties was so large and so stable that it had literally eliminated opposition from the political system. In this sense one is tempted to turn the Pulzer argument about 'responsible party government' against the Pulzer argument about 'stable coalition' and point out that responsible party government, which by and large existed in West Germany, not only needs a two-party system but also a clear alternative between governmental majority and oppositional minority. If the mechanisms of economic distribution and informal power-sharing have rendered the outcome of elections as insignificant as they did in the case of Austria, the electorate no longer has a clear choice between governments.

What Pulzer identified as one of the key reasons for the success of West German democracy, he neglected in his analysis of Austria. If he had applied the significance of responsible party government to the Austrian Second Republic as well, he would have found that it qualifies his argument on stable coalitions. All of this does not disprove the finding that the stability induced by continuous coalition government helped to pacify social conflicts and to stabilize Austrian democracy. But, with hindsight, it adds a qualification, namely that all things have a time and a price, even in the realm of 'stable coalitions'.

The Haider phenomenon in Austria, then, represented something old and something new—old in the sense that the Austrian contribution to the success of National Socialism and the contribution of individual Austrians to the Holocaust were never matters of public controversy in the way they became in Germany after 1968. The process of self-cleansing did not go very far. It represented something new in the sense that any system that stifles competition from within nourishes competition from without. This leads to three observations. First, it is of course difficult to quantify precisely what role the old and the new played: to what extent the votes for the Freedom Party were votes sympathetic to anti-foreigner, anti-European rhetoric and to what extent they were the natural reaction to two cartel-parties. Secondly, there was a link between the old and the new. The cartel of power that emerged in 1945 was also a cartel of political discourse. If Austria had for decades not come to terms with the degree of its involvement in the Nazi war and in Nazi crimes, this was a direct consequence of a political class that did not wish to confront unwelcome truths. Thirdly, the Austrian reaction against governments of stable coalition was a reaction against two political parties, not against the institutions of parliamentary democracy. If fifty years of stifled competition produced a party outside 'the system', this party was only outside the system of 'cartel power', not an extra-parliamentary opposition.

Since the late 1970s, the conditions for responsible party government in Germany, have declined, without, however, undermining the principle as such. One complicating factor consists of the larger number of political parties represented in the Bundestag, which makes the link between electoral choice and government formation more tenuous. On this note one might be tempted to argue that the FDP's change of coalition partner in 1982 was an example of the weakening of responsible party government, since it was not the outcome of electoral choice. Still, one might question whether the FDP's change really did violate the principles of responsible coalition. There was a clear declaration on the part of the SPD/FDP coalition that it would continue if re-elected in 1980; the two parties then kept their promise. Moreover, both CDU/CSU and FDP leaders announced explicitly after the change of government in 1982 that their government was only a caretaker government that lacked legitimacy as long as it was not reinforced at the polls. Both points suggest a vindication of responsible party government in 1982–3.

Perhaps the 1998 Bundestag election is a better case in point. With a Chancellor candidate who personalized the SPD's stretch into the centre ground, it was far from clear that the resulting coalition would be one between the SPD and the Greens. On the contrary, many voters speculated, and aspired to, a 'grand coalition' between the SPD and the CDU/CSU.[26] Even though it seems in retrospect as though politics had polarized along a left/right divide, with the left victorious, we can argue that the vote was in fact one for the political centre. This thesis is supported by the two key groups who had shifted from the CDU to the SPD: middle-aged middle-class voters in the West, middle-aged blue-collar workers in the East.[27] Neither group is recognized for its polarizing tendencies. The thesis is also supported by the relatively rapid decline in popularity of the new government. The mandate was weaker than it first appeared; it was situational and temporal, rather than the outcome of a long-term realignment.[28] William Paterson illustrates this fact in Chapter 13 by examining the SPD's policy reorientation in co-operation with the British Labour Party, following the resignation of Oskar Lafontaine as Finance Minister and SPD chairman.

On a similar note, we can assume that governmental majorities after German elections are smaller now than they used to be, in part because the two major parties have suffered from dealignment, in part because the PDS's presence in the Bundestag strengthens the opposition, without being politically acceptable as part of the governmental majority. Finally, we cannot exclude the possibility that one of the three smaller parties—FDP, Greens, PDS—will disappear in the medium term, thus increasing volatility even more. In a society that is less structured, and a party system that is less ordered than was the case for West Germany in the 1950s and 1960s, electoral volatility will inevitably increase, and shake one of the foundations of responsible party government.

A further complicating factor, as Max Kaase points out in Chapter 14, lies in the fact that the accountability of German governments is undermined by the humdrum constraints of federalism. If this was complicated enough in the 1960s, it has since become a hotbed of unaccountability. The process of financial equalization clouds the economic performance of individual *Land* governments, and eliminates incentives for sound budgetary policies. The mixing of federal with party politics, moreover, generates dividing lines that are not only harmful to decision-making, but also cloud political accountability. While this was particularly salient in the 1997 attempt at tax reform, we have since learnt that it will become the rule rather than the exception. True, federalism will cloud the voters' choice of government, rather than render it impossible in the way that a multi-party system does. Yet its dispersion of authority might heighten a sense of political immobilism and voter disempowerment, and, as an outcome, political disaffection. As the case of Austria has shown, political disaffection of this nature is not conducive to stable coalition or to the parties of the political centre.

This analysis is also vindicated by the influences of European integration. With the arrival and development of the Single Market, member states of the European Union have gained an additional layer of government. In large areas of economic and social policy, the locus of decision-making is neither in *Land* capitals nor in national capitals but in Brussels. Since Austria only acceded to the European Union in 1995, this has come as an even more radical change there than in Germany. The processes of European integration obfuscate responsible party government, since decisions in the Council of Ministers are taken not only far away but also behind closed doors. The result is a lack of accountability, a web of bureaucratic-administrative rules, an empowerment of executive over legislative organs, and an undermining of government responsibility *vis-à-vis* the electorate. This is a challenge to responsible party government and one that will critically affect the politics of EU member states in the future.

## *Conclusion*

This Chapter has covered historical ground from the Napoleonic Wars at the beginning of the nineteenth to the institutional set-up of the European Union in the twenty-first century, and has tried to identify some of the core themes that emerge from Pulzer's scholarship. Let us test these, briefly, on their contemporary relevance. If the twentieth century was Janus-faced, and the observer in question engaged and committed, what can we take away at the dawn of the new era?

First, the rats might die again. Not, perhaps, in the same town, yet we have reason to assume that the despair with the conditions of modernity is recurrent. While the challenge to the principles of liberal democracy does not have to come from what we have traditionally identified as the right or the left, we can rest assured that the challenge is never overcome for good. It is not limited to a particular time nor to a particular place. Even after the war, the troubles of McCarthyism in the United States and the authoritarian tendencies of parts of the students' revolution in Western Europe underlined the fact that liberalism is a fragile construction, and that liberal democracy has to be tended and nurtured. What can we do in order to maintain it? Education by itself is not enough. Where did German anti-Semitism slumber between 1895 and 1918? In the youth movement and the students' organizations, that is, in those organizations that should have been immune from the totalitarian temptation, if the intellectual standard of their members had been the key factor. Neither youth nor education are, by themselves, a guarantee of enlightened politics. Too many intellectuals in the twentieth century ended up 'excusing the inexcusable, and defending the indefensible'.

What we can assume instead is that the institutions of liberal democracy are benign even if not perfect. In part we can conclude this from the consequences of their failure. In part we can conclude it from the fragility of their existence. This is an insight that will survive the twentieth century and will recurrently prove its relevance in the twenty-first. A pertinent reminder for its underlying significance was the debate about globalization, which dominated the public arena for much of the 1990s. All too quickly, globalization was described as a threat first, and an opportunity second. While it is true that markets themselves do not guarantee the survival of liberal democracy, it would be courageous to maintain that all state activity is benign and all market activity dangerous. An economy based on market principles is, amongst other things, the necessary correlative to political liberty. As Pulzer observed in an essay on Joseph Schumpeter, 'market institutions of some kind, without which there cannot be individual autonomy, are a pre-condition of competitive politics'.[29]

Secondly, political parties continue to have crucial functions in liberal democracies. Again, they are far from perfect. They may abuse their continued existence in order to establish themselves as a cartel that is more concerned with the advantages it brings to its members than with politics as public service.[30] Their activities have to be checked by the judiciary and by the independent media. Yet in the widespread criticism of German parties in the first half of the 1990s, Pulzer's voice was conspicuously absent. His argument on the democratizing and stabilizing functions that political parties played in Austria and West Germany after the war would have sat uneasily with a fundamental criticism of their current role. This is an important realization at a time when party affiliation becomes more volatile and when politics in all EU member states has to deal with a new, central level of government at which political parties have not yet found their role.

If we wonder what the future might hold, then, we may take cues from Pulzer's scholarship for the analysis of a political system that is still very much in the process of democratization: that of the European Union. Do Pulzer's observation on political parties and democratization have any significance here? Two observations may be made. First, the absence of clear and comprehensible lines of division between the competencies of EU and nation-state organs weakens the principle of responsible party government in member states. The persistent use of EU institutions as scapegoats not only weakens popular trust in these institutions but also in government as a whole.

The second point concerns a parallel between the emerging EU polity and the political systems that Pulzer examined in Austria and Germany. If sectoral and national interests meet the political arena unmodified by party mediation, political conflicts are exacerbated rather than pacified. It is thus at least arguable that political parties will eventually play an important role in the politics of the European Union too. In this view they would have to aggregate interests and facilitate the governance of a political system where power is highly dispersed, where democratization is incomplete, and where sectoral and national conflicts will become only more acute as society—through the European Union's enlargement to Eastern and South-eastern Europe—becomes more heterogeneous. Peter Pulzer, the committed observer of a Janus-faced century, has imparted a spirit of inquiry and the tools of analysis that help in dealing with the challenges ahead. We could not ask for more.

# Notes

1. Thanks to Jonathan Lipkin, Jan Palmowski, and Jonathan Wright.
2. Albert Camus, *La Peste*, (Paris: Gallimard, 1947), 279 (author's translation).
3. Peter Pulzer, *Political Representation and Elections in Britain*, 3rd edn. (London: George Allen & Unwin, 1975), 102.
4. With *Jews and the German State, German Politics 1945–1995, Germany, 1871–1945*, and the contributions to Michael Meyer's *German-Jewish History in Modern Times*, the record of the 1990s was quite different.
5. David Sorkin, '"Historian of Fate." Fritz Stern on the History of the German Jewry. An Appreciation', in Marion F. Deshmukh and Jerry Z. Muller (eds.), *Fritz Stern at 70* (Washington, DC: German Historical Institute, 1996), 34.
6. Peter Pulzer, *The Rise of Political Anti-Semitism in Germany and Austria* (London: Peter Halban, 1988), pp. ix–x.
7. Ibid. 55.
8. See *Rise of Political Anti-Semitism*, introduction to the revised edition, and Peter Pulzer, *German Antisemitism Revisited* (Rome: Archivo Guido Izzi, 1999).
9. *Rise of Political Anti-Semitism*, p. xiv.
10. Daniel Jonah Goldhagen, *Hitler's Willing Executioners* (New York: Alfred Knopf, 1996). For more detail see also Pulzer's review of Goldhagen: 'Psychopaths and Conformists, Adventurers and Moral Cowards', *London Review of Books* (27 Jan. 1997).
11. Albert S. Lindemann, *Esau's Tears: Modern Anti-Semitism and the Rise of the Jews* (Cambridge: Cambridge University Press, 1997); Goldhagen, *Hitler's Willing Executioners*.
12. *Rise of Political Anti-Semitism*, 186.
13. Karl Jaspers in Hannah Arendt, *Elemente und Ursprünge totalitärer Herrschaft* (Munich and Zürich: Piper, 1986), 12.
14. Peter Pulzer, 'Why was there a Jewish Question in Imperial Germany?', *Year Book of the Leo Baeck Institute*, 25 (1980), 133–46.
15. Peter Pulzer, 'Jews and Nation-Building in Germany', *Year Book of the Leo Baeck Institute*, 41 (1996), 207.
16. In the social sciences the *dependent variable* is taken to refer to what one tries to explain, while the *explanatory variable* refers to what explains it. In the present context we can argue that the failure of Jewish emancipation (dependent variable) was caused by the failure of German liberalism (explanatory variable).

The particularities of Jewish life and Jewish politics are an independent variable that had no bearing on the failure of liberalism. See also Ch. 6 below, by Jan Palmowski.

17. Both quotations are taken from Pulzer, 'Jewish Question in Imperial Germany', 139; see also Michael Stürmer, *Das Ruhelose Reich, Deutschland 1866–1918*, special edn. (Berlin: Siedler, 1994), 95–119.

18. Thomas Mann, 'Von deutscher Republik', in Hermann Kurzke and Stephan Stachorski (eds.), *Thomas Mann Essays* (Frankfurt am Main: S. Fischer, 1993), ii. *Für das neue Deutschland 1919–1925*, pp. 126–66.

19. Pulzer, *Rise of Political Anti-Semitism*, 320.

20. For instance David Blackbourn and Geoff Eley, *The Peculiarities of German History* (Oxford: OUP, 1984).

21. On liberalism's inability to comprehend anti-Semitism correctly despite its earnest attempts see Jan Palmowski's contribution to this volume.

22. Peter Pulzer, *German Politics 1945–1995* (Oxford: OUP, 1995).

23. Ibid. 1.

24. If we accept that the House of Lords is not powerful enough to render the description of bicameralism accurate.

25. Peter Pulzer, 'Between Collectivism and Liberalism: The Political Evolution of Austria since 1945', in Kurt Richard Luther and Peter Pulzer (eds.), *Austria 1945–95* (Aldershot: Ashgate, 1998), 232.

26. Pulzer, 'The German Federal Election of 1998', *West European Politics*, 22/3 (1999), 241–9.

27. Stephen Padgett, 'The Boundaries of Stability: The Party System Before and After the 1998 Bundestagswahl', *German Politics*, 8/2 (1999), 88–107.

28. Ibid.

29. Peter Pulzer, 'The Contemporary Relevance of Joseph Schumpeter', in Joseph P. Strelka and Ilona Slawinski (eds.), *Die Bukowina in Vergangenheit und Gegenwart* (Berne: Peter Lang, 1995), 168.

30. Richard S. Katz and Peter Mair, 'Changing Models of Party Organization and Party Democracy', *Party Politics*, 1/1 (1995), 5–27.

# 4

## Peter Pulzer's Writing on Political Anti-Semitism and the Jewish Question in Germany and Austria: An Assessment

### *Andrei S. Markovits*

### *Introduction*

I remember it well. It was in the fall of 1968—as a 20-year-old senior in Columbia University's College—that I first encountered Peter Pulzer's *The Rise of Political Anti-Semitism in Germany and Austria*. I had never heard of Peter Pulzer but I found the title of the book not only intellectually intriguing but also profoundly compelling on a deeper, autobiographical level. This, after all, was precisely the time that I had first begun to learn in a systematic and serious way about the absolutely crucial role that anti-Semitism had played in Austria's and Central Europe's political history during the first half of the twentieth century. Tellingly, I immersed myself in this subject at an Ivy-League university in New York City's Morningside Heights, just a bus ride away from the heavily Jewish Upper West Side where my uncle—following Auschwitz— owned a small candy store. This world, though light years away from Vienna which I had left for good in 1967, seemed also peculiarly close to a Vienna about which I had heard but which I most certainly did not encounter in the nine years that I lived there—(between 1958 and 1967) as a sort of extended way station between the city of my early childhood, Timisoara (Temesvar) in Romania, and my final destiny as an adult, the United States. To be sure, I knew something about Vienna's, Austria's, Hungary's, and Romania's igno-minious recent past having been the only child of a Holocaust-ravaged family of Hungarian-speaking bourgeois Jews from Romania's Banat district. I remember distinctly how my father could not quite make up his mind whom to root more against, the underdog Germans or the mighty Hungarians—the vaunted *arany csapat* (golden team)—in that memorable World Cup final in the Wankdorf Stadium in Berne played on 4 July (of all dates) 1954. It was clear that, just as much as he hated them both, he was equally culturally and emotionally tied to both. I knew—and felt—from my earliest childhood the deep ambivalences that my parents had for all things German: on the one hand hating and fearing its every side; yet on the other still cherishing its culture, its music, its poetry, its language. To my parents the Germans writ large, thus including the Austrians and all other German-speaking peoples— mirroring in many ways the German right's image of the German *Volk*—were truly both the people of the poets and thinkers (*Dichter und Denker*) and as that of the judges and gallows (*Richter und Henker*). My parents were exactly the kinds of Jews whom Pulzer describes so articulately as the archetypes of German, Austrian, and Central European Jewry: urban, bourgeois, commer- cial, liberal, secular, non-Yiddish-speaking, and deeply identified with German culture with which they were both at least as conversant as (and perhaps even more identified than) with their native Hungarian.

While I was never confronted with any kind of overt anti-Semitism during my eight years in one of Vienna's most exclusive Gymnasia, I never felt com- fortable there, if only because I was one of three Jewish students in the entire school. For reasons that were not totally clear to me at the time, I was most definitely 'othered' (to use contemporary jargon) in every aspect of my Viennese existence: in school, among my playmates, on the soccer field. Indeed, it was mainly because I was Jewish that my father insisted—and I gladly agreed—that I attend college in the United States. Making it in America proved too daunting a task for him when we emigrated to New York after my mother's death. Indeed, it was in good part due to his deep immersion in German and Hungarian culture—in a long-destroyed Central European world—that he decided to return to Europe and settle in Vienna which he feared and hated, and which never accorded him any genuine comfort until he died thirty years later. Yet, he could not shed his cultural preferences which meant that he lived restlessly betwixt and between a world that he loved but whose culture remained alien to him (the United States); and one that he loathed but whose cultural codes he knew in the most intimate way (Austria as a contemporary representative of a bygone Central Europe). My leaving Vienna and re-immigrating to the United States after having finished the Gymnasium with a *Matura* degree was to be a vicarious resolution to my father's tortured predicament.

It is in this context that Pulzer's *The Rise of Political Anti-Semitism in Germany and Austria* has meant much more to me than the classic it has become in the fields of modern European history, Jewish history, comparative politics and—of course—German studies. I am not exaggerating by stating that, together with Karl W. Deutsch's *The Nerves of Government*, Pulzer's study changed my life. The book spoke to me on so many different intellectual and personal levels that my reading it proved a decisive factor in my wanting to emulate it in a larger sense, and the only way to do that was to become an academic. In rereading my old copy published by John Wiley and Sons in 1964 for this contribution to the *Festschrift*, it became clear to me more than ever before how deeply influential Peter Pulzer's book had been in my life. Alas, it would not be fitting to reproduce some of the many comments that I wrote on the book's pages even though their sheer quantity and content would clearly reveal to the reader just how much Pulzer's book affected me. My modest contribution here should thus mainly be seen as a personal expression of acknowledgement and gratitude to Peter Pulzer.

I would like to focus first on those aspects of Pulzer's work on anti-Semitism and the 'Jewish Question' in Germany and Austria that I have found particularly important and original. I then proceed to highlight the vast differences that inform the lives of Jews in today's world, including Austria and Germany, in contrast to the world that Pulzer has analysed so eloquently in his work. We will see that the lives of Jews at the turn of the twenty-first century are a good deal less precarious and subject to constant hostility and humiliation than was the case at the *fin de siècle* of the nineteenth century that has formed the core of Pulzer's work. I will also briefly address the changes that have occurred in the public presence and awareness of the 'Jewish Question' and the Shoah in particular since Pulzer published his seminal study in the 1960s. I will end on a somewhat pessimistic note by highlighting some of the continuities that have survived the twentieth century and whose presence Pulzer correctly identified as deeply troublesome at its beginning. I see no reason to find them less alarming at its end.

## Pulzer's Contributions

Anybody writing on anti-Semitism and the Jewish Question after the Shoah has to confront the two following epistemological problems: first, the obvious need and tendency to explain events preceding the Holocaust through its overwhelming prism, that is, to explain historical events in a *post-hoc* fashion. Though perfectly understandable and intellectually justifiable, this still leads to distortions of a reality that might not do proper justice to its agents and structures. The second problem pertains to an inherently comparative approach to anti-Semitism. For, even if not explicitly stated, the question inevitably arises: why was the Shoah conceived and executed in Germany and Austria and why not elsewhere in Europe, France or Russia for example, though other countries could well have qualified as appropriate candidates if the level of anti-Semitism was to be the major gauge for this unique disaster's cause? Pulzer's central point that forms the main conceptual axis for all his work on the Jewish Question and anti-Semitism in Germany and Austria counters these two epistemological problems effectively. He states repeatedly that the crux for this Austrian and German 'exceptionalism' lay in the contentious issue of citizenship that beset these German lands throughout the nineteenth century. Simply put, the problem was whether Jews, either as non-Christians or as non-Germans, could ever qualify as full citizens. Neither the Basic Rights of the German People, as adopted by the Frankfurt Parliament in 1848, nor the Law on the Equality of All Confessions passed by the parliament of the North German Confederation in 1869, stilled this debate'.[1] In other words, not even the most progressive pieces of legislation and the most emancipatory political moments of the nineteenth century could reconcile these complex issues of political and cultural identities in Germany and German-speaking Austria at least to a degree that might have relegated them from the public realm to that of the private as was the case in most Western countries, from the United States and Britain, to Holland and Belgium but even in viciously anti-Semitic France where the revolutionary emancipation measures were never rescinded even by the reactionary regimes that emerged periodically throughout the nineteenth century. And Pulzer further strengthens his argument by stating: 'As is almost always the case, a debate about the Jews is not only a debate about the Jews. It was primarily a debate about the character of the German nation in response to the challenge of the French Revolution and the Napoleonic invasions.'[2] In other words, the development, trajectory, form, and content of the Jewish Question in Germany—and the specificities of German anti-Semitism—were a clear manifestation of how Germany and the Germans dealt with the vicissitudes and complexities of the modernization process and the advent of modernity in the course of the nineteenth century. With the Germans being unable to find a generally accepted answer to the question 'What is a German?' they were equally unable to offer a reply to the vexing query 'Can a Jew be a German?' There were many more Jews—both in absolute numbers and as a percentage of the total population—in some European countries than in Germany, where with their 600,000 souls Jews comprised all but 1 per cent of the total population. There was a much greater degree of anti-Semitism as measured by physical violence and other unpleasant manifestations of overt discrimination against Jews in some European countries than in Germany. In short, many countries exhibited patterns in which the individual parts of the complex known as the Jewish Question appeared a good deal uglier than in Germany. And still, in the German situation the whole was a lot more acute and pernicious than the sum of its parts for the reasons so clearly delineated by Pulzer. The Jews had become willy-nilly the personification and the embodiment of modernity which—to many Germans, élites and intellectuals in particular—represented a mixed blessing at best. To be sure, Pulzer's case seems particularly convincing because he compares Germany with Europe's western countries. But what about places such as Russia, Romania, or the eastern regions of the Habsburg Empire such as Galicia as opposed to the Cisleithanian German-speaking core territory featuring Vienna, which, after all, forms the essence of Pulzer's Austrian case? Did Russians and Romanians have fewer problems than Germans resolving such central issues of modernity as the relationship between state and nation; and that of citizen in relation to either as well as both? Pulzer's conceptual case would have been more compelling still had he broadened his comparison to include Europe's eastern half as well.

To Pulzer's great credit, he anchors his explanation for anti-Semitism's unique configuration in Austria and Germany squarely in the realm of politics. Economic issues were important, as were those of religion. But the primacy of politics, according to Pulzer, remains uncontestable in a proper understanding of this German and Austrian 'exceptionalism'. This constitutes an essential conceptual point that deserves explicit praise because it clearly anchors the problem much more thoroughly than alternative 'independent variables'. Not only was the crux of the Jewish Question in Austria and Germany predominantly political, it was also a reflection of the constellation of German and Austrian politics respectively, not of Jewish politics. Countries such as Britain, France, Holland, Belgium, and the United States surely had anti-Semitism, often with an ugly and offensive tone, but—following Pulzer's argument centered on the primacy of politics and the struggle over modernity—these countries did not have a Jewish Question. This made a world of difference in the quality of anti-Semitism as a political phenomenon in Germany and Austria on the one hand; and the western countries of Europe on the other. Pulzer makes it quite clear between the lines that the controversies surrounding modernity as a crucible in the formation of new social identities and political allegiances simply had not yet reached Europe's eastern half by the middle of the nineteenth century the way they did its western part, with Germany being on the cusp though clearly tilting towards the western pattern, most certainly as the century drew to a close. Nowhere are the marked differences between Eastern and Western Europe made more explicit in Pulzer's writings than in his categorization of the Jews. Adopting Ezra Mendelsohn's well-known differentiation between Eastern European and West European Jews—the former still virtually unassimilated, Yiddish-speaking, adhering to religious Orthodoxy, living in rural areas or small towns (the *shtetl*), very poor, having a high birth-rate and a very low rate of intermarriage; the latter in contrast highly assimilated, having abandoned Yiddish as a language and Orthodoxy as a religious expression, living in large metropolitan centers, often a country's capital city, financially comfortable, perhaps even wealthy, with a very low birth-rate and a comparatively high rate of intermarriage—Pulzer makes it amply clear to the reader that the Jewish world of relevance to his concern clearly belongs to the West European category. In fact it did so with a vengeance in that one would have been hard put to find a Jewish community that was more acculturated to its macro-environment than the German. Or, as Pulzer's studies make so amply clear, perceived itself to be so acculturated and desired nothing more than a total acculturation that became its tragic trademark. For one thing was amply clear: the more the Jews in Germany desired and perpetuated this acculturation—the more they wanted to be German citizens of the Jewish faith—the more determined (and ultimately successful) the resistance became on the part of the Germans to deny the Jews precisely this very wish. No matter how German a Jew had become, he was—in the all-important perception of the Germans—still not a true German. The Germans never accepted the Jews' desire to be accepted publicly as Germans like any other German citizen while being allowed to remain Jews in their private realm, as expressed most commonly in some form of religious practice, most typically of the Reform kind which had very little in common with Jewish Orthodoxy.

While Pulzer's theoretical focus and empirical emphasis rest almost exclusively on an investigation of anti-Semitism and the Jewish Question as they pertained to the gentiles in Germany and Austria, there are many instances in which we get an illuminating glimpse of the Jews' wishes, hopes, and fears— in short of Jewish life in Austria and Germany.

Pulzer's work highlights the extreme objective ambivalence of Jews in Austria and Germany between 1870 and the 1930s. On the one hand, Pulzer conveys masterfully how the Jews reached an objectively favourable, indeed enviable, position in the urban centres of Austria and Germany (meaning in essence Vienna, in the former's case, and Berlin, in the latter's, with a smattering of Frankfurt and Hamburg thrown in for good measure) in a matter of a few decades. Their upward mobility was truly impressive. They became richer, were better educated, and occupied socially more attractive occupations such as lawyers, doctors and journalists than the average gentile bourgeois Austrian (Viennese) or German. Pulzer's numbers and analytic narrative simply leave no doubt that modernity was good to the Jews. This favourable objective situation also had a subjective consequence and corollary: Jews in Vienna, Berlin, and the other German big cities identified overwhelmingly with their newly rewarding environment. They adopted their environment's language, culture, mores to a degree that rendered them virtually (and objectively) indistinguishable from their non-Jewish bourgeois neighbors. Most important, Jews not only spoke, read, and wrote German—they *felt* German. Examples abound in Pulzer's work that make this point unmistakably clear and confirm yet again what we know so well from the vast literature on this subject. On the crucial collective identity of class, one could in fact see the Jewish fate in Germany and Austria as a success story in bourgeois acculturation, if not complete assimilation. But class is merely one—albeit important—expression of collective identity. It was another, that of ethnicity, which rendered this Austrian/German environment perhaps objectively rewarding for the Jews but far from welcoming. And this leads us to the negative dimensions of the ambivalence that informed the Jewish existence in Germany and Austria. Pulzer's work makes it amply clear that anti-Semitism was a growing force in daily life in *fin de siècle* Germany and Austria. Not in terms of the votes attained by anti-Semitic parties, which were minuscule in Germany (but less so in Austria where the most popular mayor in Vienna's history was elected repeatedly on an explicitly anti-Semitic platform); not in any kind of violence against Jewish property and people which, too, was negligible (especially when compared to the routinized pogroms in Russia); not even in major public acts of hatred like the Dreyfus case that engulfed France at the time; but in terms of the daily discriminations by key institutions such as universities, schools, the judiciary, the civil service, clubs of all kinds; as well as the constancy and ubiquity of anti-Semitic discourse in everyday life. Anti-Semitism, as opposed to Jew-baiting, became part of public and private life in all facets of German and Austrian society by the end of the nineteenth century. No space was exempt from it, not even Social Democracy, a point that Pulzer raises and acknowledges but that would have deserved a much more critical treatment than he offers in his work. And the Jews put up with this ignominious discrimination and humiliating situation. They accepted this burden as a 'bearable handicap', not because they did not see it and suffer from it but because they had simply no better alternative. In the well-known terminology of precisely such a German Jew (Albert O. Hirschmann): the Jews in Austria and Germany had no real 'exit option'. Pulzer is superb in rejecting the often-raised *post-hoc* accusation waged against the German Jews of being blinded by the objective comforts of their situation which rendered them oblivious to, even dismissive of, the rising danger around them. He summarizes the Jews' precarious predicament in their objective and subjective realities by appropriately quoting Fritz Stern (another German Jew) repeatedly: 'German Jews throve visibly—and suffered invisibly'.[3]

Pulzer describes the Jews' singularly successful and creative contributions to virtually every intellectual and artistic facet of German and Austrian life (to be precise yet again, meaning Berlin and Vienna) but he, too, like all others who have written on this topic, fails to offer a proper explanation for this singular phenomenon. Why did the Jews flourish so much in these two cities? Why were they so creative in every intellectual endeavour, from music to medicine, from literature to law, from philosophy to physics? Why did they strive so desperately to become German, to be embraced by the gentile—the 'real'—Germans the way they embraced German language and culture? Why did they expend so much energy to attain what Gershom Sholem so tellingly described as a 'one-sided and unreciprocated' love affair that bore no resemblance whatsoever to the alleged German-Jewish symbiosis that continues to be invoked with much fanfare by Germans to this day? Still, why did the Jews so longingly want this symbiosis that the Germans refused to extend to them?

Not having an exit option surely is part of the story. Being comparatively well off in relation to the surrounding German and Austrian population as well as the Jews in most European countries (especially the ones to the east of

Germany and Austria comprising the bulk of European Jewry at the time) is another. But these are negative, defensive reasons. There surely must have also been many positive, affirmative reasons that Pulzer—like most others writing on this complex issue—fails to mention, let alone present in a comprehensive analytic fashion. To be sure, the topic of his lifelong research has been anti-Semitism and the Jewish Question in Germany and Austria, which means that the primary focus of his interest lies with the gentile Austrians and Germans, not the Jews. Still, I am convinced that even as fine and careful a scholar as Peter Pulzer cannot help but be influenced by the hindsight of the Holocaust in trying to understand this enigma. Given the enormity of this tragedy, the Jews' desperate, all-out efforts to form a symbiosis with the increasingly hostile Germans and Austrians all the way up to the 1930s appears sad beyond words. Yet there was something intangible that rendered the Jews' existence in Austria and Germany between 1870 and 1938 if not symbiotic with that of their environment, then certainly special. The Jews of Berlin and even more so Vienna, attained a density in genius and creativity that remained unmatched by that of their co-religionists in London, Paris, Brussels, or Amsterdam; as well as Warsaw, Bucharest, St Petersburg, and Moscow. Only the Jews of Budapest could perhaps be classified in the same league of creativity in depth and breadth as those in Vienna. And confirming further the singular meaning of German culture and language to the Jews of Central Europe was the fact that much of the creative contribution on the part of the Budapest Jews occurred in German rather than in Hungarian. The Jewish contribution to human knowledge emanating from *fin de siècle* (nineteenth century) Vienna can only be compared to those of Babylon during the second exile; Granada under the Moors; and the United States of the *fin de siècle*—in this case that of the twentieth century. I remain very optimistic that in stark contrast to the previous three cases that brought the Jewish people exile, death, and destruction, Jews will continue to flourish in their American existence by dint of a crucial ingredient that none of the three previous places offered the Jews: full political acceptance as equal citizens.

## Positive Developments

In a variant to Theodore Adorno's famous saying that after Auschwitz it is barbaric to write poetry, I would claim that it is patently absurd to speak of an improvement of Jewish life anywhere, most certainly in Europe. Still, with this caveat in mind, and with the ever-present awareness that the executors of the anti-Semitic ideas, feelings, attitudes, and policies so meticulously studied by Peter Pulzer throughout his academic career were in fact frighteningly successful in eradicating much of Jewish life and culture in Europe in the span of barely one decade, it is fair to say that the world as a whole—and Europe in particular—is a much safer and more comfortable place for Jews in 2000 than it was in 1900. The foremost reason for this, of course, is the continued presence of a solid exit option for every Jew in the form of the state of Israel. With Isreal making the acceptance of every Jew in the world as its automatic citizen—the so-called Law of Return—the cornerstone of its very legitimacy as a Jewish state, Jews have been able to avail themselves of this option for fifty years, whenever things got bad for them as a collective or also as individuals.

The other major reason is, of course, the triumph of liberal democracy which—to reiterate Pulzer's main point—has been without a doubt the only form of political rule to have consistently and reliably proven itself to be at least a fair if not an outrightly welcoming arrangement to the Jews. In significant contrast, matters in dictatorships were completely random and incalculable: thus, though most dictatorships of the right were inimical and often murderous to the Jews, this was not the case with Franco's Spain and even Mussolini's Italy until the German influence became overbearing. Conversely, dictatorships of the left seemed initially to be supportive of Jews as human beings, as resistance fighters, as workers, as anti-fascists; though things looked a lot gloomier when these regimes were confronted with the support of Jews as Jews. As we sadly know from such events as the doctors' plot in the Soviet Union, the Slansky trial in Czechoslovakia, the Pauker case in Romania, the Rajk affair in Hungary, the Merker incident in the German Democratic Republic, and the array of anti-Semitic intrigues and accusations throughout communist rule in Poland, dictatorships of the left, though definitely less lethal to the Jews than those of the right, were hardly supportive of them as a group, even if they fostered many a Jew's political career as an individual. With liberal democracy having become safely ensconced as most of Europe's preferred form of political rule, a framework of governance and a constitutional mechanism of conflict management have been institutionalized that are fair to the Jews in that they accept them as politically equal citizens. This was simply not the case one hundred years ago and, as Pulzer teaches us, constitutes the difference between potential life or death for the Jews. Indeed, while it does not eliminate anti-Semitism, it most certainly obliterates the Jewish Question. Central Europe in 2000 continues to have the former but unlike the Central Europe of 1900 it does not have the latter.

This institutionalization of liberal democracy also entailed the development of much greater social and political tolerance in the course of the second half of the twentieth century as compared to what was acceptable in its first half. The Western world, meaning the numerous countries in which liberal democracy had become the hegemonic political rule by the end of the twentieth century, has developed a hitherto unprecedented level of tolerance in its everyday culture towards most 'others', especially weaker and hitherto voiceless ones, be they gays, lesbians, blacks, women, foreigners, animals—and

Jews. This is not to say that these societies have abolished hatreds and antag-
onisms towards 'others', but they have made their public discrimination,
humiliation, and harm not only politically unacceptable, hence illegal; but
perhaps more importantly still, they rendered them socially illegitimate. Wife
beating has become as unacceptable as torturing animals. And when neo-Nazi
thugs chase an Algerian to his death in a small town in eastern Germany, then
most of German society sees them as contemptible criminals not as harmless
pranksters or—worse still—as heroes, as would have been the case seventy
years before. Briefly put, these societies—Austria and Germany included—
have become much more compassionate on all levels than they were fifty years
ago, let alone in 1900 when anti-Semitism and the Jewish Question flourished
in the two countries featured in Pulzer's studies. And this growth in compas-
sion pertains above all to the political class for whom liberal democracy has
become the sole political regime enjoying unconditional acceptance.

There is yet another positive development that is worthy of mention in our
context: the Holocaust's near-ubiquitous presence in the political culture of
these liberal democracies. As Pulzer correctly states in the introduction to the
second edition of his *The Rise of Political Anti-Semitism in Germany and
Austria* (1988), the Shoah—though obviously known to scholars, intellectuals, and, of course, the affected (both victims and perpetrators)—was simply
not part of public discourse in 1964 when the first edition of Pulzer's book
appeared. Indeed, it is telling that the words 'Holocaust' and 'Shoah', now virtually part of the vernacular in countries such as Germany, Austria, the United
States, and Israel, were simply unknown in the 1960s. It was not until the
Auschwitz trial in Frankfurt in 1964 that the Holocaust as such—though not
with that word—became part of a larger public debate in Germany for the
very first time. Prior to that event, the Holocaust had virtually no public presence in either Germany or Austria. Interestingly, though very understandably,
the Holocaust was not a major topic of discussion among Jews in Europe, the
United States, and even in Israel. To be sure, the Nazi crimes against the Jews
furnished the basis for Konrad Adenauer's discussions with Nahum
Goldmann that later led to Germany's first reparation payments and acts of
restitution to individual Jewish victims of the Third Reich and the Jewish people as a collective. But the magnitude of the horror committed by this singularly heinous event in modern history was simply too formidable and
temporally too near for it to be part of a public debate in any relevant society,
Jewish, Israeli, American, German, or Austrian.

Things began to change by the end of the 1960s. In addition to the
Auschwitz trial in Frankfurt, there were a number of other trials in Germany
that gained attention. Moreover, the first Bundestag debate about an extension
of the statute of limitations concerning Nazi crimes garnered much publicity
when it occurred in 1969. Moreover, the student movements that shook the
complacency of many Western societies in the late 1960s also changed the dis-

course about the Holocaust. While these movements were not particularly concerned about the fate of the Jews during Nazi rule, they raised issues about fascism and repression that helped catapult the large complex of National Socialism into the public arena. This, was particularly the case in Germany where the so-called '68–ers' made Germany's role in the Second World War part of their overall attack on their parents and the so-called 'establishment' into which they lumped together Nazi Germany and the Federal Republic in a rather indiscriminate and careless fashion. Still, Auschwitz had entered the vernacular. The term 'Holocaust' did not become part of the public discourse until 1978 when NBC (one of the large American television networks) aired a four-part series with that title featuring the fate of a Jewish and a German family from Hitler's rise to power until the destruction of the Third Reich. Exhibiting all the usual problems that are inherent to products of popular culture, the film also featured one of popular culture's major benefits: the dissemination of a message to a huge audience well beyond the reaches of scholarship and high-brow journalism. The Holocaust had become part of Western culture. It had entered the public space of precisely those countries that were governed by liberal democracies. The 1980s witnessed the proliferation of thousands of Holocaust-related projects, courses, museums, monuments, centers, journeys, books, films, and many other forms of communication. Indeed, by the end of that decade the term 'Holocaust' had become synonymous with 'atrocity' as well as 'evil' in the vernacular of many Western societies. This led to two results. On the one hand, there occurred a complete relativization of the term. Anti-abortionist pro-lifers in the United States have constantly referred to abortion as a 'Holocaust'; animal rights activists have used the term in their advocacy of animal rights; and virtually every large-scale massacre be it in Bosnia or Cambodia, in East Timor or Rwanda, has been termed a 'Holocaust' at one time or another. On the other hand, there is no question that the term and the concept 'Holocaust' has become synonymous with ultimate evil in the world. Stalinism might have killed a larger number of people than did the Nazis; the Khmer Rouge most certainly murdered a larger percentage of their target population than did the Germans during the Second World War; but the Holocaust and Auschwitz have become symbols of the twentieth century's ultimate evil well beyond the confines of German, Jewish, European, and American culture. They stand for a singular shame on a global scale.

## *Potential Negative Developments*

Nothing guarantees liberal democracy's eternity. We are daily witnesses to constant attacks on the institutions and values of liberal democracy in virtually every country ruled by it at the beginning of the twenty-first century: be it via the shadowy militia groups and armed organizations of the radical right in the United States that—by themselves—amount to little but as part of a much larger conservative and right-wing backlash clearly represent a serious anti-liberal potential that could challenge if not overthrow America's liberal democratic traditions, institutions, and values; or the considerable anti-democratic sentiment in Germany, particularly in the areas of the former German Democratic Republic; the xenophobia of the French left as well as the right; and right-wing populist movements of the Jörg Haider kind in Austria and elsewhere. Liberal democracy is confronted with a constant barrage on its very being that could potentially topple it, especially under conditions of serious economic hardship and in countries—such as Germany and Austria—where this form of political rule did not attain its hegemonic presence via an endogenous development but through a forced imposition 'from above' following a military defeat. All of liberalism's real or perceived problems that Pulzer delineates so sharply as having been perhaps the most salient reasons for the mobilization of political anti-Semitism into such a potent and pernicious force in Germany and Austria of the late nineteenth and early twentieth centuries still exist: its featuring the primacy of market forces in the economy and that of the individual in polity and society; its rationalism; its inherent attacks on traditions and all forms of *Gemeinschaft*; its rootless cosmopolitanism; its trust and belief in science; and, of course, its unbounded optimism. Just as, at the end of the nineteenth century, the forces of liberalism undoubtedly caused major displacements of large numbers of people who then resented the system that caused them such hardship; so, too, are we witnesses of parallel developments one hundred years later, now captured by that ubiquitous term of 'globalization'. To be sure, in both cases the perceived dangers and harm far exceeded those caused in reality, but in politics perception has always been a much more powerful force than reality. This has been especially the case in the politics of fear and resentment which, as Pulzer tells us, was so essential for the growth of political anti-Semitism in Germany and Austria. This form of politics is alive and well at the beginning of the twenty-first century, just as it was at that of the twentieth. In one of his writings Pulzer makes the interesting point that a politics of pessimism offered a fertile ground for the mobilization of resentment against the Jews in Germany and Austria. Pessimism is alive and well today, just as it was one hundred years ago. It offers a fulcrum for all kinds of resentments that—under certain circumstances, certain 'critical junctures'—could easily be mobilized into a political force that might seriously challenge, perhaps even topple, the current liberal democratic order. Add to this the continued power of nationalism and a potentially ugly brew could ooze into the currently sparkling waters of liberal democracy. This need not lead to the disasters that rendered the twentieth century into the most murderous in human history but Pulzer's thorough scholarship and acute analysis provide us with sound reasons to remain cautious. There can be no higher praise of an academic's work than that.

# Notes

1. Peter Pulzer, *Jews and the German State: The Political History of a Minority* (Oxford: Blackwell, 1992), 15.
2. Ibid.
3. Ibid. 24; see also *Emancipation and its Discontents: The German-Jewish Dilemma* (Centre for German-Jewish Studies, University of Sussex, Research Paper 1, Summer 1997), 19.

# II

Liberalism and Anti-Semitism in Austria
and Germany

# 5

# Anti-Semitism and Ethno-Nationalism as Determining Factors for Austria's Political Culture at the *Fin de Siècle*

## *Anton Pelinka*

In the nineteenth century, Habsburg Austria was among the late-comers of Europe—in political as well in economic terms. Austria did not develop a stabilized system of constitutional rule until 1867, and even then the constitution of the Austrian part of what had become Austria-Hungary did not fulfil the criteria of a parliamentary system. The prerogatives of the emperor to make decisions about government prevailed despite the existence of a directly elected parliament.

At the turn of the century, Austria belonged—with respect to constitutional developments—to the same league as Germany, Russia, and the Ottoman Empire. But unlike all these other empires, Austria was neither a 'nation-state' as Germany claimed to be since 1871, nor was it defined by a clearly established hegemonic nation, as was the case with the Russians and Turks. The specificity of Austria-Hungary was the absence of an ethnically or lingustically defined nation which was identified with the Empire.

This was especially the case with the Austrian part of the dual monarchy. The Hungarian part was characterized by the Magyars' claim to be the leading nation of multinational Hungary. In the Austrian part, Cisleithania, none of the different nationalities could make such a claim officially. It was especially the Austrian part which justified the characterization of Austria-Hungary as a 'multinational' empire: an empire with a multitude of different nations but no dominant nation.[1]

## The Nationality Question

Austrian identity at the *fin de siècle* was based on this peculiarity: among all the other sovereign states based on a clearly defined and clearly understood national identity or national hegemony, Austria was unique. It was a reminder of the past, when sovereignty was linked to feudal lords and not based on 'the people'. It was the undisputed understanding that there was no 'Austrian people', no 'Austrian nation'. Austria was a kind of feudal umbrella, benignly sheltering and cajoling (the viewpoint of the ruling interests), ruthlessly dominating and oppressing (the viewpoint of opposing interests) a variety of peoples and nations. The official semantics of Cisleithania for these peoples was 'Nationalitäten' (nationalities), and the official criterion for defining them was linguistics: everybody who spoke German belonged to the German nationality; everybody who spoke Polish belonged to the Polish nationality. But there was no equality among the different nationalities. As in the Hungarian part, in Transleithania, there was a hierarchy in Cisleithania too: based not, as in Hungary, on an official understanding, but on an informal one. The Germans in Austria were considered to be the leading nationality.

This rank order—putting the Austrian Germans at the top of the list— found expression in many ways. One of the phenomena which can be used to indicate German dominance in Austria in the ninetenth century was the assimilation pattern of Austrian Jews. As a result of emancipation and as a consequence of secularization, Jews had to define themselves nationally by opting for a language replacing Yiddish, the language of the ghetto. For reasons of political security, they usually associated with the dominant, 'historic' nationalities. In the Hungarian part of the Habsburg Empire, the dominant nationality was Magyar, and most of the Jews in Transleithania became Hungarian. In the Austrian part, the dominant nationality was German— with the exception of Cracow and Galicia, where Polish competed with German for dominance.[2]

At the end of the nineteenth century, the great majority of Austrian Jews spoke German, considered themselves German, and officially, as the census shows were regarded as German. This assimilation pattern reflected the hierarchy of Austrian nationalities: the 'non-historic' nationalities (Czechs, Slovaks, Slovenes, Ukrainians) were considered peasant nationalities. Assimilation worked in favour of 'historic' nationalities. Most Bohemian and Moravian Jews had not opted for Czech, and Galician Jews had not chosen Ruthenian (Ukrainian) language and nationality. Within two generations, the majority of the Austrian Jewry—descendants of the millions of Central and Eastern European Jews—had been Germanized. They had opted not for the languages, cultures, and nationalities of the Habsburg Empire's political periphery but for its dominant centre. And the centre—in its political as well as its cultural meaning—was German.

Vienna was German. The Jews migrating to Vienna (and to some of the urban sub-centres of Austria) seemed to accept the informal requirement of this migration pattern: the acceptance of German not only as the dominant language but as the only accepted nationality. Czech and Italian, Polish and Ruthenian, Slovene and Romanian were the identities of the periphery. Acceptance by the centre required germanization.

Vienna was German, not a multicultural melting pot accepting different ethnic or national cultures on an equal basis. In that respect, all the established political movements and parties agreed. The 'populist' policies of Karl Lueger, Vienna's mayor at the turn of the century, whose pro-Habsburg attitudes made him anything but a pan-German, insisted on a clear ranking order: Vienna had to be German. Non-Germans were not welcome. Migrants from non-German-speaking parts of Austria were accepted only if they were germanized. But germanization was not enough in one case—in that of Jews. Jews could not be accepted as German, even after their germanization.[3]

It was the secularization of anti-Semitism which prevented this assimilation process from ending successfully. Despite their ability to assimilate, the Jews were still considered Jews. Speaking German as well as any other Austrian German did not help. Celebrating Goethe and Schiller as the quintessence of German culture, together with all the other Austrian Germans, did not help either. And as a consequence of secularization, the ultimate instrument of assimilation was no longer effective: baptism had helped Jews find acceptance in an environment defined by religious anti-Semitism, but even baptism could not help in an environment defined by secular, racist anti-Semitism.[4] This was the new version of anti-Semitism Europe had developed in the nineteenth century. No matter what 'the Jew' did, what he (or she) wanted to do: 'the Jew' was never allowed to opt out of Jewish identity. Jews were not allowed to define Jewish identity; it had to be defined by others, especially by the anti-Semites.[5]

This pattern was by no means uniquely Austrian. But in Austria, the pattern coincided with the specific Austrian lack of national identity. Austria was the only country in Europe where hegemonic nationalism worked against the very existence of the state, of the country. Russian and Turkish nationalism might have worked against a specific political system, against the interests of the Tsar or the Sultan. Polish nationalism worked against the dominant interests of Berlin and St. Petersburg and to a lesser extent also against the dominant interests of Vienna. But in Austria the politically and culturally hegemonic German nationalism was directed against the very existence of an empire which claimed to be transnational. The ultimate consequence of German nationalism in Austria, of pan-Germanism, was to destroy Austria by uniting it with the German Empire.

## The Political Culture of Subsystems

The specific Austrian lack of any kind of nationalism linked with the concept of Austria became a significant factor for the development of a specific Austrian political culture. And the secularized version of anti-Semitism became an important part of that peculiar political culture based on non-Austrian identities.

Austria as a state with a multi-ethnic and transnational understanding was unable to develop a political identity based on mass loyalty and mobilized by national sentiments. National sentiments worked against Austria including the nationalism of the *de facto* dominant nationality, the (Austrian) Germans. Czech nationalism worked for the establishment of a Czech (or Czechoslovak) state, created out of Austrian (and Hungarian) territory. Polish nationalism worked for the re-establishment of the Polish state which necessarily had to include the Austrian parts of the former Poland. The same was true of Romanian and Ruthenian and Italian and Slovenian nationalism: in the final consequence, their national ambitions could not be reconciled with the concept of a transnational empire under the Habsburgs. But because even the nationalism of the nation which considered itself (and was seen by the others) as the dominant nation was directed against the concept and the existence of a multinational Austria, there was no countervailing power of a centre-based nationalism. There was no role such as that played by Turkish nationalism in the Ottoman Empire and by Russian nationalism in the Tsar's empire. There was no nationalistic reserve power which could have been mobilized against the centrifugal effects of nationalism, because there was no nationalism in Austria which was not centrifugal. From the viewpoint of national identity, the centre of Austria was an empty place.

To compensate for this lack of a unifiying national political culture, Austria—and especially the German-speaking part of Habsburg Austria—developed political identities and loyalties based on class, religion, and ethnicity. The labour movement became a 'camp' (*Lager*), a subsystem with some qualities of a nation. The movement of political Catholicism established a similar subsystem around the Catholic Church. And the most nationalistic elements of German Austrians developed a subsystem based on the priority of German identity over class and religion. The functions of these subsystems were the same as those of the Dutch pillars (*zuilen*): most organized social life did not happen on an integrating national but on a separating subnational basis.[6] Socially, socialists met only socialists, for example, to develop specific 'socialist' curricula for continuing education; and Catholics only Catholics, for example in specific Catholic youth organizations; and pan-Germans, together with other pan-Germans, were united in 'German' gymnastics clubs.

The prevailing anti-Semitism denied Austrian Jews full integration into this system of 'camps'. As religious Jews, they were not tolerated in the Catholic-conservative camp. And the rise of secular anti-Semitism even within the Catholic segment of society prevented baptized Jews from feeling welcome among Catholics. From the 1880s, the pan-German camp became the van-guard of the most outspoken version of anti-Semitism based on 'blood' and 'race'. What was a subtextual agenda for political Catholicism was the official agenda of pan-Germanism: a Jew is defined by 'blood', by 'race'. 'Bourgeois' Jews were not accepted or did not feel accepted by the two political-ideological camps with a more or less bourgeois background. The Jewish bourgeoisie was forced to abstain from politics, to establish a specific (national) Jewish instru-ment for political participation, or to become integrated into the only 'camp' which was not openly anti-Semitic—the socialists.

The socialist 'camp' and its political arm, the Social Democratic Workers' Party (SDAP), was free of programmatic anti-Semitism, but its rank and file was not free of anti-Semitic prejudice.[7] One of the side effects of Jews joining the socialist camp was that they were tempted to play down their Jewishness. Social Democratic Jews tended to be socialist first and foremost. And they tended to distinguish themselves from the only other political options Austrian Jews had—from Zionism and other forms of Jewish nationalism—by ignoring the existence of anti-Semitism within the socialist camp and overlooking the impact anti-Semitism had generally on Austrian society and politics.

By joining (or at least sympathizing with) the SDAP, bourgeois Jewish intellectuals played an important role in the development of Austrian polit-ical culture. This fact was responsible for the *de facto* non-existence of Austrian political liberalism after the 1880s and for the decisive role assimi-lated bourgeois Jews played within the socialist camp. Jewish intellectuals pro-vided the Austrian labour movement with some of its strongest elements, beginning from Victor Adler, the integrative figure of the founding period of the SDAP, to Otto Bauer, the party's leading figure in the inter-war period, and to Bruno Kreisky, the dominant politician of post-1945 Austria.

## Anti-Semitism Preventing Austrian Liberalism

The substructure of European liberalism in the nineteenth century was usually defined by the more secularized segments of the bourgeoisie. The laicist attitude characterized—in addition to its political pro-constitution and economic pro-market policies—liberal parties all over Europe in the nine-teenth century. 'Laicism' was the attitude typical of liberal parties, defining their differences and specificities. Political Catholicism by its very nature defended the traditional prerogatives of the Church against the forces of the bourgeois revolution. The not only anti-Semitic but also generally ethno-nationalistic and xenophobic attitudes of the pan-German 'camp' were incompatible with genuine aspects of liberalism—incompatible with all the roots liberalism had in European enlightenment and rationalism. The anti-rationalistic agenda of the two bourgeois (in the sense of non-proletarian) 'camps' prevented any alliance between liberal thinkers and the political right.

That was the beginning of one of the main characteristics of Austrian polit-ical culture and the Austrian party system: the absence of any specific liberal party. When the liberals—a loose alliance of different organizations—lost control over the Austrian parliament at the end of the 1870s and a conserva-tive coalition dominated the government, liberal politicians, among them Victor Adler, joined the socialists. Others, like Karl Lueger, helped to establish the Christian Social Party; or founded the Alldeutsche Partei, the most extreme of the blatantly racist anti-Semitic elements of the pan-German 'camp'. Nothing was left to be used as the basis for a liberal party, a liberal movement, a liberal 'camp'.[8]

The term *freiheitlich*, sometimes translated as 'liberal', has been used in con-nection with the Pan-German camp.[9] This term describes the 'non-clerical' or 'anti-clerical' aspects of the pan-Germans *vis-à-vis* the 'clericals', the represen-tatives of political Catholicism. The pan-Germans tried to implement some of the laicist agenda of liberalism; in that respect they were allied with the left. But considering the anti-liberal positions of the Pan-Germans in all other areas—especially against the pro-market and pro-freedom traditions of eco-nomic and cultural liberalism—*freiheitlich* cannot be translated into 'liberal' in any (Western) European sense. Liberalism was anathema to the pan-Germans, especially in the inter-war period, when they became very much the proto-Nazi springboard of the Austrian NSDAP.[10]

The most secular element of the Austrian bourgeoisie was the Jewish ele-ment. Because of their post-ghetto experience, Austrian Jews traditionally had a strong positive attitude toward all the values represented by Enlightenment, rationalism, and the bourgeois revolution. The non-political spheres of Austrian society prospered due to the influence the liberal Jewish bourgeoisie enjoyed during the first decades of the twentieth century. Most of the inter-nationally renowned Austrian writers (from Arthur Schnitzler to Stephan Zweig, from Joseph Roth to Hugo von Hofmannsthal) were of Jewish descent. Many eminent Austrian academics (from Sigmund Freud to Paul Lazarsfeld, from Lise Meitner to Ludwig Wittgenstein) had a Jewish identity. And Jewish entrepreneurs had a much more significant role in shaping the Austrian econ-omy than the percentage of Austrians with Jewish backgrounds (less than 5 per cent between 1918 and 1938) would have led one to expect.[11]

But this kind of liberalism was not transformed into politics. Despite—or because of—the Jewish intellectuals, scientists, and entrepreneurs who had such a strong impact on Austrian society, anti-Semitism prevailed and prevented any visible integration of bourgeois Jews into the two bourgeois 'camps'. And the dominant pattern of assimilation prevented a more significant political articulation of Zionism and other varieties of Jewish nationalism. Austrian liberalism was dead because anti-Semitism had killed it politically.

The impact bourgeois Jewish intellectuals had on the socialist camp strengthened the anti-Jewish sentiment of the right. The propaganda of the moderate right (especially of the Christian Social Party, the political arm of the Catholic-conservative camp) and of the extreme right (from Schönerer's Pan-German People's Party to the Austrian NSDAP) tried to exploit existing anti-Semitism for political purposes. Marxists and Jews were equated, and the socialist labour movement was portrayed as the manipulation of naïve Aryan workers by sly Jews.[12]

Marxism was not the only ideology to be considered a Jewish plot. Economic liberalism—capitalism—was also seen as a Jewish invention. For the anti-Semites, the 'Manchester school' of economics with its implications was linked to Jewish emancipation and Jewish prosperity.[13] This 'anti-Semitic anti-capitalism' preached by Christian Socials and Pan-Germans was a possible link to latent anti-Jewish sentiments among socialists.

This anti-capitalist effect was another reason for weakening liberal energy in Austria. Karl von Vogelsang, the main ideologue of the early Christian Social movement, rejected racist and religious anti-Semitism but promoted 'economic' anti-Semitism. In his version of political Catholicism, Jews embodied the 'spirit of 1789'—for political as well as economic progress, for enlightenment and constitutionalism, for free-market philosophy and personal greed.[14]

Jews who did not want to abstain from politics had only one alternative to joining Social Democracy: Theodor Herzl's concept of a Jewish state and a Jewish nation, to be created by people moving from all over Europe to this Zion, was a product of Austrian (and European) anti-Semitism. Herzl felt rejected by society despite his acceptance of German language and 'culture', despite his assimilation. He accepted the secularized version of anti-Semitism because he defined a Jewish identity independent of religion. Herzl established a Jewish national identity.[15]

Despite Herzl's impact on Jewish history, the immediate response to his concept in Austria was not overwhelming. Most Austrian Jews did not opt for Zionism—at least not until the *Machtergreifung* of the NSDAP. In Austria, the option for the politically active majority of Jews was not Zionism. Most Jews considered the socialist 'camp', not Palestine, their political homeland. For the politically most active elements among Austrian Jews, a Marxist Zion—the classless society—was much more attractive than a specific Jewish Zion. Zionism would have forced them to accept the fact that there was no escape from their Jewish identity.

The political left had realized that Zionism challenged in principle its monopoly on Jewish votes. The Austrian left, consisting for all purposes of a single political party even after the creation of the notoriously unsuccessful Communist Party of Austria, developed a distinct dislike for Zionism. Herzl and his Zionist movement were put into the same category as other variations of 'bourgeois nationalism'. Because leftist tendencies within Jewish nationalism such as the 'Bund' did not prosper in German-speaking Austria, the SDAP was able to keep most of the Jewish vote at the end of Habsburg Austria and during the inter-war period despite the Zionist challenge.[16]

When Habsburg Austria imploded in 1918, the political culture of the sub-societies, of the 'camps', functioned as a kind of 'reserve power'. The old élite—the Habsburgs and the feudal aristocracy, the army's feudal officers' corps, and the leading bureaucrats—was finished politically. As a result of military defeat and the break-up of the multinational empire, German-speaking Austria—the 'rest'—was forced to establish a parliamentary regime (according to the will of its parties) and to stay independent from Germany (against the will of all parties).

The parliamentary regime was defined by the existing structure of the 'camps'. Until 1918, the political parties had been prevented from gaining a decisive role in the governing process. The emperor's prerogatives, in combination with the fragility of the multinational parliament, secured a *de facto* pre-democratic political process despite a parliament which—since 1907—had been elected on the basis of all-male suffrage.

The political parties and the 'camps', which gave the parties power only outside the central political process, had used their energy to imprint their respective ideologies on Austrian society. From 1918, they had the chance to shape the new republic's political system according to their ideas. The constitution of 1920 reflected the compromise between Social Democrats and Christian Socials.

The political parties started to occupy the political system's 'black box', which had excluded them until the Empire's end, as perfectly organized subsystems which were capable of fulfilling most social functions in autonomy from the centre. Many aspects of education were defined by the 'camps' and within the 'camps'. Social and cultural life hardly existed outside the 'camps'. And from the very beginning of the republic, the 'camps' took over a new function: they started to arm themselves. All the main parties had their own paramilitary forces, armed for civil war. And when Austrian pan-Germanism was absorbed by the Austrian NSDAP at the beginning of the 1930s, it took on a new dimension.

This process of domestic armament resulted in the civil wars of 1934: in February the Christian Social forces, allied with government troops, crushed the Social Democratic militia. In July, the uprising of the SS was suppressed by the government and its allies, the paramilitary units of the Vaterländische Front which had replaced the Christian Social Party.

## The 'Function' of Anti-Semitism

During the decades of the rise and stabilization of Austria's political culture, anti-Semitism was used to emphasize differences. For two of the three 'camps', anti-Semitism was a criterion to distinguish themselves from the socialists; the socialists tried to ignore anti-Semitism. Between the two 'pillars' of the right, the big stick was the claim that the other camp was not really anti-Semitic.

When the National Socialist regime in Germany organized its first anti-Jewish boycott in April 1933, the *Christlichsoziale Arbeiter-Zeitung*, the news-paper of the Christian Social workers' movement, commented that this boycott was not really anti-Semitic: the SA troops watching the Jewish shops were also protecting the Jewish owners and Jewish property; such a brief, lim-ited boycott could not be called serious; and the whole affair demonstrated that the Nazi Party did not dare to implement its anti-Jewish rhetoric.[17] There was a kind of competition between the Pan-German 'camp' (by 1933 already completely dominated by Austrian Nazis) and the Christian Socials about the role of 'true' anti-Semitism. When in 1933 Nazi propaganda accused both Pope Pius XI and Engelbert Dollfuss, the Catholic authoritarian dictator killed by the Nazis in July 1934, of being of Jewish origin, some Christian Socials treated this 'exposure' as the worst possible kind of slander.[18]

'The Jew' was used as an instrument to define identity, to create loyalty, and to make political mobilization possible. 'The Jew' fulfilled all the requirements of 'the other': when many of the leftist leaders had a Jewish background, this was seen as a decisive argument in stressing the difference from the left. The left, the SDAP, was depicted as manipulated by 'the other'. The socialist 'camp' and its institutions—party, labour unions—were considered Jewish puppets.

In the two anti-Semitic 'camps', there was no 'real' Jew who could have been used as an argument against the other. 'The Jew' had to be invented. 'The Jew' did not represent a specific part of the electorate for which Christian Socials and Pan-Germans were competing. They were competing for the role of the most credible anti-Semite, of the most convincing Jew-baiter. In 1938, the outcome of this competition was obvious: Pan-Germans-turned-Nazi easily outmanoeuvred the Christian-conservative 'camp', which for many reasons had hesitated to implement its anti-Semitic rhetoric by making it official policy.

The Social Democrats did not have to compete seriously for Jewish votes either. As the Zionist movement was not successful enough in Austria to break up the Social Democratic monopoly of Jewish votes, the left retained these votes without really having to fight for them. The SDAP could even exploit

some of the anti-Semitic clichés polemically by portraying the 'typical' capitalist as the 'typical' Jew.[19]

The Jewish community was ghettoized. Jews played no significant role in
the political market. No political party—with the exception of the less than
successful attempts of Jewish Nationalists—tried to win Jewish voters as
Jews.[20] In order to participate in Austrian politics at the end of the Empire and
in the inter-war period, Jews had to leave their Jewish identity behind. The
prominent Jewish representatives in the SDAP tried to make people forget
their Jewish background—an endeavour which could not succeed due to the
prevailing anti-Semitic society.

The memoirs of Julius Deutsch provide an interesting example of this
process. Minister of Defence in the Austrian Republic's first cabinet and leader
of the social democratic militia Republikanischer Schutzbund, Deutsch survived the defeat of 1934, went into exile and came back after 1945. In his
memoirs, he did not even mention that he was Jewish—both by birth and by
any possible definition of the anti-Semitic Austrian environment.[21]

The liberation from the ghetto was the result of enlightenment, secularization, and constitutional reforms, a legal process that ended in 1867, when
Austria became a constitutional monarchy. But this liberation could not prevent the survival of a virtual ghetto defined and controlled by an anti-Semitic
society. Unlike Tyroleans or Protestants or artisans, Jews could not be treated
as one of the many segments of society with a certain impact on politics. As a
result, Jews found themselves in a very peculiar situation: they were allowed to
enter politics and be successful at it only as part of the socialist 'camp', but
the precondition was that within this 'camp' they had to forego their Jewish
identity. Paradoxically, this sacrifice was never really honoured: Julius Deutsch
and all the other Jews in Austrian politics were never allowed to cease being
Jews.

Jewish politicians had to renounce their Jewishness. But by doing so, they
fell into one of the traps which anti-Semitism had established: secularized
anti-Semitism insisted that Jewishness was part of 'blood' and 'race', which
never could be abandoned, and that any attempt to do so was seen as proof of
a 'typical Jewish' tendency to deceive. There was no way out: pre-Auschwitz
Austria was a foreshadowing of things to come.

The political culture of the sub-societies, of the three 'camps', which was
founded in the 1880s and dominated the First Republic politically, was based
on the specific role society had reserved for Jews. Jews were the synonym for
the 'others'. Because the non-Jewish society developed its identity by distin-
guishing itself from the Jews, it needed a simple as well as hostile understanding of what Jewishness implied. It did not matter that Jewishness was
defined in different and even contradictory ways. It did not matter that secularization and the rule of law should have overcome any prejudice based on
'blood' or on religious creed. All that mattered was that society needed Jews

because it needed 'others'. The function Jews had in the development of a specific Austrian political culture can be seen as a confirmation of Jean-Paul Sartre's understanding of anti-Semitism and of the 'Jewish Question': anti-Semitism does not reveal anything about Jews—but it reveals everything about anti-Semites. If there were no Jews, anti-Semites would have to invent them.[22] This was exactly the case in post-1945 Austria. The Jewish community, which prior to 1938 had consisted of more than 200,000 members, was down to less than 10,000.[23] But anti-Semitism had not died with the Nazi Party's rule. The political culture of Austria had survived. The re-established structures of the socialist and the Christian conservative 'camp' were soon to be complemented by the revival of the pan-German 'camp', which no longer favoured annexation to Germany although it consisted almost exclusively of former members of the NSDAP.[24]

The Social Democrats (now called SPÖ) were anxious not to be seen as a Jewish party. For that reason, the party leadership did not encourage—to say the least—Jewish exiles to return.[25] The Christian Socials (now renamed the Austrian People's Party, ÖVP) did not want to be reminded of the rhetorical anti-Semitic excesses of their old guard before 1938.[26] In correspondence with the Allied policy formulated in Moscow in 1943, Austria defined itself as a victim of Nazism and thereby absolved itself of any specific responsibility for the Holocaust.

The proof that Austria had changed came when Bruno Kreisky became leader of the SPÖ and Chancellor. Kreisky dominated Austrian politics in the 1970s and early 1980s despite his Jewish heritage. Kreisky's Jewish identity was not hidden; he was seen as a Jew and he accepted that perception.[27] Kreisky's political success proved that someone from the ghetto could win elections in Austria. But the Kreisky era was marked by conflicts which pitted Jew against Jew. His ongoing dispute with Simon Wiesenthal cast Kreisky in the role of the 'good' Jew fighting against the revengeful Jew who would not accept the refusal to discuss responsibility for the Holocaust.[28] By defending an SS officer against Wiesenthal, Kreisky acted as a great reconciler. Kreisky was the Jew who seemed to forgive the anti-Semites for being anti-Semitic.

Kreisky's second intra-Jewish conflict was with Israel. Kreisky criticized some of Israel's attitudes—especially towards the Palestinians—in sometimes very harsh words. Kreisky used his Jewish identity to legitimize his position, which was unique among Western statesmen in the 1970s. It was acceptable for him to speak out against the Jewish state because nobody could accuse him of being anti-Semitic. The response of Israel—government as well as society—was very hostile.[29] Kreisky got his message heard: despite being a Jew, he confronted Jews and even the Jewish state. Because he was a Jew, he dared to do things others did not.

While Kreisky's success was proof of some changes, it was not proof of the end of anti-Semitism. The Waldheim affair was a revival of the old patterns of anti-Semitism: the campaign of 1986 was dominated by undertones of Jewish conspiracy. 'Jewish greed' and 'Jewish hatred' played an important role during and after the presidential campaign.[30] There was no Jewish vote of any significance, nor was there a Jewish segment of Austrian society seen as important enough in quantitative terms to merit much political attention. But the Jews continued to be of great interest. They still have a function to fulfil—which in reality is not their function but that of those who still consider Jews the 'others'.

# Notes

1. Robert A. Kann, *The Multinational Empire: Nationalism and National Reform in the Habsburg Monarchy, 1848–1918*, 2 vols. (New York: Columbia University Press, 1950).
2. Peter Pulzer, *The Rise of Political Anti-Semitism in Germany and Austria*, rev. edn. (London: Peter Halban, 1988), 132.
3. Ibid. 156–183.
4. Robert S. Wistrich, *Anti-Semitism: The Longest Hatred* (London: Mandarin, 1992), 43–53.
5. Jean-Paul Sartre, 'Betrachtungen zur Judenfrage', in *Drei Essays* (Berlin: Ullstein, 1960).
6. Arend Lijphart, *Democracy in Plural Societies: A Comparative Exploration* (New Haven, Yale University Press, 1977), 41–4.
7. Bruce F. Pauley, *From Prejudice to Persecution: A History of Austrian Anti-Semitism* (Chapel Hill, NC: University of North Carolina Press, 1992), 133–49.
8. Peter Pulzer, *The Rise of Political Anti-Semitism*, 122–31.
9. Klaus Berchtold (ed.), *Österreichische Parteiprogramme 1868–1966* (Vienna: Verlag für Geschichte und Politik, 1967).
10. See e.g. party platforms of the two 'moderate' pan-German parties of the inter-war period, the Grossdeutsche Volkspartei and the Landbund, in Berchtold *Österreichische Parteiprogramme*, 439–83.
11. Steven Beller, *Vienna and the Jews, 1867–1938: A Cultural History* (Cambridge: Cambridge University Press, 1990).
12. Pauley, *From Prejudice to Persecution*, 148.
13. Pulzer, *Rise of Political Anti-Semitism*, 138–41.
14. Ibid. 126–7.
15. Robert S. Wistrich, *The Jews of Vienna in the Age of Franz Joseph* (Oxford: OUP, 1989), 347–496.
16. John Bunzl, *Der lange Arm der Erinnerung: Jüdisches Bewußtsein heute* (Vienna: Böhlau, 1987), 43–61.
17. Anton Pelinka, *Stand oder Klasse? Die Christliche Arbeiterbewegung Österreichs 1933–1938* (Vienna: Europa, 1972), 227–8.
18. Ibid 229.
19. Pauley, *From Prejudice to Persecution*, 140–4.
20. Marsha L. Rozenblit, *The Jews of Vienna, 1867–1914: Assimilation and Identity* (Albany : State University Press of New York, 1983), 175–93.
21. Julius Deutsch, *Ein weiter Weg: Lebenserinnerungen* (Zürich: Europa, 1960).
22. Sartre, 'Betrachtungen'.

23. Helga Embacher, *Neubeginn ohne Illusionen: Juden in Österreich nach 1945* (Vienna: Picus, 1995), 44–58.
24. Anton Pelinka, *Austria: Out of the Shadow of the Dark* (Boulder, Colo.: Westview, 1998), 15–30.
25. Adolf Sturmthal, *Democracy Under Fire: Memoirs of a European Socialist* (Durham NC: Duke University Press, 1989), 174–7.
26. Pauley, *From Prejudice to Persecution*, 302–3.
27. Pierre H. Secher, *Bruno Kreisky: Chancellor of Austria* (Pittsburgh: Dorrance Publishing Co., 1993).
28. Ruth Wodak *et al.*, '*Wir sind alle unschuldige Täter*': *Diskurshistorische Studien zum Nachkriegsantisemitismus* (Frankfurt am Main: Suhrkamp, 1990), 282–322.
29. Helga Embacher and Margit Reiter, *Gratwanderungen: Die Beziehungen zwischen Österreich und Israel im Schatten der Vergangenheit* (Vienna: Picus, 1998), 156–98.
30. Richard Mitten, *The Politics of Antisemitic Prejudice: The Waldheim Phenomenon in Austria* (Boulder, Cola: Westview, 1992).

# 6

## Between Dependence and Influence: Jews and Liberalism in Frankfurt am Main, 1864–1933

### Jan Palmowski

'German history is not a one-way street to Auschwitz.'[1] Peter Pulzer's aversion to historical teleology has characterized his own œuvre consistently, while at the same time few historians have been as keen to consider history, and the forces shaping it, in the longue durée. In one of his most important contributions to scholarship, Pulzer has developed a rationale for the relationship between Jews, liberalism, and anti-Semitism which was closely intertwined, but never predetermined. The decline of liberalism from its endemic crises until its final collapse in 1928–32 did not make anti-Semitism inevitable, but possible.[2] While insisting that Jews and liberals must never be equated,[3] Pulzer's first seminal work on the rise of political anti-Semitism in Germany and Austria showed how close was the connection between the anti-liberal turn of the Empire and the first-generation leaders of anti-Semitism in the 1880s.[4] Electoral studies carried out since have confirmed the closeness of this link between liberalism, especially and increasingly on the left, and Jews, for Wilhelmine and Weimar Germany.[5] So close had this relationship become by 1930 that the collapse of the left-liberal Deutsche Demokratische Partei (DDP) exposed Jews as a 'dependent variable' of German history, defenceless against the growth of virulent popular anti-Semitism.[6] Liberalism's implosion in the last years of the Weimar Republic left Jews without recourse to a natural ally, foisting upon them an existential dilemma of having to opt for the party that was least hostile to their concerns.[7] Pulzer's work on liberalism and anti-Semitism was ground-breaking not just for Jewish history, of course—the growth of bourgeois illiberalism was, after all, intrinsic to the collapse of the Weimar Republic.[8]

This chapter seeks to explore further the relationship between liberalism and anti-Semitism from the beginning of the Empire to the end of the Weimar Republic, in an urban setting. The cities proved the greatest strongholds of liberalism throughout the Empire,[9] and even during the Weimar Republic, liberals retained disproportionate influence over urban government. At the same time, local government, boosted by Miquel's finance reforms of 1891/3, retained an important role in the German polity, even during the Weimar period. For despite the limitations on raising local revenues imposed by Erzberger's finance reform of 1920,[10] the recurrent political impasse at the national level ensured, throughout the 1920s, 'an increase of urban preponderance in politics'.[11] At the municipal level, the Republic faced some of its greatest challenges, and could celebrate some of its greatest achievements.[12] The urban level is important not just for the study of German history since 1871 in general, or the development of liberalism in particular. In the Weimar Republic, Jews had become the 'town dwellers par excellence', with more than 50 per cent of the Jewish population of Weimar Germany living in ten cities with more than 100,000 inhabitants.[13] These cities became the hubs of Jewish cultural, economic, scientific, and religious life.[14] Although the first wave of anti-Semitism had a strong base in small towns and agrarian areas dominated by insecure peasants and tradesmen,[15] from the turn of the century, and particularly after the First World War, the relationship between Jews, liberalism, and anti-Semitism crystallized in the cities.

Frankfurt am Main is no more 'typical' an example than any other town, and yet the city is particularly well suited for an investigation into the links between Jews and liberal politics in its urban setting. It had the second highest number of Jewish residents (after Berlin) in absolute numbers, and the highest proportion of Jews in relative terms, at 10.13 per cent of the total population in 1880, 6.33 per cent in 1910, and 6.29 per cent in 1925.[16] Frankfurt's Jewish communities were significant not just in numerical terms—they were pioneers in Jewish religious life, as well as in the divisions affecting intra-Jewish relations.[17] An important centre for Jewish enlightenment in the early nineteenth century, to which the *Philanthropin* school bore witness,[18] the city was also home to a major Orthodox renaissance in response. In 1851 the Israelitische Religionsgesellschaft broke away from the liberal community and attracted the Orthodox leader Rabbi Raphael Samson Hirsch as its head. Jewish life in Frankfurt contributed not just to Jewish religious, but also to Jewish cultural and intellectual achievement and self-confidence. Apart from Hirsch, Rabbis Nehemia Anton Noble and Caesar Seligmann exerted influence far beyond the city's boundaries,[19] while later on Max Liebermann and Theodor Adorno represented Jewish participation in Weimar culture in general.[20] The wealth of many Jewish citizens especially before 1918 distinguished not just Jewish charitable life, but was central to innumerable civic projects in general. Most remarkably, Germany's first civic university was founded largely with the help of private Jewish donations. Removed from the direct influence of the Prussian state, it became the first university in Prussia where the state was unable to veto new appointments on grounds of religion. As a result,

Frankfurt University became a major refuge for Jewish appointments. Through Martin Buber, who taught at the university from 1924, and Franz Rosenzweig, director of the Freies Jüdisches Lehrhaus, Frankfurt became a centre for attempts at the cultural and intellectual renewal of Jews in the Weimar Republic.[21]

Frankfurt was also a centre of German liberalism, and left liberalism in particular. Liberals dominated its municipal administration throughout the Empire, and even after the last municipal election in 1912, liberals had a comfortable majority in the council, with forty-four out of seventy-one seats,[22] against twenty-three seats for the SPD. Even during the 1920s, with the combined liberal vote well below 20 per cent, the left-liberal Democrats (DDP) in particular continued to exercise remarkable influence over the *Magistrat*, as both First Mayors of the Weimar period, Georg Voigt and Ludwig Landmann, were DDP party members. A second factor of left-liberal importance was the *Frankfurter Zeitung* founded by Leopold Sonnemann, which not only determined the organizational and programmatic shape of Frankfurt left liberalism, but also gave it an organ of international repute. Finally, a number of private donors generated considerable funds for liberalism not just in Frankfurt. Perhaps the most notable example is Charles Hallgarten, without whose funding Freidrich Naumann's national political career would have been impossible.[23] Grass-roots strength, the aid of the newspaper press, and generous funding all combined to ensure for Frankfurt liberalism disproportionate influence and strength.[24]

The coincidence of Jewish and liberal strength was not accidental, for the former deeply affected the latter. Apart from Leopold Sonnemann, who represented the city in the Reichstag from 1871 to 1884, a substantial number of the *Frankfurter Zeitung*'s editors were Jewish, and the Democrats' first deputies for the Prussian Abgeordnetenhaus, Guido Weiß (elected 1869) and Josef Stern (elected 1882) both worked for the newspaper.[25] Charles Hallgarten was deeply religious, and promoted not just Naumann's National Socials, but also the Verein zur Abwehr des Antisemitismus (League to Combat Anti-Semitism).[26] In the eyes of conservative opponents, Jews became a shorthand for the left-liberal Democrats, as is clear from a number of police records which noted specifically the attendance of Jews at party meetings.[27]

There is no question that Frankfurt liberalism before 1918 owed its success and strength to the nature and extent of its Jewish support. Yet in the Weimar Republic, this major asset turned into a critical liability. Frankfurt liberalism had failed to transform the city into a permanent bastion of tolerance and enlightenment. In contrast to cities like Leipzig, but similar to Breslau and Hamburg, Frankfurt is paradigmatic for a city with a strong imperial liberal tradition in which Jews appeared to be remarkably integrated at a political and social level, but which nevertheless failed to display any particular resilience towards anti-Semitism after 1918.[28] In August 1932, nineteen years after the erection, in Frankfurt, of Germany's first memorial to Heinrich Heine, the National Socialist Party gained 38.4 per cent of the popular vote in the city, just above the national average of 37.4 per cent. In this symbolic victory, Hitler had taken the bastion of 'Jews and Democrats'.[29] The intimate programmatic and ideological symbiosis between Jews and liberals was manifestly not enough to stop the eruption of anti-Semitism. On the contrary, what had been liberalism's greatest strength before 1914 turned out to be its major weakness after the First World War, as its Jewish links rendered liberalism unable to comprehend and respond adequately to anti-Semitism. This study of the relationship between liberalism and anti-Semitism in Frankfurt suggests that, from the inception of 'modern' anti-Semitism in the 1880s, there was no major turning-point in the growth of anti-Semitism paving the way for Hitler's triumph. The fundamental problem was liberalism's failure to comprehend and respond to precisely those aspects of mass politics which were conducive to anti-Semitism, even before the First World War. From the start, liberalism in Frankfurt as elsewhere was unable to respond to the concerns of popular illiberalism. Just like its Jewish constituency, liberalism, too, became a 'dependent variable' of German history.

After a debate that had occupied the citizens of the Free City of Frankfurt for half a century, Jews finally received full political and legal emancipation in 1864, two years before Frankfurt was annexed by Prussia in the Austro-Prussian War. Some Jews, like Ludwig Braunfels or the radical Maximilian Reinganum, had been politically active before and during the 1848 Revolution. Moreover, Ralf Roth has shown recently that on many levels Jews had been integrated into some of the city's leading bourgeois clubs since the 1830s.[30] Still, politically and socially, the city was dominated by a Protestant élite, and it is difficult to say whether this would have changed markedly without the political jolt of the city's loss of independence.

Annexation proved to be a complete shock to the city's public life, and its effects were felt for several years. Frankfurt had not been at war with Prussia, and its occupation was considered unlawful and unjust. The fact that Prussian troops treated the population worse than that of other occupied territories only heightened the general sense of grievance prevailing even amongst those who, in principle, favoured a small German solution under Prussian leadership. At a popular level, this anti-Prussian mood manifested itself through small but frequent acts of public defiance, such as the general disquiet during official church prayers for the Prussian royal family,[31] or the new vogue for wearing dress in red and white, the colours of the city.[32] Among the upper echelons of society, new Prussian residents who in these early days were usually from the military or the civil service were ostracized, for instance by being refused admission into the bourgeois clubs. In this context, the fact that

Germany's only Conservative Jewish deputy, Baron Meyer Carl von Rothschild, was elected in the city for the North German Parliament in 1867 is not necessarily a proof of Jewish political integration.[33] On the contrary, it is difficult to see how anybody but a relative outsider could have stood for this election, an act which signified, after all, an implicit acceptance of the status quo. The fact that he was a Conservative in this increasingly liberal city only proves the point that Rothschild was not a political insider.

The political confusion and vacuum created imperatives, but also opportunities, for political beginnings, and from late 1867 a new political élite emerged which was strongly influenced by Jews. Thus, the city's first permanent and popular political organization, the Democratic Association, was formed by Leopold Sonnemann and his *Frankfurter Zeitung*, in conscious and open hostility to the previously dominant local élites. This new élite around Sonnemann was legitimized by frequent popular meetings, and justified by its electoral success. By 1871, the Democrats were strong enough for Sonnemann to be elected to the new Reichstag, a major achievement given that Sonnemann was not only Jewish, but also a relative newcomer who had resided in the city only since 1849. From the 1870s until 1918, the Democrats dominated the city council, and, as the largest and best-organized local branch of the German People's Party, they exercised disproportionate influence beyond the city boundaries. Many of the most important Democratic city councillors were Jewish, such as Reinganum and the long-serving Martin May. If they were non-Jewish, they were often linked to the *Frankfurter Zeitung*, as was the case with the Democrat Reichstag deputies who followed Sonnemann, Carl Holthoff (1877–9), and Rudolf Oeser (1907–12).

It was not just the Democrats whose leadership and popular membership was closely associated with Jews.[34] The Progressive Party, too, had a large Jewish membership.[35] Until the 1890s, the party was led by the Jewish Berthold Geiger, while other members included long-serving councillors such as Theodor Stern (1872–1900) and Ignaz Creizenach (1867–72, 1876–1900). Only the leadership of the third large political grouping, the National Liberals, was determined more by the city's Protestant élite, although many Jews were still very much in evidence, such as Otto Braunfels (councillor 1884–1908) and Emanuel Marcus (councillor 1878–1903).[36] Given the importance of Jews for the competing liberal parties, and given their sheer numerical importance as part of the electorate, in the 1870s the different liberal parties even vied publicly for Jewish support, claiming to be the genuine representatives of Jewish interests.[37]

Jews were a guiding force in Frankfurt liberalism, but this does not necessarily make it easy to identify ways in which different and often conflicting Jewish identities determined politics in the city. One of the central personal animosities in the city's political life involved Berthold Geiger and Leopold Sonnemann. Both party leaders had very domineering characters and stood in many respects for opposite ends: the former was pro-Prussian and against public efforts to address the social question, the latter was anti-Prussian, and a pioneering and passionate advocate of social policy as a mediator between the middle and the working classes. If anything, their Jewishness increased their differences, for Geiger was as religiously active as Sonnemann was indifferent.[38]

At the same time, the Jewish influence particularly among the left-liberal Democrats helps to explain their persistent commitment to a tolerant, rational society free from superstition. It was for these ideals that Frankfurt Democrats never tired of invoking the name of Robert Blum and the 1848 Revolution in festivals and meetings.[39] Among Jewish Democrats, there was no satisfaction at the *Kulturkampf*,[40] on the contrary: the *Frankfurter Zeitung* was one of the few liberal allies of the Roman Catholics in this period.[41] Time and again, Frankfurt Democrats warned that intolerance against Catholics was principally an extension of the discrimination suffered for so long by the Jews. The *Kulturkampf* was simply contrary to the kind of society, and the relationship between state and society, that Frankfurt Democrats wished to see.

In the same way that Frankfurt Democrats distinguished themselves from other liberals in their solidarity with Roman Catholics over state repression in the *Kulturkampf*, they alienated themselves from the Roman Catholic hierarchy in their support for the separation of Church and State, especially in education. Here was an issue where liberalism in Frankfurt and the Jewishness of many of its carriers coincided and reinforced each other.[42] For at the heart of the municipal agendas of National Liberals, Progressives, and Democrats was a commitment to non-denominational primary school education. Ever since 1866, Frankfurt liberals held that denominational schools stood in the way of progress, enlightenment, and religious toleration. In 1882, Josef Stern, an editor of the *Frankfurter Zeitung* and Democratic candidate for the state elections, confirmed in a public rally that the party's (and his own) commitment to non-denominational education was closely tied to the 'Jewish question'. This commitment had been invigorated by the intolerant laws of the previous ten years of the *Kulturkampf* in which the majority imposed upon the rights of the minority. Stern pointed out that, just like his own father a generation earlier, in 1862 he had been unable to find a position anywhere as a secondary-school teacher owing to his being Jewish. From this personal experience, Stern vowed to fight for parity not just for his fellows in faith (*Glaubensgenossen*), but for the rights and equality of all estates and confessions.[43]

The Jewish and liberal policy of non-denominational education was realized with astonishing success. It was not too difficult to open non-denominational schools during the *Kulturkampf* era, but throughout Prussia the vast majority of schools established thereafter were denominational, and usually exceptions were made only in areas such as Nassau, where non-denominational schools had a long tradition. By 1906, out of 37,761 primary schools in Prussia, all but 900 were denominational. Frankfurt liberals were, by contrast, remarkably successful in resisting state pressure to open denominational schools. From 1886 to 1906, only two out of nineteen schools were opened as Roman Catholic primary schools, the rest were non-denominational. This success was enabled by the unique solidarity of all liberals on the subject, which often prevailed in the frequent confrontations with the state ministry of education. The city council made sure that nobody was elected into the city's executive, the *Magistrat*, who did not declare their support for non-denominational schooling. This also ensured the vital support of the First Mayors, Johannes Miquel (1880–90) and Franz Adickes (1890–1912), both of whom were able to support the liberals' endeavour with the substantial prestige and influence which they commanded in Berlin.[44]

Education was the most important policy issue on which the Jewish influence on Frankfurt liberalism was tangible, direct, and unambiguous.[45] There was no more important public concern to Jews than education,[46] while the abolition of clerical influence over publicly financed education was one of the few issues that all Jews from both communities could agree upon. There were few other issues which fell so plainly within the purview of local government, as it was charged with the responsibility for the funding of primary-school education.[47] Because of this local dimension, education remained one of the few spheres which liberals could truly influence, at a time of growing liberal marginalization in state and national affairs. In the early twentieth century, the education of the young with liberal, tolerant, and rational values was, perhaps, the only chance left to liberals to create their ideal society 'from below'. In Frankfurt, Jews seized the opportunity offered to them by education, and encouraged liberals towards a single-mindedness and a unity of purpose that was truly unusual. During the Empire, then, Frankfurt acquired a system of education dedicated to creating an enlightened and rational youth, from a non-denominational system of primary education to the creation of a civic university, a municipal project largely made possible through the sponsorship of Jewish donors.[48]

The issue of education demonstrates the potential and the possibilities which enabled Jews to overcome their dependence on German politics and society and to play an active part in determining them instead. And yet, the realm of education policies also delineates the limitations of such efforts. Liberal acceptance of non-denominational education was not simply contingent upon Jewish influence, but it depended crucially on the position of the city's Christian liberal élites. For reasons which were peculiar to Frankfurt, these were also supportive of non-denominational schooling. The Lutherans were broadly supportive of the liberal goal of religious tolerance and harmony, less out of a positive commitment than because of the relative religious indifference that marked Lutheran parish life during the Empire.[49]

Much more important for the liberals were the Calvinists. These had very intimate connections to the National Liberal Party and its leadership. In the German Reformed Church, five out of fourteen elders (including one of the pastors) were members of the National Liberal Party in 1893. One of these was the much-respected Gustav Humser, who presided over the City Council for twenty-five years until 1904. Three out of seventeen delegates of the French Reformed Church to the Frankfurt Reformed Synod were National Liberals in 1900, with a fourth being a city councillor who was without party allegiance, but who worked closely with the National Liberals. Both communities kept alive their memory of the persecution which had brought them to Frankfurt in the first place, and the subsequent discrimination suffered at the hands of the Lutheran majority until 1806. Frankfurt Calvinists were opposed to any form of religious discrimination and looked forward to a tolerant society guided by mutual denominational understanding. Calvinists such as the National Liberal Otto Grimm, who was responsible in the *Magistrat* for the city's schools, were only too happy to endorse the principle of non-denominational education.[50]

Even where the Jewish influence was strongest, amongst the Democrats, the political and social aims were shared and reinforced by another denominational pariah, the German Catholics. Founded in the mid-1840s as a reaction against the perceived superstition of the Roman Catholic Church (and notably its display of the Holy Cloak at Trier in 1844), the movement's ideals were closely linked to those of the radical liberals and democrats of the 1848 Revolution, and after its failure the movement lost much of its momentum.[51] German Catholics opposed the hierarchies of the established Protestant and Roman Catholic Churches. While admitting the existence of a mysterious and higher force, they regarded Christ simply as a great reformer and model.[52]

With less than a thousand full members until the turn of the century, the Frankfurt community, although one of the largest in German Catholicism, had a relatively limited potential to exercise overall influence in the city. Still, its spiritual leader, Pfarrer Sänger, became one of the most active Democrats in the 1890s, second only to Leopold Sonnemann and Heinrich Rößler. Rößler, too, was spiritually very close to German Catholicism, as he held that scientific education and rational thought alone could permanently liberate from superstition and prejudice.[53] In 1914, Rößler affirmed his criticism of established religion when he became chairman of the Weimar Cartel, a federation of 'free-thinking' and free religious organizations with which the German Catholic community was linked in association.[54] Rößler and 'Pastor' Sänger gave the Democrats' non-denominational education policies not just important personal support and intellectual input. They also enabled this issue to be presented not as a specifically Jewish issue, but as one that was objective irrespective of particular interests, and inherent to the Democrat goal of a 'progressive', tolerant, and enlightened society.

The fact that Jews, Calvinists, German Catholics, and, indeed, many Lutherans could agree on the aim of realizing a tolerant and rational civic society in Frankfurt was reflected not only in the creation of the educational system described above. With regard to Frankfurt's Jewish population, it meant that in official dealings of the municipal authorities and within the liberal parties, anti-Semitism was completely inadmissible and unacceptable, as in many ways it negated everything Frankfurt liberalism stood for and sought to achieve. This did not mean, of course, that anti-Semitism had vanished. In fact, it continued to persist throughout the imperial era, but, because it was pushed below the public political surface, it was much harder to grasp, for the politicians then as for historians now. Prejudice against Jews was widespread among the bourgeoisie, in private and public discourse, extending even to physical caricatures of Jews in the popular satirical newspaper, *Frankfurter Latern*, which was financed in part by Leopold Sonnemann.[55] Jews were disadvantaged in their access to the local bureaucracy, and the local teacher's association (Verein akademisch gebildeter Lehrer) excluded from membership those teaching at the city's Jewish schools.[56] Not without reason was Charles Hallgarten concerned to warn that, despite the public rhetoric, anti-Semitism was as potent in Frankfurt as elsewhere.[57]

The main carrier of anti-Semitism in Frankfurt was the *Mittelstand*, composed of economically insecure artisans and tradesmen, as well as house owners. Before 1866, artisans and tradesmen had consistently opposed Jewish emancipation and had often voted conservative in the local elections.[58] When, in the late 1870s, the three liberal parties had acquired total control over the city council, these sections of the population had lost their political voice. The different liberal parties were always concerned to attract the important *Mittelstand* vote through promises of low taxation or better schooling. Yet resentment remained, as ultimately even the National Liberals could not fulfil the core concerns of the *Mittelstand*; its demand for the reintroduction of guilds, even if they were voluntary, was inimical to the liberals' conception of economic progress, as were *Mittelstand* appeals for preferential tenders of municipal contracts.

During the 1890s, *Mittelstand* groups such as craftsmen, house owners, and taxpayers, became more assertive in municipal politics. One of the *Mittelstand's* allies was the anti-Semitic Deutscher Verein, established in 1894, which gave an institutional and political base to Herman Laaß, the creator and proprietor of the 'Jew-free' hotel Kölner Hof. In 1903, Laaß stood for the Reichstag, and with 4,500 votes obtained 11 per cent of the popular vote. The *Mittelstand* bettered this performance in the 1904 council elections, whereupon its representatives formed the second largest group in the city council, with fifteen out of sixty-four seats. These elections of 1904 are extremely revealing, for they were fought almost exclusively on the issue of non-denominational education, an issue which had been raised by plans of the Prussian state to introduce a law for the upkeep of primary schools. In heated debates about the kind of society that Frankfurt should be, the *Mittelstand* was strengthened greatly by a new ally, the Free Protestant People's Association, formed in 1903. Created in response to the Liberals' stubborn pursuit of non-denominational education, it considered itself free from the collusion of the Protestant establishment with the Jewish-dominated left liberal city authorities. It was, therefore, openly anti-Semitic, and fought for a Germany infused with Protestant, Christian values. In its battle against the 'Jewish-progressive-democratic' party in Frankfurt, the Free Protestant People's Association, too, made education the touchstone of their political vision.[59]

Not every *Mittelstand* voter was anti-Semitic, of course. For the 1908 municipal council elections, the *Mittelstand* nominated a Jewish candidate, who was duly elected in an area which was 35 per cent Jewish. Yet despite the existence of a Jewish *Mittelstand*, this election of Josef Fromm showed ultimately that being Jewish and standing for general *Mittelstand* interests was incompatible, as Fromm joined the left liberals soon after his arrival in the council.[60] The political success of the *Mittelstand*, and the function of anti-Semitism as a unifying element of an otherwise extremely heterogeneous and ill-defined movement, highlights the importance of anti-Semitism in late Wilhelmine Frankfurt: moreover, it signals the failure of the liberal vision, more than thirty years after it had become the basis of political action, of a civic society in which religious intolerance would no longer be possible. The liberal election defeat of 1904 had been brought about not simply by the ideal of non-denominational education, but also by the sheer determination and persistence with which liberals sought to achieve their goal, irrespective of the wishes of at least part of the population. The uncompromising nature of the liberal determination to eradicate anti-Semitism through education had provided anti-Semites with their greatest electoral fillip.

Liberals were highly aware of the significance of the 1904 election results, and drew their lessons accordingly. Since the *Mittelstand* with its anti-Semitism and anti-capitalism formed a much greater ideological challenge than socialism, they agreed to co-operate even with the SPD in the 1906 run-off elections. This prevented the *Mittelstand* from repeating its performance of 1904 and, by 1911, the *Mittelstand* presence in the council had been reduced to three seats. At the same time, it is striking that as soon as the liberals were no longer directly threatened by the *Mittelstand*, they were happy to enlist its support against the SPD, even if this necessitated an accommodation with its anti-Semitism. In the 1907 national elections, the Democrats took care not to nominate a Jewish candidate, and put up Rudolf Oeser instead, lest they offend the *Mittelstand*.[61] The *Mittelstand* approved, and contributed to

Oeser's success in the run-off elections, the first time in thirty years that the liberals beat the SPD. Despite the liberal rhetoric to the contrary, anti-Semitism had become so pervasive among large sections of Frankfurt society that, provided its presence was not too overt, Frankfurt liberals resigned themselves to its existence.

The problem with the liberal conception of progress and enlightenment was that it found it difficult to include those left behind by the processes of economic and social change, while the Frankfurt liberals' quest for a rational society could not comprehend the persistence of irrational emotions. In addition, the liberals' hope of creating a civic community that was an island of liberal tolerance and rational spirit was simply unobtainable in a society characterized by mass mobility. From 1871 to 1910, the city's population grew from 91,040 to 414,576. By 1910, around 120,000 of the population lived in areas which had been incorporated into the city since 1871, and of the 295,000 that lived in the area of the former Free City, only about 130,000 were native to Frankfurt.[62] In other words, the liberal conception of Frankfurt distinctiveness with a pronounced tradition of tolerance and enlightenment became very difficult to communicate to an urban population the majority of which had no particular roots in the city.[63] Under conditions of mass migration, as every city had to cope with the similar problems of urbanization and economic change, cities had, in effect, fewer and fewer means to distinguish themselves and to create a society in isolation from the outside world.

Nowhere was the opening up of the city to the outside world more visible than in Frankfurt Protestantism. Until 1871, all the Lutheran pastors appointed in the city had come from Frankfurt, while from the 1890s, the appointment of a native citizen became the exception rather than the rule.[64] In consequence, theological disputes were carried into the city, which magnified greatly intra-denominational disputes. Pastors were increasingly torn between 'liberal' Lutherans who followed the critical theology of Ritschl and Harnack, such as Friedrich Naumann, Martin Rade, and Wilhelm Bornemann, and 'positive' Lutherans who largely rejected this new theology. Outsiders started to dominate not just the Lutheran clergy, but also the Protestant congregation, which trebled between 1870 and 1900.[65] After the turn of the century, the majority of Frankfurt Protestants would have found it extremely difficult to identify with the traditions of tolerance upheld by Frankfurt's Protestant civic élite.[66]

The changing nature of Frankfurt Protestantism is critical, for it contained the withdrawal of its pivotal open support of the Jewish and left-liberal ideal of a society free from religious hatred and aggression. From around 1900 the beginning of Protestant anti-Semitism can be witnessed in Frankfurt, not just through the Free Protestant People's Association. In 1898, Julius Werner succeeded the liberal Martin Rade as pastor to the Paulskirche. Werner belonged to the positive theological camp, and for this reason alone his appointment had been controversial. There is no doubt, however, that he was popular, not least because he was extremely active in his parish, and influential in raising parochial activism in others. At the same time, in his speeches and writings he was clearly anti-Semitic, supporting 'Christianity, Germanness, monarchy, and social reform', while urging his flock to defy everything that was contrary to these ideas, such as any newspaper in Jewish hands.[67] As a member of the anti-Semitic Deutscher Verein, Werner remained controversial and a relative outsider within the Lutheran Church establishment. Still, Werner's appointment, and the creation of the Free Protestant People's Association discussed earlier, signalled that, from the turn of the century, Protestantism was no longer a firm bulwark against anti-Semitism. This added to the liberals' difficulty in preventing the growth of anti-Semitism. Their influence continued to make anti-Semitism unacceptable officially, but they were losing the fight to contain anti-Semitism below the veneer of public rhetoric. Liberals had failed to create in Frankfurt a civic community free from religious prejudice, in isolation from the currents prevailing in the rest of the Empire. Frankfurt was simply not 'an oasis in the desert', Leopold Sonnemann's assurances to the contrary notwithstanding.[68]

In the Weimar Republic, the paradox of Frankfurt public life grew exponentially: Jews dominated public life as never before, while, at the same time, anti-Semitism reached unprecedented proportions. In Frankfurt as in Germany as a whole, many Jewish socialists were leading figures in the Revolution of 1918, such as Toni Sender, one of the local leaders of the Independent Socialist Party, and Hugo Sinzheimer (SPD), the police president appointed by the workers' council. Even though the DDP was much more centralized and shaped by the political circles of the capital than its imperial predecessor,[69] a number of Frankfurt Jews were prominent in the left-liberal German Democratic Party (DDP), the successor to the local Democrats. The party's founding members included Sally Goldschmidt, editor of the *Frankfurter Zeitung* (and city councillor throughout the Weimar Republic) and Moritz Julius Bonn. Even the National Liberal successor, the German People's Party (DVP), enjoyed, in Frankfurt, important Jewish support. Rudolf Lion was one of only two DVP members who sat in the city council throughout the Weimar Republic, while Richard Merton led the party from 1928.[70] Apart from party politics, Jews became central to the city's administration. In 1924, the council elected the agnostic Jew Ludwig Landmann, a member of the DDP, as First Mayor. His energetic policies were supported by Bruno Asch (SPD), who was also Jewish, and who in the *Magistrat* oversaw the city's finances. Ernst May, the grandson of the Democrat Martin May, was responsible in the *Magistrat* for the large-scale construction of modern flats and apartment blocks which became the hallmark of the 'New Frankfurt' of the Landmann years.[71] Bearing in mind that, from 1927, the *Magistrat* member responsible for culture was Max Michel, this means that the four positions whose influence on Frankfurt public life was, perhaps, most profound were all occupied by Jews.[72] Considering the strong Jewish participation in the city's cultural and intellectual life of the period, one might even suggest that the 'new Frankfurt' was very much a product of Jewish leadership.[73]

The strength of Jewish influence in the city had its problems, for it increased the difficulty of formulating a public response to anti-Semitism. The liberal *raison d'être* of civic tolerance and confessional harmony before the war had been unable to admit to, let alone confront, the existence of anti-Semitism as a broad current which encompassed more than particular fringe groups like sections of the *Mittelstand*. In the Weimar Republic, the Jewish descent of Frankfurt's leading politicians not only facilitated the adoption of anti-Semitism by the parties opposed to the status quo. It also made it inordinately difficult for Frankfurt's political leadership, as an interested party, to present anti-Semitism as a general social ill. This is evidenced by a comparison of two incidents involving anti-Semitism which demonstrate, at the same time, the changing stance of the Protestant Church on the issue.

On New Year's Eve 1917, Pastor Kübel, a proponent of liberal Lutheran theology, gave a sermon in which he identified Jews as unpatriotic war profiteers on the back of the Christian population. At this point, he was criticized sharply not only by the League to Combat Anti-Semitism, but also by the (Christian) First Mayor, Voigt, and the city council. Still, it is remarkable that Kübel was supported unanimously by his Lutheran colleagues.[74] Kübel refused to answer this particular charge, though in his autobiography, written after the Second World Warr, he denied being anti-Semitic.[75] Even so, he was president of the local branch of the Fatherland Party, and after the war, his patriotism induced him to join the anti-Semitic German National People's Party (DNVP), which in Frankfurt was run by Hermann Laaß, amongst others.[76] As Jonathan Wright has shown, Protestant clerical support for the DNVP was nothing extraordinary in national terms,[77] but in the historical and clerical context of Frankfurt this action by a theologically liberal pastor represented an extraordinary shift. The growing Protestant association with anti-Semitism reflected a national trend,[78] but would have been unthinkable in Frankfurt before 1900.

In 1923, the city offered some of the property it owned near the church of St Catherine for sale, to enable the building of shops in this central location. When all those interested in buying up the land turned out to be Jews, the Lutheran pastors united in protest against this 'profanization' of the church, arguing that this would disrupt denominational harmony. After much public controversy, the Jewish buyers withdrew their offer, and the land remained unsold.[79] What is remarkable here is not only the new-found Lutheran unity against the Jews, or the way in which the pre-war liberal ideal of denominational harmony was invoked for completely opposite ends, the making of an anti-Semitic demand. It is also striking that, in marked contrast to the dispute about Kübel in 1917/18, the municipal authorities were no longer united on the issue—while the city council was unable to agree on the matter, the *Magistrat* considered itself unable to take a firm stance.

Not only did the Lutheran hierarchy become more (openly) anti-Semitic and nationalist over the period, Protestantism also continued and reinforced its engagement in party politics begun in 1903. The threat of the Republic removing still further clerical influence from public life in general, and education in particular, led to the formation, after the war, of a direct successor to the Free Protestant People's Association, the German-Protestant People's Association.[80] It only took part directly in local elections in 1929 and 1933, and otherwise sought to influence public life through acting as a pressure group. With the SPD and KPD being unacceptable to the People's Association from the beginning, the DDP with its strong Jewish links found it impossible to accommodate the People's Association's demands. By contrast, the DVP competed throughout for the committed Protestant vote, though in the early years of the Republic the party emphasized its commitment to Christian values while trying to retain its commitment to 'cultural tolerance'.[81] In the end, it was the DNVP which was best placed to respond to the People's Association and become, in Frankfurt as elsewhere, 'the' Protestant Party. The party included in its ranks leading members of the German-Evangelical People's Association, emphasized its support for the rights of all (Christian!) Churches, and underlined throughout its unambiguous preference for denominational education.[82]

The left-liberals had lost their Protestant base, while popular and political anti-Semitism was evident on many levels. Protestant support ensured that the DNVP, together with the political *Mittelstand* organized in the *Wirtschaftspartei*, gained 19.7 per cent of the popular vote in the 1924 council elections, more than the combined vote of the two liberal parties. More tangibly, in 1924, a *völkisch* gathering attracted 4,000 disgruntled citizens, by the late 1920s anti-Semitic disturbances had become common occurrences on the city's streets, and throughout the period, Jews were constantly exposed to spontaneous public expressions of hostility.[83] Even though the Democrat ideals were increasingly shown to have failed, the DDP continued to press ahead with its agenda, helped by a coalition with the SPD and the left-wing Frankfurt branch of the Centre Party. The DDP developed a view of itself as embodying the 'spirit of the new era'.[84] At the same time, its strong active and passive ties to the Jews quickly led to its being labelled, among its opponents, as the 'Judenpartei'.[85] In addition, whereas the Democrats' links to the 'German Catholic' community had been an added bonus before 1918, this now rendered the DDP doubly vulnerable, as it enabled its political opponents to charge the party with being un-Christian without having to resort to open anti-Semitism.[86] Opposition to the DDP and the rejection of the Weimar Republic and its values became closely linked, especially as this was the party which was also identified, as mentioned above, with the cultural 'modernity' of the Landmann era.[87]

In fact, Democrats did not merely embrace the 'modernity' of Landmann's policies, they also displayed a nostalgia for the past. In addition to their support for the 'new Frankfurt' of Landmann and May, they looked back to the principles of 1848 through celebrations of 'their' martyr, Robert Blum, and through demonstrative loyalty to the black, red, and golden flag of the Revolution and the Republic.[88] In this way, Democrats cemented their links with the majority of Jews, who, at this time of peril, were more than ever committed to the principles of 1848.[89] This, in turn, did little to lessen the scorn and animosity of the Democrats' opponents. Although Jews never had a more faithful ally, they could not have had a worse or more ineffectual one; everything the Democrats, the self-proclaimed 'core unit (*Kerntrupe*) of the Republic',[90] did and stood for attracted the bitter hostility of those opposed to it. From nationalist hostility towards the DDP, it was but a small step towards anti-Semitism. Even though in Frankfurt, the party continued to fight for its ideals even after its transformation into the *Staatspartei*, its declining electoral strength rendered it ineffective in obtaining its goal. This was acknowledged even by its greatest ally, the *Frankfurter Zeitung*, which, from 1928, distanced itself from the DDP, in order to encourage whichever party was best placed to ensure the survival of the left-liberal ideals of 1848 and of Weimar.[91]

If the left-liberal Democrats suffered from their close association with the Weimar Republic, the 'new Frankfurt', and active Jewish participation in public affairs, this was not true for the right-liberal successor to the National Liberals, the German People's Party (DVP). As shown above, in the imperial era, the National Liberals had shared the Democrats' vision for a tolerant Frankfurt, but their support was carried mainly by the memory of the indigenous Frankfurt Calvinist communities. The shift in Frankfurt Protestantism from the turn of the century, therefore, affected the right-liberals more deeply even than the Democrats. The DVP was still supported by a number of wealthy Jews, but the party, and its organ, the *Frankfurter Nachrichten*, never fought openly against anti-Semitism. Whereas the left-liberal *Frankfurter Zeitung* waged a constant battle against anti-Semitism and highlighted its prevalence in Frankfurt and throughout the Republic, the right-liberal *Frankfurter Nachrichten* only reported it in the most extreme cases, as it concentrated on the threat from the political left.[92] The DVP's recurrent emphases on the party's 'German' and 'Christian' character, in the context of Weimar, suggest quite strongly that the party was open to accommodating anti-Semitic resentment without being openly anti-Semitic itself. As the party of Bismarck's unification, the DVP considered itself the guardian, on behalf of the entire bourgeoisie, of the 'national and Christian foundations of German culture',[93] a concept which contained the not too implicit exclusion of Jews.

It is striking, then, that the DVP was at its most radical under the leadership of Richard Merton. He was the son of the baptized Jew Wilhelm Merton, one of the city's most prominent philanthropists of the late imperial era, whose donations formed the heart of the civic university. Merton was elected councillor in 1928, and immediately changed the party's course. Up to 1928, despite reservations, the DVP had lent its support to the policies of Ludwig Landmann and his civic administration. Under Merton's leadership, the party distinguished itself by instigating a campaign against the 'Landmann system'. Merton refused all co-operation with the SPD, Centre Party, and DDP, and accused the 'system' of incompetence, corruption, and the squandering of funds.[94] This timely policy shift found fertile ground among a *Mittelstand* suffering from renewed poverty and uncertainty, and increased popular support for the DVP, against the national trend. After the council elections held in November 1929, the Democrats' strength shrank from seven to four seats, while the DVP gained two seats to join the Centre Party and the Communists as the second largest grouping in the council, with eleven seats each. As late as 1932, Richard Merton managed to increase the DVP's share of the vote sufficiently for him to be elected to the Reichstag in November 1932.

Merton's DVP showed that it was possible for a liberal party to survive the Depression, though at a cost. In the pyrrhic victory for liberalism, the gains of the intransigent DVP in 1929 actually deprived the carriers of Landmann's policies (SPD, DDP, and Centre Party) of a majority, thus making the council unmanageable, half a year before the parliamentary collapse of the Reichstag. So indistinguishable had Merton's language become from that of the far right, that he was asked by a local National Socialist unaware of Merton's Jewish background to join them, since he was really 'one of them' ('Sie gehören doch eigentlich zu uns').[95] Even though Merton and others were opposed to National Socialism, the transition from the kind of liberalism proposed by the DVP in its late years to the Third Reich was seamless. In an article on 'The New Germany' on 19 March 1933, Heinz Gorrenz, a long-standing correspondent of the *Frankfurter Nachrichten*, wrote that just as liberalism, under the black, white, and red banner, had led Germany to its period of greatness (*Blütezeit*), so the recent 'National Revolution' had the potential to return the people to its glory.[96] Evidently, liberalism could only succeed if it gave itself up and surrendered to anti-Semitism. In Frankfurt as elsewhere, Jews had lost all political support, partly despite Jewish political engagement as in the DVP, and partly because of it, as in the DDP.

Frankfurt is a paradigm for the relationship between liberalism and anti-Semitism, because of its dramatic transformation from one of the greatest liberal strongholds of the German Empire into a city with disproportionately high Nazi support in the dying years of the Weimar Republic. In both of these conditions, the role of the city's hugely influential Jewish communities was critical. Jews were Frankfurt liberalism's most important support, without which its strength and influence until 1918 would have been unthinkable. In fact, this link was so strong that it is even possible to delineate particular liberal policies which can be traced back to Jewish concerns. It is difficult to imagine Frankfurt liberalism being as insistent and determined to realize a system of non-denominational education without its Jewish background. Indeed, the whole self-understanding, especially (but not exclusively) of left liberalism, was directed towards the Jewish concern for perfect religious tolerance and harmony.

Yet even in this instance, Jewish influence and success was a dependent variable. The position of Jews in local politics and society was determined crucially by the attitudes of Frankfurt's other faiths, notably the city's different Protestant communities, with their various influences upon the different liberal parties. It is highly unlikely that Frankfurt, a city never noted for the religious fervour of its population, was unusual in this regard.[97] Anthony Kauders has demonstrated that some of the differences in anti-Semitism between different municipal contexts relate to their different denominational traditions.[98] The case of Frankfurt confirms this impression, and shows how important it is to take into account Protestantism in its different facets and peculiarities: attitudes towards Jews cannot be summarized neatly for 'Roman Catholicism' and 'Protestantism' in Germany as a whole. In Frankfurt, the Jewish influence on liberalism during the Empire was possible only because it agreed broadly with the traditions and peculiarities of Frankfurt's Protestant liberal élite. The withdrawal of Protestant hostility towards anti-Semitism marked the defeat and failure of the Frankfurt liberal and Jewish vision of civic enlightenment and peace. It also meant that, during the Weimar Republic, the DDP's engagement for religious equality became identified, rightly or wrongly, as a predominantely Jewish concern, in contrast to the party's political opponents to the right, who emphasized their Christian (and Protestant) identity. Jewish influence on political and public life proved to be an extremely double-edged sword.

Frankfurt in the Weimar period was unrecognizeable compared to the Frankfurt of 1900. Anti-Semitism had become publicly acceptable, the conservatism which the liberals had managed to suppress until 1914 had transformed the DNVP into the city's second largest party during the Republic's 'golden years', and even the liberals themselves were divided between left and right, by completely different visions about the kind of community Frankfurt should be. And yet, the growth of public anti-Semitism and the failure of liberal attempts to overcome it had their roots in the beginning of modern anti-Semitism as such, and especially the advent of mass politics and economic change in the 1890s.

The perspective of the 'longue durée', from emancipation to persecution, relativizes the importance of the First World War as a watershed in the growth of anti-Semitism. There is no question that after the war anti-Semitism took on an order of magnitude that was quite unprecedented, and that much of it is related to the experiences of the later war and immediate post-war years (notably the census on Jews serving in the military, the radicalization of the right, and the 1918 Revolution). Moreover, the experience of Frankfurt confirms that nothing in the pre-war years made the prevalence or force of anti-Semitism after 1918 inescapable. And yet, the war did not create anti-Semitism out of thin air. Beneath the predominant liberalism in public discourse, modern anti-Semitism had developed in Frankfurt since the 1880s, from the 'Jew-free' Kölner Hof, to the sermons of Julius Werner, and on to the anti-Semitic literature which related to Frankfurt Jews.[99] And it was in the years before the war that Frankfurt Jews became identified with cultural modernism,[100] long before the beginnings of the 'new Frankfurt'. Clearly, the social and economic impact of the war created fertile conditions for anti-Semitism to spread and radicalize, but the causes of modern anti-Semitism as such go back further. Urban transformation and internal migration, economic hardship, and cultural uncertainties from the 1880s made the ideal of universal civic tolerance and enlightenment virtually unobtainable, and they made the concept of a civic community which could isolate itself from its surroundings completely illusory. This was not just evident in the city's Protestant Church, which, faced with the integration of masses of Protestant immigrants among pastors and parishioners, increasingly lost its distinctive ethos. At the end of the 1890s, liberals had to admit, even in Frankfurt, to their failure to domesticate the economically insecure *Mittelstand*, as well as the anti-Semitism with which it aligned itself. Earlier, the National Liberals had come closest to integrating the *Mittelstand*, though in the end their identification with the First Mayor, Franz Adickes, limited their ability to respond to *Mittelstand* resentments against the municipality. The National Liberals' political successor, the DVP, only managed to respond wholeheartedly to *Mittelstand* concerns from 1928, but by this time, the DVP's principled opposition to the municipality blended in perfectly with (and in this way reinforced) the anti-Semitic tendencies of its new clientele.[101]

Their intimate relationship with liberalism hindered many Jews from responding in time to the challenges of anti-Semitism. Of course, if even in Frankfurt anti-Semitism could spread with such force during the Republic, it is difficult to see what exactly the Jews as a 'dependent variable' of history could have done. Clearly, the attempt to return to the inner strength of Judaism and to convince their opponents with rational arguments, the option advocated by the Israelitische Gemeinde until about 1930, was ineffective.[102] Too many Jews had stopped believing in the religious values of Judaism,[103] while the liberal expectation that irrationality could be overcome by rational insight proved a tragic fallacy. This explains, but does not excuse, why the growing anti-Semitism of Frankfurt society was never really discussed in the newspaper of the Israelitische Gemeinde during the 1920s. The hope that anti-Semitism could be overcome by the unassailable integrity of the Jewish individual and the inner strength of the German *Geist* simply showed just how strong were the roots of the Jews in the ideals of the bourgeoisie and its erst-while political ally, liberalism.[104] Discussions about possible new political and ideological directions, now that liberalism had collapsed, were only initiated in the newspaper of the Israelitische Gemeinde in 1930. This carried the implicit acceptance that Jewish values and actions internally, and a reliance on liberalism externally, were not enough in the fight against anti-Semitism.[105] In an apparent age of collectivism, many Jewish writers pondered about the collective nature of religion, and the extent to which this was compatible with socialism.[106] Still, these considerations were of an extremely general nature and inconclusive at best. The relationship between liberalism and Jews in Frankfurt remained strong until the very end. On the eve of the first national boycott of Jewish shops (1 April 1933), the Israelitische Gemeinde issued a statement which is striking for the persistence of its liberal assumptions. 'If there is no voice raised in our defence, may our witness be the stones of this town, . . . in which the relationship between Jewish and non-Jewish citizens has always been particularly close.'[107] To the last, Jews put their faith in the liberal vision of a city distinguished by its particular denominational harmony and progress. Tragically, not even a liberal voice was left in its defence.

# NOTES

1.  Peter Pulzer, 'Warum scheiterte die Emanzipation der Juden?', in Peter Alter, Claus-Ekkehard Bärsch, and Peter Berghoff (eds.), *Die Konstruktion der Nation gegen die Juden* (Munich: Fink, 1999), 283.
2.  Peter Pulzer, *Jews and the German State: The Political History of a Minority, 1848–1933* (Oxford: Blackwell, 1992), esp. ch. 4.
3.  Ibid. 324.
4.  Peter Pulzer, *The Rise of Political Anti-Semitism in Germany and Austria*, 2nd edn. (London: Peter Halban, 1988). Greater focus on the relationship between liberalism and anti-Semitism is in Pulzer, 'Legal Equality and Public Life', in Michael A. Meyer (ed.), *German-Jewish History in Modern Times iii. Integration in Dispute 1871–1918* (New York: Columbia University Press, 1997), 153–95; and Pulzer, 'The Return of Old Hatreds', in Meyer (ed.), *German-Jewish History iii (1871–1918)*, 196–251. A succinct summary of his argument is Pulzer, *German Antisemitism Revisited* (Rome: Archivio Guido Izzi, 1999), here 29–31. In agreement is Reinhard Rürup, *Emanzipation und Antisemitismus: Studien zur 'Judenfrage' der bürgerlichen Gesselschaft* (Frankfurt: Fischer, 1987), here 116–41.
5.  Martin Liepach, *Das Wahlverhalten der jüdischen Bevölkerung: Zur politischen Orientierung der Juden in der Weimarer Republik* (Tübingen: Mohr Siebeck, 1996).

6. Peter Pulzer, 'Conclusion', in Wolfgang Benz, Arnold Paucker, and Pulzer (eds.), *Jüdisches Leben in der Weimarer Republik—Jews in the Weimar Republic* (Tübingen: Mohr Siebeck, 1998), 271–9, here 278.

7. Pulzer, *Jews and the German State*, 278–323.

8. Werner Jochmann, *Gesellschaftskrise und Judenfeindschaft in Deutschland 1870–1945* (Hamburg: Christians, 1988), 171–94.

9. James Sheehan, 'Liberalism and the City in Nineteenth-Century Germany', *Past and Present*, 51 (1971), 116–37.

10. On Erzberger's finance reforms and its implications for municipal activism, see Wolfgang R. Krabbe, *Die deutsche Stadt im 19. und 20. Jahrhundert* (Göttingen: Vandenhoeck & Ruprecht, 1989), 165–72.

11. Pulzer, *Rise of Political Anti-Semitism*, 319.

12. The contribution of local government to the achievements and failures of the Weimar Republic, and the ways in which it affected crucially public perceptions of the Weimar state, has been highlighted by Ben Lieberman, *From Recovery to Catastrophe: Weimar Stabilization and Political Crisis in Weimar Germany* (New York and Oxford: Berghahn, 1998).

13. *Gemeindeblatt der Israelitischen Gemeinde Frankfurt am Main* (*GIG*) (Mar. 1928). 'Der deutsche Jude und die Großstadt'. Avraham Barkai, 'Population Decline and Economic Stagnation', in Michael A. Meyer (ed.), *German-Jewish History in Modern Times*, iv. *Renewal and Destruction 1918–45* (New York: Columbia University Press, 1996), 33.

14. Paul Mendes-Flohr, 'Jews within German Culture', in Meyer (ed.), *German-Jewish History*, iv (1918–45), 170–94.

15. Apart from Pulzer's own work, see Dan S. White, *The Splintered Party: National Liberalism in Hessen and the Reich, 1867–1918* (Cambridge, Mass.: Harvard University Press, 1976), 134–44.

16. Monika Richarz, 'Demographic Developments', in Meyer (ed.), *German-Jewish History*, iii, 30 (table 1.9). This table severely understates the number of Jews living in Frankfurt in 1871. For the percentage in 1880, see *Statistische Jahresübersichten der Stadt Frankfurt am Main 1911/12* (Frankfurt, 1912), 21. The precise figures are in *Frankfurter Israelitisches Gemeindeblatt*: 'Ein jüdisches Standardwerk', *FIG* (Apr. 1931); 'Die Frankfurter Juden in Zahlen und Bildern' (June 1931).

17. For an account of the Frankfurt divisions within the wider religious context, see Stephen M. Lowenstein, 'Religious Life', in Meyer (ed.), *German-Jewish History*, iii, esp. 114–17.

18. Arthur Galliner, 'The Philanthropin in Frankfurt: Its Educational and Cultural Significance for German Jewry', *Year Book of the Leo Baeck Institute* (*YLBI*), 3 (1958), 169–86. Inge Schlotzhauer, *Das Philanthropin 1804–1942: Die Schule der Israelitischen Gemeinde in Frankfurt am Main* (Frankfurt: Kramer, 1990).

19. See, for instance, 'Nehemias Anton Nobel', *GIG* (Jan. 1928).

20. 'Bei Max Liebermann', *GIG* (Oct./Nov. 1926).

21. Paul Mendes-Flohr, 'Jewish Cultural and Spiritual Life', in Meyer (ed.), *German-Jewish History*, iv. 137–48.

22. Thirty-two seats were gained by the left-liberal Progressive People's Party (a fusion of Progressives and Democrats), and twelve by the National Liberal Party.

23. Bundesarchiv Potsdam 90 Na 3 n. 147 fos. 13–16, 20–1, 30. Letters from Naumann to Hallgarten, 1902–7. See also Hallgarten's obituary, written by Friedrich Naumann, in the *Frankfurter Zeitung* (1908). It was reprinted in *Ost + West: Illustrierte Zeitschrift für das gesamte Judentum* (May 1908), a copy of which is in the Institut für Stadtgeschichte (IfSG) S2/427. Charles Hallgarten.

24. Jan Palmowski, *Urban Liberalism in Imperial Germany: Frankfurt am Main, 1866–1914* (Oxford: OUP, 1999), 52–6, 322–6.
25. Ernst Kahn, 'The Frankfurter Zeitung', *YBLI*, 2 (1957), 228–35.
26. Theodor Barth, 'Charles Hallgarten', *Mitteilungen aus dem Verein zur Abwehr des Antisemitismus* (29 Apr. 1908). This article is also in IfSG S2/427. Charles Hallgarten.
27. Hessisches Hauptstaatsarchiv Wiesbaden (HStAW) 405 n. 1065 fos. 268–9. *Zeitungsbericht* (police report), 19 Nov. 1870.
28. Ina Lorenz, *Die Juden in Hamburg zur Zeit der Weimarer Republik: Eine Dokumentation* (Hamburg: Christians, 1989), i, pp. cxxxiv–clv. Till van Rahden, 'Mingling, Marrying, and Distancing: Jewish Integration in Wilhelminian Breslau and its Erosion in Early Weimar Germany', in Benz *et al.* (eds.), *Jüdisches Leben*, 197–221, here 208–10. Cornelia Rohr, 'Kommunaler Liberalismus und bürgerliche Herrschaft in den Städten Frankfurt am Main und Leipzig 1900–1924', *Jahrbuch für Liberalismus-Forschung*, 4 (1994), 167–77.
29. Dieter Rebentisch, 'Frankfurt am Main in der Weimarer Republik und im Dritten Reich 1918–1945', in *Frankfurt am Main: Die Geschichte der Stadt in neun Beiträgen* (Sigmaringen: Thorbecke, 1991), 423–520, here p. 474. Dieter Rebentisch, 'Frankfurt am Main und das Reich in der NS-Zeit', *Archiv für Frankfurts Geschichte und Kunst* (*AFGK*), 57 (1980), 243–67, here 245. On the anti-Semites' identification of Frankfurt with Jews, see also Inge Schlotzhauer, *Ideologie und Organisation des politischen Antisemitismus in Frankfurt am Main 1880–1914* (Frankfurt: Kramer, 1989), 37.
30. Ralf Roth, *Stadt und Bürgertum in Frankfurt am Main: Ein besonderer Weg von der ständischen zur modernen Bürgergesellschaft 1760–1914* (Munich: Oldenbourg, 1996), 339–42, 528–9. Political emancipation followed economic and social integration of some Jews not just in Frankfurt, but in much of Western Europe. Pierre Birnbaum and Ira Katznelson (eds.), *Paths of Emancipation: Jews, States, and Citizenship* (Princeton, NJ: Princeton University Press, 1995), here 24–5. See also Werner E. Mosse, 'From "*Schutzjuden*" to "*Deutsche Staatsbürger Jüdischen Glaubens*": The Long and Bumpy Road of Jewish Emancipation in Germany', in Birnbaum and Katznelson (eds.), *Paths of Emancipation*, 87.
31. Hermann Dechent, *Kirchengeschichte von Frankfurt am Main seit der Reformation* (Leipzig and Frankfurt: Kesselringsche Hofbuchhandlung, 1921), ii. 472.
32. Wolf-Arno Kropat, *Frankfurt zwischen Provinzialismus und Nationalismus: Die Eingliederung der 'Freien Stadt' in den preußischen Staat (1866–1871)* (Frankfurt: Kramer, 1971), 24–6, 46–9. HStAW 405 n. 40 fos. 47–52, 75–7, 112–14. *Zeitungsberichte* Jan.–Mar., May, and Nov. 1868.
33. Ralf Roth, 'Liberalismus in Frankfurt am Main 1814–1914: Probleme seiner Strukturgeschichte', in Lothar Gall and Dieter Langewiesche (eds.), *Liberalismus und Region: Zur Geschichte des deutschen Liberalismus im 19. Jahrhundert* (Munich: Oldenbourg, 1995), 41–85, esp. 74.
34. Evidence for Jewish participation in popular politics comes from the observations of the police officers present at party gatherings. Often, all attendants were simply categorized as 'Jews', which demonstrates official perceptions of the party. There were times, however, when exact attendance figures were given for Jews. In 1879, the officer reported that one meeting was attended by forty-three Jews and nine Christians. HStAW 407 n. 138/1 fo. 108. Democratic Association Meeting, 17 Nov. 1879.
35. HStAW 407 n. 150/1 fos. 159–61, 172. Progressive Liberal Meeting, 29 Mar. 1884.
36. For an introductory (if sometimes inaccurate) overview of Jewish members of the

city council, see Paul Arnsberg, *Die Geschichte der Frankfurter Juden seit der Französischen Revolution* (Darmstadt: Roether, 1983), iii. 528–41.

37. See, for instance, the letter 'Zur Stadtverordnetenwahl'. *Frankfurter Zeitung* (23 Nov. 1870, 1st edn.).

38. The son of the liberal Rabbi Abraham Geiger was a co-founder of the 'anti-baptism-committee', whose aim was to strengthen Jewish identity and pride. He was also a member of the anti-Zionist committee from 1913. Rachel Heuberger, and Helga Krohn, *Hinaus aus dem Ghetto . . . Juden in Frankfurt am Main 1800–1950* (Frankfurt: Fischer, 1988), 125. Arnsberg, *Geschichte der Frankfurter Juden*, ii. 47.

39. *Frankfurter Zeitung* (13 Nov. 1868, 2nd edn.; 6 Nov. 1870, 1st edn.). Note also the way the Democrats celebrated the 25th anniversary of the opening of the Reichstag through an invocation of the principles of 1848. *Frankfurter Zeitung* (20 Mar. 1896, 4th morning edn.).

40. Pulzer, 'Legal Equality and Public Life', 181–2.

41. Adolf Kullmann, *Die Stellungnahme der* Frankfurter Zeitung *zum Kulturkapf,* D. Phil. thesis (Würzburg, 1922). *Die Geschichte der Frankfurter Zeitung 1856 bis 1906* (Frankfurt: Societätsverlag, 1906), 224–30.

42. The importance of education as a touchstone for the relationship between Jews and liberals in the municipal context is not unique to Frankfurt. For the case of Breslau, see Till van Rahden, *Juden und andere Breslauer: Die Beziehungen zwischen Juden, Protestanten und Katholiken in einer deutschen Großstadt von 1860 bis 1925,* D. Phil. thesis (Bielefeld, 1999), 187–221.

43. HStAW 407 n. 138/2 fo. 138. The speech was also reported in *Frankfurter Zeitung* (17 Oct. 1882).

44. The ways in which Frankfurt liberals realized the non-denominational system of education is treated in more detail in Palmowski, *Urban Liberalism,* 151–60, 314–15.

45. For Breslau, Till van Rahden has pointed out a number of other areas of Jewish influence, though these concerned Jews more specifically, such as the naturalization of Jewish immigrants, and the award of an honorary citizenship to Jews. Van Rahden, 'Juden und andere Breslauer', 270–325.

46. On the importance of education in general, see Shulamit Volkov, 'Jüdische Assimilation und Eigenart im Kaiserreich', in Shulamit Volkov, *Jüdisches Leben und Antisemitismus im 19. und 20. Jahrhundert* (Munich: Beck, 1990), 142–3.

47. Rudolf Gneist, *Die Selbstverwaltung der Volksschule: Vorschläge zur Lösung des Schulstreites durch die preußische Kreis-Ordnung* (Berlin: 1869). On the importance of non-denominational education, see also Rudolf Gneist, *Die confessionelle Schule: Ihre Unzulässigkeit nach preußischen Landesgesetzen* (Berlin: 1869). Support by the right-liberal Gneist encouraged Frankfurt liberals in their unity on this subject.

48. Richard Wachsmuth, *Die Gründung der Universität Frankfurt* (Frankfurt: Englert & Schlosser, 1929). Paul Kluke, *Die Stiftungsuniversität Frankfurt am Main 1914–1932* (Frankfurt: Kramer, 1972). The Jewish donations are detailed in Arnsberg, *Geschichte der Frankfurter Juden,* ii. 292–9.

49. Rudolf Ehlers, *Zur Verständigung über die Frankfurter Kirchenfrage: Für und gegen die Schrift: 'Die protestantischen Gemeinden der Stadt Frankfurt in Preußen'* (Frankfurt, 1868), 3–4.

50. For a more detailed discussion on the relationship between National Liberals and Calvinists, see Palmowski, *Urban Liberalism,* 171–4.

51. The best survey on the German Catholic and 'free religious' movements is still Friedrich Wilhelm Graf, *Die Politisierung des religiösen Bewußtseins: Die*

*bürgerlichen Religionsparteien im deutschen Vormärz: Das Beispiel des Deutschkatholizismus* (Stuttgart: Frommann-Holzboog, 1978).

52. Carl Sänger, *1845–1895. Geschichte der freireligiösen Bewegung und der deutschkathol. (freien religiösen) Gemeinde zu Frankfurt a. M. Festschrift zur Feier des funfzigjährigen Bestehens der Gemeinde* (Frankfurt, 1895). 'Grundsätze der Deutschkatholischen (freien religiösen) Gemeinde zu Frankfurt a.M.', in *Satzungen der im Jahre 1845 gegründeten Deutschkatholischen (freien religiösen) Gemeinde mit dem Sitze in Frankfurt a.M.* (Frankfurt, 1892), especially 21–2.

53. Heinrich Rößler, *Lebenserinnerungen* (Frankfurt, 1906), here 64–5.

54. The German Catholic community was associated with the Weimar Cartel through the League of Free Religious Communities in Germany (Bund freireligiöser Gemeinden Deutschlands). Frank Simon-Ritz, *Die Organisation einer Weltanschauung: Die freigeistige Bewegung im Wilhelminischen Deutschland* (Gütersloh: Chr. Kaiser/Gütersloher Verlagshaus, 1997), 159.

55. Heuberger and Krohn, *Hinaus aus dem Ghetto*, 121.

56. Ibid.

57. Charles Hallgarten, *Neues über den Antisemitismus* (Frankfurt, 1897), 9–10.

58. Ursula Bartelsheim, *Die Politisierung und Demokratisierung der kommunalen Selbstverwaltung: Kommunalpolitik in Frankfurt am Main 1850–1900*, Ph.D. thesis (Frankfurt University, 1995), 63–4.

59. See, for instance, *Frankfurter Zeitung* (29 Nov. 1904, 3rd morning edn.), 'Vor der Entscheidung'.

60. Arnsberg, *Geschichte der Frankfurter Juden*, ii. 484.

61. Pulzer, *Jews and the German State*, 125, 186–7.

62. *Statistische Jahresübersichten 1911/12*, 11, 21. The statistics do not distinguish between those born in the area of the Free City, and those born in the incorporated areas. The estimate of 130,000 is derived by applying the ratio of the population between traditional and incorporated areas of the city to the total figure of 180,983 born in all of Frankfurt.

63. As important are the high number of migrants, which would have been particularly difficult to incorporate into any traditional civic vision. In 1906, the population growth of 25,000 was determined less by the excess of births over deaths (which amounted to around 5,000), than by the excess of those who came to the city over those who left. *Statistische Jahresübersichten der Stadt Frankfurt am Main 1907/08* (Frankfurt, 1908), 13, 15.

64. Hermann Dechent, *Kirchengeschichte*, ii. 492–3.

65. In the Empire, the number of Protestants rose from 62,196 in 1875 to 175,909 in 1900, to 250,505 in 1910. *Beiträge zur Statistik der Stadt Frankfurt am Main*, ed. Statistische Abteilung des Frankfurter Vereins für Geographie und Statistik (Frankfurt, 1882–1885), 23. *Statistische Jahresübersichten 1911/12*, 21.

66. The Protestant immigrants were, on the whole, more religiously active than the traditionally rather lethargic Frankfurt Protestants. Hermann, *Kirchengeschichte*, ii. 503, 527.

67. Julius Werner, *Deutschtum und Christentum: Gedenkreden* (Heidelberg, 1906). Julius Werner, *Der deutsche Protestantismus und das öffentliche Leben* (Hagen i. W., n.d.), esp. 83–4.

68. Leopold Sonnemann in 1880. The full quotation is in Roth, 'Liberalismus in Frankfurt', 42.

69. The importance of Berlin is evident, for instance, in the DDP's foundation. Larry E. Jones, *German Liberalism and the Dissolution of the Weimar Party System 1918–1933* (Chapel Hill, NC: University of North Carolina Press, 1988), 17–25.

70. Frankfurt was unusual in that the real influence of Jews in politics did not decline after 1918–19, mainly by virtue of the indirectly elected positions in the municipal administration. Moreover, in contrast to Breslau, for instance, the Liberal parties in Frankfurt were stronger than the national average, though their rate of decline was broadly similar. Van Rahden, 'Mingling, Marrying, and Distancing', 207. In general, see Liepach, *Wahlverhalten*, 16–26.

71. Dieter Rebentisch, *Ludwig Landmann: Frankfurter Oberbürgermeister der Weimarer Republik* (Wiesbaden: Steiner, 1975), esp. 132–6.

72. In addition, both the director of the municipal theatre, Alwin Kronacher, and the principal director of the opera house, Herbert Graf, were Jewish. Barbara Köhler, 'Die Nationalsozialisten in der Frankfurter Stadtverordnetenversammlung 1929 bis 1933', *AFGK*, 14 (1985), 439–84, here 456.

73. This point would deserve more detailed examination, analogous to that conducted for *fin de siècle* Vienna by Steven Beller, *Vienna and the Jews 1867–1938: A Cultural History* (Cambridge: Cambridge University Press, 1989).

74. See the collection of newspaper cuttings on the affair in IfSG, Magistratsakte S442/ii, which contains articles from the *Sonne* and the *Frankfurter Zeitung* (10–20 Apr. 1918), as well as the Lutheran response in *Die Gemeinde* (27 Apr. 1918).

75. Johannes Kübel, *Erinnerungen* (Villingen-Schwenningen: Selbstverlag, 1972), 107–15, also 63–4. See Kübel's personal file in IfSG/2818, esp. his sermon on 26 Jan. 1919, on the eve of the Kaiser's birthday.

76. On the DNVP's anti-Semitism, see Pulzer, *Rise of Political Anti-Semitism*, 292–5.

77. J.R.C. Wright, *'Above Parties': The Political Attitudes of the German Protestant Church Leadership 1918–1933* (Oxford: OUP, 1974), 49, 51, 54–8.

78. On the 'theological' justification of Protestant anti-Semitism in the Weimar Republic, see Marijke Smid, 'Protestantismus und Antisemitismus 1930–1933', in Jochen-Christoph Kaiser and Martin Greschat (eds.), *Der Holocaust und die Protestanten* (Frankfurt: Athenäum, 1988), 38–72, here 50–5.

79. Karl Maly, *Das Regiment der Parteien: Geschichte der Frankfurter Stadtverordnetenversammlung*, ii. 1901–33 (Frankfurt: Kramer, 1995), 364–5. *Frankfurter Nachrichten* (16 June 1923, Beiblatt).

80. Karl Veidt and Georg Struckmeier, *Hundert Jahre St. Paulskirche: Jubiläumsfestschrift zum 9. Juni 1933* (Frankfurt: Paulskirchengemeinde, 1933), 50.

81. 'Die Mitte und ihr Gegenspiel', *Frankfurter Nachrichten* (28 Apr. 1920).

82. See for instance, the election notice for 'Protestant men and women', in *Frankfurter Nachrichten* (28 Feb. 1919), IfSG S3/022.311, Deutsch-Nationale Volkspartei.

83. 'Eine "völkische Wählerversammlung"', *Frankfurter Zeitung* (5 Apr. 1924, Abendblatt) 'Wahlkundgebung der Demokraten', *Frankfurter Zeitung* (12 Nov. 1929, 2nd morning edn.). 'Jubiläumsfeier des Philanthropins', *GIG* (Jan. 1930). Avraham Barkai, 'Jewish Life in its German Milieu', in Meyer (ed.), *German-Jewish History* vi. 45–71, here 50.

84. With a quarter of the total vote, the DDP emerged as the city's strongest bourgeois party in the national elections of 1919 which, according to the *Frankfurter Nachrichten*, were a test for an acceptance of the 'Verständnis für den Geist der neuen Zeit', *Frankfurter Nachrichten* (20 Jan. 1919, Beiblatt). On the programmatic identification of Frankfurt's Democrats with the Weimar Republic, see also Rohr, 'Kommunaler Liberalismus', 175–6.

85. Pulzer, *Jews and the German State*, 220–5. Frankfurt was by no means exceptional in this regard. See, for instance, Roland Flade, *Juden in Würzburg 1918–1933* (Würzburg: Freunde Mainfränkischer Kunst und Geschichte, 1985), 75–8.

86. Note the Democrats' defence against charges by the Centre Party that Ludwig Heilbrunn, who was, of course, Jewish, was a member of the Free Religious (German Catholic) community. Its appeal to the 'decent' German contrasted to DVP and DNVP appeals to the 'Christian' German. *Frankfurter Nachrichten* (26 Jan. 1919).

87. In general, see Ben Lieberman, 'Testing Peukert's Paradigm: The "Crisis of Classical Modernity" in the "New Frankfurt", 1925–1930', *German Studies Review*, 17 (1994), 287–303.

88. Of the numerous examples, see esp. *Frankfurter Zeitung* (18 May 1928, Abendblatt); *Frankfurter Nachrichten* (20 Jan. 1919).

89. 'Bücherschau', *GIG* (Mar. 1927).

90. *Frankfurter Zeitung* (19 Aug. 1928).

91. Günther Gillessen, *Auf verlorenem Posten: Die Frankfurter Zeitung im Dritten Reich* (Berlin: Siedler, 1986), 36–43.

92. For instance, the National Socialist student riots at the University of Berlin were given their due coverage, but the fact that Jewish students were thrown out of the window was mentioned, yet not discussed. *Frankfurter Nachrichten* (13 Nov. 1929). This was a marked contrast to the engaged (and disgusted) discussion in the *Frankfurter Zeitung* (13 Nov. 1929, Abendblatt).

93. *Fankfurter Nachrichten* (27 Sept. 1930). See also *Frankfurter Nachrichten* (6 Nov. 1932, 1st Beiblatt; 1 Jan. 1933.

94. Richard Merton, *Wie Oberbürgermeister Dr. Landmann regierte: Fünf Jahre Frankfurter Kommunalpolitik* (Frankfurt, 1929).

95. Richard Merton, *Erinnernswertes aus meinem Leben* (Frankfurt: Knapp, 1955), 75. This confirms Peter Pulzer's suspicion that, on the whole, Jews in Frankfurt did not vote for the DVP, even if the party was headed by a Jew. Pulzer, *Jews and the German State*, 308–9.

96. *Frankfurter Nachrichten* (19 Mar. 1933). In the months before its dissolution in the summer of 1933, the DVP continued to distinguish itself as the party of German unity, of Bismarckian greatness. Yet throughout, it hovered uneasily between using this identity sometimes in criticism, and sometimes in support, of Hitler. IfSG S3/01761, Demokratische Volkspartei.

97. The relationship between anti-Semitism and Protestantism in the Weimar Republic is described most extensively in Gerhard Lindemann, '*Typisch jüdisch*': *die Stellung der Ev.-luth. Landeskirche Hannovers zu Antijudaismus, Judenfeindschaft und Antisemitismus 1919–1949* (Berlin: Duncker & Humblot, 1998). Lindemann confirms a growing Protestant hostility towards Jews and a greater emphasis on Christian definitions of the Volk, although the political impact of this is outside the scope of the study (ibid. 50–88).

98. Anthony Kauders, *German Politics and the Jews: Düsseldorf and Nuremberg 1910–1933* (Oxford: OUP, 1996).

99. See, for instance, anon. [Germanicus], *Die Frankfurter Juden und die Aufsaugung des Volkswohlstandes* (Leipzig, 1890). Schlotzhauer, *Ideologie und Antisemitismus*, ch. 2.

100. Anthony Kauders, 'Legally Citizens: Jewish Exclusion from the Weimar Polity', in Benz *et al.*, *Jüdisches Leben*, 162.

101. The introduction of modern anti-Semitism into public life through the organization of the insecure sections of the *Mittelstand* in the 1890s has been confirmed for the case of Hamburg. Lorenz, *Die Juden in Hamburg*, i, pp. cxxxvi–cxl. In general, see Albert Lichtblau, *Antisemitismus und soziale Spannung in Berlin und Wien 1867–1914* (Berlin: Metropol, 1994).

102. See, for instance, 'Die Mission des Judenthums', *FIG* (Apr. 1930).
103. Note the article by Kurt Epstein, a student who exposed the inadequacy of ten years of intensive debate about the quantity of Jewish religious education in schools by pointing out the need for quality and enticement instead, since most Jewish youths, especially from the affluent 'Westend' district, had very little contact with the Jewish religion altogether. *Jugend und Gemeinde* (Jan. 1932).
104. 'Aussprache: Verantwortung', *FIG* (Jan. 1930). 'Wissen und Verändern', *Jugend und Gemeinde* (Apr. 1932), esp. the article 'Passitivät und Mitarbeit'.
105. The discussion was carried out in the new supplements to the *FIG* entitled *Jugend und Gemeinde*, which appeared from Sept. 1931. For a particularly interesting discussion on different political ideologies, see *Jugend und Gemeinde* (Aug. 1932). See the 'responses to "spiritual" anti-Semitism' in *Jugend und Gemeinde* (Nov. 1932).
106. ' "Überwindet den Massenmenschen"' *Jugend und Gemeinde* (May 1932).
107. The full quotation is: 'Wenn keine Stimme sich für uns erhebt, so mögen die Steine dieser Stadt für uns zeugen, die ihren Aufschwung zu einem guten Teil jüdischer Leistung verdankt, in der so viele Einrichtungen vom Gemeinsinn der Juden künden, in der aber auch das Verhältnis zwischen jüdischen und nichtjüdischen Bürgern stets besonders eng gewesen ist.' *FIG* (Apr. 1933).

# 7

# Liberalism and Anti-Semitism in Germany: The Case of Gustav Stresemann

## *Jonathan Wright*

Peter Pulzer has described the legal process of emancipation of the Jews in Germany as a kind of bargain: the Jews would be emancipated and, in return, become assimilated. However, as he points out, it was left unclear what Jews would have to do, or to give up, in order to be accepted. 'As a consequence, there ensued a dialogue of the deaf: as long as Jews were not prepared to abandon all forms of separate culture, said some, they could not demand complete acceptance. As long as they were not offered complete acceptance, said others, they could scarcely be expected to renounce their traditions.'[1] This problem has parallels in the situation of other minorities, but in Germany, as Pulzer explains, it was aggravated by a series of unfavourable conditions: a bureaucracy with a dogmatic enlightenment view of citizenship hostile to other cultures, a new nation-state tempted to define national identity by excluding outsiders, and, paradoxically, the survival of the domestic jurisdiction of individual German states like Prussia, which were neither secular nor liberal, and continued to practise discrimination against Jews in public employment. To these were subsequently added the traumas of a lost war and a disputed Republic.[2] Unsurprisingly in these circumstances the 'Jewish Question' not only remained unresolved but acquired a political dimension and, at times of crisis, political momentum. The career of Gustav Stresemann illustrates some of the complex forms the question assumed in the life of a leading liberal politician.

Stresemann was born in 1878 in an unfashionable part of Berlin. His father ran a small business making and distributing bottled beer, and the family home doubled as a bar. It was a lower middle-class, Protestant, and left-liberal milieu. It is possible that Stresemann had one grandparent of Jewish descent, his paternal grandmother, Marie Dorothea Meyerhoff.[3] Whether, if so, this had any influence on him is unknown. His attitudes as a young man corresponded, in any case, to those of his background. In 1895–6, concealing his identity as a sixth-former, he wrote a number of 'Letters from Berlin' for a Dresden weekly. In these, he was cheerfully dismissive of Conservatives, Social Democrats, orthodox Protestantism, Ultramontanism, the anti-Semitic ex-court preacher Adolf Stoecker, the National Liberals, and the Colonial Society alike.[4] This left-liberal creed was repeated in his autobiographical essay in his last year at school, aged 19, where he described the deep impression made on him by liberal Protestantism and his belief in 'the greatest possible tolerance in all matters of faith' which, however, would not prevent him from attacking 'the anti-national character of the degenerate form of Catholicism in ultramontanism'.[5]

This last comment is a reminder of the ambiguous relationship between liberalism and nationalism. Looking back in August 1923, shortly before he became Chancellor, Stresemann wrote that the strongest influence on his early political career had been 'the ideas of a national, democratic and liberal (*freiheitlich*) persuasion, as they were expressed in the spirit of the Paulskirche in the 1848 period'. This liberalism was also 'the pioneering champion of the German fleet, German unity, German greatness'. As Stresemann admitted, the authors he had then admired like Konrad Krez and Georg Herwegh 'could perhaps now sound to many, who today call themselves Democrats, like pan-Germans'.[6] This ambiguity helps to explain some of the paradoxes of Stresemann's career, pre-war and wartime nationalist and annexationist but also advocate of constitutional reform and parliamentary government, post-war a sometimes violent critic of the Republican parties but, after a painful period of adjustment, the Republic's leading statesman, a force for consensus at home and conciliation abroad. This ambiguity can also be seen in his attitude to anti-Semitism, which was less than straightforward.

Stresemann's first encounter with anti-Semitism came as a student. He matriculated at Berlin University in the summer of 1897, at a time when the majority of *Burschenschaften* (student fraternities) were deciding to exclude Jews from membership as part of a general drift towards apeing the reactionary, socially exclusive *Korps*. Stresemann joined a small break-away group, the Allgemeiner Deutscher Burschenbund (ADB) founded in the 1880's to keep alive the original liberal ideals of the movement. In his second semester he was elected the 'spokesman' of his Berlin group, the Neo-Germania, and after transferring to Leipzig in 1898 he became the 'spokesman' of the equivalent there, the Suevia. In 1923 he recalled:

The ADB did not at that time endorse the racial principle, and the Berlin *Burschenschaft* included Jewish members in its ranks. In the period when Stresemann had just taken on the office of spokesman of the *Burschenschaft*, the strong anti-Semitic movement broke out in the ADB, Neo-Germania, as well. Meetings which lasted until well after midnight wrestled with the position to be adopted on this question. The young spokesman succeeded at that time in getting the old principle of the ADB accepted, not to bow to the racist view in this matter, but to adopt the position that everyone, whose character and attitude to *Deutschtum* offered a guarantee that they shared the ideas and feelings of the *Burschenschaften,* should also be allowed to take part in the *Burschenschaft,* the same ideas ... which were later laid down in the programme of the Deutsche Volkspartei.[7]

There is no direct confirmation of Stresemann's recollection of these events, but there is no reason to doubt its accuracy. In the pages of the ADB journal, the *Allgemeine Deutsche Universitätszeitung,* of which he became editor in 1898, he linked anti-Semitism to his standard targets of religious intolerance and class prejudice. In one article, he wrote that the liberal ideals of the *Burschenschaften* required them

to uphold the equal rights of all citizens and therefore to oppose anti-Semitism and disguised class rule. Just as they could not accept that being an adherent of the Jewish religion was a reason for rejection from the state's employment, so equally they could not accept, without protest, the contempt shown from above for the intelligence of the entire middle class, by the preferential treatment of the aristocracy in the officer corps, senior administrative appointments etc.

The article concluded: 'If there are associations which call themselves '*Burschenschaften*' but are anti-Semitic and reactionary then ... that only shows that these *Burschenschaften* have only inherited one thing from the old *Burschenschaften,* the name.'[8]

The later history of this issue provides a less clear-cut picture. In 1919, the ADB reversed its position and decided to exclude Jews. According to a former member of the Neo-Germania, while influential left-wing politicians remained silent, Stresemann was one of the very few to oppose this surrender. He did not however resign, telling someone who did that he intended to take more trouble with the ADB and perhaps it would be possible 'to bring it back on track'.[9] Stresemann kept in touch with the *Burschenschaft* and spoke at its national rally by the Kyffhäuser mountains (a place of national pilgrimage with legendary associations with Emperor Frederick Barbarossa) in 1923, twenty five years after he had held the first rally there in 1898.[10] He clearly valued the link with his student past and decided not to make a public stand against the ADB's anti-Semitism. His reasons can only be guessed at. In the immediate post-war period his position on 'the Jewish Question' was more equivocal than it had been as a student. His own political future was in doubt and there were not many votes to be gained by taking a stand on the issue. Later, from 1923, he was increasingly concerned about the political attitudes in Germany's universities and tried to win over student audiences to support for the Republic.[11] In neither phase would he have wanted to break his links with the *Burschenschaft* in which he had first made a name for himself. It is noticeable that in the obituary number of the ADB journal for Stresemann there is only a veiled reference to his opposition to anti-Semitism.[12]

The *Burschenschaft* had an important influence on Stresemann's life in another way. Through a fellow member of Suevia at Leipzig, Kurt von Kleefeld, he met the Kleefeld family and married one of the three sisters, Käte, in 1903. Her father was a Berlin manufacturer of Jewish descent, who had become a Protestant. The Kleefelds were well-to-do and the wedding was celebrated in the *Kaiser Wilhelm Gedächtniskirche* in a fashionable quarter of Berlin. In the perspective of the time, Stresemann had married above himself, 'but Jewish'.[13] In the short term, this was no disadvantage. The marriage was by all accounts a very happy and successful one. Stresemann admired his father-in-law, both as a businessman and for his interest in literature, art, and music.[14] Käte had two children, both sons. The elder, Wolfgang, had a pronounced musical talent to the pleasure of his father.[15]

Stresemann also enjoyed rapid success in his career before 1914 both in business and politics. He made his name with the Association of Saxon Industrialists, which he built up into an effective lobbying organization on behalf of the small-scale, exporting industries of Saxony, and in 1911 he became the effective director of the equivalent national organization.[16] In politics, he transferred his loyalties from the left-liberals, whom he found too negative and dogmatic, to the National Liberals and succeeded in getting himself elected to the Reichstag in 1907 as its youngest member, aged 28. There he soon established himself as a rising star of the left wing of the National Liberals and the protégé of the party leader, Ernst Bassermann, whose wife was also, like Käte, of Jewish descent. This led the chairman of the Pan-German League, Heinrich Claß, to describe them as 'Jewish affiliated' in a well-known anti-Semitic text.[17] Through his business and political interests, Stresemann came into contact with circles where distinguished Jews were prominent. Particularly important was the Hansa-Bund, formed in 1909 as a broad alliance of banking and industry to resist the influence of the Agrarian League and the Conservative Party.[18]

Stresemann was an enthusiastic supporter of the new organization, which reflected both his business and political views. He hoped it would provide a powerful counter to the agricultural and heavy-industry lobbies with their twin programme of protectionist tariffs and opposition to constitutional reform. His Association of Industrialists established close connections with the Hansa-Bund and in 1912 he became a member of its central organization, with responsibility for industrial matters and contact between the centre and individual branches. His brother-in-law, Kurt von Kleefeld, was one of the two deputy managers of the organization and its chairman was Jakob Riesser, another baptized Protestant from a famous Jewish political family. Riesser's uncle, Gabriel, as Vice-President of the Frankfurt Parliament of 1848, had been largely responsible for the inclusion of civil and political equality for Jews in the Basic Rights of the German People.[19] Jakob Riesser was also a member, like Stresemann, of the National Executive of the National Liberal

Party and later of Stresemann's *Deutsche Volkspartei*. Partly because of Riesser's position within it, the *Hansa-Bund* was regarded by friends and enemies alike as an organization that would help to promote equal rights for Jews.[20]

Through Bassermann, Stresemann also came into contact with Albert Ballin, the managing director of the Hamburg–America Line, the world's greatest steamship company and one of the most prominent Jews in the Empire.[21] Together with others, they founded in 1914 a German-American Economic Association, of which Stresemann became an executive member.[22] Through Ballin, Stresemann also experienced at first hand another form of prejudice in the Empire. When he and Bassermann were guests of Ballin's at the Kiel naval regatta, the Kaiser visited the ship but, to Ballin's embarrassment, declined to allow the National Liberal leader and Stresemann to be presented to him.[23] When Ballin died in November 1918, Stresemann praised him as an acute businessman with a vision that spanned the continents and a kind and generous host.[24]

Before the First World War, Stresemann was able to ride the two horses of nationalism and liberalism without much fear that they would pull in different directions. During the war, the debate over war aims made this more complicated. The groups supporting constitutional reform, the Social Democrats, left-liberals and Catholic Centre Party, became in 1917 also a coalition pressing for a compromise peace 'of understanding', while the forces of the right, the Conservative Party, the High Command, and the Court, resisted constitutional reform and held out for total victory. Stresemann, who became leader of the National Liberals in the Reichstag in September 1917, following the death of Bassermann, continued to try to have a foot in both camps. The National Liberals supported the inter-party committee of the majority parties on constitutional reform but the High Command on war aims. The division became increasingly bitter as the war progressed. One symptom of the conflict was the use of anti-Semitism by the right to brand their opponents as unpatriotic. For the first time, Stresemann's judgement was also affected and an anti-Semitic note entered his vocabulary.

In a memorandum written at the beginning of 1916, he expressed his discontent with what he saw as Chancellor Bethmann Hollweg's weak leadership. In particular he suspected that Bethmann Hollweg wanted to keep open the possibility of peace with Britain, in return for restoring Belgian independence, in order to concentrate on the war with Russia. This 'false peace'—false because it would only provide an armistice until Germany's enemies attacked once again—would be, he feared, attractive to the German public, whose morale was growing weaker. Among the influences leading public opinion in this direction, he mentioned the two leading liberal newspapers, the *Berliner Tageblatt* and the *Frankfurter Zeitung*, both Jewish-owned and the former edited by the most famous journalist from a Jewish background, Theodor

Wolff.[25] He noted that these newspapers were prepared to give up Belgium but wanted the Russian Empire destroyed. He went on:

In order to understand this whole attitude, one must remember that for many of these writers, namely for the whole daily press in Jewish hands, the decisive factor is the anti-Semitic stance of the Russian government and many of them view this world war purely from the standpoint of the Jewish pogroms. These intellectual circles have for decades [shown] a completely ape-like attraction for France and England . . . because of the ruling democratic system there, whilst a strong monarchy such as exists in Russia and Germany seems undesirable to them. Therefore, they have invented the slogan that Germany must not lose its connection with the culture of Western Europe, and would like to show consideration for France and bring about an understanding with England, while on the other hand they are ready for far-reaching annexations in the East.[26]

This memorandum was not for publication and did not represent a full statement of his views. In the Reichstag the following year, he contrasted the success of parliamentary institutions in Britain in mobilizing support for the war with the failures of the imperial government in Germany.[27] In 1918 he also showed no hesitation in supporting the break-up of the Russian Empire. But he continued to oppose all thought of a compromise peace in the West and became a leading advocate of unrestricted submarine warfare in the hope that this would prove decisive against Britain. His difference with Theodor Wolff and the *Berliner Tageblatt* on this issue, and the exposed and disastrous position Stresemann took on it, had lasting effects on their relationship.

Another issue during the war which marked a shift in Stresemann's attitude towards anti-Semitism was the so-called 'Jewish census' in October 1916. Matthias Erzberger, a leading member of the Centre Party, proposed to the Reichstag budget committee that there should be a survey of the people involved in the various procurement agencies (which had been set up to manage supplies of food and essential materials) and that this information should include their religious denomination. The ostensible purpose was to dispel a widespread view, damaging to the agencies' reputation, that they were in the hands of a Jewish clique. The proposal was adopted by a majority on the committee, with the National Liberals voting in favour, against the votes of the Social Democrats and the left-liberals. In fact, nothing came of the survey, which was opposed by the government, and the Reichstag took no further action on it. But the proposal was naturally deeply offensive to German Jews, implying as it did that there were grounds for suspecting their contribution to the war effort and thus, whatever the intention of some of its supporters, appearing to confirm the propaganda of anti-Semites. The situation was made worse by the fact that the army carried out its own survey, which was humiliating to Jewish soldiers.[28]

Stresemann was one of the National Liberal representatives on the committee. Defending their stance in a newspaper article against the criticism of the *Berliner Tageblatt* and others, he took the line that their purpose had been to counter the rapidly growing anti-Semitic agitation by depriving it of one of its arguments. He admitted that in principle they should have voted against the proposal, on the grounds that religious belief was not relevant to state employment, but he argued that, in practice, exceptions had always been made. For instance, if Catholics or Protestants were given privileged treatment the disadvantaged side would protest. To have opposed the proposal would simply have allowed anti-Semites to argue that the Liberals were covering up abuses. The National Liberal members of the Reichstag knew that the anti-Semitic propaganda was highly exaggerated and therefore they—and the Jews—had every interest in the true position being clarified. He rejected the suggestion that their support for the proposal showed that they harboured anti-Semitic tendencies, pointing out that the National Liberal Party included 'a large number of outstanding Jewish citizens as colleagues and is proud to have them'. To suggest otherwise and to make the issue one of 'for or against anti-Semitism' was to play party politics. This would serve only the cause of those whose influence German liberalism as a whole should resist 'by enlightenment and calm, sober explanation of the facts'.[29]

It is not difficult to see the weaknesses in Stresemann's argument. By acknowledging that there was a case to rebut, the National Liberals appeared to endorse the anti-Semitic campaign, whatever Stresemann's disclaimers. It was also unrealistic to imagine that such propaganda could be stilled by sober facts. This was the beginning for Stresemann of a way of dealing with 'the Jewish Question' by accepting, unlike the left-liberals, that there was a question to be answered, an awkward compromise which continued into the post-war period. It is, however, important to distinguish Stresemann's position from that of the racial anti-Semites, like the pan-German Claß. Writing to a friend, he referred to the confiscation of Claß's pamphlets on war aims as an example of Bethmann Hollweg's over-reaction to his opponents but, at the same time, he noted Claß's 'folly of wanting to solve the Jewish question in conquered Poland by sending the Jews to Palestine'.[30]

Defeat and revolution in October-November 1918 intensified the divisions which had taken shape during the war. Stresemann was no longer able to maintain the balancing act between left and right, with the twin policies of reform and victory. Instead, the National Liberal Party broke up with the majority defecting to join the left-liberals in the new Democratic Party (DDP). Stresemann found himself unwanted by the leaders of the new party, a 'compromised' politician because of his wartime reputation as an annexationist. Only a year before, at the age of 39, he had become leader of the National Liberal Party. Now it seemed that his political career was over. Among the founders of the DDP were prominent Jews, including Theodor Wolff, and it was supported by the Jewish-owned press.[31] Stresemann's family was also represented in the person of Kurt von Kleefeld, who made a wounding reference to Stresemann as 'my poor, unfortunate, misguided brother-in-law'.[32] Among the defectors from the National Liberal Party to the Democrats were also politicians of Jewish descent. Stresemann was particularly bitter about Robert Friedberg, a prominent member of the right-wing of the party and chairman of the national executive, whom he accused of capitulating to the Democrats by eventually accepting their terms for a merger on his own authority.[33]

Stresemann was resentful and disoriented. He saw the DDP as controlled by the extreme left wing of German liberalism, the circle represented by the *Berliner Tageblatt*. Their criticisms of the German Empire now seemed to him exaggerated and unpatriotic in defeat. With the remaining National Liberals he formed the *Deutsche Volkspartei* (DVP). In the elections to the National Assembly in January 1919, it secured 4.4 per cent of the vote and twenty-two seats. This was just enough to make it viable but in 1912, by comparison, the National Liberal share of the vote had been 13.6 per cent. The future of the DVP clearly depended on whether it could recover the approximately two-thirds of its constituency, which had gone over to the DDP, giving them in 1919 18.5 per cent of the vote and seventy-seven seats. In these circumstances Stresemann was bound to look for issues on which the Democrats were vulnerable. Anti-Semitism, which had been given new momentum on the right by defeat and revolution, with the Jews as an obvious scapegoat, was clearly one such issue. However, there were also constraining factors. Stresemann remained a liberal and the DVP retained from the National Liberal Party distinguished Jews among its members. Among these were a group of bankers, including Max Warburg, whose financial support was important.[34] In addition, Stresemann himself now came more openly under attack from anti-Semites because of his marriage. Under these contrary pressures, he tried to face both ways, blaming the Jews for not disowning the views of the Jewish-owned press while at the same time denying any anti-Semitic motive.

In an article about the failure of negotiations for a united liberal party in December 1918, he declared that National Liberals had nothing in common with those in the Democratic Party who had decided that 'Deutschland, Deutschland über alles' should no longer be sung: 'This is where the spirits separate.' He quoted with approval a National Liberal who had said, 'A party which includes me and Theodor Wolff is inherently false'.[35] In the same vein, he declared to the first DVP party conference in April 1919 that they had been ready for a liberal union but they refused to join with 'that left democratic wing ... from which we are divided like fire and water, from which we are divided by a consciously German outlook on one side from cosmopolitan ideas on the other'.[36] He repeated this comment in his speech to the second party conference in October 1919. He also violently attacked the communists for spreading revolution and associated them with immigration from the east, in words which were clearly intended to refer to Jewish immigration and, as the report on the conference made clear, were warmly appreciated:

This Communist idea and its application, which has resulted in animal bestiality, I am certain its origin does not lie in the German soul. They are foreign elements (*loud agreement*) which have put themselves at the leadership of this movement, and with total conviction and unanimity the German People's Party in the National Assembly opposed open frontiers for the immigration of these elements. (*Applause*) We want our German nation to be kept German. (*Applause*) We do not want to become a playground for the perverse, theoretical passions of people without home or fatherland. (*Stormy applause*)'[37]

The issue also arose in relation to the party programme. A statement by the party chairman in the National Assembly, Rudolf Heinze, that the DVP 'rejected anti-Semitism in any form' had exposed the party to attacks from the nationalist right.[38] In discussions on the executive committee, Stresemann was clearly concerned to find a more flexible formula. Explaining a reference in the draft programme to 'international tendencies to disintegration' under the heading of 'Nationality and Family' he said, according to the minutes,

we must take a stand in some form on the Jewish question. It was clear that we could not take part in the anti-Semitic agitation which was now widespread. When Jewish organizations approached him as a result of this agitation about the position of our party, he had repeatedly told them that the Jews themselves were the best promoters of the agitation. They had it in their power to remove the ground from under its feet if they found patriotic Jews, who had the courage to oppose the despicable behaviour of the Jewish press. *Der Ulk* of the Mosse publishing house and *Die Weltbühne* of Siegfried Jacobson [sic] and others degraded everything that was holy to national-minded Germans in the most infamous fashion. However, no Jew had been found who would distance himself from this behaviour. It was therefore no wonder that anti-Semitism was spreading ever more widely.

Stresemann added that it was not only Jews who were involved and he named a number of prominent gentile pacifists. He also referred to other abuses— 'almost Russian conditions, with bribery part of the agenda'—again adding 'Unfortunately it was not only Jews who were involved'.[39]

The party programme duly affirmed the importance for the German people of maintaining a consciousness of 'its particular national nature' (*seiner völkischen Eigenart*) and declared its opposition to 'all attempts at repressing our German feelings in favour of cosmopolitan and to us foreign opinions'. The party 'wanted to keep the German nation German and therefore opposed the flooding of Germany with people of foreign origin which has occurred particularly since the revolution'.[40]

These thinly disguised concessions to anti-Semitism caused concern to Jewish organizations and to the DVP's Jewish members. Prompted by Jakob Riesser, the executive committee considered the matter again and adopted a new resolution to be used in answer to enquiries.[41] This reflected the different views in the party, renewing the criticism of Jews involved in left-wing activities but making it clear that Jews as such were not responsible and that patriotic Jews were welcome in the DVP:

A series of regrettable recent events have allowed a revival of anti-Semitism; in particular, a relatively large number of members of the Jewish community at home and abroad have taken a leading role in attempts at revolution and acts of violence.

The German People's Party rejects any generalization of the criticism, which is justified in such cases, as inaccurate and unjustified. Its programme demands full equality for all citizens; it also emphatically rejects, however, all revolutionary and similar efforts, which want to replace commitment to the national state and German national character with a cosmopolitan citizenship, which represses our German feeling in favour of international opinions. The Party is further convinced that the moral and economic recovery of our nation can only succeed if we return to the old principles of loyalty, honesty, impartiality and incorruptibility in public service and in commercial and social life. All other attitudes will be resisted by the German People's Party, wherever they come from.

Whoever shares this position and stands unconditionally behind the nation is welcome in the ranks of the German People's Party, whatever his religious faith.

An influential member of the Reichstag party, Paul Moldenhauer, probably reflected a widely held view of this decision when in his memoirs (albeit written during the Third Reich) he described the party's attitude as a compromise between its liberal principles and its 'instinctive, strong disapproval of the Jews, particularly in the especially subversive form in which we encountered them in politics, literature and art'. He said at the time he had expressed the view that 'The Democratic Party must be preserved as it has the historic task of gathering together the subversive elements of Jewry and thus freeing the German People's Party of them' and he went on: 'Basically we were all racially minded and against the Jews and we found it disturbing that the party leader was married to a Jew.'[42]

The new party resolution did not result in any change of tactics on Stresemann's part. The same day, he replied to an enquiry from the Central Association of German Citizens of the Jewish Faith, saying that he was a Christian and that as a Christian he deplored the growth of anti-Semitism, which he saw as a great danger for their common fatherland. He added that he was married to a Jew. However, he went on, since he condemned anti-Semitism, he believed he was entitled to say that he was astonished at the short-sightedness of Jewish organizations in not recognizing that 'some of the worst *agents provocateur* [sic] for anti-Semitism were to be found in Jewish circles'. He criticized the *Berliner Tageblatt*, which was commonly seen as 'the mouthpiece of German Jewry', for its repeated allegations that German landowners and farmers had extended the war for selfish reasons, an accusation which was bound to cause resentment when so many of them, who had been Prussian officers, now lay in foreign soil. He quoted other examples from the *Ulk*, edited by Kurt Tucholsky, and suggested that the Central Association should dissociate itself from these and such sentiments.[43] After the Kapp *putsch* in March 1920, he pressed the attack home, saying that Galician Jews had been standing at every street corner in the west of Berlin preaching Bolshevism and he urged the foundation of an 'association of national Jews' to dissociate Jews from these groups and from the destructive criticism of the Jewish press.[44]

The Central Association does not appear to have responded to Stresemann's letter.[45] However, in 1921 an Association of National German Jews was founded by a Dr Max Naumann who was a member of the DVP.[46] Although there is no direct evidence, it seems possible that this was at least in part in response to Stresemann's repeated suggestions. Certainly its programme of total commitment to the German nation and opposition to the tendency of the Central Association to co-operate with parties of the left was exactly what Stresemann had in mind. It was reported that Stresemann had addressed one of its early meetings.[47] He does not appear, however, to have made use of it in subsequent debate. It quickly became involved in a bitter feud with the Central Association, to which senior Jewish members of the DVP belonged. Stresemann would therefore not have wanted to become involved with Naumann's group too closely.

The issue of anti-Semitism also arose between the DVP and the German National People's Party (DNVP) on the right. As an amalgamation of the old Conservative Party, Christian Social, and anti-Semitic groups, anti-Semitism was rife within it although, at first, unofficially. Since in 1919–20 the DVP and the DNVP were competing for the anti-Republican Protestant vote, there was a natural rivalry between them. Just as Stresemann was tempted to use anti-Semitism against the DDP, the DNVP was tempted to use it against the DVP. Apart from the DVP's equivocal stance on the issue, another ready weapon was the argument that Stresemann, the party leader, was married to a Jew. Stresemann found himself on the defensive. In a letter to the Chairman of the DNVP, Oscar Hergt, he complained that at a recent meeting, DVP agents had reported that

in the most different parts of the German Reich, the German National Party was alleging that the German People's Party was not nationally reliable, as its Chairman, Dr Stresemann was married to a Jew. This allegation is untrue. If I have so far not refuted it in public, it is because I find it offensive to be answerable to anyone at all in such a matter.

Stresemann maintained that the way the allegation was being circulated showed that it must have been organized by the central party authorities. He added that the DVP agents wanted to reply in kind with anti-Semitic material against DNVP leaders. He had opposed this idea, saying that he did not believe that the DNVP leadership was responsible. Instead, he asked Hergt to use his influence to stop this kind of campaigning. Hergt replied denying that there had been any instruction of the kind from the central party organization and offering to make clear his disapproval of such personal attacks at a forth-coming meeting of the provincial organizations. At the same time, he accused the DVP of a systematic campaign against the DNVP, following Stresemann's criticism of them at the DVP conference.[48]

Despite this exchange, the DVP thought it necessary to address the issue in a party publication, which offered advice on how to campaign.[49] It said the allegation by DNVP agitators that Stresemann was married to a Jew was 'pure invention' and it pointed out that there was no difference between the official positions of the two parties on the Jewish Question. It added that if party members found they were up against opponents who insisted on making per-sonal attacks, they could make use of material about the Jewish connections of prominent members of the DNVP, which they quoted from the *Demokratische Rundschau*.

This defensive stance showed the degree to which Stresemann and the DVP felt vulnerable on the issue. It is noticeable that he denied that Käte was a Jew, although to the Jewish Central Association, he had specifically mentioned the fact. The ambiguity between Jewish faith and Jewish descent allowed him to claim both. He was clearly not prepared to give anti-Semites the satisfaction of confirming that he was married to a Jew. To one enquiry, he replied sharply: 'my wife neither is nor was a Jew. If racial anti-Semites believe they can find Jews among her ancestors and from this deduce Jewish blood, that is an occu-pation which I am happy to leave to those gentlemen. They will probably find a great deal of material of this kind about all parties.'[50]

The elections of June 1920, following the Kapp *putsch*, transformed the political landscape. The DVP, recapturing most of the old National Liberal constituency, won 13.9 per cent of the vote and sixty-five seats, while the DDP lost half its share of the vote and was reduced to thirty-nine seats. The tables were turned and Stresemann savoured his triumph over his old enemies in the *Berliner Tageblatt*. He was particularly gratified that the DVP had taken five Berlin seats to the DDP's two. Had it not been, he wrote, for the fears of Jewish voters about the alleged 'blood-thirsty anti-Semitism' of the DVP, the DDP would not have won any Berlin votes at all.[51] As a result of the elections, the Republican coalition parties, SPD, Centre, and DDP, lost their majority and the DVP became a contender for power. This was exactly what Stresemann had hoped for. He did not want to remain in opposition as a lesser partner of the DNVP. Even as he had attacked the republican parties in 1919, he had looked forward to the day when the DVP would be able to take part in government. The DVP became a member with the Centre Party and DDP of a minority coalition, which remained in power until May 1921. The DVP then left in protest at what was seen as the weakness of the Foreign Minister and the SPD replaced it. Stresemann did not himself hold office but, as party leader, he did his best to keep the DVP in power and to find ways for it to rejoin the government after May 1921. He became the leading advocate of a 'great coalition', stretching from the DVP to the SPD, which would consolidate parliamentary democracy at home and represent national unity abroad. He faced persistent opposition from those within the DVP who preferred an anti-Republican course, particularly given the unpopularity of German governments as they struggled with the consequences of the Versailles Treaty.

The major themes of Stresemann's speeches became the danger of polarizing the nation and the importance of accepting the Republic as the only basis on which recovery could take place.[52] The veiled anti-Semitism of his attacks on the *Berliner Tageblatt* disappeared. They were no longer relevant, as the DDP was no longer a threat and the DVP was now its partner in government. Stresemann's own attitudes also developed in important ways in this period. He overcame his resentment at the way he had been spurned by the Republican parties in 1918–19. At the time of the Kapp *putsch* in March 1920, he did not feel any instinctive loyalty to the Republic. This changed over the following three years as his influence grew and he became increasingly aware that the alternatives to the Republic were civil war, revolution from the left, and dictatorship from the right. His attitude was also affected by his awareness of the limited room for manoeuvre for German governments, as they faced mounting Allied pressure over reparations. As Chairman of the Reichstag Foreign Affairs Committee from June 1920 he was in regular contact with German Foreign Ministers and became an acknowledged expert on foreign policy. To his objective of consolidating parliamentary government by a great coalition was added the complementary objective of persuading the Allies that the European economies were interdependent and that European recovery depended on allowing German recovery.

Among the influences on him in this period was Walther Rathenau, one of the most fascinating and distinguished German Jews of his generation. Stresemann did not share Rathenau's philosophical interests or his semi-socialist theories on the organization of the economy. But Stresemann was attracted by his intelligence and inventiveness and his willingness to put his gifts at the service of the Republic, becoming Minister for Reconstruction in 1921 and Foreign Minister from January 1922 until his assassination in June 1922. Rathenau may have flattered Stresemann by letting it be known that he regarded him as his successor.[53] In fact their relations were not close. Apart from the difference between their temperaments, the speculative theorist from a great Jewish industrial dynasty on the one hand and the professional politician from Berlin's Protestant lower middle class on the other, there were also political tensions between them. There was a natural rivalry between Rathenau and the Ruhr industrialist, Hugo Stinnes, who was a powerful influence within the DVP.[54] Stresemann found himself at times in their cross-fire. Rathenau's appointment as Foreign Minister by the Centre Party Chancellor, Josef Wirth, was also resented by the DVP, as Rathenau was a member of the

DDP, and it came at a time when the DVP were hoping to rejoin the coalition. His appointment was seen as an affront by the Stinnes wing of the party. Stresemann was doubly disappointed as he had worked to get the DVP back into government and had expected to take office himself, possibly even as Foreign Minister.[55]

Nevertheless, Stresemann admired Rathenau's gifts and was appalled at his assassination. In a perceptive appreciation in the party journal, *Deutsche Stimmen*, he praised Rathenau as a man who had combined wealth with culture.[56] He contrasted Rathenau's literary achievements with the crass materialism of the German Empire. Instead of being angry in a racist way about the disproportionate influence of Jews on German public opinion, he suggested that the question that ought to be considered was whether 'this superiority does not derive in part from the fact that the whole Jewish education and disposition remained far more directed towards intellectual questions, even though its share in business grew more than in other walks of life'. Stresemann described the contradictions in Rathenau's character, his love–hate relationship with the Empire, his support for annexationist goals in the war and his admiration for Ludendorff, but also his opposition to unrestricted submarine warfare. Stresemann praised his skill as a government adviser and minister, particularly in negotiations with the French, although he criticized Rathenau's tendency to make over-optimistic assumptions about what the German economy could bear. Stresemann stressed Rathenau's dedication to German national interests abroad and his support for a great coalition at home. Those who had known him were not blind to his faults—his erratic association of ideas and his love of ostentation—but they saw a finely cultured man, whose kindness of spirit and manner was incapable of giving offence and should have meant he had no enemies.

Stresemann responded to Rathenau's assassination by identifying the DVP more closely with the Republic. He supported legislation against terrorism, making possible the two-thirds majority necessary to allow the suspension of some civil rights. Stresemann took this stand despite the opposition of a sizeable minority of his party, who feared that the legislation would be used in a partisan fashion against the right by the Wirth government. In a defining speech to the Reichstag, Stresemann accepted that Rathenau's assassination, following the earlier assassination of Matthias Erzberger, showed that there were terrorist organizations in Germany, not simply individual assassins, something he had previously refused to believe, and he advocated the harshest punishment within the law for the murderers.[57] He appealed for the crime not to be turned into a new battle cry of Republicans against monarchists but instead for mutual acceptance among all those who were prepared to work for the existing state. Germany would never find peace so long as it tore itself apart in conflicts about the past. Republicans should accept the good faith of all those who were loyal to the constitution, whatever their personal

convictions, and the extreme right should stop blaming Republican governments for all the misery of the German people. In a second speech, he added
that the desperate international situation made it imperative to allow the issue
of the form of state to rest.[58]

Stresemann's appeals for co-operation found an increasingly sympathetic
hearing in the Centre Party and the DDP. The SPD, however, which had
just negotiated a merger with the Independent Socialists on its left, was not
prepared to join a government with the DVP. Disagreement on this issue
led to the breakdown of the coalition in November 1922. Many, including
Stresemann, thought he might be asked to form a government. President
Ebert, however, turned instead to the non-party head of the Hamburg–
America shipping company, Wilhelm Cuno, who formed a government of
'experts' in which the DVP was represented but again without Stresemann.
After the French and Belgian occupation of the Ruhr in January 1923,
Germany's financial situation rapidly deteriorated and it became clear that
the Cuno government did not have the authority to continue. On 11
August, the SPD decided to end its toleration of the government and
declared its readiness to form a great coalition. Stresemann was now the
unanimous choice of the coalition parties and Ebert asked him to form a
government. Stresemann had at last achieved his goal but in circumstances
which, as he confided to Käte, made it 'all but political suicide'.[59]

There is no need here for a detailed account of Stresemann's administration
but some aspects of it are relevant to our theme. He appointed as Minister of
Finance the Social Democrat (formerly Independent Social Democrat),
Rudolf Hilferding. Hilferding was, apart from Rathenau, the only Minister at
Reich level in the Weimar Republic of the Jewish faith.[60] Born in Vienna, he
became a left-wing socialist and published before the war an important trea-
tise on 'finance capital', sometimes referred to as the fourth volume of *Das
Kapital*. Stresemann intended his appointment, together with that of Hans
von Raumer, a member of the DVP and director of the association of the elec-
tronic industry, as Minister of Economic Affairs, to symbolize the great coalition. Stresemann had been impressed by the way they had co-operated
previously to produce a joint programme for the Wirth government to present to the Allied reparations commission in 1922.[61] Unfortunately, this success
was not repeated in government. Hilferding was indecisive about currency
stabilization—in the caustic words of his party colleague, Otto Braun, he was
'too clever to be a Minister'[62]—and both he and Raumer were replaced when
the government was reconstructed in October. Nevertheless, Stresemann's
appointment of a prominent Jew to the cabinet, so soon after the assassination of Rathenau, was a bold decision which provoked a predictable reaction.
As Stresemann started to prepare public opinion for the abandonment of passive resistance to the French in the Ruhr, since the cost of supporting it was
destroying the currency, nationalist groups saw their opportunity. According

to a report to the Reich Chancellery on public opinion in the Ruhr, such people spoke of Stresemann as a traitor and said he should suffer the same fate as Erzberger and Rathenau as soon as possible. They claimed that the Ruhr could have held out much longer, if it had not been sold out as in 1918 by a 'Government of Jews'. 'Hilferding, the Austrian Jew, and Stresemann, the half-Jew, naturally had no understanding for national dignity and the honour of the German name.'[63]

More serious was the reaction in Bavaria, where paramilitary nationalist groups, including the Nazi SA, had congregated under the protective arm of the Bavarian authorities, themselves hostile to the Republican government in Berlin. The suspension of passive resistance was followed by the appointment by the Bavarian government of Gustav von Kahr as Commissioner with dictatorial powers, setting off the train of events which culminated in the Hitler *putsch* in November. One aspect of Kahr's regime deserves mention here. In October, he authorized the expulsion of Jewish families who were by origin immigrants from Eastern Europe, even though some of them had been resident in Bavaria for as long as twenty or thirty years, on the flimsiest of pretexts. This was clearly a measure intended to court popularity with the Nazis and their sympathizers.[64]

Stresemann had himself been concerned at the success of Nazi propaganda against Jewish immigration from the east and the way in which new immigrants were allegedly profiting from inflation. In February 1923, before he took office, he wrote that the government had to sail between the Scylla of fascism and the Charybdis of communism. What made Hitler powerful was his exposure of abuses which everyone felt. 'The East Galician immigration, which has whipped up anti-Semitism among us, gets him the applause of the unthinking mass by making the Jews responsible for everything.' The sufferings of the German middle class through inflation were the breeding ground for all kinds of extremism. People despaired of justice as the law stuck to the principle that a mark equals a mark, regardless of the way inflation undermined savers and creditors. Stresemann lashed out at the profiteers:

Germans and non-Germans, of the latter above all those who came to Berlin from Galicia, and began their shady existence in the Grenadierstrasse, then moved to the Landsberger Straße and already often live on the Kurfürstendamm. They have the instinct of vultures who know where something is rotting. They have a firm belief in the decay of Germany . . . Following the examples of Russia, Poland and Austria, they have now fallen on us. They buy houses and sell them with a profit of many paper millions. These houses carry mortgages. The middle class, betrayed by the state, still had this reserve. Will all these people, who have gained hundreds of millions from property, be allowed to betray their mortgage creditors as well?[65]

Stresemann did not find it possible in government to follow up his own polemic and safeguard those who lost by inflation. However, his attitude to the Bavarian expulsions was clear. When he first heard of it, he said 'That cannot be allowed' and promised to investigate.[66] There were soon ample reports confirming the expulsions and Nazi violence against individual Jews and Jewish property.[67] Stresemann was not in a position to intervene directly on this issue, or against the growing threat of a march on Berlin (in imitation of Mussolini's 'march on Rome' the previous October), as the army would not act against the Bavarian authorities. By contrast, the army was more than happy to depose the left SPD–Communist coalition in Saxony, which threatened simultaneously to embark on social revolution. This double standard led the SPD to withdraw from Stresemann's government in protest and among the reasons the Minister of the Interior, Wilhelm Sollmann, gave was the failure to take a position 'against the medieval expulsions of Jews from Bavaria'. To this Stresemann replied simply that 'On the question of the persecution of the Jews, the members of the cabinet were of one mind'.[68] In fact, after the failure of the Hitler *putsch*, Stresemann pressed successfully for the expulsions to cease, in view of the danger of Polish retaliation against the German minority.[69]

This ugly incident was a warning of the dangers faced by Jews if the Weimar Republic should be overthrown by the Nazis. In a wider sense, therefore, Stresemann's commitment to the Republic and his skill in managing the multiple crises which threatened its survival during his administration are part of our story. He faced, in summary, the occupation of the Ruhr and the threat of separatism, the collapse of the currency, the twin threats from the left in Saxony and Thuringia and the Right in Bavaria, the highly conditional loyalty of the army and an attempt by its commanding officer, General von Seeckt, to force his resignation, and similar pressure from within the DVP itself. He withstood all these challenges with courage and a sometimes desperate determination and thus made a vital contribution to the survival of the Republic into easier times. His speech in the debate on a vote of confidence, which finally brought down his government in November 1923, contained an eloquent defence of parliamentary democracy as the only form of government which could reconcile the deep divisions of German society. He recalled the attempts of the Prussian reformers, Stein and Hardenberg, to create representative institutions after Prussia's defeat by Napoleon. He suggested there were parallels of almost photographic likeness between that period and their own—both being concerned with creating a state after a lost war. As an example, he pointed out that Stein had then been attacked by conservative opponents as a 'Jacobin' and his taxation reforms condemned as turning Prussia into 'a modern Jewish state'.[70]

Stresemann's policy as Foreign Minister, in all the successive coalitions until his death in October 1929, is in the same way indirectly linked to our theme. If the Weimar Republic was to survive it had to find a way of accommodating itself to the post-war international order. Stresemann tried to reconcile German interests in revision of the Versailles Treaty with the security interests of

Germany's neighbours. His policy of peaceful revision, of which the high points were the Dawes Plan, the Locrano Treaties and German entry into the League of Nations, became stalled after 1926, as the tension between German aspirations and French fears increased. Stresemann hoped that economic co-operation, perhaps in the form of a European customs union, might provide a way of overcoming French fears; but hopeful beginnings, like the agree-ment between the major West European steel producers in 1926, were not enough to change the political climate before the Depression undermined any hope of further progress. For racist groups, this policy was tantamount to a surrender to international, Jewish capitalism. As Graf Reventlow put it, 'He [Stresemann] is well-known to be closely connected to Jewry, personally politically and in his whole outlook.'[71]

The details of Stresemann's foreign policy, and controversies about its interpretation, need not concern us. It is of interest here, however, that some of his strongest support came from the Jewish owned, left-liberal press. The old hostility between him and Theodor Wolff gave way to mutual respect. At the time that Stresemann formed his government in 1923, Wolff acknowledged that few German politicians had learnt as much from the past as Stresemann.[72] When the Locarno Treaties were signed, Wolff praised him for standing up to the nationalist opposition.[73] When Stresemann died, Wolff described him as a statesman who had pursued a persistent course, through changing coalitions, to lead Germany out of isolation back to a respected posi-tion among the powers. He described Stresemann as someone with 'the ambi-tion of the creative, of the far-sighted, of the historically well-read, of those who live through deeds and want to live on through them beyond their own time'.[74] Stresemann badly needed this support against the increasingly vicious attacks of the press empire of Alfred Hugenberg, who in 1928 became leader of the DNVP. One of Stresemann's last interviews was to brief Theodor Wolff on the Young Plan, to counteract Hugenberg's campaign for a referendum against it backed by the entire racist right, the DNVP, the NSDAP, the ex-servicemen's *Stahlhelm*, and the Pan-German League.[75] It is noticeable that among Stresemann's biographers, there were three Jewish journalists: Antonina Vallentin, a long-standing admirer, Rudolf Olden of the *Berliner Tageblatt*, and later Felix Hirsch who had also worked for the Mosse press.[76] Among the congratulations which Stresemann received on his fiftieth birthday was a warm letter from another leading Jewish newspaper proprietor, Franz Ullstein.[77] There was perhaps even a tendency among some Jewish intellectuals to idealize Stresemann as the type of open-minded German gentile they wanted to believe in.

As this support suggests, the last phase of Stresemann's career saw him return to his left-liberal roots. After the Reichstag elections of 1928, he helped to bring about another great coalition under an SPD Chancellor. This was bit-terly resented by the right wing of the DVP. Stresemann's increasing difficulties with his own party led him to contemplate a united liberal party with the DDP, once the Young Plan had been safely adopted. As Theodor Wolff said in his obituary notice, what had seemed impossible with him in November 1918, now only seemed possible under his leadership. His death helped to deprive the new party of whatever chance it may have had of winning over a significant proportion of the DVP vote.[78]

Among the tributes paid to Stresemann at his death was one from another founding member of the DDP, Albert Einstein.[79] He described Stresemann as someone toughened by having to make his own way from a modest background and by his battle with illness. But he possessed an ear for language and literature which gave him a special talent as a speaker. He also had a rare sensitivity to the ideas and feelings of others. His great achievement had been 'to win over important political groups, against their own political instincts, for an ambitious policy of European reconciliation'. His distinctive quality, like that of all great leaders, had been not to represent a particular type, whether of class, profession or country, but to 'work directly as an individual through his intellect and as the bearer of an idea'.

This appreciation echoed one of the qualities Stresemann associated with Jews—their intellectual and cultural distinction. On several occasions, he warned that in the concentration on economic progress and material welfare since the Empire, Germans had neglected the life of the mind and he held up Jews as the exception.[80] Stresemann's own love of literature and history brought him into contact with the cultural life of Berlin. He was a regular theatre-goer and glad recipient of complimentary tickets for new performances from Max Reinhardt, the famous Jewish theatrical producer at the Deutsches Theater. He was a member, and subsequently honorary member, of the prestigious Deutscher Bühnenklub, addressing them in 1927 on his favourite subject of Goethe—and whether when Goethe spoke of his 'main occupation' he was referring to Faust or, as Stresemann believed, to another manuscript subsequently lost.[81] Stresemann's pleasure in these occasions may be sensed from a diary entry in 1922: 'Supper in the Bühnenklub. Met well-known actors and singers. Very lively!'[82] Stresemann never belonged to the avant-garde of Weimar culture. His tastes were traditional and, as Eschenburg put it, bore 'a trace of the petit-bourgeois'.[83] But he firmly believed in the importance of maintaining intellectual standards. He pointed out that the University of Berlin had been founded after Prussia's defeat by Napoleon, because the King believed that education was vital to national recovery.[84] He also supported student exchanges with foreign countries to help to overcome Germany's isolation.[85] In his own pleasure in literature and his belief in the national importance of culture, he valued the special contribution made by Jews. The eminent and popular Jewish playwright, Ludwig Fulda, whom Stresemann had helped to recover a home in the Alps expropriated by the Italian authorities, said Germany could have experienced no greater good fortune than to be led by the man who was summoned 'to reconcile the land of Goethe and the land of Bismarck by an inner Locarno'.[86]

Such hopes were to be tragically disappointed. Fulda, stripped of his honours by the Nazis, committed suicide in March 1939. Stresemann's family was more fortunate. They emigrated to the United States in 1938–9, where Wolfgang, encouraged by a fellow *émigré* and former family friend from Berlin, Bruno Walter, became an orchestral conductor, and his younger brother, Joachim, pursued a career in business. Both became American citizens. Wolfgang returned to Berlin in 1956 and became the manager of the Berlin Philharmonic Orchestra in 1959, a position he held until 1978 and again from 1984 to 1986. Käte also returned to Berlin in 1968, where she died in 1970.[87]

The theme of Stresemann and the Jews provides an interesting perspective on his career. At each stage he was confronted with the 'Jewish Question'. He responded as a student by sticking to his ideals and as a young politician and businessman by ignoring the issue, but during and after the war he was affected by the growing current of anti-Semitism which was fed by the effects of revolution and inflation. This aggressive phase, both emotive and opportunistic, gave way gradually after the 1920 elections to an appreciation of what was at stake if parliamentary democracy failed, a development completed when he became Chancellor in 1923. Stresemann wanted 'to be the bridge between the old Germany and the new', building a firm basis of support for the Republic.[88] Among those who understood and supported what he was doing were the Jewish intellectuals from whom he had been divided by mutual dislike at the end of the war. Both had the imagination to conceive of building a more cohesive society and a more secure Europe. These were the ideals which Stresemann came to represent for men like Wolff, Einstein, and Fulda. In a sense, like them he was also an outsider, whose vision of Germany remained that of the 1848 Revolution at a time when liberal ideals were out of fashion. In his tribute, on Stresemann's death, Einstein wrote that members of his generation no longer doubted that his ideas would prevail. Stresemann had himself, however, become doubtful and depressed in his last year. Unfortunately, his pessimism proved correct. He had not been able to integrate the Protestant middle class securely behind the Republic. Within a year, under the impact of the Depression, they began to defect in large numbers to the National Socialists and his successors in the party leadership hurried to join the trend and dissociate themselves from his legacy. Stresemann's leadership, as his supporters recognized, was unique. His policy did not survive his death, but it offered his Jewish friends, and not them alone, a tantalizing vision of how things might have been different.

In his post-war memoirs the Jewish consultant physician, Hermann Zondek, who looked after Stresemann from 1928 recalled: 'I was very moved by Stresemann's death. Not only for personal reasons. I felt that with him had passed away a personality, perhaps the last one, in whom the German masses had confidence and whom they were ready to follow in the battle against the rising tide of National Socialism.'[89] After Stresemann had suffered the first stroke on the night of 2 October 1929, Zondek asked one of his senior colleagues, Professor Friedrich Kraus (a gentile), to come to share the responsibility with him. They both knew the situation was hopeless. Seeing how deeply moved Zondek was, Kraus said: 'I feel for you. You are losing a great friend. More it is a loss for Germany but most of all for German Jewry. It is dying tonight.'[90] Although these words carry a heavier load of meaning in retrospect than was probably intended at the time, they show the degree to which Stresemann had become a symbol in some quarters for the survival of a liberal and decent Germany.

# Notes

I am grateful to Peter Oppenheimer for reading and commenting on this chapter.

1. Peter Pulzer, *Jews and the German State: The Political History of a Minority, 1848–1933* (Oxford: Blackwell, 1992), 33.
2. Ibid. 32–4, 334–7.
3. Kurt Koszyk, *Gustav Stresemann: Der kaisertreue Demokrat. Eine Biographie* (Cologne: Kiepenheuer & Witsch, 1989), 27–8.
4. *Dresdner Volks-Zeitung. Freisinniges Wochenblatt für Stadt und Land* (29 Dec. 1895–13 Dec. 1896; Koszyk, *Stresemann*, 56–66.
5. *Gustav Stresemann Schriften*, ed. Arnold Harttung (Berlin: Berlin Verlag, 1976), 4–5.
6. *Gustav Stresemann. Vermächtnis*, ed. Henry Bernhard (Berlin: Ullstein, 1932), i.2–3.
7. Ibid. i. 5; Norbert Kampe, *Studenten und 'Judenfrage' im Deutschen Kaiserreich: Die Entstehung einer akademischen Trägerschicht des Antisemitismus* (Göttingen: Vandenhoeck & Ruprecht, 1988), 196–9.
8. 'Burschenschaft und Politik', *Allgemeine Deutsche Universitätszeitung*, 12/7 (1 Apr. 1898), 65.
9. Dr H.C. 'Ein noch unbekanntes Kapitel: Stresemanns Kampf gegen Judenhaß', *8 Uhr Abendblatt*, 235 (8 Oct. 1929).
10. Dr. Caliebe, 'Dem alten Neogermanen!', *Burschenschaftliche Wege*, 20/6 (Nov. 1929), 54.
11. Stresemann to the Burschenschaft Suevia, 20 Aug. 1923, *Stresemann Schriften*, ed. Harttung, 12–13. Theodor Eschenburg, 'Stresemann und die Studenten', *Nord und Süd*, 52/11 (Nov. 1929), 998–1008.
12. *Burschenschaftliche Wege*, 20/6 (Nov. 1929), 54.
13. Interview with Theodor Eschenburg, 4 Sept. 1998.
14. Felix Hirsch, *Stresemann: Ein Lebensbild* (Göttingen: Musterschmidt, 1978), 37.
15. 'Wolfgang performs his sonata. A great concept full of talent.' Stresemann diary

entry, 17 Apr. 1921. Politisches Archiv des Auswärtigen Amts, Berlin: Nachlaß Stresemann, 361.

16. Hans-Peter Ullmann, *Der Bund der Industriellen* (Göttingen: Vandenhoeck & Ruprecht, 1976).

17. Daniel Fryman [Heinrich Claß], *Wenn ich der Kaiser wär: Politische Wahrheiten und Notwendigkeiten* (2nd edn., Leipzig: Theodor Weicher, 1912), 205. The book continued to be reprinted in the Weimar Republic, its 7th edn. appearing in 1925.

18. Siegfried Mielke, *Der Hansa-Bund für Gewerbe, Handel und Industrie 1909–1914: Der gescheiterte Versuch einer antifeudalen Sammlungspolitik* (Göttingen: Vandenhoeck & Ruprecht, 1976).

19. Pulzer, *Jews and the German State*, 324–5.

20. Ibid. 184–5.

21. Lamar Cecil, *Albert Ballin: Business and Politics in Imperial Germany, 1888–1918* (Princeton, NJ: Princeton University Press, 1967).

22. Hirsch, *Stresemann*, 58.

23. Stresemann to Frau von Roon (née Bassermann), 22 Nov. 1928; Nachlaß Stresemann, 290.

24. 'Politische Umschau', *Deutsche Stimmen*, 30/45 (10 Nov. 1918), reprinted in *Stresemann Reden und Schriften 1897–1926*, ed. Rochus von Rheinbaben (Dresden: Carl Reissner, 1926), i. 206–11.

25. Pulzer, *Jews and the German State*, 170–1; Wolfram Köhler, *Der Chef-Redakteur Theodor Wolff: Ein Leben in Europa 1868–1943* (Düsseldorf: Droste, 1978), 171–7.

26. 'Die militärische und politische Lage des Deutschen Reiches', dated 'Anfang 1916'. It is not clear what the purpose of the memorandum was, possibly as background for a report to a National Liberal party audience. Nachlaß Stresemann, 159.

27. Reichstag speech, 29 Mar. 1917; reprinted as 'Neue Zeiten', *Stresemann. Reden und Schriften*, ed. Rheinbaben, i. 172–92.

28. Pulzer, *Jews and the German State*, 204–6.

29. 'Reichstag und konfessioneller Burgfriede', text for a newspaper article, according to a marginal note for the *Deutsche Kurier* (28 Nov. [?Oct.] 1916); Nachlaß Stresemann, 156.

30. Stresemann to Friedrich Uebel, 16 Jan. 1915, Nachlaß Stresemann, 145; *Stresemann Schriften*, ed. Harttung, 148–51.

31. Pulzer, *Jews and the German State*, 217–21. Lothar Albertin, *Liberalismus und Demokratie am Anfang der Weimarer Republik* (Düsseldorf: Droste, 1972), 54–9.

32. Stresemann's diary entry for 15 Nov. 1918; Nachlaß Stresemann, 362.

33. Stresemann's diary entry for 20 Nov. 1918; Nachlaß Stresemann, 362. Wolfgang Hartenstein, *Die Anfänge der Deutschen Volkspartei 1918–1920* (Düsseldorf: Droste, 1962), 25–33.

34. Pulzer, *Jews and the German State*, 232–3; Alfred Vagts, 'M.M. Warburg & Co. Ein Bankhaus in der deutschen Weltpolitik 1905–1933', *Vierteljahrschrift für Sozial- und Wirtschaftsgeschichte*, 45 (1958), 378–9.

35. 'Politische Umschau', *Deutsche Stimmen*, 30/50 (15 Dec.1918), reprinted as 'Liberalismus oder Demokratie' in Gustav Stresemann, *Von der Revolution bis zum Frieden von Versailles* (Berlin: Staatspolitischer Verlag, 1919), 63.

36. Stresemann, *Von der Revolution*, 158–9.

37. *Bericht über den Zweiten Parteitag der Deutschen Volkspartei* (Berlin: Staatspolitischer Verlag, [1919]), 17, 22.

38. *Archiv der deutschen Volkspartei*, 1 (18 Feb. 1920), 35.

39. Minutes of the meeting of the Geschäftsführender Ausschuß, 13 Sept. 1919; Bundesarchiv Koblenz, R 45 II/50. Eberhard Kolb and Ludwig Richter (eds.),

*Nationalliberalismus in der Weimarer Republik. Die Führungsgremien der Deutschen Volkspartei 1918–1933* (Düsseldorf: Droste Verlag, 1999), i, 189–90.

40. *Grundsätze der Deutschen Volkspartei* (Berlin: Staatspolitischer Verlag, 1920), 6–7.
41. Riesser to Stresemann, 19 Dec. 1919; Nachlaß Stresemann, 208; Minutes of the meeting of the Geschäftsführender Ausschuß, 28 Jan. 1920; Bundesarchiv Koblenz, R 45 II/51. Kolb and Richter, *Nationalliberalismus*, 219–20; Larry Eugene Jones, *German Liberalism and the Dissolution of the Weimar Party System 1918–1933* (Chapel Hill, NC: University of North Carolina Press, 1988), 71. Later Riesser wrote that anti-Semitism was '*doubtless* well represented' in DVP circles but 'at any rate it has never found official expression in the Reichstag party'; Riesser to his son Hans, 19 July 1922; Bundesarchiv Koblenz, Kleine Erwerbung, 549/1–2.
42. Paul Moldenhauer, 'Politische Erinnerungen'; Bundesarchiv, Koblenz, Nachlaß Moldenhauer, 1, pp.119–20. Moldenhauer's views were not those of an extremist. Although at first a member of the party's right wing, he later moved to the centre and served as Reich Economics Minister and then Reich Finance Minister from November 1929 to June 1930.
43. Stresemann to the Zentralverein Deutscher Staatsbürger jüdischen Glaubens, 28 Jan. 1920; Nachlaß Stresemann, 220.
44. Stresemann to Dr Berckemeyer, 3 April 1920; Nachlaß Stresemann, 217. Also text for a newspaper article, 'Die wirklichen Ursachen des Antisemitismus', 22 April 1920; Nachlaß Stresemann, 222.
45. Another Jewish organization, the Verein zur Abwehr des Antisemitismus, quoted Stresemann from a speech in Sept. 1919 as saying that 'A liberal party cannot champion anti-Semitic principles with their one-sided view of the question of guilt and its excrescences', omitting the kinds of criticisms which Stresemann normally added against sections of the Jewish community. Donald L. Niewyk, *The Jews in Weimar Germany* (Baton Rouge, La.: Louisiana State University Press, 1980), 73–4.
46. Pulzer, *Jews and the German State*, 234–5.
47. Carl J. Rheins, 'The Verband nationaldeutscher Juden 1921–1933', *Year Book of the Leo Baeck Institute*, 25 (1980), 263; Niewyk, *Jews in Weimar Germany*, 172.
48. Stresemann to Hergt, 22 Dec. 1919, Hergt to Stresemann, 30 Dec.1919; Nachlaß Stresemann, 208.
49. *Archiv der Deutschen Volkspartei*, 1 (18 Feb. 1920), 35–8.
50. Stresemann to Dr Ettling, 12 Apr. 1921; Nachlaß Stresemann, 360.
51. 'Wahlausfall und Regierungsbildung', *Deutsche Stimmen*, 32/25 (20 June 1920).
52. e.g. his speeches to the party conferences of 3 Dec. 1920 and 1 Dec. 1921; Bundesarchiv Koblenz, R 45 II/26,27.
53. Wolfgang Stresemann, *Mein Vater Gustav Stresemann* (Munich: Herbig, 1979), 212.
54. On Stinnes's relations with Stresemann, see Gerald D. Feldman, 'Hugo Stinnes, Gustav Stresemann, and the Politics of the DVP in the Early Weimar Republic' in Wolfram Pyta and Ludwig Richter (eds.), *Gestaltungskraft des Politischen: Festschrift für Eberhard Kolb* (Berlin: Duncker & Humblot, 1998), 421–42.
55. Stresemann to a party colleague, Johann Becker, 18 Dec. 1921; Stresemann Nachlaß 227, printed in *Stresemann Schriften*, ed. Harttung, 231–2.
56. 'Politische Umschau', *Deutsche Stimmen*, 34/27 (2 July 1922).
57. 5 July 1922, reprinted in *Gustav Stresemann, Reichstagsreden*, ed. Gerhard Zwoch (Bonn: Pfattheicher & Reichardt, 1972), 115–33.

58. 18 July 1922, *Verhandlungen des Reichstags*, 1. Wahlperiode 1920, vol. 356, 8708–12.
59. Stresemann to Käte, 28 May 1923; Wolfgang Stresemann, *Mein Vater* 224.
60. Pulzer, *Jews and the German State*, 272.
61. *Vermächtnis*, ed. Bernhard, i. 144.
62. Otto Braun, *Von Weimar zu Hitler* (New York: Europa, 1940), 126–7.
63. 'Bericht über die Haltung der Parteien im Ruhrgebiet', 15 Sept. 1923; Karl Dietrich Erdmann and Martin Vogt (eds.), *Die Kabinette Stresemann I und II* (Boppard: Harald Boldt, 1978), 285.
64. George and Roberta Earley, 'Bavarian Prelude, 1923: A Model for Nazism?', *The Wiener Library Bulletin*, 30/43–44 (1977), 53–60.
65. 'Vom Rechte, das mit uns geboren', *Deutsche Stimmen*, 35/3 (5 Feb. 1923). Stresemann's argument about mortgages is not entirely clear. Borrowers, of course, benefited from inflation because they could repay the mortgages with devalued currency. Stresemann appears to be referring to the practice of house owners themselves issuing mortgages on parts of their property (or other property belonging to them) to other occupants. This practice made them mortgage creditors and therefore at risk of losing this asset. I am grateful to Professor Peter-Christian Witt, Kassel, for this reading.
66. Discussion with party leaders, 29 Oct. 1923; Erdmann and Vogt (eds.), *Kabinette Stresemann*, ii. 872.
67. Report of an eyewitness, 31 Oct. 1923; ibid. 926–33.
68. Minutes of the cabinet meeting, 2 Nov. 1923; ibid. 949–50.
69. Pulzer, *Jews and the German State*, 226–7.
70. Speech to the Reichstag, 22 Nov. 1923; *Stresemann. Reichstagsreden*, ed. Zwoch, 155–206.
71. Graf E. Reventlow, *Minister Stresemann als Staatsmann und Anwalt des Weltgewissens* (Munich: J. F. Lehmanns Verlag, 1926), 15. Reventlow moved from the racist Deutschvölkische Freiheitspartei to the NSDAP, which he represented in the Reichstag from 1924. He attacked Stresemann in a foreign affairs debate in June 1929 for describing the Jewish author, Emil Ludwig, as 'an exponent of the German spirit', declaring that Stresemann was 'an exponent of the Jewish spirit . . . admittedly only by adoption but that makes it stick all the better'. *Verhandlungen des Reichstags*, vol. 425, 2859 (24 June 1929).
72. *Berliner Tageblatt*, (13 Aug. 1923), reprinted in *Theodor Wolff: Der Journalist. Berichte und Leitartikel*, ed. Bernd Sösemann (Düsseldorf: Econ, 1993), 184–6.
73. *Berliner Tageblatt* (30 Nov. 1925), in *Wolff*, ed. Sösemann, 215–17. Stresemann briefed Wolff to counteract the DNVP press attacks on Locarno; Stresemann's diary entry for 22 Sept. 1925. *Vermächtnis*, ed. Bernhard. ii. 179; Kurt Koszyk, *Deutsche Presse 1914–1945: Geschichte der deutschen Presse*, iii (Berlin: Colloquium, 1972), 178. Stresemann to Wolff, 5 Nov. 1925, and subsequent correspondence; Bundesarchiv Koblenz, Nachlaß Wolff, 18.
74. 'Erinnerung', *Berliner Tageblatt* (6 Oct. 1929); *Wolff*, ed. Sösemann, 262–6.
75. 11 Sept. 1929; *Vermächtnis*, ed. Bernhard, iii. 563–6.
76. Antonina Vallentin, *Stresemann: Vom Werden einer Staatsidee* (Leipzig: List, 1930); Rudolf Olden, *Stresemann* (New York: Dutton, 1930); Felix Hirsch, *Stresemann: Ein Lebensbild* (Göttingen: Musterschmidt, 1978).
77. Ullstein to Stresemann, 10 May 1928; Nachlaß Stresemann, 320.
78. On the refounded DDP, the Deutscher Staatspartei, see Pulzer, *Jews and the German State*, 288–313.
79. 'Stresemanns Mission', *Nord und Süd*, 52/11 (Nov. 1929), 953–4.

80. In his tribute to Rathenau (above, p. 115); also speeches to DVP students, *Die Zeit*, 5/33 (2 Feb. 1925) and to the Überseeklub in Hamburg, 16 Apr. 1925, *Vermächtnis*, ed. Bernhard, ii. 295.
81. *Vermächtnis*, ed. Bernhard, ii. 363–76. Nachlaß Stresemann, 344.
82. Diary entry for 30 Dec. 1922; Nachlaß Stresemann, 362.
83. Theodor Eschenburg, 'Gustav Stresemann', in Eschenburg, *Die improvisierte Demokratie* (Munich: Piper, 1964), 145.
84. Speech at the opening of the Harnack Building of the Kaiser-Wilhelm-Gesellschaft, 7 May 1929; *Vermächtnis*, ed. Bernhard, iii. 489.
85. Speech on receiving an honorary degree from Heidelberg University, 5 May 1928; *Vermächtnis*, ed. Bernhard, iii. 487–8.
86. Fulda to Stresemann, 22 July 1927; Nachlaß Stresemann, 109.
87. Information from Wolfgang Stresemann, 26 Mar. 1993 and his obituary in the *Süddeutsche Zeitung*, (9 Nov. 1998).
88. Stresemann to Wilhelm Kahl, 13 Mar. 1929; *Vermächtnis*, ed. Bernhard, iii. 439.
89. Hermann Zondek, *Auf festem Fusse: Erinnerungen eines jüdischen Klinikers* (Stuttgart: Deutsche Verlags-Anstalt, 1973), 142.
90. Ibid.

# 8

## Compromised Republicans: The *Vernunftrepublikaner* and the Transformation of Liberal Thought from Weimar to the Federal Republic

### *Jan-Werner Müller*

How is one to write the history of liberalism in a country with a famously illiberal tradition—a country which lacked what Friedrich Naumann once called *Elementarliberalismus* (basic liberalism) and in which, it seems, liberal parties suffered a permanent crisis?[1] Is it simply the story of decline and fall, missed opportunities and bourgeois weaknesses, even hypocrisies? Were there particular theoretical weaknesses in German liberal thought, or was liberalism doomed because of social factors which had little to do with the peculiarities of German liberal ideology? And was the gradual liberalization of the Federal Republic after the Second World War a 'velvet revolution without ideas', a strange rebirth of liberalism without liberal thought, as has sometimes been claimed?[2]

More specifically, there is the question of whether and how to historicize the political thought of the Weimar Republic.[3] Most immediate post-war treatments of the topic tended to tell a linear narrative of increasing extremism, the 'destruction of reason' and the triumph of an irrational vitalism.[4] As Joachim Fischer has argued, such treatments, while valuable as part of *Vergangenheitsbewältigung* (coming to terms with the past), often failed to consider the particular philosophical problems and ideological challenges German thinkers were facing at the time. Similarly, they fail to take into account the particular intellectual resources which they had available after the destruction of German idealism, the crisis of historicism, and the rise of *Lebensphilosophie* (philosophy of life).[5] The point then is not simply to contextualize Weimar thought, but the need to relate it to the legacy (and burdens) inherited from pre-war thought and the Second Reich. One also has to pose the question, as Fischer has suggested, whether the 'Weimar Republic' is even an appropriate framework of reference. This historical bracket already implies that 'republic' or democracy had to be central concerns for political thinkers at the time.[6] They are then simply measured by their stance towards democracy, a test which many liberals will fail.[7]

The various possible answers to the republican challenge also raise the specific question of how to read the history of the *Vernunftrepublikaner*. Recently, the Weimar extremes, in particular the 'Conservative Revolution', have yet again come under close, sometimes scholastic scrutiny, but relatively little has been said about either the genuinely liberal centre or those who, out of 'reasonableness', decided provisionally to subscribe to democratic values. There are obvious reasons for this. Since the *Vernunftrepublikaner* often decided to support the republic out of purely pragmatic considerations inspired by 'historical necessity', there was not much to theorize or historically to reconstruct. And since so many abandoned their republican beliefs later on, it became clear that liberal beliefs were indeed held with little sincerity and probably not worth much further investigation. And yet, at a time when historical 'transformations' and 'transitology' have been at the top of many social scientific research agendas, the *Vernunftrepublikaner* merit a closer look. Far too little is still known about how precisely processes of ideological conversion and 'deconversion' take place and how thought patterns in particular are transformed over time.[8] Moreover, as many theorists of democratic transitions have pointed out, *Vernunftrepublikaner* are crucial for so-called 'institutional strategies' in democratization to succeed. Anna Sa'adah, in an important contribution, has usefully distinguished between two different strategies of democratization and political reconciliation: on the one hand, an institutional strategy assigns

chronological and causal priority to the creation of a community of behavior, and ... emphasizes the ability of institutions and procedures to engender a pattern of behavior that may not correspond to the inner convictions of the past political commitments of individual actors, but that can (hypothetically) be expected ultimately to reshape political culture and common perceptions of justice as actors bring their beliefs into harmony with their actions.[9]

On the other hand, cultural strategies set a priority on 'the creation of a community of conviction, in the sense of a self-conscious constitutional consensus supported by a democratic political culture'.[10] In other words, institutional or procedural strategies occur in a top–down manner, as democratic institutions are imposed from above, and define political trust in terms of outward reliability, rather than in terms of true convictions or trust-as-trustworthiness. They are essentially Hobbesian: if the right institutions and incentives are in place, undemocratic inclinations will be kept in check—and, so the hope goes, eventually be overcome as not only the behaviour, but also the political values of citizens are reshaped. Cultural strategies adopt a bottom–up perspective and focus on the creation of a genuinely democratic political culture, where institutional strategies put order first. Clearly, *Vernunftrepublikaner* are essential in institutional strategies, as they can be relied upon to accept a democratic system at least rationally and act accordingly, and every new democracy will have its fair share of them. But how exactly do they come to 'convert' even in an ever so superficial way and how can their democratic commitments be strengthened?

Finally, without facile claims for current relevance, one might say that becoming *Vernunftrepublikaner* is precisely what much of current Anglo-American liberal political theory asks citizens to do: to put aside what their 'comprehensive doctrines of the good' demand of them, and agree to what appear to be political arrangements, which 'no one could reasonably reject'.[11] Moreover, Weimar was characterized by precisely the strong 'value pluralism' which Max Weber had first identified and which current critics of 'political liberalism' who argue instead for 'agonistic democracy' take as their starting-point. Apart from the value of exploring a neglected part of Weimar history, there might be theoretical value in reconsidering the political psychology of the *Vernunftrepubikaner*, especially since the liberal imagination, even after 1989, remains haunted by the spectre of the failure of Weimar democracy.

In this chapter, I seek to reconstruct a more subtle and nuanced picture of the *Vernunftrepublikaner* than has previously been painted, a task which will be limited to intellectuals in the rather narrow sense of writers, historians, and philosophers who commented on the affairs of the republic. In other words, the *Vernunftrepublikaner* among policy-makers, most famously Stresemann, will not come under consideration here. At the same time, I would like to trace the story further by examining how liberal thought developed after 1945. It is well known that Weimar liberals such as Theodor Heuss and Theodor Eschenburg returned to the political stage as the founding generation of the Federal Republic.[12] As is also well known, in the early Federal Republic, the FDP, the official party-political home of liberalism, was rather 'national-liberal' and harboured a new generation of *Vernunftrepublikaner*. And yet, something had changed in the thought patterns of both liberals and the new *Vernunftbundesrepublikaner*. I shall return to this shift—or rather, learning process—at the end of this chapter and shall suggest that it was in the attitude towards institutions and liberal authority that this process was most manifest.

# *Reasons for the Republic: The* Vernunftrepublikaner *after 1918*

*Herzensmonarchisten,* monarchists of the heart, as Friedrich Meinecke called them, were not converted to the republic overnight, nor were they all converted for the same reason. Meinecke himself, probably the most famous academic *Vernunftrepublikaner,* had already become more democratic during the war. He had advocated a negotiated peace and, like Adolf von Harnack, Ernst Troeltsch, Hugo Preuss, Gerhard Anschütz, and Fritz Hartung, campaigned against the three-class Prussian voting system. Like them, he was slowly moving away from the mixture of social liberalism and imperialism which Friedrich Naumann had espoused, but, like Troeltsch, retained a conception of 'German freedom' and German liberalism defined against the West.[13] Both Troeltsch and Meinecke were still shocked by the sudden and complete collapse of the monarchy. But they quickly came to accept the republic both as a 'historical necessity' and as a bulwark against even more political chaos caused by the political extremes, the 'Bolshevik' one in particular. Troeltsch claimed in 1918 that 'democracy had left the sphere of mere doctrine . . . and had become a pure practical necessity'.[14] At the same time, Troeltsch affirmed the need for social pacification and an integration of all classes, as well as a peculiarly German 'spiritual-ethical conception of democracy'.[15] He criticized the new constitution, but at the same time stressed the importance of an inner affirmation of the idea of republicanism which had to precede any criticism: 'Only when one has honestly affirmed it (the republic), can one begin to think about giving it the participation and counterweight of the aristocratic and conservative weights which are indispensable to any society, without being suspected of wanting to dissolve the very system which has saved the Reich and on which the Reich further depends.' 'Saving the Reich' and 'rescuing the state' were priorities for many *Vernunftrepublikaner*: the republic was merely a means to an end. After the Empire had failed to integrate all classes and 'the masses' into the state, democracy seemed to be the only state-form capable of doing so. The state was more important than the state-form. As in the case of Hans Delbrück, the reason for the republic was *Staatsräson* (reason of state). He claimed that 'whoever loves the German *Volk* has to serve faithfully the republic today', and agreed with fellow *Vernunftrepublikaner* who argued that only a republic could restore state authority, check separatist tendencies, prevent the further loss of territory, and have any hope of revising the Treaty of Versailles.[16]

Since they closely followed Naumann in placing so much value on social integration, liberals such as Troeltsch were paradoxically also more 'social' than 'democratic'. They could advocate alliances with the SPD not out of any concern with the republic, but with the social question and with what

Naumann had called the *Menschwerdung der Masse* (the humanization of the masses). As Michael Freeden has pointed out, social liberal tendencies were particularly pronounced in the basic ideological programme of German liberals, but remained closely connected with a romantic organicism which conceived of the nation as a living and growing personality.[17] In that sense, the crisis after the First World War only accelerated a thought process already under way: the liberals overcame their inherited fear of 'the masses' and showed themselves to be surprisingly 'accommodationist' in their willingness to integrate the *Volk* into the state.[18] As Meinecke claimed, 'today the republic is the form of government which least divides us', and which allowed 'to make one nation out of two'.[19]

At the same time, liberals sought to combine social policies with a strong executive or 'substitute Kaiser', which, Meinecke stressed, was also to preserve German state traditions and to succeed where the real Kaiser had failed. Many liberals, such as Moritz Julius Bonn, would of course have preferred a constitutional monarchy along British lines, but, in the absence of suitable royals and with the end of what Helmuth Plessner called 'natural legitimacy', they turned to vaguely defined ideas such as Meinecke's *Volksstaat* (people's state). In that sense, the vision of a socially integrated republic with a strong executive became a continuation of the *soziales Volkskaisertum* (popular social monarchy) which Naumann had advocated.[20] Behind the conceptions of a strong executive in turn stood Max Weber's idea of plebiscitarian presidential democracy, with its inherent distrust of parties and its pacification of the masses through strong leadership and a strong *bürgerliche* (bourgeois) élite forged in parliamentary battles.[21]

Social liberalism was not, however, the only factor in the liberals' conversion to the republic after the First World War. Among academics and intellectuals, a probably even more significant reason was a fundamental concern with the survival of a German *Kultur* (culture) in contrast to mere Western *Zivilisation* (civilization). The liberals were in many cases among what Fritz Ringer has identified as the 'modernist mandarins'. They were members of the German academic community who believed in their superiority *qua Bildung*, that is, education and self-cultivation, and their own status as a *Geistesaristokratie* (intellectual aristocracy). The modernist mandarins, unlike the majority of mandarins, however, showed themselves open to some democratic reform before the war. Now they felt that accepting the new regime would allow them to steer and moderate it from within. Most importantly, they hoped that accommodation would allow them to salvage the mandarin tradition and the aristocratic values which, as Troeltsch put it, 'were capable of living on'.[22]

A concern with *Kultur* was also at the heart of Thomas Mann's famous conversion from the ardent wartime nationalism and German exceptionalism displayed in the *Reflections of an Unpolitical Man* to the cautious advocacy of republicanism in 'About the German Republic' in 1922. Mann had not converted from *Kultur* to *Zivilisation*, but rather come to the conclusion that *Kultur* would best be safeguarded in a democracy. Democracy was of course not itself the site of cultural life, but provided the framework for what he called 'national life' or the 'German *Volk*', which always exceeded the letter of the constitution.[23] As in Willy Hellpach's concept of 'conservative democracy', democracy was a more effective means of social integration or of achieving some form of cohesion and *Gemeinschaft* (community) under modern conditions. Like Meinecke and other liberals, Mann was not impervious to the social question, but the 'socialism' he called for was closer to Spengler's 'Prussian socialism', that is, to a *Volksgemeinschaft* (a people's community) of national solidarity and common duties, rather than to a form of Marxism. Mann also continued to oppose socialist internationalism, re-emphasizing the 'fact' that 'the human can be realized in the national'.[24] 'Politics', which Mann had collapsed into *Zivilisation* in the *Reflections*, remained the enemy throughout, and he consequently arrived at a rather paradoxical notion of an 'apolitical democracy' as the desirable political form for the Germans. This apolitical entity was in turn to be suffused with a humanism which brought Mann closer to the 'civilization' of the West, but which also yielded no particular political principles in favour of democracy. Like Hans Castorp in the *Magic Mountain*, Mann did not truly transcend the poles of the Western Enlightenment of a Settembrini and the Eastern apocalyptical mysticism of a Naphta, but found an uneasy compromise leaning towards Settembrini and signified by such vague concepts as 'the Middle' and 'Humanity'.[25]

The 'accommodationists' were on weak theoretical territory from the very start. There was something inherently temporary in the 'republicanism of reason', when Meinecke claimed that 'if one cannot have what one loves, then one must love what one has', a stance that even after the crisis of historicism and idealism betrayed a liberal temperament which took the real for the rational.[26] The liberals' defence of democracy was based on 'reason', but only in the sense of historical reasons and quasi-sociological assessments, rather than on a principled, philosophical view of democracy. Their pragmatism, leaning sometimes this way and sometimes that, following what Meinecke called the *Lebensgesetz des Ausgleichs* (vital law of balancing), remained in constant danger of tipping over into opportunism. It also led to what Peter Gay has called a 'curious, rather limited Machiavellianism', as avoiding conflict and protecting the core of German culture became their priority.[27] While to some extent *any* liberal stance will be faced with this situation, the *Vernunftrepublikaner* performed a particularly precarious *Gratwanderung* (balancing act), to use one of Meinecke's favourite metaphors, since they found it impossible to resolve even in their own minds dualisms such as power politics versus ethics, while at the same time fundamentally abhorring politics. But not only is democracy a form of politics, democracy is a form of controlled conflict, in which the yearning for some unproblematic form of social cohesion and collective belonging such as the *Volksgemeinschaft* or even the *Volksstaat* can never be satisfied. A fundamental aversion to politics *qua* conflict made it all the more difficult to come to a principled defence of democracy.

In the same vein, many of the *Vernunftrepublikaner* were curiously unconcerned with the shape and durability of institutions. If, as Mann pointed out, the 'national life' and the *Volk* always exceeded the written letter of the constitution, and if one cared primarily about that 'national life', then violations of that letter were by definition less serious. Nationalism took precedence over liberalism, but did not specify any particular institutional set-up, which is why in the end it was not so difficult after all to refashion the idea of the social monarchy as a conservative democracy.[28] And while German liberalism had always been more etatist than its British and French counterparts, it was not actually 'the state' understood in terms of concrete institutions which the republic was to have salvaged, or the state understood as a Weberian *Anstalt* (public institution), but instead an almost metaphysical concept which could be conceived interchangeably with the notion of the Reich.[29] In short, reasoning one's way towards the 'spirit' of the republic did not translate into support for its institutions, even at the best of times.

## Principles for the Republic: Liberal Philosophers during Weimar

But what about liberalism beyond pragmatism? After all, in the intellectual and cultural hothouse that Weimar was, not only the philosophical extremes flourished—although they grew much better in an immoderate climate. There were, after all, intellectuals who, in the spirit of *Neue Sachlichkeit* and the 'cold personality', kept a distance and resisted the temptations of the past, abhorred the yearning for 'community', and sought to fashion self-consciously realist and modern social theories.[30]

One of the most ingenious and complex defences of *Gesellschaft* against the proponents of *Gemeinschaft* on both the right and the left was offered by Helmuth Plessner in his 1924 'Limits of Community'.[31] Plessner, drawing on his complex, dualist philosophical anthropology which closely resembled that of Max Scheler, viewed society itself as essentially a consequence of the 'natural', that is unavoidable, 'artificiality' which human beings were fated to live.[32] He sought to anchor the inherent dignity of society in his philosophical anthropology, and in particular in his view of humans being in need of both human fellowship *and* distance. The complete self-revelation and social warmth which proponents of *Gemeinschaft* were yearning for was, according to Plessner, actually 'inhuman'—

graciously keeping a distance, wearing 'social masks', and hiding one's 'true identity' were as necessary to a proper social life as infrequent moments of true *Gemeinschaft*. Through this defence of an almost aristocratic ethos of 'distance', Plessner wanted to make the German bourgeoisie face the challenges of industrial society, without resorting either to romanticism, as was the case with the Youth Movement, or to the extreme communitarianism which the advocates of a *Volksgemeinschaft* espoused—and most of all, without succumbing to the challenge of communism. He constructed a peculiar justification of 'society' beyond Western liberal theories, which he saw as discredited by the hypocrisy of the victorious Western powers after the First World War. Instead, he tried to argue from within the context of Germany's own 'spiritual and political possibilities'.[33] In that sense, he did not quite fill the vacuum which the absence of 'a vital tradition of political liberalism' and the 'inadequate and partial incorporation (of the Enlightenment) into German society' had left.[34] But he did provide an essentially individualist theory to make the Germans face up to modern society, employing the philosophical resources available so as to find a new underpinning for an ethos of political action after Europeans generally had lost faith in the idea of 'progress' and in a humanist ethos.

However, Plessner's despair over the growth of the 'masses' as well as his defensive stance *vis-à-vis* communism increasingly made him adopt arguments drawn from vitalism, which in turn justified authoritarianism. Plessner, having affirmed society, technology, and politics through an anthropological foundation centred on the constitution of the human soul and underpinned by vitalism, was left without theoretical resources to defend himself against a politics which effectively amounted to a form of authoritarian communitarianism. Plessner's 'Limits of Community', despite its main thrust as a liberal search for individual dignity within modern society, had already contained a call for the kind of 'authoritarian liberalism' typical of figures like Weber and Meinecke, since it denied any possibility of democratic self-determination or democratic deliberation to reach political compromises. Instead, in the early 1930s, Plessner developed his ethos of distance into a view of politics as defined by friend–enemy relations, and increasingly, drawing on vitalism, emphasized the need for self-assertion and the role of sheer power in human life. His delicate attempt at reconciling an aristocratic ethos of distance adapted for the bourgeoisie, an ethics of the state, and a realist insight into the role of power came under increasing strain. Eventually, he came to the insight that his ethos of *Gesellschaft* was indeed aristocratic, that is, only for a few, and that the politics of these few would always have to be based on groundless, existential decisions.[35] Subsequently, in his famous 1935 reconstruction of the ideological background of the Third Reich, *The Belated Nation*, Plessner indirectly admitted that his attempt at providing a new 'political humanism' through combining the values of *Gesellschaft*, an ethos of distance, and decisionism had failed, and had in fact played into the rise of even more authoritarian and decisionist theories.

Like Plessner, the philosopher of pedagogy Theodor Litt sought to find a 'middle way', or rather a reconciliation between the 'idea' and reality. Litt, whose work focused mainly on *staatsbürgerliche Erziehung* (civic education), argued that there was no universally 'best' political constitution, but that the quality of any existing constitution depended on whether it fitted and augmented the 'whole concrete life of an association'.[36] Like Plessner, Litt was eager to overcome inherited dichotomies. He rejected an opposition between individual and society, arguing instead that there was a 'dialectical' relation between them. Human associations could only be conceived in terms of the daily, dynamic interaction between individual and society, rather than as organic entities or in terms of purely normative relations, as in social contract theory.[37] This phenomenological approach proved attractive to legal theorists such as Hermann Heller and Rudolf Smend, who sought to transcend the positivism and neo-Kantian formalism espoused by Hans Kelsen.[38] Litt's theory helped Smend in particular to overcome a notion of the state as an unchanging 'substance', and instead see it as an ongoing process, in need of daily realization and renewal through the action of its citizens. Heller, even more than Smend, who was hardly a republican and who remained attached to organic conceptions of the state, also emphasized the character of the state as constituted through conscious acts of will, and tried to give theories of the state a more sociological cast. In short, Litt's model of the interaction between individual and society helped to infuse a sense of the state as depending on something akin to Renan's 'plebiscite de tous les jours' into the still either organicist or excessively formalist German *Staatsrechtslehre* (theories of the state).

At the same time, Litt—somewhat akin to Plessner—rejected the dichotomy between the bodily nature of human beings and their cultural achievements. As a logical extension of this postulate, he also refused any dichotomy between the state, concerned mainly with survival, on the one hand, and culture on the other. He claimed that, by providing the institutional space and protection for cultural activity, the state actually relieved the conscience of each individual and took on the moral burden of providing order which each citizen would otherwise have to shoulder. Since violence was an inevitable part of human life, given its *Leiblichkeit* (concrete embodiment), *Sittlichkeit* (ethical life) and state violence for the sake of order were not opposed to each other. Nevertheless, while *Geist* (spirit) and 'state' could approach each other, they could never coincide. Spirit could, however, 'civilize' the state under favourable conditions, that is, conditions of peace and order.

Still, a basic antinomy between state and violence on the one hand, and *Geist* and individual conscience on the other, remained. Litt sought to mediate it by pointing to the 'irrationality of the concrete reality of life', which for him was another way of saying 'history'. No universal, a historical judgements could be made on matters of state, an appropriate balance of culture and violence would have to be found for each particular situation. In other words, while first embarking on a detour to overcome inherited antinomies of *Geist* and violence, culture and state, Litt actually arrived at a thorough 'historicization and nationalization of moral decisions'—a position, in fact, not far from Meinecke's pre-war historicism and justification of German power politics.[39] Litt concluded that changes in state-form belonged to the state's overall fate, so that respect for the current Weimar Constitution could be combined with an appreciation of the Wilhelminian heritage and an 'openness towards the future'.[40] In the end, Litt came out strongly in defence of the republic in his 1930 lecture 'Idea and Reality of the State in Civic Education'. At the same time, he reiterated the point that the state could not be divorced from power, as Germany's *Traumpolitiker* (politicians living in dreams) were wont to believe. However, the sense of wavering and of the temporariness of all political arrangements suffused even this defence.

Karl Jaspers was typical of what Jürgen Habermas has called 'liberalism at its most defensive', and of an existentialist strand of liberalism in Weimar in particular.[41] Politics, for Jaspers as for his teacher Weber, was essentially struggle, and a matter of collective self-assertion. Only the potential of violence lent politics its seriousness, but at the same time this should never reach the extreme of denying the existence of the adversary. Struggle should never be sought for its own sake, but only be accepted if absolutely necessary. Only then could it lead to a *Grenzerfahrung* (an experience at the limits) and possibly yield what Jaspers called 'transcendence'. All these rather vague existentialist claims seemed to indicate that only politics, faced with an attitude of existential resoluteness, enabled men and women to be fully human.

Like Plessner and Litt, Jaspers indirectly sought to sharpen the bourgeoisie's sense of politics and power, while offering ill-defined ethical limits on power politics, thereby continuing Max Weber's pre-Weimar balancing act between an ethics of conviction and an ethics of responsibility. Jaspers wrote nothing on Versailles or on the rise of National Socialism, but instead in his 1931 *Spiritual Situation of the Age* focused on the rise of 'the masses'. There he contended that technology and the masses had essentially produced each other.[42] The masses seemed to be destined to dominate, but were in fact incapable of governing. Instead, the domination of technology and mechanization over the masses had caused the rise of *Lebensangst* (anxiety). The answer to these problems lay in a turn to the state, which had to be a 'substantially bound power'.[43] Such general cultural criticism and attempts at reconciling a mandarin culture sheltered by the state with state violence offered little in the way of concrete support for political institutions.[44] But they revealed much about a bourgeoisie under threat, its intellectuals caught in Weber's dichotomies. They were only able to offer quasi-metaphysical state 'substances' as answers, or to escape into the value-free formalism of Kelsen's Pure Theory of Law. No wonder that many of these 'liberals in panic' eventually turned to more authoritarian ground. On such ground, however, they could not compete with real advocates of 'state substance', such as Carl Schmitt.

Meanwhile, Meinecke, in his role as historian-cum-philosopher, tried to revise the historicist treatment of Bismarck and the Second Reich which he had offered in his pre-war 'Nation-State and Cosmopolitanism'. His 1924 'Die Idee der Staatsräson' was not to be just a piece of intellectual history, but also an advocacy of the idea of 'reason of state' as a bridge between the 'power impulse' and moral responsibility.[45] He contended that every state had to be inspired by *Geist*, lest it be given over to 'the demon'. The primary 'demon' in the 1920s seemed to be mass nationalism, which made Meinecke call upon the implied statesman of *Staatsräson* to fight the 'Machiavellism' of the masses.[46] But he found it difficult to give any clear advice on how to contain them or to draw a clear line between power politics and moral conduct. Instead, he offered a dialectical movement between the two, which in the end failed to transcend the basic dualism—and historicism—at the heart of his theory, a fact which did not go unnoticed by theorists like Carl Schmitt eager to exploit liberal weaknesses.[47] Since reasons of state were historical and therefore relative, no universal judgements as to responsible political action could be made. Like Litt, Meinecke seemed to reproduce the dilemmas of Weber's 'warring gods', that is the value pluralism which according to Weber chararcterized the modern condition. And as Henry Pachter has pointed out, Meinecke's 'Hamlet nature' therefore remained 'vulnerable to the irrationalist attack from the nationalist right and to the rationalist assault from the left'.[48] In the end, Litt and Meinecke seemed simply to surrender to the 'irrationality of concrete life' and trust that the great personality would somehow succeed in an ethical 'balancing act'—guided by the spirit of Weber's ethics of responsibility. Even the liberal qualifications for such 'personalities', however, were increasingly in doubt: traditional notions of *Bildung* imploded with the Weimar avant-garde, and individual property was of less distinction in a commercialized mass culture.[49] Nevertheless, liberals continued to subscribe to E. Leidig's dictum from 1919 that 'democracy hates the geniuses ... but liberalism yearns for geniuses'.[50] The premium on personalities also showed in Meinecke's political commitments. He had never quite given up on his idea of a *Vertrauensdiktatur* (trusteeship dictatorship) based on popular will, and it was only consistent that he found himself on the side of those eager to strengthen the Reich presidency in the early 1930s.[51] Such somewhat holistic conceptions of a new politics of the 'people's state' under a powerful executive were often complemented by the hope for a European-wide 'new humanism' of the type Ernst Robert Curtius called for. Such a source of social cohesion, however, could also take the shape of the nationalist 'Third Humanism' which members of the George circle propagated.[52] The dichotomy between élitist conceptions of liberalism and an opening towards the masses was covered with a vague concept like humanism—just as the wavering of the DDP between a 'small, pure party' of genuine liberals and a liberal mass party in Naumann's image was left unresolved by the resort to overarching concepts like the 'nation' and the 'people'.[53]

Throughout, then, liberal philosophers remained patricians deeply disturbed by the rise of the 'masses', but at the same time unsure about their own relationship to power. The very yearning for the aristocratic personality seemed to be an indication of liberalism's vanishing social base, but at the same time proved unworkable as a solution to the dilemmas of power politics versus ethics.[54] In the end, the *Vernunftrepublikaner* and liberal philosophers, not unlike the ill-fated DDP, had less and less space to manœuvre. The *Gratwanderung* which Meinecke had advocated was becoming increasingly difficult, as the political *Grat* itself, the space in which to perform a balancing act, was getting ever more narrow.[55] Some, like Thomas Mann, turned vigorously to the Social Democrats, realizing that social integration remained the main challenge for the Weimar Republic, and that the liberal parties had failed to accomplish that task. Others turned to the nationalist right, attracted not least by its supposed 'dynamism' and the priority it unashamedly gave to *Gemeinschaft*.[56] The erstwhile left-liberal Theodor Wolff, for instance, supported the fusion of the DDP with the nationalist Jungdeutscher Orden, while Meinecke in the spring of 1933 was impressed by the 'tremendous dynamic force' of the National Socialists.[57] Heuss, in the infamous collective decision of the then *Staatspartei*, which was created through the fusion of the DDP and the Jungdeutscher Orden, eventually voted in favour of the Enabling Law, apparently thinking that if *parliamentarism* had to be left behind, a legal *Machtergreifung* would at least help to protect the rule of law.[58] In the end, however, the crisis of Weimar *was* a crisis of parliamentarism: once that ground had been abandoned both practically and theoretically, liberals had no convincing answer to National Socialism. But which lessons would liberals draw from their 'honourable impotence'[59] and 'speechlessness' at the end of what for them had always remained a *Vorbehaltsrepublik*, that is, a 'republic accepted with reservations' (Karl Dietrich Bracher)?

## After the 'German Catastrophe': Humanism, Institutions and Authority

Even immediately after the war, liberal historians and philosophers offered ready-made explanations of the Nazi period, which was almost universally described in a language of 'catastrophe', 'tragedy', 'fate', and the 'demonic'.

Sweeping narratives of the German *Irrweg* (wrong track) focused on the failed revolutions from the peasants' revolt onwards, on the 'Prussianization' of Germany after 1871, and—yet again—on the evils of massification. Especially the latter pattern of explanation proved popular, since it allowed blame to settle on an amorphous entity, 'the masses', which seemed to universalize and therefore under-specify guilt, while at the same time opening the path to reasserting traditional liberal values of the individual and unique 'personality'.[60] Meinecke and Gerhard Ritter now saw massification and 'proletarian national feelings' at the root of the 'totalitarian dictatorships'. For Ritter, massification had begun with the French Revolution, and a direct line ran from this first appearance of the free reign of the hedonistic desires of the masses through what Meinecke was to call 'democratization, Bolshevization, fascisization'.[61] And yet again the discourse about 'massification' expressed an underlying distrust of popular democracy, continuing what can only be called the ontologization of bourgeois anxieties so typical of the inter-war period.

Meinecke and Ritter also called for a revision of the German image of history. However, this revision never extended further than shifting some of the concepts and categories inherited from before 1933. Meinecke, returning to the very dualism of power and culture which he had sought to overcome in the 1920s, criticized German militarism and overemphasis of the *Machtstaat* (state of power), which had to be redressed in favour of 'culture'. Moreover, once again taking up his teleology of 'cosmopolitanism to nation-state', Meinecke now wanted to return to a more cosmopolitan ethics. Ritter also condemned the 'cult of power', but sought to isolate the Third Reich from previous German traditions by explaining National Socialism through a grand history centred on the pathological aspects of modernity *per se*. The nation-state remained the framework of etatist historical analysis, centred on what Ernst Schulin has aptly called a 'politically and morally tamed historicism'.[62] Other, even more conservatively inclined liberals fell back on a Goethe-inspired humanism which was complemented by advancing the notion of the *Abendland* (Occident) and its European Christian values as a rallying point against both the communist threat from the East and against the immediate past.[63] Moreover, most of the proponents of a new humanism continued in their aversion to parliamentarism, and parties in particular. Especially in the early post-war years, the authoritarian presidentialism familiar from the final phase of Weimar, with its emphasis on the 'great personality' rising both above parties and the masses, still enjoyed considerable prestige.[64]

At the universities, and in the humanities in particular, only a minority called for a reckoning with the immediate past or for the drawing of any liberal 'lessons' from the 'German catastrophe'. In philosophy, only Julius Ebbinghaus, Litt, and, most prominently, Jaspers, engaged with the question of guilt. Litt, in a deeply ambivalent, but highly influential argument, claimed that the horrors of the Nazi period had, on one level, constituted an 'unmasking of man' and yielded a 'clarity of knowledge of ourselves'. The 'truth which makes us free' about the universal evil of which man was capable proved to be the insight which the Germans had learnt from their time in the 'abyss of error, pain and guilt'[65]. Ebbinghaus called for a revival of traditional Kantianism and a thorough 'self-enlightenment' of the Germans about their behaviour in the past twelve years.[66] Most importantly, after a long silence imposed by the Nazis, Jaspers published *The Question of German Guilt* in 1946. It established the fundamental parameters for post-war discussions of German guilt and its connection to the German nation-state—to such an extent, in fact, that left-wing intellectuals like Günter Grass and Jürgen Habermas would time and again return to Jaspers's categories during the course of the 'Bonn Republic'.

Jaspers drew a distinction between criminal, political, moral, and metaphysical guilt.[67] He rejected the thesis of 'collective guilt', arguing for the concept of 'collective responsibility' instead. He linked the question of guilt with the question of German unity, claiming that both a democratic political identity and a sense of social cohesion could only be achieved if the Germans shouldered collective responsibility. But Jaspers's account of the institutional expression of this imperative to assume guilt—lest it be imposed—remained ambiguous: had the Germans once and for all squandered their nation-state, allowing what he called the 'true German as world citizen' to emerge, or was the German nation to be a 'pariah' for a certain time only, potentially regaining its statehood after a period of purification?[68] The first option was suggested by Jaspers's remark in a letter to Hannah Arendt that 'Germany is the first nation that, as a nation, has gone to ruin', and by his admission—which horrified Arendt—that 'now that Germany is destroyed, I feel at ease for the first time'.[69] Jaspers rejected the nationalism which he had previously adopted from his teacher Weber, denying that a liberal political identity and a nation-state framework could go together for the Germans. Yet he still identified with a German high culture, which could supposedly be rescued from the Third Reich, and he clung to the élitist and ethnic notion of the *Kulturnation* (culture nation) as an untainted source of social cohesion. He was, moreover, primarily occupied with the German *Wesen* (nature), with the meanings of being German after the war. As Dagmar Barnouw has pointed out, Jaspers's psychological and personal approach to the Germans' 'political victimization and moral responsibility' was largely 'informed by a diagnostic and therapeutic empathy'.[70] Not only did this approach obscure the more socio-political reasons for the rise of Nazism; it also betrayed a certain German self-centredness, including the nucleus of the argument that Germans, after their historical 'catastrophe', were more than other peoples in a position to contribute to the renewal of human existence 'from its origins' for which Jaspers called. Jaspers also insisted, however, that, as much as moral guilt was a question for one's individual conscience, the only way to deal with German guilt as a whole was through free public communication and what he called the 'solidarity of charitable struggle', instead of mutual moral condemnations.[71] This claim, rooted in Jaspers's philosophy of free and universal communication between equals, was subsequently taken up by numerous intellectuals, most importantly Habermas, who established a link between remembrance and a democratic political culture. Jaspers had also wished for free and equal communication about the democratic foundations of the West German Constitution.[72] While one should be wary of anachronism and teleology in this context and while Jaspers hardly overcame his 'fear of the masses' completely, it might not be too much to say he instead began to approximate the idea of an open public sphere in which equals would deliberate freely according to commonly agreed procedures.

Other liberal intellectuals also revised their underlying assumptions, often combining what have above been referred to as institutional and cultural strategies, with a clear emphasis on the former. In particular, intellectuals close to and sometimes in politics showed a concrete concern with the quality of political culture and what Heuss called 'political style', which had been absent from Weimar.[73] At the same time, they sought to emphasize the importance of caring for liberal political institutions. Theodor Eschenburg, who had been a student of Heinrich Triepel and close to Stresemann in the 1920s, strongly believed in legal-rational *Herrschaft* (domination) and in the strenuous protection of the integrity of institutions by following their procedures. Heuss also emphasized the always limited and temporary mandate of legal *Herrschaft* in the democratic state, thereby stressing the more legal-institutional—rather than charismatic—aspects of the Weberian legacy of political thought. He was against the 'perfectionism' of the Weimar Constitution, against too strong a fixation on paragraphs and details, instead stressing the importance of creating a tradition of respect for a democratic political culture.[74] Such concerns also made political scientists like Dolf Sternberger and Wilhelm Hennis advocate a kind of neo-Aristotelianism in which civic virtue played a central role alongside a respect for political office and its authority.[75] Sternberger in particular sought to move away from the Weberian preoccupation with *Herrschaft*, instead promoting the idea of *Staatsfreundschaft* (friendship towards the state)—a precursor of his later concept of 'constitutional patriotism', which was then further developed by Habermas.[76] Where inter-war liberals had appealed to the 'nation' as the only factor providing social cohesion, Sternberger and other liberals conceived of a liberal 'civil religion' centred on the constitution and a common democratic ethos. Against Weber and Schmitt with their conception of politics as struggle, moreover, Sternberger also sought to redefine the 'concept of the political' as being about 'the area of all endeavour to seek and secure peace'.[77]

For Eschenburg in turn, sometimes called a 'liberal with a sense of order', institutions were both the subjects and objects of politics.[78] More importantly, they were also the outcome of collective learning processes, and always in danger of being damaged by strategic, Machiavellian action which not only violated their spirit, but also eroded the political culture at large. Institutions therefore had to be fashioned as barriers to such strategic action. Eschenburg, with numerous books such as *Institutional Concerns in the Federal Republic* and a stream of articles in *Die Zeit*, assumed the role of a journalistic-cum-academic 'guardian of the Constitution' in West Germany, seeking to protect the authority of existing institutions—and the authority of political office in particular.[79] Litt also wanted to strengthen respect for the state in his books and lectures in the 1950s. The state, he claimed, was never just a means. In fact, state and society always formed an interacting whole, proving the truth of Naumann's dictum that 'the state is us'.[80] In short, liberals more concerned about actual theories of the state concluded from the failure of the Weimar Republic that strong democratic institutions and their authority had to be protected. To some extent, this meant falling back on German statist traditions. But when Eschenburg, Heuss, Jaspers, and Litt spoke of the state, they did not mean what the *Vernunftrepublikaner* meant by the state or the Reich. Theirs was a commitment to concrete institutions without the metaphysical content which Smend, under Litt's influence, had first sought to eliminate from German understandings of the state. Moreover, liberals no longer saw the state as being over and above a society whose divergent social and economic interests had to be fashioned according to the common good by a strong state. This privileging of the political over the social had been a legacy of German thought since Hegel and betrayed a basic distrust of civil society and social contract theory in particular.[81] In the 1950s, it became much more attenuated with the rise of theories of 'neo-pluralism', which accepted the interplay of interest groups within society as well as social integration between state and society in the ways which Smend had first envisaged. Part of this new-found acceptance, which also meant the end of Weimar anti-parliamentarianism, was the recognition of political parties as quasi-constitutional bodies.

None of this meant, however, that party-political liberalism had simply detached itself from nationalism or other 'substances'. On the contrary, the FDP became the haven not just for old 'national liberals', but even for old National Socialists.[82] Nevertheless, theoretically liberals were moving away from the notions of a German essence to which previous *Vernunftrepublikaner* and liberals had clung. Democracy was not merely a temporary state-form, as Litt had claimed in the 1920s—instead, its institutions had to be meticulously protected, sometimes to the extent that 'the people' were excluded. All had strong anti-plebiscitarian feelings and were concerned about an excessive value pluralism extending to the right or the left. A tradition of mandarin cultural criticism did not disappear overnight, as the 'loss of the middle' continued to be mourned in the 1950s. But the strenuous reconciliation of opposites, which had consumed the energies of so many Weimar liberals, diminished in favour of a commitment to the values 'eternally' enshrined in the Basic Law. Such concerns were later denigrated as being purely about 'formal democracy' or still tainted by the problems of Weberian authoritarian liberalism. But whatever the truth of such accusations may be, these sincere commitments to democratic institutions, no matter how distrustful of the people, stand in marked contrast to the inherent wavering of *Vernunftrepublikaner* and liberals in the inter-war years. It seemed that, after all, German liberals had learnt 'the second lesson' of modernity. The first had been the renunciation of nostalgia. The second was that a republic 'might deserve wholehearted support—or, rather, that it might become deserving if enough deserving persons supported it'.[83]

# Notes

Thanks to Jerry Cohen, Patrick Cohrs, Henning Tewes, and Jonathan Wright. Part of this articke draws on thinking I first developed in *Another Country: German Intellectuals, Unification and National Identity* (New Haven and London: Yale UP, 2000). I thank Yale University Press for allowing me to use this material here.

1. Some of these issues are explored in Konrad H. Jarausch and Larry Eugene Jones (eds.), *In Search of Liberal Germany: Studies in the History of German Liberalism from 1789 to the Present* (New York: Berg, 1990), in particular Jarausch and Jones, 'German Liberalism Reconsidered: Inevitable Decline, Bourgeois Hegemony, or Partial Achievement?', 1–23. For the idea of a permanent crisis of German liberalism, see Peter Pulzer, *Jews and the German State* (Oxford: Blackwell, 1992), 324.

2. Mark Lilla, 'The Other Velvet Revolution: Continental Liberalism and its Discontents', *Daedalus*, 123/2 (1994), 129–57.

3. For a general discussion of the historiographical dilemmas with regard to Weimar, see Detlev J. K. Peukert, *The Weimar Republic: The Crisis of Classical Modernity*, tr. Richard Deveson (London: Penguin, 1993).

4. Kurt Sontheimer, *Antidemokratisches Denken in der Weimarer Republik: Die politischen Ideen des deutschen Nationalismus zwischen 1918 und 1933* (Munich: Deutscher Taschenbuch Verlag, 1978).

5. Joachim Fischer, 'Plessner und die politische Philosophie der zwanziger Jahre', in Volker Gerhardt, Henning Ottmann, and Martyn P. Thompson (eds.), *Jahrbuch Politisches Denken* (1992), 53–77.

6. Ibid. 55–6.

7. On the basic theoretical positions of Weimar liberal philosophers, see Norbert J. Schürgers, *Politische Philosophie in der Weimarer Republik: Staatsverständnis*

_zwischen Führerdemokratie und bürokratischem Sozialismus_ (Stuttgart: J. B. Metzlersche Verlagsbuchhandlung, 1989), 61–87.

8. For the notion of 'deconversion' and a number of important insights into the liberalization of political thought after 1945, see A. D. Moses, 'The Forty-Fivers: A Generation Between Fascism and Democracy', _German Politics and Society_, 17/1 (1999), 94–126.

9. Anne Sa'adah, _Germany's Second Chance: Trust, Justice and Democratization_ (Cambridge, Mass.: Harvard University Press, 1998), 3.

10. Ibid.

11. John Rawls, _Political Liberalism_ (New York: Columbia University Press, 1993).

12. See also Ralf Dahrendorf , _Liberale und andere: Portraits_ (Stuttgart: DVA, 1994) for some insightful characterizations of the 'mind-sets' of liberal personalities in the 20th century.

13. Troeltsch in 'Deutscher Geist und Westeuropa', Meinecke in 'Die deutsche Erhebung von 1914'.

14. Quoted in Rolf Vierhaus, 'Die Ideologie eines deutschen Weges der politischen und sozialen Entwicklung', in Rudolf von Thadden (ed.), _Die Krise des Liberalismus zwischen den Weltkriegen_ (Göttingen: Vandenhoeck & Ruprecht, 1978), 96–114; here 100.

15. Ibid.

16. Fritz Ringer, _The Decline of the German Mandarins: The German Academic Community, 1890–1933_ (Hanover: University of New England Press, 1990), 202.

17. Michael Freeden, _Ideologies and Political Theory: A Conceptual Approach_ (Oxford: OUP, 1996), 213. See also Karl Holl _et al._ (eds.), _Sozialer Liberalismus_ (Göttingen: Vandenhoeck & Ruprecht, 1986).

18. On the fear of the masses, see Helmut König, _Zivilisation und Leidenschaften: Die Masse im bürgerlichen Zeitalter_ (Reinbek: Rowohlt, 1992).

19. Meinecke quoted by Ringer, _Decline_, 203, and Kurt Töpner, _Gelehrte Politiker und politisierende Gelehrte: Die Revolution von 1918 im Urteil deutscher Hochschullehrer_ (Göttingen: Musterschmidt, 1970), 119.

20. Ibid. 112. See also Hans Peter Bleuel, _Deutschlands Bekenner: Professoren zwischen Kaiserreich und Diktatur_ (Munich: Scherz, 1968).

21. Wolfgang J. Mommsen, _Max Weber and German Politics 1890–1920_, tr. Michael S. Steinberg (Chicago: University of Chicago Press, 1984).

22. Ringer, _Decline_, 203.

23. Daniel Argelès, 'Thomas Manns Einstellung zur Demokratie: Der Fall eines "progressiven Konservativen"' in Manfred Gangl and Gérard Raulet (eds.), _Intellektuellendiskurse in der Weimarer Republik: Zur politischen Kultur einer Gemengelage_ (Frankfurt: Campus, 1994), 221–31.

24. Quoted in Donald Prater, _Thomas Mann: A Life_ (Oxford: OUP, 1995), 129.

25. Harvey Goldman, _Politics, Death, and the Devil: Self and Power in Max Weber and Thomas Mann_ (Berkeley, Calif.: University of California Press, 1992), 145–6.

26. Meinecke quoted in Töpner, _Gelehrte Politiker_, 116.

27. Peter Gay, _Weimar Culture: The Outsider as Insider_ (New York: Harper & Row, 1968), 24.

28. The most important exception were the 'neo-liberals' such as Walter Eucken, Alexander von Rüstow, and Wilhelm Röpke, who shared some of the distrust of the 'masses' typical of liberal philosophers, but were generally less nationalist than the _Vernunftrepublikaner_. See A. J. Nicholls, _Freedom with Responsibility: The Social Market Economy in Germany 1918–1963_ (Oxford: Clarendon Press, 1994).

29. Hans Vorländer, 'Leidenswege des Liberalismus in Deutschland', in: Werner Bruns

and Walter Döring (eds.), *Der selbstbewußte Bürger: Die liberalen Perspektiven* (Bonn: Bouvier, 1995), 41–51.

30. Helmuth Lethen, *Verhaltenslehren der Kälte: Lebensversuche zwischen den Kriegen* (Frankfurt am Main: Suhrkamp, 1994) and *Neue Sachlichkeit 1924–1932: Studien zur Literatur des 'Weißen Sozialismus'* (Stuttgart: J. B. Metzlersche Buchhandlung, 1970).

31. Helmuth Plessner, 'Grenzen der Gemeinschaft: Eine Kritik des sozialen Radikalismus', in *Gesammelte Schriften*, eds. Günter Dux *et al.* v. 7–133.

32. Rüdiger Kramme, *Helmuth Plessner und Carl Schmitt: Eine historische Fallstudie zum Verhältnis von Anthropologie und Politik in der deutschen Philosophie der zwanziger Jahre* (Berlin: Duncker & Humblot, 1989), 51.

33. Helmuth Plessner, 'Die verspätete Nation: Über die politische Verführbarkeit bürgerlichen Geistes (1959)', in *Gesammelte Schriften*, vi. 7–223; here 44–5 (originally published as *Schicksal deutschen Geistes am Ausgang seiner bürgerlichen Epoche*, Zürich: Max Niehans, 1935). In his judgement from the mid-1930s, he argued that 'it is furthermore a fact that the war propaganda of the Entente, the treaty of Versailles and the coalition games of the republican parties completely devalued the concepts of freedom, democracy, self-determination of peoples, progress and world peace, in one word, the value system of the Western-type political humanism'. Moreover, ever since the 17th century, Germany had become alienated from Western natural-law traditions and failed to develop its own 'political humanism'. See ibid. 51–2.

34. Jeffrey Herf, *Reactionary Modernism: Technology, Culture and Politics in Weimar and the Third Reich* (Cambridge: Cambridge University Press, 1984), p. ix.

35. Helmuth Plessner, 'Macht und menschliche Natur: Ein Versuch zur Anthropologie der geschichtlichen Weltsicht (1931)', in *Gesammelte Schriften*, v. 135–234.

36. Schürgers, *Politische Philosophie*, 192.

37. Ulrich Scheuner, 'Was bleibt von der Staatslehre Theodor Litts? Theodor Litt und die Staatslehre in der Weimarer Republik und der Bundesrepublik Deutschland', in Peter Gutjahr-Löser *et al.* (eds.), *Theodor Litt und die Politische Bildung der Gegenwart* (Munich: Olzog, 1981), 175–92.

38. Cf. Peter C. Caldwell, *Popular Sovereignty and the Crisis of German Constitutional Law: The Theory and Practice of Weimar Constitutionalism* (Durham, NC: Duke University Press, 1997).

39. Schürgers, *Politische Philosophie*, 199.

40. Ibid. 209.

41. Jürgen Habermas, *Philosophisch-politische Profile* (Frankfurt am Main: Suhrkamp, 1971), 100.

42. Karl Jaspers, *Die geistige Situation der Zeit*, 5th, partially rev. edn. (Berlin: de Gruyter, 1933), 28.

43. Ibid. 73.

44. See also Dagmar Barnouw, *Weimar Intellectuals and the Threat of Modernity* (Bloomington Ind.: Indiana University Press).

45. See also Henry Pachter, 'Friedrich Meinecke and the Tragedy of German Liberalism', in *Weimar Etudes* (New York: Columbia University Press, 1982), 135–70.

46. Friedrich Meinecke, *Die Idee der Staatsräson in der neueren Geschichte* (1924; Munich: R. Oldenbourg, 1963), 481–510.

47. Carl Schmitt, *Positionen und Begriffe im Kampf mit Weimar-Genf-Versailles* (1940; Berlin: Duncker & Humblot, 1988), 45–52.

48. Ibid. 162.

49. Dieter Langewiesche, *Liberalismus in Deutschland* (Frankfurt am Main: Suhrkamp, 1988), 239.
50. Quoted in ibid. 255.
51. Friedrich Meinecke, 'Republik, Bürgertum und Jugend', in *Politische Schriften und Reden*, ed. Georg Kotowski (Darmstadt: Siegried Toeche-Mittler, 1958), 369–83; here 379–80.
52. Hans Manfred Bock, 'Ernst Robert Curtius und die Aporien des "unpolitischen" Intellektuellen', in Gangl and Raulet (eds.), *Intellektuellendiskurse*, 234–44.
53. Modris Eksteins, *Theodor Heuss und die Weimarer Republik: Ein Beitrag zur Geschichte des deutschen Liberalismus* (Stuttgart: E. Klett, 1969), 105.
54. See also Kurt Klotzbach, *Das Eliteproblem im politischen Liberalismus: Ein Beitrag zum Staats- und Gesellschaftsbild des 19. Jahrhunderts* (Cologne: Westdeutscher Verlag, 1966).
55. Jürgen C. Hess, 'Die Desintegration des Liberalismus in der Weimarer Republik', in Hans Vorländer (ed.), *Verfall oder Renaissance des Liberalismus? Beiträge zum deutschen und internationalen Liberalismus* (Munich: Olzog, 1987), 91–116.
56. In May 1933 Meinecke was impressed by the Nazis' 'dynamic force', but, I hasten to add, he had vigorously fought against them before 1933. See *Ausgewählter Briefwechsel*, ed. Ludwig Dehio and Peter Classen (Stuttgart: K. F. Koehler, 1962), 138.
57. Werner Jochmann, 'Der deutsche Liberalismus und seine Herausforderung durch den Nationalsozialismus', in von Thadden (ed.), *Die Krise*, 115–28; here 124.
58. This is plausibly argued by Jürgen C. Heß in his '"Die deutsche Lage ist ungeheuer ernst geworden": Theodor Heuss vor den Herausforderungen des Jahres 1933', *Jahrbuch zur Liberalismus-Forschung*, 6 (1994), 65–136.
59. Gay, *Weimar Culture*, 23.
60. For a liberal 'total antifascism' from a liberal point of view which opposed the individual personality to 'massification', see Wilhelm Röpke, *Die deutsche Frage* (Erlenbach-Zürich: Eugen-Rentsch, 1945).
61. Friedrich Meinecke, *Die deutsche Katastrophe* (Zürich: Aero, 1946) and Gerhard Ritter, *Europa und die deutsche Frage* (Munich: Bruckmann, 1948).
62. Bernd Faulenbach, 'Historistische Tradition und politische Neuorientierung: Zur Geschichtswissenschaft nach der "deutschen Katastrophe"', in Walter H. Pehle and Peter Sillem (eds.), *Wissenschaft im geteilten Deutschland: Restauration oder Neubeginn nach 1945?* (Frankfurt am Main: Fischer, 1992), 191–204; here 198–9.
63. Axel Schildt, *Zwischen Abendland und Amerika: Studien zur westdeutschen Ideenlandschaft der 50er Jahre* (Munich: R. Oldenbourg, 1999)
64. Hans Mommsen, 'Von Weimar nach Bonn: Zum Demokratieverständnis der Deutschen', in Axel Schildt and Arnold Sywottek (eds.), *Modernisisierung im Wiederaufbau: Die westdeutsche Gesellschaft der 50er Jahre* (Bonn: Dietz, 1993), 745–58.
65. Theodor Litt, *Von der Sendung der Philosophie* (Wiesbaden: Dieterich'sche Verlagsbuchhandlung, 1946), 24–5.
66. Helmut Fahrenbach, 'Nationalsozialismus und der Neuanfang 'westdeutscher Philosophie' 1945–1950', in Pehle and Sillem (eds.), *Wissenschaft*, 99–112.
67. Karl Jaspers, *Die Schuldfrage: Ein Beitrag zur deutschen Frage* (Zürich: Artemis, 1946), 10–14.
68. Anson Rabinbach, 'The German as Pariah: Karl Jaspers's *The Question of German Guilt*', in *In the Shadow of Catastrophe: German Intellectuals between Apocalypse and Enlightenment* (Berkeley, Calif.: University of California Press), 129–65; here 138.

69. *Hannah Arendt-Karl Jaspers-Briefwechsel 1926–1969*, ed. Lotte Köhler and Hans Saner (Munich: Piper, 1985), 82 and 93.

70. Dagmar Barnouw, *Germany 1945: Views of War and Destruction* (Bloomington, Ind.: Indiana University Press, 1996), 146.

71. Jaspers, *Die Schuldfrage*, 17.

72. Kurt Salamun, *Karl Jaspers* (Munich: C. H. Beck, 1985), 105.

73. Theodor Heuss, 'Freiheit als Aufgabe' (1946), in Peter Juling (ed.), *Was heisst heute liberal?* (Gerlingen: Bleicher, 1978), 31–4

74. Karl Dietrich Bracher, *Theodor Heuss und die Wiederbegründung der Demokratie in Deutschland* (Tübingen: Wunderlich, 1965).

75. See also Hans Maier *et al.* (eds.), *Politik, Philosophie, Praxis: Festschrift für Wilhelm Hennis zum 65. Geburtstag* (Stuttgart: Klett-Cotta, 1988).

76. Reinhard Mehring, 'Bürgerliche statt demokratische Legitimität: Dolf Sternbergers Auseinandersetzung um den Begriff des Politischen', in Andreas Göbel *et al.* (eds.), *Metamorphosen des Politischen: Grundfragen politischer Einheitsbildung* (Berlin: Akademie, 1995), 233–46.

77. Dolf Sternberger, *Die Politik und der Friede* (Frankfurt am Main: Suhrkamp, 1986), 76.

78. See also Hermann Rudolph (ed.), *Den Staat denken: Theodor Eschenburg zum Fünfundachtzigsten* (Berlin: Siedler, 1990).

79. Theodor Eschenburg, *Institutionelle Sorgen in der Bundesrepublik* (Stuttgart: C. E. Schwab, 1961). See also Eschenburg's treatment of the Weimar Republic in *Die improvisierte Demokratie: Gesammelte Aufsätze zur Weimarer Republik* (Munich: Piper, 1964).

80. Theodor Litt, 'Kulturpolitik als Prüfstein freiheitlicher Staatsgestaltung', in Walter Erbe *et al.* (eds.), *Die geistige und politische Freiheit in der Massendemokratie* (Stuttgart: DVA, 1960), 126–50; here 150.

81. See for instance Chris Thornhill, *Political Theory in Modern Germany* (Cambridge: Polity, 1999).

82. Peter Lösche and Franz Walter, *Die FDP: Richtungsstreit und Zukunftszweifel* (Darmstadt: Wissenschaftliche Buchgesellschaft, 1996), 24–48.

83. Gay, *Weimar Culture*, 25.

# III

## Citizenship and Human Rights

# 9

## Jacobinism Redefined: Second Empire Municipalism and the Emergence of Republican Citizenship

### *Sudhir Hazareesingh*

It is a commonplace among political and intellectual historians that the principles of modern French citizenship were fashioned by the democratic and republican state—initially by the Revolution of 1789 and later in more substantive form by the Third Republic (1875–1940).[1] An analogous point is sometimes made through the assertion that, unlike in Britain and Germany, where the nation preceded the state, in France it was the state which preceded (and thus created) the nation.[2] Modern France thus appears as the archetype of the 'statist' political community, in which public institutions—whether Napoleonic, Bourbon, Orleanist, or republican—consistently played a defining role in articulating the principles which held together the political community.

In this orthodox account of the modernization of French political and civic culture, special emphasis tends to be placed on the last three decades of the nineteenth century. After the fall of the Second Empire in 1870 France became a fully-fledged political democracy, with the emergence of liberal institutions and the development of basic political and associational freedoms.[3] In Pierre Rosanvallon's *Le Sacre du citoyen*, the early Third Republic appears as the defining moment in the emergence of republican citizenship, particularly from the perspective of mass electoral participation.[4] The territorial transformation of France into a nation-state is also generally seen to follow this chronology. In the words of Eugene Weber: 'the ideology of the nation was still fragmented and informal in the middle of the nineteenth century. French culture only became truly national in the final years of the nineteenth century'.[5] Historians of French republicanism also agree that it was in the later parts of the nineteenth century that this critical ideological modernization took place.[6] Indeed, in sociological terms this 'republican' sense of collective identity is largely seen as a product of the Third Republic's education system, which was founded in the early 1880s as a centralist instrument for disseminating the key values of the new republican order.[7] It is this 'Jacobin' project, whose premises had to accepted even by those in the periphery who opposed its ideological and cultural content, which is broadly seen to define the modern cultural notion of 'Frenchness'.[8] Hence—and as the logical culmination of all these developments—the prevailing conclusion that it was also under the Third Republic that the contours of a democratic, republican, individualist and secular notion of citizenship were fully defined.[9]

It would be difficult to deny the part played by the Third Republic in the emergence of the modern democratic polity, and the civic culture which accompanied it. However the overwhelming focus on the late nineteenth century has produced an unduly narrow account of the intellectual and political forces which have fashioned France's democratic modernity. In particular, it has overlooked the political significance of the Second Empire (1852–70), during which many of the basic parameters of the modern French notion of citizenship were defined. By the end of the 1860s—and arguably even earlier—all political groups had clear and strong views on the principles which held the political community together; the question of citizenship was therefore at the centre of political debate long before the advent of opportunist and radical élites in the 1880s and 1890s. Highlighting the existence of this range of views before the Third Republic is also an important means of exploding what might be called the myth of republican agency: the notion that the modern paradigm of citizenship in France was the creation of republicans *alone*. Many key notions about civic and political life (such as political freedoms, mass participation, local democracy, and political accountability) were also shared by a number of political groups during the Second Empire—notably by liberals and legitimists. And while it is true that the republicans were politically responsible for the codification of these civic principles, they were by no means the exclusive bearers of the ideological values which underlay them.

A closer inspection of the political culture of the Second Empire also allows for an extension of the intellectual framework within which the notion of citizenship is conventionally discussed, in two ways. First, those who view the Third Republic as the defining moment for the emergence of the principles of modern citizenship tend to offer a bipolar account of its genesis: a secular, democratic, and individualist republican paradigm is thus typically contrasted with a religious, authoritarian, and communitarian construct.[10] However, the range of ideological views about membership of the political community was much broader in nineteenth-century France. For not only were there Bonapartist, legitimist, Catholic, liberal, and republican approaches to citizenship before 1870, but also vibrant arguments within each of these political traditions over the question. This ideological complexity will be fully illustrated in this chapter in our discussion of the republican case.

Secondly, and more ambitiously, re-examining the debates of the Second Empire suggests that the types of issue which are conventionally deemed relevant to identifying the principles of good citizenship need to be broadened. Given that citizenship is largely about defining what keeps a political community together, the natural tendency has been to focus on debates about 'the nation' as the fulcrum of its emergence. Indeed, in many writings, no real distinction is made between the concepts of 'nation' and 'citizen'.[11] To define citizenship, from this angle, is to identify the ways in which the French state 'created' a sense of collective identity, either in political and juridical terms, or through the establishment of distinct cultural norms. But while the 'Jacobin' project of nation- and state-building undoubtedly played a central role in the development of the modern French polity, this was not the only way in which France came to acquire a sense of collective identity. Indeed, such feelings can emerge alongside and even independently of the problematic of 'nationhood'. For, as we shall see below, being part of the same political community is also about living together in a localized space: defining proper relations with one's neighbours, creating institutions of sociability, administering communal properties, electing local councillors, and articulating the relationship between localities and the political and administrative centre. In short, powerful notions of the rights and duties of citizens are embedded in experiences (and expectations) about local and territorial collective life.[12]

## *Second Empire Republicans and the Problem of Decentralization*

How and why did this ideological consensus about the principles of citizenship emerge during the Second Empire? The short answer is that French political élites came to reconsider the basic principles of collective life in the course of a wide-ranging public discussion about the shortcomings of administrative centralization. This debate convinced them of the need to devolve greater political powers to communal and departmental institutions. 'Decentralization' thus became a central object of intellectual reflection, and it was through their cogitations about territorial politics that political élites came to rethink their principles of citizenship. This proposition will be illustrated here through an examination of the transformation of republican attitudes towards the issue of decentralization between 1852 and 1870. By the end of the Second Empire, liberal republican élites had elaborated a new synthetic approach to territorial politics which drew from other political undercurrents (both within and outside the republican movement) and defined the parameters of modern republican citizenship.

It is worth noting that the republicans were in effect a highly decentralized movement under the Second Empire:[13] in the absence of a firm connection with the seat of power in Paris after 1851, the movement fragmented into a 'mosaic of disparate organizations'.[14] There none the less remained institutional and ideological elements of commonality. Republican conceptions of constitutional reform and change, for example, remained within the broad framework of the classical republican tradition during this period.[15] During the 1850s and 1860s, the republican movement was also united in its condemnation of the Second Empire's centralized practices, which vested control of local government in the hands of the administration. Even the Bonapartist regime's cautious efforts towards promoting greater local liberty in the 1860s found little favour among republicans, who suspected the government of using the issue of decentralization as a cynical ploy to rally political support in the provinces.[16] Thus in 1870 the republicans collectively declined to participate in the deliberations of the Commission of Decentralization, and reiterated their demand that mayors be chosen by their communes rather than appointed by the government.[17]

There was also general agreement among republican élites that the cities of Paris and Lyon should be governed by elected municipal authorities,[18] and that the powers of the prefectoral authorities should be drastically curbed.[19] Underlying these specific proposals was a broader sense among republican élites that the paradigm of communal sociability was the urban collectivity: the town and the city were the prime bearers of republican citizenship, not the village. In 1871, some republicans even went so far as to propose a system of special representation for towns and cities in order to counter-balance the preponderance of rural interests in the National Assembly.[20] However, this was the limit of the internal republican consensus. Contrary to the widespread view, Second Empire republicans were not 'Jacobin and centralist'[21] in their conception of territorial government. In fact, there was a wide-ranging and often passionate debate within the party over the structure of the future republican state and the principles governing membership of the political community.

Three broad paradigms of citizenship were in contention. Jacobins offered a restatement of their classical principles of strong and purposive centralized government, in which the good life was clearly and unambiguously defined around the public institutions of the state. Radical decentralists made the case for a fundamental restructuring of the local government system along federalist lines, as a means of sponsoring an individualistic and associational form of citizenship. Finally, between these two extremes, municipalist republicans argued for a moderate form of self-government, in which individual territorial units retained substantive affiliations to the centre, and citizenship was defined in terms of the reconciliation of local and national political values. It was this third version which emerged as the dominant republican par-

adigm by the end of the Second Empire, both reflecting and helping to consolidate the emerging ideological consensus in France over the principles of
good citizenship.

## The Jacobin Framework

Like its forebears during the 1790s, Jacobin republicanism under the Second
Empire expressed an attachment to the core values of nationalism, civil and
political egalitarianism, collectivism, and centralization. To be a Jacobin in
France in the 1850s and 1860s was often a matter of style as much as substance: it was a flamboyant and often aggressive manner of politics, which was
confident about its values and suspicious of the motives of its opponents—
both within and outside the republican movement.[22]

However, Jacobinism was not an exclusive ideology: its advocates could be
found across the entire republican political spectrum, from revolutionists on
the extreme left to moderate constitutionalists. It should also be noted from
the outset that self-styled 'Jacobin' republicans of the Second Empire were
not systematically committed to violence. Revolutionist republicans such as
the Blanquists were the exception, and their invocation of the revolutionary
violence of the 1790s was intended to inspire contemporary political
action.[23] But during the Second Empire most of those who defended the
methods used by the Revolution in the 1790s were constitutionalist republicans, who sought to achieve their ends through legal and peaceful means. As
the intra-republican debate over the Terror demonstrated in 1865–66,[24] this
Jacobinism was in part a means of establishing a distinct historical lineage,
and defining a specific cultural identity in relation to other political undercurrents within the republican party. Central to this identity was the vener-
ation of the 'tradition of 1789', and this revolutionary fetishism was
epitomized by Charles Delescluze's newspaper *Le Réveil*, which was dated
according to the revolutionary calendar.[25]

The essential feature of Jacobin theory was its emphasis on the transcendental nature of state institutions. Common to all advocates of Jacobinism was
an abiding attachment to the liberating role of the state.[26] During the Second
Empire, the wide-ranging public discussions about reformulating the relationship between state and society were thus viewed with considerable distaste
by Jacobin republicans. In the reproving words of Étienne Vacherot: 'the
domain of the state cannot be at the mercy of fashionable opinions that sometimes seek to restrain it, and at others to expand its limits'.[27] The Jacobin state
was the only effective instrument for promoting the general interest, and the
guarantor of principles which were eternally and universally valid: national
independence, order, justice, freedom, and equality. These principles appeared

self-evident to all Jacobins. Here is Vacherot again: 'military unity is the condition of national independence. Political unity is the prerequisite of internal order. Unity of legislation and taxation are the conditions of civil equality. Indeed what would remain of a nation if it had no independence, no order, and no equal justice for all?'[28]

One of the essential social purposes of the Jacobin state was to ensure the protection of weaker sections of society. In the words of the republican socialist Louis Blanc: 'what will happen if we allow the most intelligent or the strongest to prevent the development of the faculties of those who are less intelligent or strong? It will result in the destruction of freedom. How should this crime be prevented? By making all the power of the people intervene between the oppressor and the oppressed.'[29] To express the point in different terms, Jacobins subscribed to the values both of liberty and equality, but accorded greater weight to the latter: 'we want freedom, all freedoms, but we want the same freedom for all. And for this we want everyone to have the power to use freedom.'[30] This formula expressed one of the core values of Jacobinism, but was at the same time deeply ambiguous. In its weak form, it signified that liberty was valuable, but only if it could be enjoyed by every citizen in some measure. More strongly (and therefore controversially), it could be taken to mean that liberty existed only when it was enjoyed by every citizen in equal amounts. Liberal, radical, and socialist Jacobins tended to subscribe to the weak view, while revolutionist Jacobins adhered to the strong. Blanqui, who belonged to the latter group, was particularly scathing about any republican scheme which did not purport to offer the same basic entitlements to all citizens: 'The individual is the key element of humanity, like the stitch in a knitted fabric. In consequence, beyond individual education, there is nothing. Administration, centralization or decentralization, and combinations and accommodations of power are all silliness and corruption. With individual education, we can have everything. Without it, nothing. Light or darkness, life or death.'[31]

It was precisely in the name of protecting the weak citizens against the strong that Jacobin republicans were suspicious of decentralization. In Vacherot's scathing formula: 'there is no worse tyranny than that of the commune'.[32] Even the modest proposals of the 1865 Nancy Manifesto, which called for an incremental transfer of power to local political bodies, were emphatically rejected[33]. Most Jacobins viewed decentralization as a scheme to weaken the republican movement: one Jacobin pamphleteer thus warned that the liberal opposition's pleas for decentralization were dangerous to the cause of liberty, because they left the republican party open to infiltration by 'the supporters of bourgeois monopoly, the Orleanists, transformed into liberals, who fraudulently introduce themselves in the ranks of democracy to take advantage of its loyalty or its weaknesses'.[34] This view was echoed by another suspicious writer: 'in 1847 we would have said decentralization is a legitimist conception; in 1865 we say, decentralization is a Catholic notion'.[35] Above all, decentralization appeared to many Jacobins as a conspiracy to turn the clock back to the pre-revolutionary era. In the estimation of the Blanquist Gustave Tridon: 'Federalism, under its modern label of decentralization, represents dispersal and disarmament; in the face of an organized and rallied reaction, this is defeat and ruin. To decentralize is to kill the provincial worker, to hand him over, gagged and bound, to the Jesuits and the clan chiefs, and to return to the darkness of the Middle Ages.'[36]

In the 1850s and 1860s most Jacobin republicans remained indefectibly attached to the defining principles of Jacobin citizenship: national sovereignty, political unity, and strong centralized government. It was only within this institutional framework that a virtuous republican citizenry could emerge. Indeed, only a strong state could prevent the subversion of the general interest by the self-regarding machinations of the provincial nobility and clergy.[37] Jacobin citizenship was in this sense an expression of vigilance against all those whose actions (consciously or otherwise) threatened to undermine the unitary and egalitarian promise of the French Revolution. These neo-Jacobin principles would find their culmination in the tragic apotheosis of the Paris Commune.[38]

## *The Federalist Response*

In opposition to this Jacobin perspective stood a democratic and self-governing culture, which sought to identify the appropriate sociological conditions for democratic governance. It was patriotic as opposed to nationalist,[39] and adopted a consensual approach in politics, in contrast to the conflictual postures of Jacobinism. It was pluralist, tolerant, and open to experimentation, in sharp distinction from the apparent Jacobin confidence in the certainty of its goals and values. This democratic and self-governing culture idealized the role of local institutions and associational life, and stressed the vital importance of the individual in the attainment of the republican ideal.[40]

Like Jacobinism, republican federalism was not a unitary doctrine. In the diverse and pluralistic intellectual atmosphere prevailing in the republican community during the 1860s, it could manifest itself in a variety of ideological forms: there were thus democratic, socialist, libertarian, and even communist forms of federalism.[41] However, all its advocates were united in their adherence to a number of core attitudes and principles. One of their defining characteristics was the very acceptance of the label 'Federalist', a concept which was proudly traced back to the revolutionary and even pre-revolutionary eras.[42] In addition to this common historical ancestry, all republican federalists were defined by the centrality they assigned to local liberty in their scheme of values. If all Jacobins were committed to the principles of unity and equality, federalists believed that decentralization was the most important organizing principle of social order, from which all other political values were deduced. Pierre-Joseph Proudhon, who was the recognized standard-bearer of the federalist cause within the republican movement, expressed this point simply: 'all my political views can be expressed in this single formula: political federation or decentralization'.[43]

The Proudhonian federation was a freely contracted alliance of communes, all of which enjoyed the full trappings of sovereignty within their respective spheres of jurisdiction. The only limits to a commune's autonomy were set by the natural interests of its neighbours. Potential conflicts of interest were to be settled by a framework of legal regulations and arbitration; the Second Empire's centralized and hierarchical system of local government was disdainfully rejected.[44] At the same time, federalist republicans were strongly critical of royalist schemes for provincial liberty, which smacked of clericalism and aristocratic paternalism.[45] But their sharpest rebuke was directed at the Jacobin project of defining and enforcing the values of the Republic from the centre. For the socialist republican Auguste Vermorel, such an approach represented an inversion of the appropriate relationship between the state and the localities:

In a Republic unity must not come from the centre and be imposed by an arbitrary order; it should result from the free will of groups and their harmonious adhesion to common principles, which are the guarantee of the greatness, independence, and prosperity of the nation. It is the communes and the departments that, instead of receiving their instructions from central government, should direct it. Central government, indeed, has no separate existence, independent of local groups, and it is in no way superior to these groups; it is only their delegate and representative, and in consequence, it is essentially their subordinate.[46]

This was a complete rejection of the intellectual foundations of Jacobinism. Human nature was seen as naturally benevolent, and not inherently flawed; the interests of the whole were not greater than those of particular groups of citizens; membership of a wider national entity had to be based on choice, not coercion; and power had to flow from the communes and departments up to the central state, not the reverse. Most fundamentally, the state had no justifiable moral or political purpose of its own; all its legitimate functions were merely expressions of the particular wills of local groups of citizens.[47] One could not assert a more contrary doctrine to the Jacobin faith in the transcendental authority of the state, and the subordination of the citizenry to its conception of the general will.

Contrary to the beliefs of many of their critics, federalists were also attached to the idea of national unity. In the words of Proudhon: 'unity in any political organism, is, at the risk of destruction, inviolable'.[48] But the unity celebrated by federalists was not the same as that proposed by the advocates of the 'one and indivisible Republic'. Federalist unity was based on communal liberty, political equality, and patriotic sentiment: its citizens were autonomous agents, who treated each other as equals, and were united in a common sense of identification with the values of the Republic.[49] Most importantly, this unity was founded on the non-coercive nature of the federalist contract, which was in itself a guarantee of its survival in the long term: 'the aggregation of parts, based on adhesion, voluntary alliance, and contractual commitment, is much more solid and generates a much more energetic form of patriotism than an annexation or absorption that is simply the product of coercion'.[50]

During the 1860s, a federalist culture thus came to flourish within the republican movement. Throughout the decade, a plethora of federalist and quasi-federalist schemes were advanced by democratic, socialist, and libertarian republican organizations in books, journals, and pamphlets.[51] This self-governing and democratic tendency represented an intellectual challenge to two phenomena which were often conflated in federalist writings: the ideological prominence of Jacobinism within the republican party, and the despotic centralism of the Second Empire. The intellectual potency of this culture came into full view after the collapse of the Second Empire, with the emergence of the Paris Commune (particularly in its early phase) and especially federalist republican movements in the provinces.[52]

But, as would be tragically confirmed by the ultimate fate of these movements in 1871, the federalist cause was also inhibited by a number of weaknesses. As a movement federalism was fragmented into diverse ideological undercurrents, each possessing different and sometimes conflicting aspirations, most notably on the questions of property ownership and redistribution. The death of Proudhon in 1865 deprived the federalist cause of its most articulate (if not necessarily coherent) advocate, and also created a growing fracture within the socialist movement between different conceptions of revolutionary change. Within the broader republican community, federalism (in its dominant Proudhonist form) was further undermined by two serious— and related—weaknesses. First, it still suffered from the pejorative connotations associated with the Girondin legacy; most notably, the fear of the disintegration of French national unity. That this apprehension remained so potent more than seventy years after the Revolution was a measure of the affective strength of the Jacobin myth in the historical memory of Second Empire republicans. But these fears of 'separatism' were also fuelled by the social exclusivism of the Proudhonists, typified in their conscious efforts to separate the working class from the bourgeois leadership of the republican party.[53] In a large part due to the influence of Proudhon, the federalist message thus came to be conflated with the doctrine that workers should seek political dissociation from the élites of the nation—a doctrine which, it should be added, was in complete contradiction with the unitary sociological assumptions of federalism.

From an ideological point of view, the principles of federalism coincided with the generous aspiration which was embodied in the republican spirit. In particular, they carried the republican demands for political liberty and self-government during the Second Empire to their logical conclusion. But there were important respects in which the federalist approach was problematic. Most critically, federalist writers tended to idealize the commune, and overestimate the extent to which republican values were already embraced by French society. A federation of communes, it will be remembered, was to be generated on the basis of the voluntary adhesion of its individual members. This acceptance, in turn, was meant to rest on a common identification with the principles and values of republicanism. However, the latter postulate represented a confusion of means with ends. It was one thing to hope that adhesion to the federation would facilitate the promotion of republican values in society. But it was quite another to expect a predominantly rural, largely illiterate, and deeply conservative society to embrace the principles of republican federalism even prior to the institutional emancipation of communes.

In addition to idealizing the commune, federalist discourse manifested a profound ambiguity over the question of freedom. In their critique of Jacobin, legitimist, and Bonapartist authoritarianism, federalist writers tended to project a liberal and pluralist conception of freedom. The state's imposition of its moral and political values on localities was thus presented as a violation of the rights of communes to exercise their free will as sovereign agents. The implications of this proposition were that the aspirations of communes were not one but multiple, and that this diversity was both a legitimate and valuable feature of the republican project. Yet at the same time, liberty was presented by some federalist writers as a goal to be 'realized'. In this conception—which was in fact closer to the classical republican notion of liberty—freedom was defined not in terms of acting according to one's will, but rather as a progression towards achieving a predetermined set of moral and political ends. From such a perspective, ethical and ideological diversity were not a manifestation of freedom, but unnecessary and potentially dangerous impediments to its realization. There was only a short step from this inference to the conclusion that these obstacles should be removed in the very name of freedom.

## Freedom and Order: Republican Municipalism

Pitched between the two extremes of Jacobinism and federalism stood the liberal republican doctrine of 'municipalism'.[54] Municipalism argued for the democratic self-government of the commune within the framework of a politically centralized state. Its synthetic doctrine consciously borrowed elements from the two other traditions. In common with Jacobin culture it affirmed the necessity of the principle of centralization, defined in terms of a unitary political, military, juridical, and financial framework for the nation.[55] But it also recognized with the federalists that the over-extension of state functions was damaging to the civic health of the polity. Just as importantly, it accepted the federalist intuition that democracy was not simply an institutional process, but a political culture. Fostering democratic institutions in France was therefore not just a matter of formally practising universal suffrage: it required establishing the conditions for the emergence of a patriotic, tolerant, enlightened, and participant political community.[56] The democratic self-government of the commune was seen as an essential instrument for achieving this new republican citizenship.

Municipalism was a liberal doctrine of territorial politics, whose key premiss was to reconcile the general interest with the particular claims of communes. The extent and limits of democratic self-government were thus outlined by the Kantian republican Jules Barni:

Instead of suffocating municipal freedoms under a system of administrative centralization, the republican state will favour their development. But at the same time it cannot suffer, under the pretext of communal independence, that the rights of citizens and the public interest should be endangered. At this double condition, the commune will be what it should be, and only what it should be: a free collectivity in a free society.[57]

The municipalist notion of self-government accordingly offered a distinct type of 'tempered' state: neither the passive and subordinate aggregation of local interests which was advocated by the federalists, nor the imperious and transcendental agent of popular sovereignty promoted by the Jacobins.[58] To the Jacobin (and imperial) notion of strong government, municipalists preferred the concept of state authority. In the words of Jules Simon: 'the more a state is free, the more its authority its limited; the more this authority is limited, the more indispensable it is that it should be strong'.[59] Strong authority could come through national political leadership, through the dissemination of moral and cultural values through the education system, and, as we shall see below, by means of a system of territorial government which reconciled order and liberty.

Municipalist doctrine highlighted the beneficial consequences of communal self-government for the development of a republican sense of citizenship. First, collective participation in local public life was seen as a crucial means of giving sense to the republican principle of political equality.[60] In addition, political education would be strengthened through the substantive interactions produced during the political process. As republican deputies in the legislative Corps repeatedly noted, an active municipal life would bring the citizenry into the public arena, and thus generate a healthy public spirit.[61] Furthermore, it would make individual citizens reason not only in terms of their own self-interest, but also in relation to the needs of others. Hence, in conclusion, the promotion of the spirit of fraternity,[62] and the logical progression from an attachment to the commune to the love of the *patrie*. Participation in the life of the city also performed an essential ideological objective in the republican project: fostering a sense of common identity which transcended class boundaries. This lyrical passage by Jules Ferry represented an idealized version of this notion of communal social solidarity:

Nothing is more conducive than an active and strong communal life to engendering this fusion of classes which is the goal of democracy, to shorten and attenuate the distances and inequalities between social groups by the indefinite availability of local functions and the exercise of offices that are not complicated but honoured and important; to make the rich more generous and the poor less bitter; and finally to awaken among the wider sections of society a feeling of political reality and respect for the law.[63]

Municipalist republicans were strongly committed to the preservation of 'order'. At the same time, it was an essential feature of their approach that territorial political stability could not be maintained by repressive and regulatory action alone, as had been attempted by the Second Empire. Furthermore, stability could come neither through the Jacobin deployment of the resources of centralist power, nor through the federalists' irresponsible and turbulent invocation of the absolute liberty of communes. Municipalism, in short, was an attempt to reconcile order and liberty. Jules Simon provided the formula which would later become one of the guiding themes of the opportunist Republic: 'the real party of order is the party of freedom'.[64]

A key element in maintaining republican order in the commune was the mayor, and here the municipalist school offered a notable contrast with both Jacobinism and Federalism. While recognizing the principle of the 'sovereignty'[65] of the commune, Jacobins circumscribed the mayor's attributions in the name of the general interest, while the latter extended them almost without limits by appealing to a radical notion of political liberty. The municipalist mayor preserved communal order by invoking the notion of authority—a key attribute in the municipalist scheme of values. The first magistrate's personal authority was derived not merely from his election by the commune, but from his social reputation and occupational respectability. The essential place of these values in the definition of municipalist authority is well represented in Eugène Pelletan's portrait of the ideal republican mayor, which strikingly anticipated the emergence of the Third Republic's *notable*:

This man, whoever he is, and who is generally a doctor, notary, businessman, veterinary, cultivator, farmer, a man of independent means, liberal by character, having no ambition other than to cultivate his assets and bring up his family; he has no need to seek influence, influence comes to him naturally; he attracts it and holds on to it; whenever advice is needed, everyone turns to him; and when there is a quarrel to be settled; he is the one chosen to adjudicate it.[66]

This passage represented the distinctive character of municipal republicanism in all its ambiguity. Municipalists sought to transcend the antithesis between federalist autonomy and Jacobin centralism by creating a communal polity which combined the best features of both political cultures, thus enabling the emergence of a type of republican citizenship which was national in substance but local in form. But this reconciliation of opposites was problematic. In the invocation of Ferry, as previously noted, class differences were to be eroded and even eliminated through an active municipalist culture. This was a formulation of the classic republican dream of a society in which social differences had no significant political consequences. Yet, paradoxically, municipalist republicanism also sought to recognize and even confirm existing class differences by appealing to the social authority of established elites. A political contradiction followed directly from this tension. On the one hand, municipalist republicanism aspired to create an active and participant political culture, in which citizens would treat each other as equals and settle their differences by the compromises of universal suffrage. On the other hand, and alongside this democratic framework, municipalists expected to promote a distinct bourgeois élite, which would owe its political fortunes mainly (if not exclusively) to the social esteem it enjoyed among the local population.

The latter point was clearly spelt out by Pelletan, who prefaced the remarks quoted above by acknowledging—in violation of the republican normative code—the pre-eminence of social distinction over democratic choice: 'one thing is often forgotten, which is that one does not create a mayor, a mayor *already exists*'.[67] In other words, the designation of the mayor by the commune merely involved giving legal expression to a form of 'natural' social leadership. But if this was true, universal suffrage was for the municipalists not merely a means of ensuring the social equality of citizens, as proclaimed in traditional republican doctrine, but also an instrument for legitimizing an emerging social elite. The opportunist Republic's celebration of the 'new social strata'[68] was thus fully anticipated in the social theory of municipalist republicanism.

## Conclusion

Reflecting on the defeat of French liberals in the 1869 legislative elections (and the general failure of Second Empire liberalism), Charles de Rémusat noted soberly: 'this fact and the failure of our opinion led many of us to judge that the Republic was much closer than many believed, indeed that this was the regime for which we had to prepare by assisting the Girondins in containing the Jacobin elements'.[69] With characteristic foresight Rémusat not only foresaw the advent of the Republic but also the triumph of a liberal form of republicanism, which indeed became the dominant political and

ideological force in France after 1877. Embedded within this liberal republicanism was a clear and coherent doctrine of citizenship, which has been
described here as 'municipalist'. As one of the leading republican newspapers
put it in 1871: 'it is in the interest of the Republic to establish independent
municipalities animated by a democratic spirit'.[70] This municipalist doctrine
was distinct both from the implacable centralization of Jacobinism and the
extreme decentralization favoured by the federalists; and as we have seen it
was fully formed well before the rise and fall of the Paris Commune in 1871.

Republican municipalism illustrates how rich a source the political culture
of the Second Empire can be for the historian of French political and territorial identity. But its triumph within the republican camp was also an illustra-
tion of broader changes within the body politic. Indeed by the late 1860s
France's political élites had come to a broadly convergent view of the core
principles of public life. This was expressed *inter alia* in a common emphasis
on a particular interpretation of the heritage of 1789; the importance of mass
participation in civic life; the inalienable quality of individual freedoms; the
rejection of bureaucratic oppression; and the need for a state which was
strong but politically accountable. This ideological convergence was manifested in a large measure through discussions of the territorial organization of
the French polity. There was a general measure of agreement over how municipal and departmental institutions should be organized and reformed, what
degree of freedom communes should be granted, and how the proper relationship between central and local government should be articulated. This
agreement demonstrated that a strong sense of what held France together as a
political collectivity was already present by the late 1860s. While this intellectual consensus was of course not uncontested, it suggests that France had
acquired a coherent notion of its core political characteristics long before the
epic battles over the definition of its 'republican' and 'national' identities in the
late nineteenth century. Thus, the Republic did not 'invent' modern French
citizenship, but merely gave a legal and political formulation to an existing
ideological consensus about the principles which should define membership
of the political community—a consensus which, as we have seen, was largely
fashioned under the Second Empire.

# Notes

1. For a recent discussion, see Renée Waldinger, Philip Dawson, and Isser Woloch
   (eds.), *The French Revolution and the Meaning of Citizenship* (Westport, Conn.:
   Greenwood Press, 1993).
2. See Pierre Rosanvallon, *L'État en France* (Paris: Seuil, 1990).
3. On the early Third Republic see Jean-Marie Mayeur, *Les Débuts de la Troisième*

*République* (Paris: Seuil, 1989); and Jérôme Grévy, *Les Opportunistes* (Paris: Perrin, 1998).

4. Pierre Rosanvallon, *Le Sacre du citoyen* (Paris: Gallimard, 1992). See also his *Le Peuple introuvable* (Paris: Gallimard, 1998).

5. Eugene Weber, *La Fin des terroirs* (Paris: Fayard, 1983), 691. For a recent response, see James Lehning, *Peasant and French: Cultural Contact in Rural France During the Nineteenth Century* (Cambridge: Cambridge University Press, 1995). On the broader historiographical debates about the origins of the 'French nation', see Suzanne Citron, *Le Mythe National: L'Histoire de France en question* (Paris: Éditions Ouvrières, 1989).

6. See Claude Nicolet, *L'Idée républicaine en France* (Paris: Gallimard, 1982).

7. The proximate intellectual origins of republican secularism are analysed in Katherine Auspitz, *The Radical Bourgeoisie: The Ligue de l'Enseignement and the Origins of the Third Republic 1866–1885* (Cambridge: Cambridge University Press, 1982).

8. On the 'mediating' influence of religion in the making of national identity in late 19th and early 20th century Brittany, see Caroline Ford, *Creating the Nation in Provincial France: Religion and Political Identity in Brittany* (Princeton, NJ: Princeton University Press, 1993).

9. Dominique Schnapper, *La Communauté des citoyens* (Paris: Gallimard, 1994).

10. See Yves Déloye, *École et citoyenneté: L'Individualisme républicain de Jules Ferry à Vichy* (Paris: Presses de la Fondation Nationale des Sciences Politiques, 1994).

11. 'Modern national citizenship was an invention of the French Revolution': Rogers Brubaker, *Citizenship and Nationhood in France and Germany* (Cambridge, Mass.: Harvard University Press, 1992), 35.

12. This argument is further developed in Sudhir Hazareesingh, *From Subject to Citizen: The Second Empire and the Emergence of Modern French Democracy* (Princeton, NJ: Princeton University Press, 1998).

13. The two classic accounts of Second Empire republicanism are Ilouda Tchernoff, *Le Parti républicain au coup d'état et sous le Second Empire* (Paris: Pedone, 1906); and Georges Weill, *Histoire du parti républicain 1814–1870* (Paris: Alcan, 1900).

14. Raymond Huard, *Le Mouvement républicain en Bas-Languedoc* (Paris: Presses de la Fondation Nationale des Sciences Politiques, 1992), 86.

15. The constitutional debates within the party are analysed in Charles Grangé, *Les Doctrines politiques du parti républicain à la fin du Second Empire* (Bordeaux: Cadoret, 1903).

16. See Paul Bethmont's speech at the legislative Corps, 8 Apr. 1867, in *Corps législatif, session 1867, compte-rendu analytique des séances* (Paris: Panckoucke, 1867), 270.

17. See the speech by Jules Favre on the question, in *Corps législatif, session 1870, compte-rendu analytique des séances* (Paris, 1870), ii, pp.157–159.

18. On the reform of the Parisian municipal system, see Jules Simon, *Paris aux Parisiens* (Paris: Degorce-Cadot, 1869).

19. For a republican satire on the prefects, see Edouard Ordinaire, *Du perfection-nement de la race préfectorale* (Paris: Voitelain, 1870).

20. See e.g. Edgar Quinet's proposals in May 1871, appendix X, in Edgar Quinet, *La République* (Paris: Dentu, 1872), 301–10.

21. A view taken by P. Benaerts *et. al.*, *Nationalité et nationalisme 1860–1878* (Paris: Presses Universitaires de France, 1968), 33.

22. On Jacobinism see Patrice Higonnet, *Goodness Beyond Virtue* (Harvard, 1998). For an overview of the fate of Jacobinism in the 19th century, see François Furet, *La Révolution 1770–1880* (Paris: Hachette, 1988); and 'Révolution française et

tradition jacobine', in Colin Lucas (ed.), *The French Revolution and the Creation of Modern Political Culture*, ii (Oxford: Pergamon, 1988). On Jacobin political philosophy, see Lucien Jaume, *Le Discours jacobin et la démocratie* (Paris: Fayard, 1989).

23. See e.g. Gustave Tridon, *Les Hébertistes*, in *Œuvres diverses de Gustave Tridon* (Paris: Allemane, 1891), 3–93.

24. These debates are analysed in François Furet, *La gauche et la Révolution au milieu du XIXième siècle* (Paris: Fayard, 1986).

25. René Arnaud, *La Deuxième République et le Second Empire* (Paris: Hachette, 1929), 273.

26. For a typical example, see Pascal Duprat, *De l'état, sa place et son rôle dans la vie des sociétés* (Brussels, 1852).

27. Étienne Vacherot, *La Démocratie* (Paris: Chamerot, 1860), p. xxii.

28. Ibid. 260.

29. Louis Blanc, 'De l'état', in *Histoire de la Révolution de 1848*, ii, appendix (Paris: Lacroix, 1870), 236.

30. Jules Labbé, *Le Manifeste de Nancy et la démocratie* (Paris: Dentu, 1865), 30.

31. Auguste Blanqui, *Critique sociale*, ii (Paris: Alcan, 1885), 116.

32. Vacherot, *La Démocratie* 224.

33. See *Un projet de décentralisation* (Nancy: Vagner, 1865).

34. Henri Marchegay, *La Liberté des proudhoniens, des libéraux, c'est l'esclavage* (Paris, n.d.), 6.

35. Labbé, *Le Manifeste de Nancy*, p.18.

36. Gustave Tridon, 'Gironde et Girondins', in *Œuvres diverses*, 130.

37. *Opinion du citoyen Paul Joly sur la décentralisation* (Tours: Ladevèze, 1866), 7.

38. On the Jacobin role in the Commune, and especially on Delescluze, see Igor Tchernoff, *L'Extrême-gauche socialiste-révolutionaire en 1870–1871* (Paris: Action Nationale, 1918), 7–10.

39. In the sense that its principles in defining membership of the national community were primarily civic and political, as opposed to cultural or ethnic. For further discussion of the contrast between patriotism and nationalism, see Maurizio Viroli, *For Love of Country: An Essay on Patriotism and Nationalism* (Oxford: Clarendon Press, 1995).

40. See e.g. Ernest Desmarest, *Les États provinciaux: Essai sur la décentralisation* (Paris: Librairie Internationale, 1868).

41. For an example of the latter, see Edouard de Pompéry, *La Question sociale dans les réunions publiques* (Paris: Degorce, 1869).

42. Pierre-Joseph Proudhon, *Du principe fédératif et de la nécéssité de reconstituer le parti de la révolution* (Paris: Dentu, 1863), 85–6. On the history of the federalist idea during the 1790s, see Mona Ozouf, 'Fédérations, fédéralisme et stéréotypes régionaux', in J. C. Boogman (ed.), *Federalism: History and Significance of a Form of Government* (The Hague: Martinus Nijhoff, 1980); Alan Forrest, 'Regionalism and Counter-Revolution', in Colin Lucas (ed.), *Rewriting the French Revolution* (Oxford: Clarendon Press, 1991); and François Furet and Mona Ozouf (eds.), *La Gironde et les Girondins* (Paris: Payot, 1991).

43. Proudhon, *Du principe fédératif*, p.116.

44. Pierre-Joseph Proudhon, *Essais d'une philosophie populaire* (Brussels, 1860), 82–3.

45. Louis Joly, *La Fédération, seule forme de décentralisation dans les démocraties* (Paris: Garnier, 1866), 28.

46. Auguste Vermorel, *Qu'est-ce que la République?* (Paris: Fayard, 1871), 25.

47. Paul David, *La Confédération française* (Périgueux: Dupont 1870), 4.

48. Pierre-Joseph Proudhon, *Théorie du mouvement constitutionnel* (Paris: Lacroix, 1870), 109.
49. For a curious neo-Proudhonian attempt to present federalism as part of the cultural heritage of the Latin race, see Louis-Xavier de Ricard, *Le Fédéralisme* (Paris: Sandoz, 1877).
50. Gustave Chaudey, *L'Empire parlementaire est-il possible?* (Paris: Le Chevalier, 1870), 48.
51. See e.g. *Esquisses d'institutions républicaines, par un des comités insurrectionnels de Paris* (Brussels, 1862), 73.
52. On the Communes in Paris and the provinces, see *Les Révolutions du XIXeme siècle* (Paris: EDHIS, 1988), vii and viii.
53. On this theme see 'Manifeste dit des soixante: Candidatures ouvrières' (1863), in *Les Révolutions du XIXieme siècle*, iv 48; Pierre-Joseph Proudhon, *De la capacité politique des classes ouvrières* (Paris: Dentu, 1865), 440; and Justin Dromel, *Bourgeois et socialistes* (Paris: Le Chevalier, 1869).
54. A concept used by Jules Ferry in his letter to the signatories of the 1865 Nancy Manifesto. See Paul Robiquet (ed.), *Discours et opinions de Jules Ferry*, i (Paris: Armand Colin, 1893), 558.
55. Alfred Naquet, *La République radicale* (Paris: Germer Baillière, 1873), 138–9.
56. Pierre Lanfrey, *Chroniques Politiques 1860–1865*, i (Paris: Charpentier, 1883), 151–2.
57. Jules Barni, *Manuel Républicain* (Paris: Germer Baillière, 1872), 23–5.
58. A vision later developed in Gustave de Molinari, *La République tempérée* (Paris: Garnier, 1875).
59. Jules Simon, *La Liberté*, i (Paris: Hachette, 1859), 263.
60. François Henri René Allain-Targé, *La République sous l'Empire* (Paris: Grasset, 1939), 104.
61. See e.g. the speech by Magnin, 8 Apr. 1867, in *Corps législatif, session 1867, compte-rendu analytique des séances* (Paris: Panckoucke, 1867), 272.
62. Jacobins such as Vacherot argued that 'fraternity' should be excluded from the core values of republicanism because it was a 'sentiment and not a right' (in *La Démocratie*, 9). But most municipalists insisted on the centrality of the concept. See e.g. Jules Simon, *Le Devoir* (Paris: Hachette, 1854), 320; Jules Barni, *La Morale dans la démocratie*, 2nd edn. (Paris: Alcan, 1885), 9–20.
63. Jules Ferry, letter to the authors of the Nancy Manifesto (1865), in *Discours et opinions de Jules Ferry*, i 559.
64. Simon, *La liberté*, ii 270.
65. See *L'Avenir national* (24 June 1870).
66. Eugène Pelletan, *Droits de l'homme* (Paris: Pagnerre, 1867), 282.
67. Ibid. 281; my emphasis.
68. *Couches nouvelles*—a term used by Gambetta in his Grenoble speech in Sept. 1872; quoted in Pierre Barral, *Les fondateurs de la Troisième République* (Paris: Armand Colin, 1968), 232.
69. Charles de Rémusat, *Mémoires de ma vie* (Paris: Plon, 1967 edn.) v. 251.
70. *La République française* (23 November 1871).

# 10

## The History of Human Rights in Germany
### David Southern

### Human Rights

The history of the twentieth century was characterized by what has been called the struggle between empirical and liberal democracy on one hand, and totalitarian messianic democracy on the other.[1] The contrast goes back to the French Revolution, when ideology entered into politics in the form of the reconstruction of society from top to bottom on an ideal basis. One philosophy regards politics as 'a contrivance of human wisdom to provide for human wants' (Burke, *Reflections on the Revolution in France* (1790), 88) and seeks to reconcile the inherently conflicting claims of the individual and those of the community without postulating some overall conflict-free system. The other sees politics as having some absolute purpose, namely, the collective and compulsory pursuit and attainment of an ideal order in which the claims of the individual and the claims of the community converge. The one espouses diversity and is relativist; the other seeks unanimity and is absolutist. The loftiness of their aims justified the idealists in the use of coercion to achieve them, so that, in Dostoevsky's phrase, beginning in a theory of total liberty they ended in a theory of total despotism.

Human rights stand at the heart of the liberal, empirical, as against the metaphysical, totalitarian view of politics. This theme has constituted the essence of Peter Pulzer's influence as a scholar and teacher. In Germany what came to the fore was the totalitarianism of the right rather than the left. National Socialist ideology defined individuals not by reference to the collective entities of state or class, but in terms of race. For historical determinism it substituted a preordained struggle for existence in which the strong would dominate the weak permanently and for ever. This concept of politics was given characteristic expression in the idiosyncratic and inflammatory language of Nietzsche, who propagated as a historical fact the devaluation of all values. The originality of Peter Pulzer's studies of anti-Semitism in Germany and central Europe has been in his detection of the emergence of a new, racial, ideological anti-Semitism towards the end of the nineteenth century, which had no connection with earlier, religious forms of anti-Semitism and which formed a potent vehicle for the passionate discontent which the processes of modernization evoked.

In Germany in the nineteenth century the forces of constitutional liberalism were always influential, but never succeeded in overcoming the dominance of autocratic conservatism and the more sinister, revolutionary-conservative elements which it increasingly attracted. The contrast was expressed as being between the ideas of Western Europe and the German spirit. Before 1918 the rivalry between these two incompatible concepts of politics in Germany was always endemic. In the Weimar Republic, it became epidemic and ended in the National Socialist dictatorship, which almost brought an end to Germany. The history of human rights in Germany has therefore been chosen as the subject of this chapter, as a counter-balance to the violent irrationalism which almost engulfed it.

## The Source of Basic Rights

What are the origins and source of human rights in Germany? The ultimate source lies in what Ernst Troeltsch called 'the ideas of natural law and humanity in world politics'.[2] In that sense basic rights derive from pre-positive legal norms, which are binding on the state itself. The immediate contemporary source is the code of basic rights (*Grundrechte*) set out in the Basic Law (*Grundgesetz*) of 23 May 1949, which provides the constitution both of the West German state established in 1949 from the Western zones of occupation and the united Germany established in 1990.

The basic rights are not self-interpreting or self-enforcing, but depend very much on the meaning and role which the judges of the Federal Constitutional Court ascribe to them. Hence the study of basic rights also requires consideration of the institutions established by the constitution, in particular the parliament (Bundestag) and Federal Constitutional Court. Whereas basic rights provisions essentially mark out the limits of parliament's powers, and say negatively what is not law, the Federal Constitutional Court, having regard to the increasingly social character of basic rights, has gone further and said positively what the law should be.

Positive law requires by definition a political legislator, who is sovereign to the extent that he is not bound by a higher order of norms derived from natural law or a paramount law of the constitution. It was Hobbes who observed that, as soon as jurists take it upon themselves to start interpreting laws, they attack the sovereignty of the state.[3] He was of course correct. The reaction of sovereigns to the interpretative activities of jurists have been various. Justinian forbade commentaries on the Digest, overlooking the fact that the Digest itself was based on commentaries on older laws.[4] When the first commentary on the French Civil Code appeared shortly after the Code itself, Napoleon observed with resignation: 'Mon Code est perdu.'[5]

Underlying the debate on basic rights is the old question of whether reason or authority is the source of law. Hobbes said the answer was authority (*auctoritas*). However, authority is not the same thing as power, implying as it does some sort of external legitimation. Hobbes essentially hedged his bets, leaving some space for personal autonomy. In Hobbes the idea of a sovereign legislature, which cannot act except through the medium of positive law, is a critical step in the evolution of the nineteenth-century rule-of-law constitutional state (*Rechtsstaat*). Hence he was rather the begetter of the *Rechtsstaat* than of Carl Schmitt's decisionist state theory—the dogma of a state whose only essential role consists in crushing opponents at home and abroad.[6] On this view, what matters is the fact of a decision, not its content.[7] Law ceases to exist as a distinct category of intellectual and practical activity. It is the metaphysical view of politics in its application to law.

## The Legal Enactment of Human Rights

Savigny observes that 'law has a double life, first as part of the whole national life, secondly as a special science in the hands of jurists . . . we call the connection of law with the general national life the political aspect, the separate academic life of law the technical aspect'.[8] Basic rights can belong to both spheres. To give basic rights greater certainty and security, they may be embodied in written, legal, constitutional form. Such provisions require a statutory basis (*Vorbehalt des Gesetzes*) and have to be implemented by ordinary laws. Basic rights enacted in this form in no way qualify the precedence of ordinary laws, and are essentially no different from laws on drains and dentists. For this reason the standard commentary on the Weimar Constitution referred to the basic rights provisions as 'having no content' (*leerlaufend*).[9]

The legal implementation of human rights has played an essential role in the realization of German democracy. The revival and development of German democracy after 1945 have been due in significant measure to the success of formal constitutional arrangements. While the main focus of the Basic Law of 1949 remains political institutions and their relationship to each other and to citizens, the dimension of basic rights (*Grundrechte*) has consistently grown in importance. German law, and German society as a whole, have become human rights-based systems.

This topic reaches back to the Enlightenment and earlier. Four essential reasons may be detected for the primacy now attached to human rights.

1. The reaction against National Socialism, whose horrors continue to traumatize.

2. The Treaty of Westphalia—the outcome of the religious wars of 1618–48—established the practice of safeguarding by international treaty the rights of minorities, in particular the right of religious freedom and the rights of aliens. This in turn gave currency to the notion that, if a freedom was to be capable of effective exercise, it had to be written down somewhere in some legal form.

3. There has been the concept beloved of jurisprudents of the legal system as a hierarchy of norms, having an existence distinct from their creators. Kelsen's *Grundnorm* is the characteristic modern expression of this approach.

4. Lutheranism attached central importance to the written word, which assumed a secularized form as a code of basic rights.

Human rights—variously called the rights of man, fundamental freedoms, basic rights—may be a static or a dynamic concept. The history of human rights in Western societies has broadly followed two phases. In the first (moral) phase, human rights serve as the banner of the cause of freedom and liberty. In the second (more technical) phase, when freedom and liberty have been broadly attained, they are refined to advance and protect interests of particular minorities and more generally to elevate things which may be merely desirable (for example, a proper level of social welfare for the disabled) into constitutionally guaranteed rights. Alternatively, in the liberal phase, basic rights are concerned with the classic, 'negative' freedoms of the individual against the state. In the second, social phase, basic rights become more concerned with assuring to the individual and groups of individuals social and economic entitlements forming part of the legal order of society.

This process can have some unexpected consequences. For example, a German tax official regarded it as unfair that he should declare his bank interest for tax purposes, while 80 per cent of his fellow citizens unaccountably omitted to do so. The problem was approached on the basis that this state of affairs violated the taxpayer's basic right of equality. The Federal Constitutional Court obliged the Federal government to introduce a withholding tax on bank interest.[10] This in turn caused capital flight (principally to neighbouring Luxembourg) and significantly increased the financing costs of German unification, as money exported out of Germany was lent back into Germany at an additional interest cost. While the issue did not fit within the classical categories of human rights, the case illustrates that human rights have an in-built tendency to expand. The categories of human rights are not closed, and as the German example shows they are capable of an ever greater and more nuanced refinement and elaboration.

For Marxists it has been a commonplace to say that human rights were merely bourgeois rights, a function of capitalist society with no inherent content or claim to special status. Certainly, the evolution of liberal rights into social rights shows the inherent fluidity of the concept. Politics is about how to adjust the claims of the individual to those of society. This involves adjusting the rights and claims of individuals against each other, as well as addressing and defining the relationship between the individual and the state. The problem of reconciling the enjoyment of those attending a noisy party with the lack of enjoyment of those in the vicinity and not attending has nothing to do with human rights and is purely a question of social regulation. The open-ended nature of human rights carries with it the danger of trivialization.

While human rights were part of the essential intellectual equipment of the Enlightenment, and their modern history begins with the American and French Revolutions, the ways in which human rights have been conceived and implemented in different societies have not been uniform. The history of human rights in Germany constitutes an important dimension in the liberalization of German political culture, and democratization in Germany more generally.

The proclamation of human rights was part of the nineteenth-century revolt against particularist absolutism. Human rights were a prominent feature of German constitutionalism from 1815 onwards. In the Weimar Republic, the definition of human rights underwent a shift from liberal rights of freedom to social rights. In the Federal Republic human rights, in the form of basic rights, have been a dominant feature in the political and legal system, so that in human rights—as in the spheres of the economy, industrial relations and federalism—one may aptly speak of a German model.

In truth, the legal enactment of human rights does not as such constitute new rights but rather recognizes existing rights. A code of basic rights embodies part of the essential consensus on which democratic government is based. It represents a state of affairs which society has attained, though also prefiguring future developments. The legal implementation of human rights is in a sense superfluous, because if a society respects human rights in general, they will exist as real constraints on and guides for political action. If a society does not respect them, formal enactments simply serve as a cloak for despotism. Codes of basic rights having the status of formal law are therefore in the main declaratory, not constitutive. They reflect values and constraints already present in society. They do not as such create new legal rules. Though conducted in the language of morality, problems of human rights in practice may resolve themselves into familiar problems of legal and legislative technique.

Law is a kind of *bureau de change* between power and morality, the resultant coinage being something which does not rest in coercion or morality alone (though these remain important elements) but which has its own logic, autonomy, and integrity. The development of German democracy has seen the growth of respect for the integrity of the legal process as a value in itself. While one of the key events of German history was Luther's defiance of the Roman Catholic Church and its temporal establishment, at subsequent crises in German history—as Peter Pulzer has pointed out in his works—the defective development of a civil society in Germany was revealed by the absence of individuals able to take a stand against the political system on the basis of some alternative set of values which attracted a wider public resonance. When Bismarck imposed taxes unconstitutionally in 1861, no Prussian Hampden emerged to refuse to pay taxes. When the Nazis took power in 1933, the liberal *Rechtsstaat*—to the extent that it had survived the period of presidential rule in 1930–33—vanished noiselessly. Carl Schmitt's extraordinary justification of the Nazi actions on 30 June 1934—'The Führer protects the law'—offers the clearest example of the misuse and hollowing out of the concepts and vocabulary of law by its most influential exponents long before later horrors were unleashed.[11]

Before the Bismarck era, in the almost complete absence of central political institutions, the legal profession took it upon itself to bring some rationality to the chaotic and fragmented state of government in Germany and to express, through legal and constitutional documents, some shared social vision. Technicians could achieve much, but, as the outcome of the revolutions of 1848 revealed, without decisive political power behind it, legal reform could only accomplish limited results.

## *Human Rights in West European Thought*

As the period of National Socialism showed, the emergence of Germany as a human rights state had no inevitability about it. The central thesis of Troeltsch was that West European and German thought and ideas had developed along different lines, and it was only in the 1920s that they began to coalesce. The secularized natural law of Western Europe he defined in these terms:[12]

the movements opposed to absolutism sought comfort and countenance in ideas of inherent and indestructible human rights which were based upon the divinely appointed order of the Universe . . . the doctrine of inherited sin has crumbled away; and its place has been taken by a convinced optimism in regard to human nature and reason and a belief that, if left to themselves, men will follow the lead of their natural interest in the community, and will solve every problem rationally by the standard of utility . . . the idea of a steadily moving Progress, and the ideal of a rational self-development of society and the State, evolved from the old and predominantly conservative Natural Law of the church . . . with all its zest for progress, the theory still remains moderate: it retains a conservative and bourgeois character.

Of the influence of Lutheranism, he continued:[13]

The intellectual thought of Germany originally shared in this general system of ideas
. . . an excess of emphasis on original sin, and a corresponding excess of emphasis on
mere authority . . . invested Lutheran doctrine with a peculiar tinge of authoritarian
conservatism . . . The result was that, for practical purposes, the natural-law ideas of
western Europe only affected Germany in the sadly attenuated form of enlightened
despotism.

The Romantic Movement finally turned authoritarian conservatism into
revolutionary conservatism:[14]

The peculiarity of German thought . . . is primarily derived from the Romantic
Movement. Romanticism . . . is a revolution against . . . the whole of the mathe-
matico-mechanical spirit of science in western Europe, against a concept of Natural
Law which sought to blend utility with morality, against the bare abstraction of a
universal and equal humanity . . . Romanticism pursued an increasingly self-conscious trend in the opposite direction of a conservative revolution.

The consequences were that law was demoralized, in the sense of being
deprived of any connection with ethics and morality. Law was bereft of its
universalizing concept, and became something particular and positive, which
belonged only to a given time and place. Morality became wholly a matter of
the inner self. The blame for the direction which romanticism took into political metaphysics he blamed on three figures: Bismarck, Nietzsche, and Marx.
The result in Germany was Troeltsch concluded, in an astonishingly prophetic
phrase, 'to brutalize romance and to romanticize cynicism' (*die Romantik zu
brutalisieren und den Zynismus zu romantisiern*).[15]

   Thus those who in the early nineteenth century and Weimar period wanted
to make Germany more internationalist, more outward-looking, with a
greater focus on human rights, were going against powerful grains of German
development and German society. The transformation of human rights, from
a programmatic aspiration to a social reality mirrored in technical legal
provisions, has been part of the growth of German democracy and its revital-
ization after 1945.


## Law as a System of Norms


Two starting-points may be selected for the process: Montesquieu's *L'Esprit
des Lois* (1748) and the German Federal Acts of 8 June 1815. Montesquieu put
forward the idea of law as a system of norms, that is, rules which were rational
in that they had an identifiable content and were general in their application:
'Laws are relationships, which necessarily result from the nature of things.'
What he put forward was the idea of a natural law based on reason, rather
than divine revelation. As Maine somewhat unkindly put it, 'the philosophers

of France, in their eagerness to escape from . . . a superstition of the priests, flung themselves headlong into a superstition of the lawyers'.[16] In Germany Montesquieu's ideas were domesticated by Feuerbach. He took the view that statutes only had the quality of law if they corresponded to some a priori rationality.[17]

On this view, positive law was not a product of the state. On the contrary, the state was a product of positive law. It was for this reason that codes of human rights were regarded as declaratory in function: they said what the law was—they did not say what was law. As the founders of the American constitutionalism put it in the Declaration of Independence (1776), 'We hold these truths to be self-evident, that all men are . . . endowed . . . with certain inalienable rights'. Basic rights were essentially conceived as a limitation on the power of the legislature, but limitations which the legislature would self-evidently respect. The psychological basis of legal positivism was the assumption of a preordained harmony between power and law. Goethe quintessentially expressed this rationalist view in the line: 'Und nur das Gesetz uns Freiheit geben kann' (And only law can give us freedom). For all his authoritarian bias, there were echoes in this of Luther's formula that truth makes us free. The role of formal constitutions and codes of basic rights was not to produce that equilibrium but to mirror and maintain it.

## German Constitutionalism

The French occupation of Germany gave German romanticism its anti-Western impetus. At the same time, with the Napoleonic conquest, the idea of a rational law embodied in codified form was given a new dimension. Notwithstanding their aim of re-establishing pre-democratic, legitimist, particularist forms of government, the Federal Acts of 1815, by which the Vienna peace-makers created the German Federation (*Bund*), also broke new ground.[18] By a resolution of 8 July 1820 the Federal Acts were declared to constitute the 'basic law' (*Grundgesetz*) of the German Bund. Article 13 of the Federal Acts required each of the federal states to introduce a 'representative constitution' (*landständische Verfassung*).[19] What this meant was a matter for the rulers of the individual states. They looked to a constitutional document to create a sense of unity and statehood where there was little sense of either. The earliest constitution was introduced in the dukedom of Nassau in 1814. In 1816 Grand Duke Karl August of Sachsen-Weimar followed this example. In 1818–19 Bavaria, Württemberg, and Baden also received written constitutions.[20]

None of these documents or the institutions which they embodied could be regarded as liberal. Their basis was the monarchic principle. They represented a concession by the monarch with regard to the exercise of his unlimited powers. The pre-existent authority of the monarch remained anterior and superior to the constitutional act. The south German constitutions expressed the classic form of the monarchic principle, by proclaiming that the ruler 'unites in himself all the rights of state authority and exercises them within the limits set by the constitution'.

The introduction of constitutions raised the question, to whom or what were official oaths of loyalty to be sworn? It is worth remembering that, from July 1934, Hitler introduced a personal oath of loyalty to himself. The real difficulties of conscience which this caused to the 20 July 1944 conspirators, who rationally knew that the regime had no claim to loyalty or respect of any kind, are difficult to understand, but testimony to the power of this symbol.

Under some pre-March 1848 constitutions, the official took an oath of loyalty to the constitution. This caused alarm to upholders of the established order. In Article 24 of the Vienna Protocols of 12 June 1834, the rulers agreed that under no circumstances were members of the armed services to take such an oath: they would swear fealty to the person of the ruler. In the Hannover constitutional crisis of 1837, caused by Duke Ernst August's revocation of the 1834 constitution, the seven Göttingen professors who protested against this action—including to their eternal credit the Grimm brothers—based their protest on the fact that they had taken an oath to the constitution. In dismissing them Ernst August observed that professors, whores, and female dancers could be obtained anywhere, if you just offered a few more talers.[21]

As the Hannover example showed, once constitutions were introduced they took on a life of their own. Though the representative basis and powers of the legislative assemblies was minimal, the longing for political freedom which these assemblies expressed and generated took in wider circles and strengthened the call for a general, German parliament, as part of the powerful but imprecise aspiration which Fallersleben encapsulated in the lapidary formula 'Einigkeit und Recht und Freiheit für das deutsche Vaterland' (Unity and justice and freedom for the German fatherland). The revolutions of 1848 and the Paul's church constitution of 1849 were the immediate outcome of this movement. Subsequent history showed how weary and indirect were the paths into which these forces might wander or be diverted.

The codes of human rights which these constitutions contained were designed to put down a marker for the future, and expressed the assumption that the legislature would only operate within the framework of the human rights set out in the constitution, so that its measures would conform with an overall standard of rationality. The Frankfurt constituent assembly was actually called into existence by a resolution of the Bund of 30 March 1848, and directly elected on an all-German basis. This of itself was a remarkable gesture towards popular representation, and indeed thereafter the democratic credentials of national German parliaments were invariably in advance of their political powers and influence. Moreover, until 1918 the Reichstag operated alongside state parliaments with largely plutocratic and unrepresentative franchises. Unlike the state constitutions issued after 1815, the Reich Constitution of 28 March 1849 was the product of sustained debate and discussion in a deliberative assembly, democratically legitimated and motivated by a high sense of political and national duty. The constitution sought to impose a set of Reich institutions on the existing fabric of the forty-one individual states of the Bund, whose existence was not to be altered, further than was necessary to accommodate the extra layer of governmental institutions. The most radical provision of the constitution was for the election on a democratic basis of a national parliament (§94). Part VI was headed: 'The basic rights of the German people' (§§130–89).[22] Capital and corporal punishment were to be abolished (§139). While many of the basic rights provisions were related to circumstances of the time, for example, matters relating to hunting rights and patrimonial jurisdiction, some of the articles—such as on the freedom of teaching and research (§152)—have reappeared almost unaltered in successive German constitutions and are to be found in the Basic Law (art. 5(3)).

## The Weimar Constitution

Until 1918 constitutionalism in Germany was identified with the absence of parliamentary government, not its presence. As Thomas Mann put it, before he became the Thomas Mann of the *Magic Mountain*:[23] 'I remain deeply convinced that the German people will never be able to love political democracy . . . and that the much despised *Obrigkeitsstaat* is and remains both the appropriate form of state for the German people and what people essentially want.'

A state with a parliamentary government had only emerged in Germany after the First World War under the conditions of organized capitalism, with elements of a welfare state based on mass democracy. 'Classical basic rights', it has been said, 'have an inherent tendency to protect the status quo.'[24] Though plausible, this is more easily asserted than demonstrated, and can easily be turned into the 'all human rights are bourgeois rights' argument. Social-democratic theorists in the Weimar period wanted to combine the heritage of civil rights and legal and political equality with a concern for social welfare and justice, by supplementing liberal freedom rights with social basic rights.[25] The traditional, liberal type of basic rights based on negative liberty were no longer regarded as adequate, and needed to be extended to found a claim to material benefits. Obstacles must be removed not only to actual, but to potential choices. Hugo Preuss, 'the father of the Weimar constitution', distrusted such provisions because they were felt to lack normative quality, and so dilute the force of the constitution as such. Accordingly, the basic rights were placed at the end of the constitution. Every interest group was able to put down a marker of its claims, so that the basic rights section became a kind of cornucopia poured out over the German people. They enumerated not only the negative freedoms of the citizen—freedom of speech, freedom of the person—but also rights and empowerments attributable to the social and political order. The Reich was to act as arbitrator in labour disputes, to ensure for workers 'a general minimum of social rights' (art. 162); every German had a moral duty to work and was to have the possibility of earning his living (art. 163); the self-employed middle class was to be 'fostered by legislation and the executive and protected against over-burdening and exploitation' (art. 164).

According to the liberal theory, basic rights were 'subjective public rights', that is, rights vested in individuals by public law and giving them a claim against the state. Thoma took this further and classified the claims which the individual might assert against the state by virtue of the basic rights provisions of the constitution under three headings:[26]

(*a*)  freedom rights, deriving from the negative status of the individual being entitled to freedom from the state;

(*b*)  participation rights, that is, the right to take part in the affairs of the state, for example, by being a candidate for election and having voting rights (these derived from the positive status of the individual to exercise his freedoms);

(*c*)  positive rights, that is, the right to be provided with economic and social benefits by the state, for example, a system of public education (these derived from the right of the individual to be enabled to enjoy in fact his abstract entitlements).

It was (*c*) which gave the Weimar basic rights a marked and novel social dimension. Carl Schmitt also adopted a threefold definition of the basic rights as (*a*) freedom rights, (*b*) guarantees of institutions, for example, of marriage and the family, and (*c*) institutional guarantees, that is, of conditions necessary for the effective enjoyment of basic rights, such as full employment and public education.[27] E. R. Huber wrote that the basic rights had ceased to be liberal freedom rights alone, which were declaratory in effect, but embodied objective elements of social order which were conferred by the state:[28]

All true basic rights of the liberal epoch are . . . subjective rights of the individual who is subject to the authority of the state. The basic rights of the Reich Constitution are to a large extent not in essence subjective rights but in the first place public principles . . . subjective public rights of the liberal epoch are recognised, not conferred. They represent the confirmation and affirmation of the natural freedom of the individual which exists before and outside the state . . . Out of the individual freedoms the basic rights have now developed into basic elements of the public ordering of the community.

The main difficulty about giving basic rights this social dimension in the Weimar period was that political direction was too weak and divided, and the material resources were simply not there, to turn these aspirations into reality. In the words of the proverb, 'If there is nothing there, even the emperor has forfeited his rights' (*Wenn nichts gibt, hat auch der Kaiser seine Rechte verloren*).

## The Judicial Power of Review

The logical outcome of the new dimension given to basic rights by the Weimar Constitution would have been a judicial power to review statute to ensure its constitutionality. The 1871 Reich Constitution had established the para-mountcy of Reich law over laws passed by the Federal states (art. 2). The *Reichsgericht* under the 1871 constitution confined its scrutiny to reviewing the validity of administrative decrees and state laws which trespassed on the domain of Reich legislation.[29] The enactment of the Weimar Constitution resurrected the question of how the supremacy of the constitution was to be vindicated: who was to be 'the guardian of the constitution'?

The change of state-form brought a reappraisal of the relationship of the courts and the political system. Hugo Preuss had long argued that the *Rechtsstaat* should be crowned by the judicial power of review of statute.[30] The Weimar National Assembly did not resolve the question. On the political right Carl Schmitt argued against the idea of making a court responsible for safeguarding the observance of the constitution.[31] The true guardian of the constitution was, he said, the Reich President, as the embodiment of Benjamin Constant's fourth power, *un pouvoir neutre qui regne et ne gouverne pas* (a neutral power which reigns but does not rule).[32]

Kelsen described a constitutional court with a power of review as a 'negative legislature': like a legislature, such a court would produce norms, but only in a negative sense. It would say what was not law, not what law was. Schmitt's argument he denounced as 'the apotheosis of Article 48'.[33] This was an accurate characterization, because what Schmitt actually did was to provide the legal justification for the triumph of irresponsible government based on the exercise of the President's powers under article 48 of the constitution in the period 1930–33. This paved the way for the Nazi take-over, which in turn fired Schmitt—in his incarnation as a latter-day Nietzsche—with admiration for successful violence and the practice of cruelty.

In the Reichsgericht the German Supreme Court in Leipzig, the existence of such a power was indirectly asserted, but it was never established in the Weimar period.[34] Walter Simons, the President of the Reichsgericht from 1922 to 1929, believed that a constitutional court 'formed a necessary counterweight to the idea of popular sovereignty . . . In a republic, governed by parliament . . . the peril exists that, without such a counterweight, under the influence of ephemeral opinions and political passions, quickly changing minorities bring disorder and insecurity into the organic development of the state form'.[35]

# The Rejection of Positivism

The Weimar period was characterized in public law by the conflict over method and direction between the proponents of the old and the new schools of constitutional law.[36] However, the division between constitutional lawyers did not coincide with political divisions, supporters of a liberal and a revolutionary conservative position respectively being found on both sides of the legal divide. Hence the wholesale failure of German law and the German legal system in the Nazi period to do anything to uphold the basic decencies of organized society cannot be attributed to doctrinal or dogmatic shortcomings alone.

Gustav Radbruch—a scholar of impeccable liberal convictions who briefly served as SPD Reich Minister of Justice in 1921–2 and again in 1923—set the fashion for the traditional, positive school of constitutional law. In his *Rechtsphilosophie* in the 1920s he had adopted the orthodox liberal position of positing a sharp divide between legality and morality: [37]

The judge, who is subject to the interpretation and service of the positive legal order, must only have regard to the doctrine of legal validity, which identifies the meaning and claim to authority of the law with its real effect. For the judge it is his professional duty to implement the will of the law striving to take effect, and to sacrifice his own sense of justice to the authoritative command of the law, only to ask what is lawful, and never to ask what is just . . . We scorn the man of religion who preaches against his conscience, but we honour the judge, who does not let himself be diverted from his fidelity to the law by his own conflicting sense of justice.

The point being made was sensible. However, it was expressed in such hyperbolic terms as virtually to mean: the greater the injustice, the greater the legality. In the wake of National Socialism, Radbruch recognized that a line had to be drawn somewhere. Authority had to be kept at bay. In a highly influential article in 1946 he observed:[38]

Positivism in truth—with its slogan 'Law is law'—rendered lawyers defenceless against laws of arbitrary and criminal content . . . It may be that the conflict between justice and legal certainty can be resolved on the basis that positive law—expressed in written form and backed by authority—must still be given precedence, even if its content is unjust and serves no useful purpose, unless the contradiction between the positive

law and justice is of such a degree, that the law as 'unjust law' must yield to justice . . .
In the light of the experiences of the last twelve years we cannot overlook what fearful
perils for legal certainty accompany the concept of 'legal injustice'. We must hope that
such injustice will remain a once and for all error and confusion of the German people. Above all else, we must protect ourselves against the re-emergence of such a state
based on injustice by overcoming legal positivism, which paralysed the ability to resist
the abuses of National Socialist legislation.

Rabruch's analysis, though noteworthy because of the recantation of his
former views, was superficial. In the first place, as the *Richtungsstreit* (the conflict over future direction) had shown, the views of jurists were not uniform.
Goldschmidt, Triepel, Marschall von Bieberstein, and many others all proclaimed in the Weimar period that laws were not holy, only justice: 'The state
does not create justice; the state creates laws, and both state and law are subordinate to justice.'[39] These views were expressed with special prominence in
relation to the revaluation-question—the attempt to compensate those who
had lost all their financial assets in the hyperinflation of 1922–3—and in
particular the famous decision of the Fifth Civil Senate of the Reichsgericht of
28 November 1923, that a papermark mortgage could not be redeemed by
paying the specified amount of papermarks.[40] Moreover, the 'justice not law'
approach had also become prominent before the First World War, in the Free
Law Movement of Ernst Fuchs and Hermann Kantorowicz.[41]

Secondly, among constitutional lawyers Rudolf Smend argued that, however appropriate literalism might be in the application of laws below constitutional level, when one reached the level of the constitution other factors
must come into play. A constitution was a 'value-order' (*Wertordnung*). Its aim
is to bind together—integrate—society. [42] Thirdly, according to the thesis of
Ernst Fraenkel, which Martin Broszat has refined and developed, the Nazi
system was characterized by two states, one a rational bureaucratic order,
which existed alongside a permanent dictatorship based on unlimited powers.
Fraenkel called these the 'Normative state' and the 'Prerogative state'.[43]
Fourthly, the real problem with National Socialism was not its exploitation of
positive law but its rejection of all law as an instrument and framework of
government.[44]

## The Basic Law

Arnold Brecht had written in 1945:[45] 'It would be advisable . . . for the new
German constitutional order to contain certain sacrosanct principles and
standards which could not be abolished or suspended by emergency decrees
of any parliamentary or plebiscitary majorities, either directly or indirectly.'
Unlike the Weimar National Assembly, which put together the Weimar

Constitution on the basis of Preuss's draft, the Parliamentary Council which met in Bonn from July 1948 to May 1949 to draft the Basic Law on the basis of the Herrenchiemsee draft was in general agreement that the new basic law should contain a basic rights section binding on all organs of government. In the classic language of natural law, article 1(2) says that 'inviolable and inalienable human rights (*Menschenrechte*) are the foundation of all human community'. Article 1(3) states: 'The following basic rights shall bind the legislature, the executive, and the judiciary'. Article 2(1) declares and establishes as the key material right, the right to free self-fulfilment, which the Federal Constitutional Court has framed as a general right to personal freedom. In Isaiah Berlin's formulation, 'it is a form of secularised Protestant individualism, in which the place of God is taken by the rational life'.[46]

Both the Christian Democrats, who in 1948 obtained a majority in both the Economic Council in Frankfurt[47] and the Parliamentary Council, and the American occupation authorities were hostile to the concept of social rights, because they were not seen as part of the free market. Conscious of the hollow resonance of much of the basic rights section of the Weimar Constitution, the members of the Parliamentary Council—working amidst conditions of economic deprivation and devastation far more severe than those which accompanied Weimar constitution-making—did not want to fill the Basic Law with empty constitutional promises. Hence, while safeguarding negative liberty, as originally conceived the Basic Law did not protect social rights, such as the right to employment, housing, a minimum standard of living.

However, while the Christian Democrats succeeded in excluding express social rights from the Basic Law, von Mangoldt (CDU) suggested by way of compromise that article 20 should contain the formula 'the Federal Republic of Germany is a democratic and social Federal state'. In article 28(1) the wording 'social *Rechtsstaat*' was introduced. In this way a vague obligation would be imposed on the state to promote social welfare, without conferring enforceable rights on individuals. By its very lack of definition, the social state (*Sozialstaat*) formula has proved capable of indefinite expansion. It marks a decisive shift from fundamental freedoms as liberties to fundamental freedoms as rights. As was said of the equally casual inclusion of the formula 'equity and good faith' (*Treu und Glauben*) in §242 of the German Civil Code of 1900, the social state provision has proved the Archimedean point from which the old legal order has been lifted from its foundations. It has grown to be one of the most important provisions of the Basic Law. The constitution has changed from being a simple defence of the individual against state power to being the groundplan of a social welfare state. Hence, the present debate on the 'Third Way' in Germany, in which the desirability and feasibility of the indefinite extension of state welfare provision is increasingly questioned, has an inescapable constitutional dimension.

The classification of basic rights applied to the Weimar Constitution has consequently been given reality and extended. Whether these are rules of interpretation or rules of substantive law has never been wholly clear. Böckenförde's fivefold classification of basic rights has been highly influential, by reason both of his academic pre-eminence and jurisprudence as a judge of the Federal Constitutional Court.[48] On this analysis, basic rights may be classified under five headings.

1. Liberal rights of freedom, that is, negative liberty against the state. Human freedom is in principle unlimited, while the authority of the state to restrict is inherently restricted.

2. Institutional guarantees, that is, obligations on the state to maintain institutions essential for the attainment and functioning of democratic political life within the constitution, such the Bundestag, the Federal Constitutional Court, a free press, freedom of teaching and learning.

3. The value theory of basic rights, that is, basic rights as the expression of a moral consensus. This essentially derives from Smend's 'integration' theory of a constitution as the embodiment of a 'value order' (Wertordnung).

4. The social state theory of basic rights (rights of participation), that is securing the right to benefits conferred by the state, which may be material (social welfare) or ideal (co-determination in industry). The state has to create the conditions for the realization of fundamental freedoms.

5. The democratic-functional theory of basic rights, that is, basic rights are recognized as part of and essential for the realization of the democratic political order. This controls their content in practice.

The critical distinction is between basic rights as subjective rights (claims of the individual on the state) and basic rights as objective norms (elements of the constitutional order which are given for individuals, being part of what civil lawyers call *ordre public*). These two approaches were described by the Federal Constitutional Court in the *Lüth*-judgment in these terms:[49] 'Undoubtedly the basic rights are intended in the first place to secure the individual's sphere of freedom from violation by public authority . . . However, it is equally true the Basic Law has in its basic rights section established an objective value order . . . The value system must be effective as a fundamental decision of constitutional law for all spheres of law.'

In applying the social state theory, the court has sought to have regard to the fact that resources are limited and the subject of competing claims. Thus in seeking to reconcile the *numerus clausus* in higher education (restriction on the number of student places in certain subjects) with the right to free choice of education and occupation (art. 12), the court said that the basic rights were subject to a 'proviso of what is possible, in the sense of the individual can reasonably lay claim to by law'.[50] The efficacy of this attempt by the Court to apply the brakes, having previously applied the accelerator, has been doubted:[51] 'If one wished to develop the right to enjoyment of benefits further, it would in the end lead to free tickets on public transport as a means of effectuating the right to freedom of travel (art. 11), if not the constitutionally guaranteed right to issue of a free motor car.'

## The Novelty of the Basic Law

Either the list of basic rights must be very long and detailed, or there must be a mechanism to resolve different claims and interests, and make the basic rights—properly interpreted—enforceable. The novelty of the Basic Law was threefold. First, it makes basic rights directly binding on all organs of government; secondly, it established judicial control of the legislature, in the form of the abstract and concrete norm control procedure; thirdly, it gave the individual directly enforceable rights against the state in the form of the 'constitutional appeal'.

The dangers of over-reliance on legal procedures to resolve political questions had been pointed out by Carl Schmitt in these terms:[52] 'The idea suggests itself of regarding the judicial resolution of all political questions as the idea of the *Rechtsstaat* and thereby overlooking the fact that the administration of justice can only be harmed by expanding it into material which is perhaps non-justiciable. The result would then be . . . not the judicialization of politics but the politicization of justice'. The difficulty arises essentially when the laws which parliament can make and which courts must interpret are themselves determined by a paramount constitution, of which a court is the sole authentic interpreter. However, the actual ambit of the political responsibilities of the Federal Constitutional Court is closely, though flexibly, defined. The direct jurisdiction of the court to hear constitutional appeals under art. 93(1) No. 4a provides the bulk of its work. The key procedural right is art. 103(1) which guarantees the right to a judicial hearing of a legal complaint. There is hardly a case which legal imagination cannot bring within the basic rights and so potentially within the Constitutional Court's jurisdiction. A constitutional appeal is only admissible if there is no alternative remedy, subject to two exceptions: (*a*) if a case is of general importance, and (*b*) if the complainant would otherwise suffer immediate and irrecoverable damages. Of constitutional appeals 97.5 per cent are rejected by the Constitutional Court in a preliminary procedure. The European Court of Justice also has a human rights competence, and in time responsibilities in this field may be transferred to it.

A disturbing development of recent years has been the long-winded nature of recent amendments to the basic rights, in contrast to the lapidary formulation of the original provisions. For example the new articles 12a and 16a go into detail more fitting for implementing legislation. However, the Basic Law

and the basic rights have emerged from the revision of constitutional arrangements following unification with their vitality and *raison d'être* unimpaired.

## Conclusion

German political theory has struggled with the question whether the state is a
partnership—in which the individuals composing it are primary—or a collective entity existing independently of the individuals composing it. Maitland
observed:[53] 'before the end of the Middle Ages the Roman word for partnership was assuming a vastly wider meaning and . . . was entering the field of
politics. "Human Society" should be a partnership of mankind; "Civil Society"
should be a partnership of citizens; "the Origin of Civil Society" should be a
Social Contract or contract of partnership'. The question was whether the
results of this contract transcend the individual contractors, establishing some
sort of group-person with a group-will in their place, or whether the state was
only another name, a collective name, for the people composing it. The
group-will theory could be developed so as to exclude both human rights and
those categorized as non-members of the group, such as Jews, Social
Democrats, or political opponents, or the ideologically suspect of any kind.

The question has often been asked, what influence did Rousseau's concept
of the general will play in German political thought? The answer is: surprisingly little. There is not even a satisfactory translation of 'general will'. German
terms such as 'group-mind' (*Gemeingeist*) and 'spirit of the people' (*Volksgeist*)
are no sort of equivalent. The theory of the general will, like that of the social
contract, is concerned with popular sovereignty. Hobbes had twinned the
social contract between ruler and ruled with a second irrevocable contract of
subjection, whereby the people undertook to obey the ruler. Rousseau vindicated popular sovereignty by seeing the social contract as being constantly
renewed through the general will: 'a plebiscite of every day' (*une plébiscite des
tous les jours*'), as Renan described it in the nineteenth century. For the
empirical-liberal school of politics, the general will was embodied in the laws
of a democratically legitimated legislature, based on the active and willing
participation of the political community.

However, the general will is a notoriously plastic concept. For the meta-
physical-totalitarian theory of politics, focusing on Rousseau's observation
that people 'must be forced to be free', the general will symbolized the objective purpose immanent in man and society which it was the goal of politics to
realize.

Neither of these concepts fitted German circumstances. There were no central, popular legislative or constitutional arrangements through which the
general will could be mediated. For those who contrasted the 'German spirit'

to that of Western Europe, Rousseau was hopelessly mired in the intellectual apparatus of the Enlightenment with its natural law based on reason and universalist values. Savigny asserted that the true source of law was not the artificial manufacture of rules by a legislature but 'the inner silently working processes of the nation' (*Volk*); law (*Recht*) is national law (*Volksrecht*); national law is the product of the spirit of the nation (*Volksgeist*).[54] In practice, Savigny regarded professors of Roman law as the true exponents of the spirit of the nation. As Hattenhauer has observed, 'It is one of the most remarkable facts of legal history that Savigny in his *On the Vocation* had laid the foundation not only of the *Volksgeist*-theory but also of the worship of legal science.'[55]

Both approaches were positivist and particularist. Neither approach was compatible with the notion of legally protected human rights, reflecting some sort of universalist values. Acceptance of common values, as Isaiah Berlin has tirelessly reiterated, enters our conception of a normal human being. This is embodied in the basic right to free self-fulfilment expressed in article 2(1) of the Basic Law. The basic rights themselves constituted the adoption by Germany of those internationalist values which Troeltsch had encapsulated in the formula 'humanity and natural law'. The contrast between 'humanity and natural law'—the values of the Western tradition—and the 'German spirit' was given literary expression in the endless debates between Settembrini and Naphta in Thomas Mann's *The Magic Mountain*. The Basic Law of 1949, and in particular its code of basic rights, constituted the victory of Settembrini over Naphta.

# Notes

1. On this interpretation, see J. L. Talmon, *The Origins of Totalitarian Democracy* (London: Secker & Warburg, 1952); K. R. Popper, *The Open Society and its Enemies*, 2 vols., 5th edn. (London: Routledge, 1966); Isaiah Berlin, *Four Essays on Liberty* (Oxford: OUP, 1969).
2. Ernst Troeltsch, 'Naturrecht und Humanität in der Weltpolitik', *Deutscher Geist und Westeuropa* (Tübingen: Mohr, 1925), 1–25. Otto Gierke, *Natural Law and the Theory of Society 1500–1800*, tr. Ernest Barker, 2 vols. (Cambridge: Cambridge University Press, 1934), i, appendix 1.
3. Thomas Hobbes, *Dialog zwischen einem Philosophen und einem Juristen über das englische Recht*, ed. Bernard Wilms (Weinheim: VCH Verlag: 1992), 8.
4. John P. Dawson, *The Oracles of the Law* (Ann Arbor, Mich.: Michigan University Press, 1968), 122–3.
5. Francois Geny, *Methode d'interpretation et sources en droit privé postif*, 2 vols., 2nd edn. (Paris: Montchrestien, 1919), i. 96.
6. Carl Schmitt, *Politische Theologie* (Berlin: Duncker & Humblot, 1933).
7. Stefan Korioth, 'Erschütterungen des staatsrechtlichen Positivismus im ausgehenden Kaiserreich', *Archiv des öffentlichen Rechts*, 117 (1992), 212–38 at 216.

8. Friedrich von Savigny, *Vom Beruf unserer Zeit für Gesetzgebung und Rechtswissenschaft* (Heidelberg: de Gruyter, 1814), 12.

9. G. Anschütz, *Die Verfassung des Deutschen Reichs vom 11. August 1919*, 14th edn. (Berlin: Beck, 1933), 12. This was the last edn. of Anschütz's work: by the time of its publication the constitution as a whole had ceased to mean anything.

10. *Entscheidungen des Bundesverfassungsgerichts* (=*BVerfGE*) 84,p. 239 (decision of 27 June 1991).

11. Carl Schmitt, der Führer schützt das Recht', *Deutsche Juristen-Zeitung* (1934), 945.

12. Troeltsch, 'Naturrecht und Humanität), 11 (Barker trans., 207–8).

13. ibid. 13 (Barker trans. 209).

14. ibid. 14 (Barker trans. 210).

15. ibid. 18 (Barker trans. 214).

16. Sir Henry Maine, *Ancient Law* (London: Dent, Everyman's Library, 1965), 53.

17. Gustav Radbruch, *Paul Johann Anselm Feuerbach: Ein Juristenleben* (Vienna: Müller, 1934; 2nd edn. 1956), 46–50; Franz Wieacker, *Privatrechtsgeschichte der Neuzeit*, 2nd edn. (Göttingen: Vandenhoeck & Ruprecht, 1967), 237.

18. E. R. Huber, *Dokumente zur Deutschen Verefassungsgeschichte* 5 vols, 3rd edn. (Stuttgart: Kohlhammer, 1986), i. 84–90; E. R. Huber, *Deutsche Verfassungsgeschichte*, 8 vols., 2nd edn. (Stuttgart: Kohlhammer, 1957), i. 640–56.

19. Hans Hattenhauer, *Zwischen Hierarchie und Demokratie* (Karlsruhe: Müller, 1971), 90.

20. Franz Schnabel, *Deutsche Geschichte im neunzehnten Jahrhundert* 8 vols. (Freiburg: Herder, 1964), iii. 104–11; Huber, *Verfassungsgeschichte* i. 319–84.

21. Hattenhauer, *Zwischen Hierarchie*, 97.

22. Jörg-Detlef Kühne, *Die Reichsverfassung der Paulskirche* (Frankfurt am Main: Metzner, 1988), 159–203.

23. Thomas Mann, *Betrachtungen eines Unpolitischen* (Hamburg: Fischer Taschenbuch, 1988), 22.

24. H. H. Hartwich, *Sozialstaatspostulat und gesellschaftlicher Status Quo'*, 2nd edn. (Opladen: Springer, 1977), 50.

25. Keith Tribe (ed.), *Social Democracy and the Rule of Law: Otto Kirchheimer, Franz Neumann* (London: Routledge, 1987).

26. Richard Thoma, 'Das System der subjektiven öffentlichen Rechte und Pflichten', in G. Anschütz and R. Thoma, (eds.), *Handbuch des Deutschen Staatsrechts*, 2 vols. (Tübingen: Mohr, 1930), i. 607–23.

27. Carl Schmitt, 'Freiheitsrechte und institutionelle Garantien der Reichsverfassung', in *Verfassungsrechtliche Aufsätze*, 2nd edn. (Berlin: Duncker & Humblot, 1973), 140–73.

28. E. R. Huber, 'Der Bedeutungswandel der Grundrechte', in Anschütz and Thoma, *Handbuch*, ii. 79.

29. *RGZ* (= *Entscheidungen des Reichsgerichts in Zivilachen*) 24, p. 3; 46, p. 69; 48, p. 84; Friedrich Dessauer, *Recht, Richtertum und Ministerialbürokratie* (Mannheim: Koehler, 1923), 1–3.

30. Hugo Preuss, *Der Rechtsstaat* (Berlin: de Gruyter, 1872), 57.

31. Carl Schmitt, 'Die Hüter der Verfassung', *Archiv des öffentlichen Rechts*, 55 (1929), 161–237.

32. It was observed of this argument, 'Thus the wolf was made to look after the sheep': J. P. Mayer, *Max Weber and German Politics* (London: Routledge, 1944), 44. Carl Schmitt only produced this argument after the election of Hindenburg as Reich President in 1925, but justified it by reference to the use of presidential legislative decrees under Art. 48 of the Constitution under the Reich Presidency of the Social Democrat Ebert (1919–25).

33. 'Wer soll der Hüter der Verfassung sein?', *Die Justiz* 6 (1930), 576–628.
34. *RGZ* 102, p. 164; 107, pp. 78, 317, 319; 111, p. 322; 118, p. 325.
35. Letter to Reich Chancellor, 30 May 1925, Bundesarchiv Koblenz, R 43 I, No. 1211, f315; 'Das Reichsgericht im Gegenwart und Zukunft', *Deutsche Juristen-Zeitung* 29 (1924), 241–6; 'Relation of the German Judiciary to the Executive and Legislative Branches', *American Bar Association Journal*, 15 (1929), 762. Simons could perhaps be described as a liberal conservative (if such a thing was possible in the 1920s).
36. There is an admirable summary of this in Korioth, 'Erschütterungen'.
37. Gustav Radbruch, *Rechtsphilosophie*, 3rd edn. (Stuttgart: Koehler, 1932), 182.
38. 'Gesetzliches Unrecht und Ubergesetzliches Recht', *Süddeutsche Juristenzeitung* (Aug. 1946), 107.
39. Erich Kaufmann, *VVDStL* (= *Veröffentlichungen des Vereines der Deutschen Staatsrechtslehrer*) 3 (1927), 20.
40. *RGZ* 107, p. 87. There is a huge literature on this topic. The best single account in English is John P. Dawson, 'Germany's Case Law Revolution', *The Oracles of the Law*, 452–502.
41. Ernst Fuchs, *Schreibjustiz und Richterkönigtum* (Leipzig: Beck, 1907); Gnaeus Flavius (=Kantorowicz), *Der Kampf um die Rechtswissenschaft* (Heidelberg: Veröffentlichungen der juristischen Vereinigung, 1906). Curiously, they held up an idealized model of the English legal system as the model which Germany should adopt.
42. Rudolf Smend, *Verfassung und Verfassungsrecht* (Munich and Leipzig: Beck, 1928).
43. Ernst Fraenkel, *The Dual State: A Contribution to the Theory of Dictatorship* (New York: OUP, 1941), p. xiii.
44. Bernd Rüthers, *Die unbegrenzte Auslegung: Zum Wandel der Privatrechtsordnung im Nationalsozialismus* (Frankfurt am Main: Fischer, 1973), 104–11.
45. Arnold Brecht, *Federalism and Regionalism in Germany: the Division of Germany* (New York: OUP, 1945), 138.
46. Berlin, *Liberty*, 138.
47. An elected assembly which was the immediate forerunner of the Bundestag.
48. Böckenförde, 'Grundrechtstheorie und Grundrechtsinterpretation', *Neue Juristische Wochenschrift*, 272 (1974), 1529–38.
49. *BVerfGE* 7, p. 205.
50. *BVerfGE* 43, p. 291.
51. Ossenbühl, 'Die Interpretation der Grundrechte in der Rechtsprechung des Bundesverfassungsgerichts', *Neue Juristische Wochenschrift*, 29/2 (1976), 2100–07.
52. Schmitt, 'Die Hüter der Verfassung', 173.
53. Otto Gierke, *Political Theories of the Middle Age*, with an introduction by E.W. Maitland (Cambridge: Cambridge University Press, 1900), p. xxiii.
54. Savigny, *Vom Beruf*, 23; Hermann Kantorowicz, 'Savigny and the Historical School of Law', *Law Quarterly Review*, 53 (1937), 326–43.
55. Hattenhauer, *Zwischen Hierarchie*, 166.

# IV

Responsible Governments and Stable Coalitions?

# 11

## Party-Building and Consociational Democracy in Post-War Austria
### *Wolfgang C. Müller*

In his essay 'The Legitimizing Role of Political Parties: The Second Austrian Republic' Peter Pulzer identifies Austria as 'the only example of a European state in which an initially unsuccessful parliamentary system turned into a successful one, and in which constitutional and party-structural factors can be held constant over half a century (1919–1969)'.[1] Indeed the contrast between the First (1918–33) and Second (after 1945) Austrian Republics is striking. While the first one ended in civil war and dictatorship, the second turned out to be a success story, combining a stable parliamentary democracy with economic prosperity. It is noteworthy that this happened under the same constitutional framework and with the same political subcultures, the so-called *Lager* (political camps), as the main collective actors.[2] The major camps in both republics were the Catholic Conservative *Lager* and the Social Democratic *Lager*. While they fought each other bitterly after a brief period of all-party or grand coalition government (1918–20) in the inter-war period, they engaged in civilized competition in the post-war period and even joined forces in a grand coalition government for the first two post-war decades (including the tiny Communist Party until 1947).

The most general approach to this puzzle is the consociational literature which sets great store on the behaviour of the élites. As Arend Lijphart has put it: 'The leaders of the rival subcultures may engage in competitive behavior and thus further aggravate mutual tensions and political instability, but they may also make *deliberate efforts to counteract the immobilizing and unstabilizing effects of cultural fragmentation.*'[3] If the leaders choose the latter strategy, consociational democracy emerges. 'In a consociational democracy the centrifugal tendencies inherent in a plural society are counteracted by the cooperative attitudes and behavior of the leaders of the different segments of the population.'[4] Austria fits in nicely. Indeed most observers recognize a learning of the élites.[5] Having been exposed first to the common experience of being victimized under Nazi rule and then having faced the Allied occupational forces for a decade, the *Lager* élites have learnt to see common interests and to work together in order to realize them. And they did so despite the continuation of the traditional *Lager* encapsulation and mutual hostility. Figure 1 summarizes this story.

Figure 1 identifies four actors (if the term 'actor' can be applied to anything as broad as a political subculture), I to IV, and four relations, 1 to 4, which make up the consociational model.[6] In the context of the consociational literature, most attention has been devoted to relations 1 and 2 which, of course, constitute its core. The existence of co-operative behaviour between the élites of the two main Austrian *Lager* has taken a variety of forms—grand coalition government, parliamentary co-operation, and intense interest-group co-operation, the so-called social partnership (*Sozialpartnerschaft*)—and is well documented.[7] Although, by today's standards, encapsulation of the subcultures and mutual hostility between them at the mass level is less well documented for the period of 'classic' consociationalism (1945–66), there is consensus among the researchers that these features characterized Austria for much of the post-war period.[8]

The consociational literature also has a clear understanding of the nature of the relations between the subcultural élites and their rank and file. In a consociational system, élites must have 'the allegiance and support of their own rank and file', the leaders must be able to carry along not only the rank and file but also the middle-level élites of political activists.[9] With regard to Austria, these relations have not been studied in the context of the emergence of consociationalism. The assumption behind this relative neglect is that, if relations 1 and 2 indeed exist, relations 3 and 4 must work according to theory. Otherwise consociationalism could not exist. Moreover, there is a body of literature which provides empirical support for consociational theory's claim about the élite–mass relationship with regard to the consociational period of Austrian history.[10] However, there is a *logical alternative* to this interpretation. To push it to its extreme, consociationalism may have *emerged* as a result of the leaders improving their grip on their followers rather than changing their minds. If the leaders in the inter-war period lacked the capacity to carry the

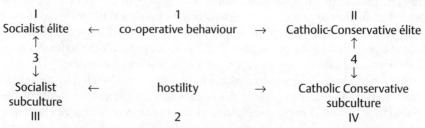

FIGURE 1. The consociational model of Austrian politics

middle-level elites and rank and file along in a policy of accommodation, then the *building up* of such capacities would be an important precondition for post-war consociationalism. This logical alternative comes in two versions. The strong one would claim that the leaders' lack of control in the inter-war period over their respective *Lager* indeed *prevented* them from following a course of accommodation. Thus, the crucial change from the inter-war to the post-war period would be the building up of this capacity (rather than the leaders changing their minds). The weak version would claim that while the leaders did change their minds, this alone would not have been sufficient to establish consociationalism. It needed to be accompanied by the building up of élite control over the own *Lager* in order to allow the leaders to engage in overarching co-operation with the élites of the other *Lager*.

In this chapter I will try to shed some light on these alternatives to the conventional wisdom of the elites' changing their minds. Given the almost complete lack of research on the power relations within the *Lager* in the inter-war period and the still nascent research on building up party organizations in the immediate post-war period, the present chapter is exploratory. While it provides some empirical information, it cannot compensate for thorough and specific historical research. The claim the chapter makes is basically that what I have numbered relations 3 and 4 are worth studying in the context of the emergence of consociationalism in Austria.

In the remainder of this chapter I will discuss the élite–mass relations within the Social Democratic and Catholic Conservative *Lager* in two separate sections. In each case I first take a brief look at the inter-war period. The question is whether the leaders were directly or indirectly constrained by their rank and file and activists in steering the course of the *Lager*. Then I look at party-building in the immediate post-war period. Here the question is whether the élites have engaged in attempts to reduce such constraints by designing new party structures, tailor-made for their control of rank and file and activists. Since it is hard to discuss relations without paying attention to the elements which are linked, I will also review changes in elite and mass characteristics. I will also briefly address factors in the external political environment, which had a direct impact on the building up of the *Lager* and intra-*Lager* relations.

## *The Social Democratic* Lager

In many respects the organization of the Austrian Social Democrats in the inter-war period was the height of the mass integration party, particularly in Vienna. Nevertheless, it suffered from severe defects. Probably the most critical was a leadership problem. According to the voluminous study by Norbert Leser, the claim of which has been substantiated by other studies, the Social

Democratic leaders combined verbal radicalism with lack of action.[11] Verbal radicalism, which is best illustrated by the threat of 'the dictatorship of the proletariat' in the 1926 Linz party programme, was taken at face value by non-socialist political forces (perhaps with the exception of their most clever and sinister leaders) and encouraged them in similar radicalism. The lack of action could be observed in almost every conflict between the Social Democrats and the non-socialist forces. Before these confrontations the Social Democrats usually defined scenarios, hammered out plans, and committed themselves to a particular course of action. However, once the scenario emerged, the plans were cancelled and no action was taken. There was also a contradiction between the Social Democrats' extra-parliamentary radicalism and their pol-icy of parliamentary toleration, so long as small concessions could be earned. Although the party's chief strategist, Otto Bauer, was pretty good at bridging these contradictions with 'theoretical' justifications, their true reason was that the party was split over its strategy. The function of verbal radicalism and rev-olutionary phraseology was to accommodate the party's radical left, which mainly consisted of the younger generation. Attempts at co-operation with the non-socialist forces were made in response to the pressure of and by the party's right, led by Karl Renner and his friends from Lower Austria. Obsessed by the idea of maintaining party unity, that is, of avoiding the break-away of any wing, the Social Democrats manœuvred themselves into a hopeless posi-tion. They encouraged the bourgeois forces to pursue a confrontational strat-egy and eventually also alienated their own rank and file by their policy of incremental withdrawal. This allowed not only the dismantling of the Social Democrats' social policy achievements of the 1918–20 period, but also of the party itself, and of Austrian liberal democracy at large.

Yet, there is a second version of the leadership problem, which appears somewhat contradictory to what has been said so far, but which is particularly important, because this view was held by Adolf Schärf, who assumed the party leadership in 1945. According to him the strategy of the Social Democrats in the inter-war period suffered from individuals taking crucial decisions in an *ad hoc* manner, without careful consideration in the party leadership bodies.[12] Indeed, Schärf attributed the Social Democrats' political isolation from 1927 onwards and the end of parliamentary democracy in 1933 to fatally wrong moves on the part of his party's key players.[13]

What happened in the post-war period? First, let us take a brief look at the Social Democrats' leaders. The Nazi regime's persecution, particularly of the Jews, had left mainly members of the party's old right in the country[14] (who did their best not to encourage the return of the old, often Jewish, left). So in some sense the Social Democratic leadership was ideologically truncated. However, there was also the new left—those young party activists who had been most active in clandestine activities against the Austrian dictatorship of 1933–8 under the label of the Revolutionary Socialists. Social Democrats and

Revolutionary Socialists in the first post-war days joined forces under the new party name of Socialist Party (Sozialistische Partei Österreichs, SPÖ). About half the party's executive members were recruited from the Revolutionary Socialists. Many of them, in the immediate post-war period, had some sympathies for their Communist 'brethren' and were critical of government co-operation with their arch enemies of the Catholic Conservative *Lager*.[15] Indeed, a sizeable minority would have preferred co-operation with the Communists and for many other party leaders it was not clear which side was to be mistrusted more: the Communists or the People's Party (Österreichische Volkspartei, ÖVP). It might thus be argued that the leadership was split again.

But what was the situation at the mass and activist level in the immediate post-war period? The experience of the inter-war years certainly had disillusioned a good part of the Social Democratic supporters. Moreover, a whole generation of the working class had not been subject to socialization in the Social Democratic subculture. The Social Democratic magazine for the party activists, *Der Vertrauensmann*, mourned in 1946 that 'the hard red core of party activists, who have devoted themselves body and soul to the party, who have supported it wholeheartedly, who have not shun away from any sacrifice and for whom full participation is self-evident, has become smaller'.[16] Looking back to the development of the first post-war decade, Fritz Klenner remarked that the 'unshakeable basis of trust' which had existed between the rank and file and the leaders of the Social Democrats in the inter-war years no longer existed.[17] Klenner also recognized that many people had joined the party for patronage reasons or considered it the 'lesser evil'. Peter Pulzer summarized this development in the elegant phrase that 'what was once a millenarian vision has become a set of routinized dogmatic attitudes'.[18]

While the party voters were certainly less ideologically oriented than in the inter-war period, this did not necessarily make them easier to handle in times when politics could not deliver rewards. This was the case in the first post-war years, when food rations were even smaller than during the war. Before the constant threat of the Communists had disappeared, the sudden rise of the League of Independents in 1949 demonstrated that the Social Democrats (just as in the 1930s) were also vulnerable to attacks from the right. Indeed, the League of Independents initially attracted many blue-collar workers in the industries built up under Nazi rule (which as nationalized industries were to become Social Democrat strongholds during the course of the Second Republic).[19] It was only in retrospect, after the Social Democrats' victories, that these challenges could be belittled.

The Communist threat to the cohesion of the Social Democratic *Lager* was organizational and electoral. Until 1949 the Social Democrats could not take the extent of their electoral advantage over the Communists for granted. Nor could they proceed from the organizational unity of the party. This became evident in 1947, when the Social Democrats' radical left wing broke away, establishing a left socialist party. In retrospect, the failure of this party makes the break-away look harmless. However, a closer look reveals that it was a major party crisis. This is best illustrated by the non-willingness of party members to pay their membership dues. Indeed, payment of membership dues dropped from 92.5 per cent in 1946 to 65.9 in 1946, indicating that more than a quarter of the party members were shaky in their party loyalty. [20] However, the Social Democrats maintained their electoral predominance as the party of the left, met the organizational challenge, and defeated the Communists whenever these tried to succeed by non-democratic means. After the failed Communist attempt at general strike and government overthrow in 1950, the Social Democrats had finally won this battle (although it took them more than another decade to drive the Communists out of the market for the working-class vote completely). They also met the challenge from the League of Independents for the working-class vote after the League had broken into this Social Democratic core constituency in 1949.

So far I have demonstrated that the post-war Social Democrats faced considerable internal conflicts at the élite level and challenges from other parties at the mass level. Thus, in some respects, the situation differed little from the inter-war period. To be sure, there were also important differences. These have been given much attention with the benefit of hindsight. However, the costs of retrospective analysis are obvious: real challenges may not be recognized and no attention may be given to the means by which they were met. In the remainder of this section I will review briefly whether the organizational design of the post-war Socialist Party made a contribution to overcoming these challenges.

In the immediate post-war period the Social Democrats considered their organizational principles, discussing in particular whether they should return to the pre-war mass organization or whether they should resort to a type of organization that reflected their experiences with both the defeat in the civil war of 1934 and the clandestine organization of the Revolutionary Socialists in subsequent years.[21] Much of the debate focused on the question whether the party should try to gain as many members as possible, or, alternatively, whether it should opt for a much smaller organization consisting exclusively of well-trained and deeply committed activists. While the former Revolutionary Socialists had demanded the adoption of the latter model, and some of the old Social Democrats favoured the unconditional return to the pre-war organizational model, the most realistic men of the party's centre-right agreed that some combination of the classic bottom–up mass organization with top–down elements was required under the special conditions of the immediate post-war period. They did not want to leave the building up of the party to chance. Thus provisional chairman Schärf concluded that 'we need the centrally directed party'.[22] Moreover, the Social Democrats from 1947 onwards made an effort to complement their classic structure of local branches with firm-level branches, thus borrowing one of the organizational ideas of the Communists. In 1950, both organizational innovations of the post-war period were given up. The classic mass organization in practice had prevailed over the alternative model, and after the Socialist trade unionists had defeated the Communists in their 1950 attempt at general strike and government over-throw, they could legitimately claim the firm level as their exclusive territory.

What distinguished the Social Democrats of the immediate post-war from the inter-war period was strong leadership and an unambiguous strategy. The Socialist Party was prepared to put up with the break-away of the radical left rather than to lead the party in a situation of deadlock. In other words, the leadership problem that had plagued the party in the inter-war period had been solved. How did this come about? Clearly, the majority of the post-war party leaders was not only less visionary but also much more realistic than those of the inter-war period. The new party leader was also a much better 'power technician' than the great orator and 'theorist' Otto Bauer. Rather than 'erring with the masses' he and his allies chose to provide leadership. I have already mentioned the temporary variation of organizational principles at the mass level. At the élite level Schärf established a system of intra-party bodies which allowed the party to give careful consideration to each organizational and political issue.[23] Until 1967, with the exception of a single year, all leader-ship bodies combined held more than sixty and in most years more than eighty meetings. This system was tailor-made for Schärf, who was extremely good at steering his proposals through the system and at killing proposals he did not like. This system also provided *collective responsibility* for the party leadership. Thus intra-party opposition at the elite level was difficult.

To summarize the story: the leaders of the post-war Socialist Party to some extent faced similar problems to their predecessors in the inter-war years. With regard to inter-*Lager* co-operation, the post-war leadership had not only changed its mind (or, more accurately, composition). Rather the new leaders were more gifted in practical politics. And they managed to adapt the party organization to their needs, both at the élite and mass levels.

## *The Catholic Conservative* Lager

The Catholic Conservative *Lager* in the inter-war period was plagued by a number of severe political and organizational problems. To begin with, given the ideological divide within the non-socialist political spectrum, it did not manage to integrate all non-socialist forces under its umbrella. The German nationalists constituted a separate political *Lager*, which fell into two parts, the Pan-German People's Party (*Großdeutsche Volkspartei*), which attracted civil servants and other urban groups, and the Rural League (*Landbund*), the organization of Protestant farmers. In many respects, the non-socialist tie between these parties was stronger than the division between Catholics and Protestants and between their Austrian or German orientation. Consequently, these parties co-operated in government and attempts were made to present a common list in elections. In 1927 the Christian Socials had a joint list with the Pan-German People's Party, in 1930 with the Rural League. However, the co-operation remained fragile. In 1930, the Pan-German People's Party decided for opposition, not willing to share government office with leaders of the Catholic Conservative's armed forces, the *Heimwehren*. Nevertheless, the *Heimwehren* broke away from the Christian Social Party in 1930, running a separate list in the parliamentary elections, the *Heimatblock*. The *Heimwehr* movement itself was plagued by cohesion problems, with some of their constituency organizations and leaders (and some of their eight MPs after the 1930 elections) being more inclined to the Nazi party than to the Christian Socials.

Moreover, even the Christian Social Party as such had great cohesion problems. In many respects it was a party of individual political entrepreneurs. These had very diverse power bases. First, there were politicians who represented a traditional organization of the Catholic Conservative *Lager*, such as the Farmers' League, Christian trade unions, or a business organization (such as the Handels- und Gewerbebund). Many of these groups lacked an effective national organization so that the power bases of individual politicians were mainly at the *Land* level. Second, there were politicians who had made it to the top of one of the Christian Socials' *Land* party organizations and/or had managed to become governor of a *Land* (*Landeshauptmann*). Third, there were politicians who had a stake in national politics, basically by having been appointed to the cabinet and building up a personal following among the party's activists and MPs. Naturally, having the support of the Catholic Church was also helpful.

Ignaz Seipel was the leading politician of the Christian Socials in the inter-war period. He was party chairman from 1921 until 1930 and Federal Chancellor in the 1922–4 and 1926–9 periods, but also had great influence on some of the cabinets in which he did not participate. Seipel had close links with the Catholic Church and the *Heimwehren*. However, being the chairman of a party with a dispersed power structure did not give him much power *per se*, nor did he control the *Heimwehren*. And his holding cabinet office depended on the intra-party constellation and the approval of the Christian Socials' coalition partners. In 1924, there was a solid majority against Seipel within the Christian Social Party, and after 1929 it was to a large extent the demands of the coalition partners' which withheld the chancellorship from Seipel.[24] As a consequence of these factors, the party leader of the Christian Socials held government office only for five and a half years during the sixteen years of the party's government participation during the life time of the First Republic.[25] With Seipel's illness and death in 1932, no individual politician could pull together the centrifugal forces of the Catholic Conservative *Lager,* let alone the much broader non-socialist camp.

The Christian Social Party was well aware of its organizational problems and was engaged in a continual struggle to increase party cohesion and discipline by reforming the formal party organization.[26] These attempts were largely ineffective. In the end the leader of the Catholic Conservative *Lager,* Chancellor Dollfuß, after establishing the dictatorship, found it more rewarding to dissolve the Christian Social Party and to try something new: the Fatherland's Front (Vaterländische Front).[27] This was a patriotic 'administered mass organization'[28] which in the end also failed: it did not become the effective mass organization envisaged by its founders.[29]

In the Catholic Conservative *Lager* there was thus no successful organizational model which could simply have been revived in the post-war period. To some extent the task had by now become easier. Steps towards the 'nationalization' of interest groups had already been made in the Christian Socials' attempt at improving their organization in the last years of the first republic and they were continued under the 1933–8 dictatorship.[30] Although these groups were abolished under Nazi rule, they constituted a reference point for the post-war organizational design. However, first and foremost, in a country controlled by Allied occupational forces there was no room for a Nazi party nor the armed *Heimwehren,* even where these had not discredited themselves in the eyes of their former supporters. Nor was there room for a party upholding the tradition of the Pan-German People's Party, which as early as the 1930s had demanded that Austria join Nazi Germany, and whose leaders and followers had later eagerly joined the Nazi party. It was not until 1949 that a party which appealed to this part of the electorate was allowed to compete in elections: the League of Independents. However, the League remained severely handicapped not only by the legacy of Nazism but also by the Soviet occupation of the most densely populated parts of Austria, which made it particularly difficult to organize and campaign for this party. The situation was different for the Rural League. It had sided with the Christian Socials after 1930 and had tried to support the moderate, democratically oriented elements among them. So, the Rural League was no more discredited than the Christan Social themselves. Consequently, Karl Renner had kept seats vacant in the 1945 provisional government for the Rural League. It was a genuine achievement of the People's Party in its efforts at party-building that it managed to integrate the Rural League in the first post-war days, by offering its remaining leaders incentives of political and private careers. This strategy paid off at the mass level. The People's Party, or more precisely, its Farmers' League (Bauernbund), experienced a substantial influx of former Rural League members in 1945.[31] The Business League (Wirtschaftsbund) of the People's Party was similarly successful in recruiting the self-employed, some of whom had compromised themselves under Nazi rule and were now looking for shelter.

The organizational model which underlay the integration of these non-socialist groups was that of an indirect party, building first and foremost on economic interests. These were organized in three leagues, the Farmers' League, the Business League, and the Workers' and Employees' League (Arbeiter- und Angestelltenbund). These leagues were organized both as legally independent organizations (Vereine), which decided their own statutes, leadership, and finances, and as constituent units of the People's Party. Although members of the leagues, according to their statutes, automatically became party members, the membership cards of the leagues did not reflect this fact and many members, in particular of the Business League, did not recognize themselves as being members of the People's Party. The Business and Farmers' Leagues were extraordinarily successful in recruiting members and winning elections in the Business and Agricultural Chambers respectively. These chambers are state-licensed interest groups with compulsory membership for all potential members. In addition to their acting as interest groups, they are important for the self-governance of the respective sector (for example, for granting licences) and for fulfilling administrative functions on behalf of the government (for example, the distribution of subsidies). Thus individual farmers and businessmen can be highly dependent on their respective chamber. The chambers, over the first two post-war decades, increased their direct impact on public policy-making by building up the arrangements of liberal corporatism, the social partnership. Moreover, the Farmers' and Business Leagues remained predominant within the People's Party until the mid-1960s. Thus, from the point of view of economic interests, farmers and businessmen did well by staying with the People's Party.

The situation is different with regard to the third pillar of the People's Party, the Workers' and Employees' League. In contrast to the two other socio-economic groups, workers and employees are not overwhelmingly attracted by the People's Party. It is the Social Democrats who organize those who are not self-employed, who control the relevant interest groups (Chamber of Labour, Trade Union Congress), and who win the vast majority of their votes in elections. Indeed, the interests of the leagues often conflict (with farmers being interested in high agrarian prices and subsidies, business in moderate wages and a minimum of social policy benefits, and employees being interested in low food prices, high wages and many social policy benefits). Given the intra-party predominance of farmers and business, it might be expected that workers and employees would not have been tied to the People's Party by economic interests but by its ideological appeal. To some extent this was true. For the Workers' and Employees' League's clientele the Christian appeal has always been more important than for the party's other groups and the more elaborate versions of Christian Social doctrine as a rule have had their origin in this organization. This is not the whole story, however. A closer look reveals that the Workers' and Employees' League mainly organizes civil servants, who form a large group in Austria (including schoolteachers, military staff, academics, and judges). At least with respect to this group, even the Workers' and Employees' League has an 'economic mission', that is, defending the interests of civil servants.

In short, the leagues could integrate Protestants, liberals and former Nazis on the basis of shared socio-economic interests.[32] At the same time, the People's Party did its best to dissociate itself from the Austrian dictatorship 1933–8 and to avoid having too narrow an appeal. To begin with, its founders chose a new name. Dropping the Catholic label and calling the party a 'people's party' was a clear and deliberate signal of openness. Although the April 1945 declaration of independence from Germany was signed by the People's Party president Leopold Kunschak 'on behalf of the Christian Social People's Party, now Austrian People's Party', the party claimed to be brand new, having nothing to do with the Christian Socials or the regime of 1933–8. While it is true that many of its leading functionaries had held positions at the second and third levels of this regime, they had as a rule belonged to the moderating forces within the Christian Social Party before the establishment of the dictatorship. Once the People's Party had fully integrated the Catholic Conservative *Lager* of the inter-war period, and with the first democratic elections approaching (held in November 1945), those who had survived from the old guard were sacked. The leader (though not yet chairman) of the Social Democrats, commented on the sacking of the old guard in private: 'The People's Party has come to a rather radical end with the past. All people, who have been associated with the Dolfuss-Schuschnigg course, have been eliminated.'[33]

Building the People's Party as an indirect party with predominant leagues was not the only alternative considered in the immediate post-war period (and indeed already during the war). The provisional leadership of the People's Party, and its general secretary, Felix Hurdes, in particular, had aimed at a party based on leagues, but with a much stronger central party organization than eventually emerged.[34] This ambition was killed once the leagues assumed power and sacked the old guard (to which Hurdes did not belong). Another ambition of the party headquarters came closer to realization: the building up of an effective mass organization. Although a contemporary observer was right in recognizing the characteristics of a cadre party rather than a mass party, and in mentioning that membership statistics were treated 'much more casually', when comparing the People's Party with the Socialist Party, it nevertheless appears that by pre-war standards the People's Party was making a real effort at building up an effective mass organization.[35]

The Christian Social Party had ceased to exist *as party* below the *Land* level, drawing on a variety of Catholic and interest organizations.[36] In contrast, the People's Party in the immediate post-war period established a party structure which, at least on paper, reached down to the local level. Although much of the local level remained a domain of the leagues, the People's Party managed to build up a solid party organization with a backbone of professional staff at the district (*Bezirk*) level, the intermediate level between the *Land* and local levels.[37] In the immediate post-war period it produced membership statistics and organizational reports, it had a much acclaimed central training institution, and routine conferences of the party and league secretaries of all levels. Although the organizational efforts were not nearly as comprehensive as those of the Social Democrats, they were a far cry from anything the Christian Socials had ever managed to achieve.

The organizational success of the People's Party was also recognized by their main competitor, the Socialist Party. After their electoral defeat in the 1956 parliamentary elections, the Social Democrats established a committee to scrutinize the experience of the campaign. After compiling much evidence the committee concluded that the People's Party's campaign had been 'decisively superior' in the 'technical and material' sense. It is particularly interesting to consider the reports by the *Land* party chairmen. According to the Carinthian chairman the People's Party 'has built up its organization so well that in many regions we have nothing equivalent to put against it'. The Vienna chairman claimed that the People's Party 'is at least equally good in all organizational respects'. The Lower Austrian chairman acknowledged that the People's Party had 'the better organization'. And the Salzburg chairman said that the People's Party's body of activists 'today is partly superior to ours'.[38]

Why did the People's Party have such an effective organization in the mid-1950s? Despite all the advantages of the leagues in recruiting members and colonising the chamber system, in the end there was an election and the voters were required to put their cross against the People's Party. Although the leagues could and indeed did campaign for the People's Party, many of the new members might have been tempted to return to or try out another non-socialist party in the privacy of the voting booth. This made it necessary—and acceptable from the point of view of the leagues—to have a strong campaign organization under the party label. And back in the 1940s and 1950s a strong mass organization was still one of the greatest assets in an election campaign. It seems that the People's Party's attempt to strengthen its mass organization ran out of steam in the late 1950s. At least the national party was decreasingly concerned with organizational issues. Relevant information ceased to be collected and stored by party headquarters and, leaving aside occasional attempts at party statute reform, national party congresses were not concerned with organizational questions nor did they receive meaningful organizational reports before the 1970s (when the People's Party had lost government office and temporarily revived its concern about mass organization). This relative neglect of 'classic' organizational matters from the 1950s onwards can be seen as connected with the rise of new means of communication, in particular non-party media, modern advertisement techniques, and public opinion research.[39] In Austria, it was the People's Party, which had a much more instrumental view of the mass organization than the Social Democrats, which championed the use of new techniques.[40]

Finally, the early success of the People's Party owes much to the ability of individuals to hold several leadership positions simultaneously. The most relevant case is Julius Raab. From the very beginning of the Second Republic until his death in 1964 he combined crucial party, interest group, and public offices which allowed him to steer his party effectively (see Figure 2). As leader of the Business League he was in command of one of the party's three constituent organizations.[41] Although this league was the smallest one in terms of members, it was powerful through its command of crucial resources, in particular money and know-how. Representing the most wealthy constituency of the people's party, the Business League was in a good position to collect political funds. And given the fact that public party finance was not introduced at a relevant scale before the mid-1970s, the capacity of political parties to raise funds did matter. The know-how, in

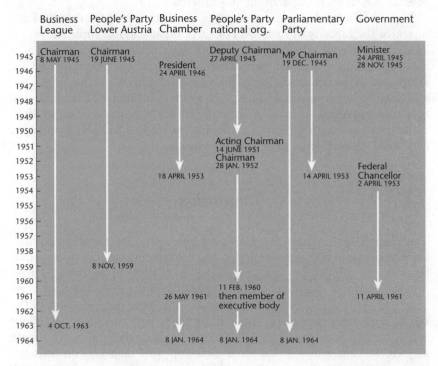

FIGURE 2. The cumulation of political positions: Julius Raab (compiled mainly from A. Brusatti and G. Heindel (eds.), *Julius Raab: Eine Biographie in Einzeldarstellungen* (Linz: Trauner, 1986))

turn, was concentrated in the staff of the Business Chamber, which since its foundation has been under the control of the Business League. As founding president of the Business Chamber, Raab was in direct control of this resource and shaped it to a considerable extent. When he resigned from this position to become Federal Chancellor, Raab handpicked a loyal successor, who had to resign when Raab returned after eight years in government. Heading the *Land* party organization of Lower Austria, the 'heartland' of the People's Party, meant to represent slightly more than a third of the party's 600,000 members, almost as much as the second-, third-, and fourth-strongest *Land* party organizations combined.[42] All this backed up Raab's power in his national party and cabinet functions. From December 1945 until his resignation as party chairman he always held one of the two leading party functions, chairman of the extra-parliamentary or parliamentary party. At the height of his power, he held the most important public office, that of Federal Chancellor. Even before that, the leaders of the Social Democrats considered him as the true leader of the People's Party, the one with whom to strike deals, and no evidence has been produced by historical research which would undermine this judgement.

To put it in a nutshell, compared to the Christian Socials the People's Party increased the capacity of its leaders by three organizational innovations: the indirect party with all-embracing leagues for farmers and businessmen, a mass organization that was particularly effective in campaigning, and the acceptance of the concentration of power in the hands of one leader. All this was eased by environmental factors such as the truncation of the ideological spectrum and Allied occupation. Nevertheless the organizational innovations made their own contribution to increasing the leaders' room to manœuvre, and hence the emergence of consociationalism.

## Conclusion

This chapter has reviewed the élite–mass link within the socialist and non-socialist camps in the inter-war period and the building up of party organizations in the immediate post-war period in Austria. In so doing, I have provided evidence shedding light on a *logical alternative* to the standard interpretation of the emergence of consociationalism in the post-war period. The standard interpretation places emphasis on the leaders changing their minds and assumes that they were equally unconstrained by their followers in both periods. The *alternative* is that the leaders improved their grip on their followers and hence increased their room for manoeuvre in the post-war period. If there was indeed such a problem in the inter-war period and if we can indeed find such a strengthening of the leaders' grip on their followers after the war, this may be considered as either a sufficient or a necessary condition for the emergence of consociationalism in the post-war period.

The review of the still very rudimentary research on power relations within the *Lager* in the inter-war period suggests that the leaders faced considerable constraints. The Social Democrats' inconsistent strategy resulted from the primacy of maintaining party unity at both élite and mass level. The non-socialist side was organizationally fragmented, comprising the Christian Social Party, the *Heimwehren*, the Rural League, and the Pan-German People's Party. The boundaries between these groups were to some extent unclear and even the Christian Social Party itself faced problems of party cohesion. Thus there is evidence to suggest that the leaders were constrained to a considerable extent by intra-bloc competition and lack of intra-*Lager* cohesion.

The review of the building of party organization in the post-war period suggests that the post-war innovations helped the leaders to pursue a coherent strategy and to increase their grip on the rank and file. This is particularly true for the People's Party's ingenious combination of interest group and effective campaign organization. The developments reviewed in this chapter are linked to other developments and alone cannot account for the emergence of consociationalism. However, they have certainly made it more likely and perhaps constitute a necessary precondition for its emergence. While I have barely scratched the surface of the important questions of intra-*Lager* relations in this chapter, I hope that it demonstrates that party-building in the immediate post-war period is an important topic for understanding Austria's post-war turn to consociationalism.

# Notes

1. Peter Pulzer, 'The Legitimizing Role of Political Parties: The Second Austrian Republic', *Government and Opposition*, 4 (1969), 324–44, here 325.
2. A *Lager* in both republics is headed by a political party and also comprises a wide variety of societal organizations and interest groups. In the inter-war period the Social Democratic and Catholic Conservative *Lager* also included paramilitary forces, the *Schutzbund* (Social Democrats), and the *Heimwehren*.
3. Arend Lijphart, 'Consociational Democracy', *World Politics*, 21 (1969), 207–25, here 211–12.
4. Arend Lijphart, *Democracy in Plural Societies* (New Haven, Conn.: Yale University Press, 1977), 1.
5. See the summary of the literature, ibid. 102–3.
6. Anton Pelinka, 'Postklassischer Parlamentarismus und Sozialpartnerschaft', *Österreichische Zeitschrift für Politikwissenschaft*, 3 (1974), 333–45 applies a similar visualization in different context.
7. See Pulzer, 'Legitimizing Role'; Wolfgang C. Müller, 'Austria: Tight Coalitions

and Stable Government', in Wolfgang C. Müller and Kaare Strøm (eds.), *Coalition Governments in Western Europe* (Oxford: OUP, 2000); Emmerich Tálos, 'Sozialpartnerschaft: Zur Entwicklung und Entwicklungsdynamik kooperativ-konzertierter Politik in Österreich', in Peter Gerlich, Edgar Grande, and Wolfgang C. Müller (eds.), *Sozialpartnerschaft in der Krise* (Vienna: Böhlau, 1985).

8. The best evidence is G. Bingham Powell, jun., *Social Fragmentation and Political Hostility: An Austrian Case Study* (Stanford, Calif.: Stanford University Press, 1970); Frederick C. Engelmann and Mildred A. Schwartz, 'Partisan Stability and the Continuity of a Segmented Society: The Austrian Case', *American Journal of Sociology*, 79 (1974), 948–66.

9. Lijphart, 'Consociationalism', 221.

10. For a convenient summary of the relevant literature in an elaborated framework see Kurt Richard Luther, 'Consociationalism, Parties and the Party System', in Kurt Richard Luther and Wolfgang C. Müller (eds.), *Politics in Austria: Still a Case of Consociationalism?* (London: Frank Cass, 1992), 65–8 and 'Must what Goes up Always Come down?', in Kurt Richard Luther and Kris Deschouwer (eds.), *Party Elites in Divided Societies* (London: Routledge, 1999), 55–8. See also the excellent study by Joseph J. Houska, *Influencing Mass Political Behavior* (Berkeley, Calif.: Institute of International Studies, 1985), which takes a different approach to élites–masses relationships.

11. Norbert Leser, *Zwischen Reformismus und Bolschewismus* (Vienna: Europaverlag, 1968), especially 502–5; Everhard Holtmann, *Zwischen Unterdrückung und Befriedung* (Vienna: Verlag für Geschichte und Politik, 1978), 65–92, and 'Die Organisation der Sozialdemokratie in der Ersten Republik, 1918–1934', in Wolfgang Maderthaner and Wolfgang C. Müller (eds.), *Die Organisation der österreichischen Sozialdemokratie 1889–1995* (Vienna: Löcker, 1996), 106, 145–6, Klemens von Klemperer, *Ignaz Seipel: Staatsmann einer Krisenzeit* (Graz: Styria, 1976), esp. ch. 5; and Anson Rabinbach, *The Crisis of Austrian Socialism* (Chicago: University of Chicago Press, 1983).

12. See Karl Stadler, *Adolf Schärf: Mensch—Politiker—Staatsmann* (Vienna: Europaverlag, 1982), 79–81, 96–7.

13. In 1927 Social Democratic protesters burnt the Palace of Justice and were engaged in bloody street battles with the police. The preparation of the demonstration was at least careless, and Schärf implies that the organizers were acting deliberately. The consequence of these events of 15 July 1927 was that the bourgeois forces took the Social Democratic verbal radicalism at face value. In 1933, in an *ad hoc* meeting in the lobby of parliament, four Social Democratic leaders decided that the Social Democratic president of parliament, Karl Renner, should resign. This triggered the resignation of the second and third presidents of parliament of the Christian Socials and Pan-German People's Party, respectively. The government used this 'self-elimination' of parliament as a pretext for establishing a dictatorship.

14. See Kurt L. Shell, *The Transformation of Austrian Socialism* (New York: State University of New York Press, 1962), 78–80; Peter Pulzer, 'Austria', in Stanley Henig (ed.), *European Political Parties* (New York: Praeger, 1970), 290.

15. Fritz Weber, *Der Kalte Krieg in der SPÖ* (Vienna: Verlag für Gesellschaftskritik, 1986).

16. See Müller, 'Die Organisation der SPÖ, 1945–1995', in Maderthaner and Müller (eds.), *Die Organisation der österreichischen Sozialdemokratie*, 276–9.

17. Fritz Klenner, *Das Unbehagen in der Demokratie* (Vienna: Verlag der Wiener Volksbuchhandlung, 1956), 61.

18. Pulzer, 'Legitimizing Role', 338.
19. See Viktor Reimann, *Die Dritte Kraft in Österreich* (Vienna: Molden, 1980), 174–82.
20. Müller, 'Die Organisation der SPÖ', 232.
21. Shell, *Transformation of Austrian Socialism*, 36–43; Weber, *Der Kalte Krieg*, 62–4; Müller, 'Die Organisation der SPÖ', 241–3.
22. In the SPÖ party executive committee meeting, July 2, 1945, cited in W.C. Müller, 'Die Organisation der SPÖ', 242.
23. Ibid. 290–93.
24. See von Klemperer, *Ignaz Seipel.*
25. See Wolfgang C. Müller, Wilfried Philipp, and Barbara Steininger, 'Die Regierung', in Emmerich Tálos, Herbert Dachs, Ernst Hanisch, and Anton Staudinger (eds.), *Handbuch des politischen Systems Österreichs: Erste Republik 1918–1933* (Vienna, Manz, 1995), 77–9.
26. Anton Staudinger, Wolfgang C. Müller, and Barbara Steininger, 'Die Christlich-soziale Partei', ibid. 167–9.
27. See Anton Staudinger, 'Bemühungen Carl Vaugoins um Suprematie der Christlichsozialen Partei in Österreich (1930–33), *Mitteilungen des Österreichischen Staatsarchivs*, 23 (1970), 297–376, here 367–76; Peter Huemer, *Sektionschef Robert Hecht und die Zerstörung der Demokratie in Österreich* (Vienna: Verlag für Geschichte und Politik, 1975), 271–7.
28. On this type of organization see Gregory J. Kasza, *The Conscription Society* (New Haven, Conn.: Yale University Press, 1995).
29. See Emmerich Tálos and Walter Manoschek, 'Politische Struktur des Austrofaschismus (1934–1938)', in Emmerich Tálos and Wolfgang Neugebauer (eds.), *'Austrofaschismus'* (Vienna: Verlag für Gesellschaftskritik, 1985), 97–107.
30. See Ernst Bruckmüller, 'Die ständische Tradition: ÖVP und Neokorporatismus', in Robert Kriechbaumer and Franz Schausberger (eds.), *Volkspartei: Anspruch und Realität* (Vienna: Böhlau, 1995), 290–2; Helmut Wohnout, *Regierungsdiktatur oder Ständeparlament?* (Vienna: Böhlau, 1993).
31. Alfred Ableitinger, 'Partei- und Organisationsstruktur', 150–1; Roman Sandgruber, 'Die ÖVP in Oberösterreich', 416; Dieter A. Binder, 'Steirische oder Österreichische Volkspartei', 567, all in Kriechbaumer and Schausberger (eds.), *Volkspartei: Anspruch und Realität.*
32. Ludwig Reichhold, *Geschichte der ÖVP* (Graz: Styria, 1975), 111; Ableitinger, 'Partei- und Organisationsstruktur', 151.
33. Minutes of the SPÖ party executive, 10 Sept. 1945.
34. Reichhold, *Geschichte der ÖVP*, 76–7. Robert Kriechbaumer, *Von der Illegalität zur Legalität: Gründungsgeschichte der ÖVP* (Vienna: Multiplex Media Verlag, 1985), 146–7 and 47–62.
35. Louise Powelson, *'The Political Parties of Austria 1945–1951'* (Ph.D., Yale University, 1953), 142.
36. Staudinger, Müller, and Steininger, 'Die Christlichsoziale Partei', 166.
37. Ableitinger, 'Partei- und Organisationsstruktur', 152.
38. Müller, 'Die Organisation der SPÖ, 1945–1995', 220.
39. These 'counter-organizational tendencies' were first described by Leon D. Epstein, *Political Parties in Western Democracies* (New York: Praeger, 1967), ch. 9.
40. See Wolfgang C. Müller, 'Inside the Black Box', *Party Politics* 3, (1997), 293–313.
41. See Wolfgang C. Müller and Barbara Steininger, 'Party Organisation and Party Competitiveness: The Case of the Austrian People's Party, 1945–1992', *European Journal of Political Research* 26, (1994), 1–29.
42. See Powelson, *'Political Parties of Austria'*, 622.

# 12

# Liberalism as a Minority Subculture: The Case of Italy

## David Hine

## Introduction

Until the 1990s, it was traditional to see the Italian political system as distinct-ive, in comparative European terms, for the persistence of ideological polar-ization and subcultural fragmentation.[1] Both the Marxist/socialist subculture and the Catholic subculture remained largely intact until as recently as the mid-1980s, despite the revisionism of the Communist Party and the long-term secularization of Christian Democracy. The effects on the party system of this mutually hostile subcultural confrontation were paralysing: the Com-munist Party was condemned to permanent opposition, and the Christian Democrat Party was permanently in power at the heart of an unstable centrist coalition. The end of the cold war dismantled that system over a decade ago. Today the Communists have completed their transition to social-democratic status, and the Christian Democrat Party has broken into pieces, though catholic influence is still strongly felt across the party spectrum.[2]

However, as we shall see later in this chapter, there is still an Italian excep-tionalism to be understood and explained. Italian party politics is today more fragmented than ever. Coalition building may not take place in an atmosphere of impending democratic collapse, as often seemed to happen in the 1950s and 1960s, but it is scarcely less complex or more stable. And in some respects there is greater uncertainty about how the rules of the political game ought to operate than at the height of the cold war, and hence intense and seemingly unending controversy over both the constitution, and ordinary legislation regulating political activity. Liberal democracy does not appear to be under imminent threat, but it is still shows some very unusual features: a party system composed of around fifteen party groups in parliament; a high turnover of prime ministers and governments (higher in the 1990s than in the 1970s or 1980s); and governments that are most effective when run, as they often have been for the last decade, by non-party technocrats. Moreover, with the era of subcultural politics now apparently past, a related but distinct element of Italian exceptionalism—the long-term weakness of liberal values—whose origins seem to lie far back in the process of nineteenth-century state-building, is once again becoming an important part of the explanation.

## *Liberal Values in Italy*

This chapter examines the relationship between the long-term weakness of Italian liberalism, and the difficulties the country experienced first in sustaining an ideologically fragmented party system after 1945, and secondly in rebuilding political life after the near collapse of the First Republic in 1992. The claim that liberal values are weak in a particular society needs some preliminary explanation. It might be taken to imply that such values are definable and comparable between societies and over time. Even if feasible, such an exercise would be well beyond the scope of this chapter, for liberal political theorists differ greatly in their views on the foundational justification of liberal values. Arguments about the relationship between liberty, equality, and democracy give rise to different conclusions about the nature of the liberal state, its institutions, its citizens' rights and duties, its neutrality between conceptions of the good, and the broad distributional thrust of the policies liberals ought to pursue.[3]

Liberal values when applied to economic issues have conventionally pointed in the direction of free markets and individual enterprise, but in the twentieth century revisionist liberalism and later Rawlsian political thought have brought major qualifications to that generalization. Even liberals concerned with liberty rather than equality have sometimes accepted that measures to increase equality are a necessary precursor to those which enhance liberty. And even when liberalism is concerned not with distributional issues, but with essentially procedural and constitutional issues such as civil rights and freedoms, and institutional checks and balances, countries vary a great deal in the practices they apply and the assumptions they make about the trade-off between programmatic purposiveness in government on the one hand, and accountability and representativeness on the other.

Concerning what liberalism *is* in the real world, as opposed to what, starting from foundational principles, liberalism *should be*, it can however be said with some confidence that over time liberal theory has undergone some very broad changes in focus, passing through several stages of development. The twentieth century has seen two important watersheds. The first divides the liberalism of the so-called liberal century (1815–1914), from 'revisionist liberalism' (itself in some respects profoundly anti-liberal) which began to emerge at its end, under the pressures of mass democracy. A second, less clear cut, watershed seems to divide the revisionist liberalism of figures like Keynes and Beveridge from the revival of something akin to classical liberalism in the last third of the twentieth century, under the intellectual leadership of figures such as Hayek and Friedman. In long-term perspective, the most important contribution of revisionist liberalism proved not its influence over liberal parties themselves (except in so far as it created serious tensions within them), but its ability to dilute the value systems of mass parties and movements such as social democracy and Christian democracy. The revival of classical liberalism, for its part, also did more to infiltrate the thinking of existing parties and movements than to generate new liberal movements or revive older ones. Both watersheds were real and important breaks in liberal thought, representing new approaches to the problems of balancing liberty against equality, and both therefore add to the difficulties of defining with precision what might be meant by a long-term weakness of liberal values.

Given these qualifications, the reader with a knowledge of Italian history might conclude that, if liberalism is to be defined only by loose labels and broad ideological trends, then Italy, far from suffering a weakness of liberal values and representing an exception to the broad trends of European development, was not entirely out of line with them. Italy's first post-unification regime was, after all, known as 'liberal Italy'.[4] It lasted until the march on Rome in 1922, and it was certainly a much more 'liberal' system, both politically and economically, than what had gone before. A constitution establishing representative and responsible government was introduced, albeit initially on a very limited franchise. Internal economic borders were removed, as were some external protective measures. The fascist interlude—an extreme form of political authoritarianism and economic autarchy—clearly constitutes a rude interruption to this trend, but after 1945 a form of constitutional liberalism, combined with Keynesian economic management and social intervention, took deep root. It certainly had Italian peculiarities, some of which were inherited from fascism, not borrowed from revisionist liberalism elsewhere in Europe. Liberalism as a political movement, as opposed to a set of values, was reduced from the dominant force before 1922 to a minor residue after 1945. Two parties, the Liberal Party and Republican Party, qualified as 'liberal' in that sense, but between them they won only some 3–5 per cent in most post-war elections.

However, this was not entirely out of line with other European experience. It is difficult to find anywhere in Europe after 1945 examples of dominant or self-confident governing parties operating under the liberal banner. British and German liberalism was reduced to minor party status after 1945, as, if less drastically, were their Benelux and Scandinavian counterparts.[5] What might be thought more important was that, despite its relatively backward and under-developed status, Italy, alone among Mediterranean states, joined the family of European liberal democracies at the first attempt, making a reasonable success of the market economy, and combining it with significant elements of social welfare and income redistribution.

There are three reasons why this interpretation is less than fully convincing. First, the liberal state that preceded fascism proves on closer inspection to have offered much less fertile terrain for liberal values than might seem to be the case simply by comparing it with the regimes which preceded and succeeded it. The regime was deeply flawed, and most liberal and virtually all Marxist historians came to regard the Risorgimento as a liberal revolution that failed, allowing pre-democratic values and means of government to reassert themselves, even before the rise of fascism.

Secondly, as already noted, the dominant parties which emerged from fascism were the Italian Communist Party and Christian Democracy and the party system then remained for several decades an ideologically fragmented and polarized one, with a large number of parties, and extreme difficulty in assembling coalitions and maintaining political stability. The Italian system lacked a basic consensus on major issues of policy—international alliances, the role of the market, the scope and nature of welfare—until well into the 1980s. Its two major parties were in their different ways suspicious of each other's commitment to liberal values: the Communists saw the Christian Democrats as a clerical conspiracy against secular values, while the Christian Democrats saw the Communists as Moscow's advance guard.

Finally, and for the contemporary system most importantly, even if the two major parties did with some hesitation adapt to revisionist liberal values in the 1950s and 1960s, they had great difficulty in taking on board any element of the classical liberal corrections of the later decades. Indeed, in European terms, what has been striking about Italy in this last period has been the absence until very recently of any serious party programme which has taken its cue from the late twentieth-century revival of classical liberal values. This absence has had far-reaching consequences for the way Italy has been governed, not just in terms of economic and fiscal management, but also in terms of the working of liberal democratic institutions.

What is also very striking is the parallel between the problems of governability of the liberal state of 1861–1922 on the one hand, and that of the postwar democratic republic on the other. The two regimes, and especially their major political crises (respectively 1922 and 1992), are far apart in time and take place in such different political and socio-economic contexts that the parallels might seem rather limited. 1922, after all, brought a collapse into authoritarianism, whereas 1992, for all the uncertainty and confusion of the subsequent decade, did not. At another level, however, Italian political culture shows striking features of long-term continuity. They are identifiable in the difficulty of linking civil society to the machinery of government, in generating genuinely national political parties, and in establishing agreed and impartial procedural rules for key areas of democratic life. The absence of a consensus on these matters is strong prima-facie evidence of the underlying weakness of the commitment of large parts of Italian society to a genuinely liberal value system.

## Liberal Italy, Coalition-Building, and Party Government before Fascism

When pro-Piedmontese Risorgimento hagiography had been discredited for good by the rise of fascism, Italian historiography came to be dominated by a perspective on national unification that stressed the long-term consequences of that process's weaknesses. Few subsequent Italian historians or social theorists, whether liberal or Marxist, have believed that the collapse of liberal Italy was not the consequence of serious systemic shortcomings. Vilfredo Pareto, Antonio Gramsci, Piero Gobetti, Gaetano Salvemini, and Benedetto Croce, diverse as they are in ideology, all share a perspective that became a key feature of Italian historiography.[6] Central to that perspective was that the relationship between social and political élites, on the one hand, and the mass public on the other, was seriously deficient. It is no coincidence that the main international legacy of Italian social theory has been in the sociology of political élites.[7] Throughout the nineteenth and twentieth centuries, Italian theorists have worried about the mass–élite relationship, and more generally about the detachment of political society from civil society. Without an organic and enduring relationship in which political leaders reflect and represent civil society, they have believed, the liberal political system will not function in an open, fair, and impartial way, to deliver a lasting relationship of trust and legitimacy between ruled and rulers. Mechanisms for obtaining and sustaining political support will quickly become distorted, and faith in the impartiality and predictability of rules will be lost.

Nineteenth-century Italy was, by the standards set by these concerns, certainly not a good laboratory for experimentation. The absence of middle-class participation in the process of national revolution and state-building, or, in large parts of the country, even any consciousness whatsoever of the process, was the central problem from which many others flowed. This was hardly surprising in a society three-quarters of which was still illiterate, and where fewer than one per cent spoke an easily understood version of Italian. The cultural fragmentation of the peninsula was not overcome by the Risorgimento, and in some respects unification actually made things worse. It was a cardinal principle of unification that a political revolution was not to be followed by a social one. Old ascriptive social élites were left in place, especially in the south, and the peasantry, isolated by language from national political debate, politically disenfranchised, and, in the absence of land reform, economically dependent on their landlords, had no chance of real input into political life. Dissatisfaction took the form of brigandage and bread riots rather than organized political opposition. Suppression rather than accommodation was the governmental response, though at times an alternative solution was accommodation with informal networks of coercive power like the *mafia* and the *camorra*, that could be used as a form of surrogate social control. Internal free trade and a common currency also proved highly damaging to the southern economy. What little industrial development there already was in the south was quickly wiped out by competition from the more efficient north, and with it the process of indigenous capital accumulation.[8]

It was not therefore entirely surprising, given the hostility or at best indifference of so many Italians, that the new state denied the principle of territorial diversity and local autonomy, and the possibility raised by recent revisionist historians that brigandage was fomented or overstated to justify centralization does not much alter the argument for these purposes. A strong central administrative system, with almost no local autonomies, was the order of the day. The federalist ideas of Carlo Cattaneo were cast aside as quickly as the republican ideas of Giuseppe Mazzini, and tight control was exercised through the prefect, the ministry of the interior, and the *carabinieri*.[9]

However, central political control could not be based on authoritarianism alone. Unification was a military annexation of the south by the north in 1861, but power relations were destined to change thereafter. Unified Italy had, in practice if not fully on paper, a parliamentary system, albeit one based on a limited franchise. Parliamentary majorities had to be sustained and this would inevitably involve southerners as well as northerners. Governments were held in power by a form of parliamentary deal-making that quickly came to erase any notion of a boundary between government and opposition. In the 1860s and 1870s there were two key lines of division in Italian parliamentary politics. The first, between north and south, was never the basis for real party division. It would have split the country, even if a real boundary between the two could have been identified, and would have left the south as the permanent minority. The second, and more promising, line of division reflected what might have been the basis for a conservative–liberal division between the predominantly but by no means exclusively northern landed aristocracy, and the emerging middle class of lawyers, professionals, and other non-propertied local leaders. It could have divided moderates from progressives over the range of issues that late nineteenth-century governments across Europe all faced—franchise reform, decentralization, education reform, public health, transport infrastructure—and helped unite the country by giving voters a sense of meaningful choice between clear alternatives. Instead, in a steady line of prime-ministerial successors from Agostino Depretis, through Francesco Crispi to Giovanni Giolitti, each of whom condemned his predecessors but adopted their parliamentary practices, prime ministers built majorities across the centre of the political spectrum. Thus was born the practice of *trasformismo*, which brought a new word into the language and guaranteed that liberal Italy would not generate party government and until the eve of the First World War would not even generate anything resembling organized political parties.[10]

The consequence of *trasformismo* was a parliamentary culture built on individualist political entrepreneurship: a political market-place of extensive locally based clientele politics associated with a high degree of corruption. In this system there were no clear boundaries to the use of the machinery of state for political advantage. The judiciary, the police, and the civil service were not permitted to operate in professional impartiality, but were reservoirs of patronage and tools for settling political scores. Long before its final compromise with fascism, this system was roundly condemned by idealist liberal thinkers such as Bendetto Croce and Piero Gobetti. For such figures the national revolution had failed, producing neither democracy nor liberalism. Not only were the mass of the peasantry excluded from voting by the political élite, but in so far as the great majority of Italians were Catholic, they excluded themselves by following the Vatican's ban on political participation in the Italian state. From this followed a failure to develop local self-government, organized political parties, and fair political rules: in short, several of the indispensable features of a fully functioning liberal democracy. The moment this exclusion was no longer possible, after the First World War, the party system became deadlocked. The Socialists and the Catholic People's Party entered politics as intransigent opponents of each other and Liberalism, and the consequence was the collapse of 1922.

## The Legacy of Liberal Failure

There is a clear line connecting liberal failures before 1922, and the nature of the political system after 1945. Between 1861 and 1922, the system was dominated by 'Liberals' who failed to establish a workable liberal democratic system, and after 1945 their heirs were punished for this. The post-war system was relieved almost entirely of representatives of the liberal tradition precisely because political liberalism was seen to have failed. It was perceived that liberal Italy had paved the way for fascism, and it had been a still powerful Liberal block in parliament that invited Mussolini to become prime minister.

At the fall of fascism the Liberals still played a modest role in the resistance movement and the short-lived Action Party (1942–7) for six months in 1945 even held the office of prime minister through its leader Ferruccio Parri, before De Gasperi's Christian Democrats asserted their dominance. The Action Party, in fact, was the closest Italy came to establishing a significant voice of post-war revisionist liberalism, committed to a combination of the market economy and a strong defence of secular and individual freedoms in civil life.[11] But within a few months of its first electoral defeat in the vote for the 1946 Constituent Assembly, at which it won less than 2 per cent of the popular vote, the Action Party broke up over alliance strategy with the larger parties, and over key aspects of economic policy. The direct heirs of the old Liberal Party (PLI) survived only in the deep south, where they competed with the monarchists and neo-fascists. Later, during the 1960s, as its southern voters defected to the Christian Democrats, the PLI made a determined attempt to transform itself into a party of northern business. This generated an early attempt to become the Italian voice of economic neo-liberalism during the 1960s. Briefly, the PLI made some headway in this enterprise, rising to 5 per cent of the vote in the 1963 election, but faded thereafter. It was eventually reabsorbed into southern clientelist practices and, in an extraordinary echo of its pre-fascist forefathers, it emerged from the political scandals of the early 1990s as one of the parties most corrupted by the use of state patronage. A third heir of the broad liberal family was the Republican Party (PRI), an offshoot of the Action Party. Strongly entrenched in certain local bases where Mazzini's republicanism could be traced back to the early nineteenth century—most notably in Emilia Romagna—the party had the satisfaction in the 1946 referendum on the monarchy of seeing its spiritual father vindicated eighty years after his defeat by Cavour. But in the megaphone politics of subcultural confrontation, its subtle message (combining liberal civil rights, indicative economic planning of an essentially market economy, the welfare state, and incomes policy) was never able to take firm root, even when its leader, Ugo La Malfa, became Planning Minister in the early 1960s. For several decades the PRI had a moral authority in intellectual circles that belied its tiny following of less than 2 per cent of the vote, and the party was always recognized in the Anglo-Saxon world as one that talked intelligible and pragmatic language in the realm of public policy. But in the end even the PRI fell victim to the clientele coalition politics of the 1980s, and emerged from the great crisis of 1992, like the PLI, deeply compromised by political corruption.[12]

The post-war party system was therefore dominated by two strong mass parties: the Communists and Christian Democrats. For most members of the future political élite, and especially those who had fought in the Resistance, this was a healthy reaction to the failures of the liberal system. If liberal Italy lacked responsible party government, they reasoned, it was because it lacked strong stable parties, linking voters to political leaders. The answer was to focus on mechanisms for building strong parties and party government. Post-war politics thus very rapidly turned into a race to colonize large areas of civil society: the labour movement, co-operatives, student organizations, agricultural workers and small farmers, commercial and retail organizations, and recreational associations, were all brought into a party fold.[13] And if the left had a natural advantage in several of the labour-movement organizations, the Christian Democrats had the enormous assistance of the Church and the six million members of Catholic Action, the lay arm of the Church, during its heyday in the 1950s.[14]

Without doubt, this competitive search for a social base by the parties, with their extensive machinery and very large memberships, did link parties to civil society far more closely than in the pre-fascist era. Given the nature of the two major parties, however, it froze the party system into a mould in which the space for real competition was very limited, and in which the opportunity for policy debate and competition was almost non-existent. With the single, partial, exception of 1976, every general election from 1948 to 1987 inclusive brought more or less the same result, and left the Christian Democrats in control of the governing coalition. The nature of party competition ensured that both the two main parties contained within themselves characteristics which departed significantly from the liberal mainstream. In the case of the Communist Party the way in which this departure manifested itself was self-evident. In its early years it was an anti-system party of the far left, whose programme was by any standards exclusive and sectarian. Not until the 1980s was the party a serious contender for government office, until then never finding the allies necessary to escape from its 25–30 per cent ceiling of support among voters.

The case of the Christian Democrat Party (DC) is more complex. As the backbone of every coalition from 1945 to 1992, it declared itself the chief defender of liberal democracy against the extremes of right and left. But the DC's liberalism also had limits and these became more visible over time. Initially, they were in evidence for the most part in the party's strongly clerical nature, and its close links with the Catholic Church, leading to advocacy of special privileges for the clergy which found their way into both the constitution and ordinary law. Gradually, however, as the Catholic element became a less important and less uniting feature of the party's support base, two other characteristics undermining the party's liberal credentials began to cut in.[15]

The first was its extensive colonization of the machinery of government and public employment: schools, health services, local government payrolls, development agencies, the financial sector, and state enterprises. Party membership became an important criteria for employment and advancement in many such areas. Most pernicious of all for the liberal state, however, was party control of appointments and career management in politically strategic sectors like the state-run broadcasting system and the judiciary, where party management affected not merely the number of voters who might have an interest in maintaining the status quo, but the presentation of politics to the mass public, and the ability to protect politicians who transgressed anti-corruption legislation, especially in the complex world of party finances.[16]

The second characteristic—no less corrosive to its liberal credentials, though less significant until the 1980s—was the party's complete failure to adjust to basic changes in European political economy. This was not surprising, because from early on the DC showed itself strongly attached to state intervention in economic life. Like most other Christian democrat parties in Europe, it advocated income redistribution and a range of welfare measures to promote social cohesion, giving it much in common with social democracy. But Italian Christian Democracy went well beyond this, seeing direct state intervention as a solution to many of the structural weaknesses of the Italian economy, including, most notably, the dramatic development gap between the northern and southern halves of the country. Its mission was of course greatly assisted by the structures and outlooks inherited from the fascist regime. The extent of state involvement in the Italian economy underwent a dramatic increase during the crisis of the 1930s, when a large part of the banking system and its industrial assets were taken into public hands to prevent an immediate financial catastrophe. After the Second World War these structures were not dismantled, and although initially public-sector managers and bankers were given extensive leeway to make independent commercial decisions, their appointment and terms of office were increasingly determined by political exigencies—with correspondingly deleterious consequences for the financial performance of the businesses involved.[17]

The interventionist mentality gradually acquired by the DC proved to be the heaviest legacy of the post-war party system—heavier even than the presence of a large communist party occupying the natural electoral space of social democracy. In the twenty years from 1970 to 1990, with the DC still dominant, Italy was unable to generate a credible party of the moderate centre-right which could articulate values of fiscal prudence, public-sector efficiency, and taxpayer accountability. Within Christian Democracy itself the expressions 'left' and 'right' had meaning only in terms of the direction of coalition alliances, and since the parties of the far right were no more attached to the neo-liberal critique of the welfare state than were the Christian Democrats, this would have had no effect on party policy, even if coalition-building had shifted in a rightward direction. Few Christian Democrats from any wing of the party were sympathetic to budgetary prudence if they came from the south. The parties which might have assumed this mantle—the Liberal Party and the Republican Party—were, as we have seen, unable to assume the mantle of neo-liberalism, and through their continued presence as minor parties of the governing coalition ended up as discredited co-conspirators of Christian Democracy.

The DC therefore steered Italy to the point in 1990 at which the annual budget deficit had reached 11 per cent of GDP, and the accumulated stock of public debt had exceeded 100 per cent of GDP (reaching 125 per cent four years later): a fiscal crisis unparalleled in any other major European economy. Throughout those two decades no national party had been able to pitch its appeal to voters in terms of significant and distinctive tax-reductions or expenditure containment. There was a diffuse awareness of the impending crisis, especially in the last years of the 1980s, but there was no capacity for leadership in such a deeply factionalized party. Christian Democrat party secretaries and prime ministers survived in office by political mediation, and this left little room for a leadership style which could appeal beyond and over the immediate concerns of patronage-based power-broking inside the party, and could focus voters' attention on the wider needs for major structural reform through deregulation, privatization, budgetary restraint, and lower debt-servicing costs.[18]

In reality, the political basis for these sorts of policies was beginning to emerge in the 1980s, but its articulation to the electorate was compromised by two important constraints. The first was the long-standing fear on the part of all voters of the centre and the right that any dispersal of votes away from the Christian Democrats and their allies would open the door to the Communist Party. The second was the confusion between the appeals of budgetary restraint and economic reform on the one side, and of territorial politics on the other. From the mid-1980s onwards, first slowly and then at an accelerating pace, a new factor began to emerge into political life, which was based on the fermentation of a growing economic and political grievance nurtured by prosperous, or at least heavily taxed, northern voters, against the central government in Rome, and against southern voters who were presented as controlling and manipulating the latter. Thus it was that the first party to exploit the demand for budgetary restraint was the xenophobic Northern League, which, because of its exotic and explicitly racist approach to immigration, could hardly count as a credible candidate to lead Italy towards the neo-liberal reform agenda. It wrapped its demands for reform in explicitly territorial and secessionist terms—northern taxpayers, it said, could reap the benefits of tax and expenditure cuts without paying any price in terms of employment or service reduction. And in so doing the League inevitably blurred issues that badly needed clarity, and sharply circumscribed the electoral and geographical limits of the neo-liberal appeal.[19] The chances of a phased escape from the failures of economic policy in the 1980s, the dimensions of which can be seen from Table 1, were therefore undermined by the peculiarities of Italy's political geography. Reform pressures were impossible to pursue for the southern electorate, and they became distorted and misdirected in the north.

Table 1. *The fiscal crisis of the Italian state, 1980–1992*

| | Deficit ratio % GDP | Debt ratio % GDP | Pensions % GDP | GDP growth | Inflation | Long-term int. rates |
|---|---|---|---|---|---|---|
| 1980 | 8.6 | 58.1 | 14.2 | 3.5 | 20.6 | 15.3 |
| 1981 | 11.5 | 60.3 | 15.8 | 0.5 | 18.1 | 19.4 |
| 1982 | 11.4 | 65.3 | 16.3 | 0.5 | 17.0 | 20.2 |
| 1983 | 10.7 | 70.2 | 17.3 | 1.2 | 14.7 | 18.3 |
| 1984 | 11.7 | 75.5 | 16.8 | 2.6 | 11.9 | 15.6 |
| 1985 | 12.6 | 82.3 | 17.2 | 2.8 | 9.3 | 13.7 |
| 1986 | 11.7 | 86.4 | 17.2 | 2.8 | 6.3 | 11.5 |
| 1987 | 11.0 | 90.6 | 17.3 | 3.1 | 5.4 | 10.6 |
| 1988 | 10.7 | 92.8 | 17.3 | 3.9 | 5.9 | 10.9 |
| 1989 | 9.8 | 95.7 | 17.6 | 2.9 | 6.6 | 12.8 |
| 1990 | 11.1 | 104.5 | 18.2 | 2.2 | 6.3 | 13.5 |
| 1991 | 10.1 | 108.4 | 18.3 | 1.1 | 6.9 | 13.3 |
| 1992 | 9.6 | 117.3 | 19.3 | 0.6 | 5.6 | 13.3 |

*Sources:* Annual reports of the governor of the Bank of Italy; *OECD Economic Outlook* (various years); G. Di Palma, S. Fabbrini, and G. Freddi, *Condannata al successo? L'Italia nell' Europa integrata* (Bologna: Il Mulino, 2000), 294–5.

The Christian Democrat Party's inability to adapt to the new demands of economic policy thus led directly to the political collapse of the early 1990s, though the precise interaction between electoral crisis, the loss of control over state patronage, judicial investigation of corruption, and the financial crisis was complex. The serious territorial imbalance in voting behaviour in the north in 1992 quickly turned the problem from a fiscal crisis into an institutional one. The governing parties' share of the northern vote dropped spectacularly while, initially at least, holding steady in the south. Their parliamentary majority disappeared but there was no alternative majority to replace it, and certainly no majority built on a neo-liberal programme of budgetary rationalization. The collapse of governing-party authority in 1992 was therefore rapidly followed by a collapse of party control over those institutions—the judiciary, the media, local government, the state-controlled financial sector, and state enterprise—which by various mechanisms had sustained an electoral majority and suppressed the detection of political corruption.[20] The lira lost 30 per cent of its value against the mark in a matter of months and the external credibility crisis which followed, exacerbated by the spectacle of nearly a third of the 1992 parliament being investigated for corruption, became so severe that the only solution commanding external confidence was the drastic resort to government through non-party technocrats.

The spectacular political collapse of 1992 is thus closely related to long-term failure of the party system of the post-war Republic, linked to the weakness of liberal values. If in the first three decades after 1945 Italy was distinct in Europe for its ideological polarization, in the last two it was distinct for the less dramatic, but no less pernicious political failure to generate responsible, party-led policy debate that retained a stable linkage between parties and voters. Italy's party system and constitutional arrangements failed to face the economic constraints of an increasingly liberalized European economic system by articulating a clear programme of adaptation to contain extensive, inadequately funded, welfare intervention, and move rapidly towards a greater role for market-driven allocative mechanisms. The pressures for change came from outside—primarily from financial markets and from the European Union—and in the face of such pressures, rather than adapt, the party system fragmented, the political class subcontracting the task of adaptation largely to non-party technocrats.

# Liberalism and the Struggle for Political Reconstruction in the 1990s

The physiology of the Italian party system, and the stance of public policy since 1992, represent sharp breaks with the past. In just two years the party which had dominated every government since 1945 broke up and disappeared. Numerous former Christian Democrat politicians survived, joining almost every party across the centre and right. Meanwhile a flush of new parties sprang up to replace those that went down with Christian Democracy. Parliament was largely renewed in the general election of 1994 (only one in five of those elected had previously been members). Only the former Communist Party, now renamed the Democratic Left Party, and the former neo-fascist MSI, now renamed Alleanza Nazionale, survived in anything like their original form, and in both cases there was an explicit change of name and programme.[21]

The change in economic and fiscal management was even more dramatic. Between 1992 and 1997, Italy finally received its long-overdue dose of neo-liberal budgetary rectitude. Massive cuts in public expenditure were imposed and, by 1996, the impact was being felt in financial market confidence, and hence Italy's real interest rates and debt-servicing costs. This in turn reduced the annual budget deficit in 1997 from 11 per cent at the start of the decade to below the EMU target figure of 3 per cent in 1997. Certainly, the price paid was a heavy one. The programme was rushed through at speed, its effect on public infrastructure provision and long-term public investment was unplanned and chaotic. It depressed business confidence, and it pushed unemployment to levels unseen since the early post-war years. It hit the under-developed south with exceptional ferocity. Italy's growth rate slipped to the bottom of the EU range and stayed there throughout the decade. But given the direction in which the rest of the EU had already decided to go, Italy by 1992 probably had little choice. Even if it had not planned to get itself into the common currency area, a major programme of adjustment would have been necessary. The majority of commentators in the early 1990s wrote off any chance that Italy might qualify for first-wave membership of European Monetary Union, yet in 1999 the country did so qualify. The rules were interpreted generously, and other countries had strong reasons for making concessions, but the public-finance revolution delivered the main goal. And the fact that, by a variety of means between 1992 and 1998, parliamentary majorities were assembled which went along with the programmes demanded by the technocrats who took over the reins of economic management, suggests that the neo-liberal message had finally got through to the political class.[22]

These bare facts of the complex process by which public policy was revolutionized might suggest that neo-liberalism did finally assert itself over the patterns laid down over the previous two decades, but the reality is more complex, and it is here that the limitations of the revolution of the 1990s, and the parallels with Italy's past, show up most clearly. The reform programme was carried out without voters ever having voted for parties that made a cohesive coalition virtue of such a programme. Most members of the Italian parliament saw themselves as having no alternative but to accept the programme dictated by the Treasury and by the European Union's convergence programme, and voted for it in parliament without ever endorsing it publicly. Voters, meanwhile, dispersed their votes across an ever wider and more disparate range of parties. No professional politician held the Treasury—by far the most powerful department of government—after 1991. It was entrusted to technocrats from either the Bank of Italy or the academic world, and their political strength *vis-à-vis* their spending ministry colleagues and parliament came entirely from their credibility in international financial markets, and from the backing of prime ministers whose removal from office would be judged harshly by those markets. Some governments—those of Carlo Azeglio Ciampi in 1993 and Lamberto Dini in 1995/6, and even the Prodi government of 1996—were composed largely (in Dini's case entirely) of non-party technocrats. None of the five prime ministers between Amato (1992/3) and Prodi (1996/8) was a conventional politician of the First Republic, and only Berlusconi (1994) was a senior figure in a significant party.[23]

No less significantly, by the end of a decade which was hailed at its beginning as one in which the party system would be rationalized and modernized, and the institutions made to work in the interests of a more purposive and open style of government, the fragmentation of the party system and the individualism of parliamentary representation had reached epidemic proportions. This happened despite the introduction of a first-past-the-post electoral system for three-quarters of each chamber of Parliament. Parties simply engaged in stand-down electoral alliances, grouping together very broad and disparate coalitions. By 1999 there were nearly twice as many parties in Parliament as at the start of the decade, and here the parallel between the contemporary pattern of parliamentary politics, and that in liberal Italy, is especially striking. It was certainly very widely assumed that the introduction of the single-ballot, simple plurality electoral system would reduce the party system, if not to a bipartite system, then at least—through coalition alliances to which individual parties had pledged themselves before the voters—to stable coalitions of parties. In these coalitions, it was hoped, the emergence of bipolar competition between leaders who were designated prime-ministerial candidates would also strengthen coalition leaders against parliamentary backbenchers or minor parties.[24]

The reality has turned out very differently. Small parties, and large numbers of individual members of parliament, have quickly learnt how to develop strong contractual bargaining power in the new system, both in the negotiations over the distribution of parliamentary constituencies before elections, and in each elected chamber thereafter. As Table 2 shows, the Italian parliaments of the 1990s have returned to the pre-1922 system of *trasformismo* with a vengeance. A very significant proportion (129 out of 630) of the deputies elected in the 1996 legislature had by 1999 migrated into different parliamentary groups. Some were forced into this as their parliamentary group fell below the threshold for official existence, and technically had to be folded into the so-called 'mixed group' (an administrative umbrella for a wide range of mini-parties). But this accounts only for about one-fifth of the total. Most of those who joined the mixed group—which grew from twenty-six in 1996 to 113 in 1999—joined because the party under which they had originally been elected broke up, or because they themselves defected. For many of these individuals, party allegiance of any kind was secondary to a personal search for maximum contractual power, and the securing of a stand-down agreement giving them the best possible opportunity for re-election.

The impact of this post-electoral fragmentation on coalition-building, and on the linkage between electoral choice and government formation, has been profound. The purpose of the electoral reform of 1993 was to bind coalitions together, by ensuring that those parties that stood together in the campaign, and operated stand-down agreements in each others' favour, were then pledged to stay together in the ensuring parliament, and—if in power—support the programme on which they were elected. Yet in both the 1994 and 1996 parliaments quite the opposite has happened. There have been serious defections across the major divide between right and left, involving both members of the majority defecting to the opposition, and members of the opposition defecting to the majority. The government of Lamberto Dini in 1995 was formed when the Northern League defected from the so-called Freedom Pole led by Silvio Berlusconi (only seven months after the 1994 general election). Similarly, the government of Massimo D'Alema was formed in 1998 (thirty months into the 1996 parliament) when some of the far-left Communist Refoundation group defected from Romano Prodi's government, and were replaced by centrists elected in stand-down agreements with Silvio Berlusconi and the conservatives. In many respects this behaviour represents a more serious denial of electoral choice under the new electoral system than it would have done under the old. Previously, parties rarely pledged themselves in advance to particular coalitions, and as a result there were never clear-cut prime ministerial candidates, as there were in 1994 and 1996. In the 1990s, there have been both electoral coalitions and prime-ministerial candidates, yet the level of post-electoral discipline has decreased dramatically, rather than tightened. It is therefore difficult to see in the two legislatures elected since the political collapse of 1992 any major progress towards responsible programmatic government. On the contrary, the final collapse of the mass

Table 2. *Parliamentary groups in the Italian Chamber of Deputies, May 1996–August 1999*

| | May 1996 | Feb. 1997 | Mar. 1998 | Oct. 1998 | Mar. 1999 | Aug. 1999 |
|---|---|---|---|---|---|---|
| AN | 92 | 92 | 91 | 91 | 91 | 89 |
| CCD–CDU | 30 | 20 | 8 | 0 | 0 | 0 |
| UDR | 0 | 0 | 27 | 26 | 19 | 0 |
| PDS–L'Ulivo | 172 | 171 | 172 | 169 | 165 | 166 |
| FI | 123 | 121 | 112 | 111 | 111 | 109 |
| Communists | 0 | 0 | 0 | 21 | 21 | 21 |
| Democr–L'Ulivo | 0 | 0 | 0 | 0 | 20 | 21 |
| NL | 59 | 58 | 58 | 55 | 55 | 49 |
| Pop–L'Ulivo | 67 | 68 | 67 | 67 | 60 | 62 |
| RC | 35 | 34 | 34 | 0 | 0 | 0 |
| RI | 26 | 20 | 24 | 23 | 0 | 0 |
| Other | 26 | 46 | 37 | 67 | 88 | 113 |
| TOTAL | 630 | 630 | 630 | 630 | 630 | 630 |

*Sources:* Data derived from information provided by the Chamber of Deputies.
*Note:* The data here refer only to the transfer of deputies from one group to another and not to the replacement of members of parliament through by-elections.

party organizations brought into being in the 1940s and 1950s has engendered a return to the *trasformismo* of an earlier era.[25]

A second striking fact about the reordering of party politics in the 1990s is the continuing difficulty visible on the centre-right in generating a clear and unambiguous coalition for neo-liberal values. In the far north and north-east, the Northern League has captured what most observers take to be a vote in favour of such policies. But it has done so through a strong populist and local- ist appeal to xenophobia, low taxes, and extensive measures of devolution. Its main plank is that northern taxpayers should not subsidize the south. In parts of the south, similarly, the principal party of the right is Alleanza Nazionale. But this party cannot be seen as the embodiment of neo-liberal values for two fundamental reasons. The first is that the party is the successor to the neo- fascist MSI, and contains within its fold a number of individuals from that background. The second is that, quite predictably from a party whose main strength is concentrated in the south, AN is in favour of an interventionist mixture of public spending and regional transfer aid, which compromises its qualifications for adherence to a neo-liberal programme in the economic sphere. Certainly AN has been one of the most vociferous opponents of pri- vatization, the effects of which would be felt most harshly among the non- viable state-owned enterprises located in the south.[26]

This leaves Silvio Berlusconi's Forza Italia as the main embodiment of neo- liberal values. However, since it has so far won only some 20 per cent of the popular vote, it has to work closely with the League, Alleanza Nazionale, and indeed those ex-Christian Democrats who have ended up on the right rather than the left. So, while Forza Italia certainly sees itself as the main voice of neo-liberalism in contemporary Italy, it is required to work in coalition with two parties which, politically, have strongly illiberal features in their make-up, and one of which is as committed to state intervention in the economy as the Christian Democrats. In any case, it is difficult on some counts to see Forza Italia itself as the embodiment of liberal values. Silvio Berlusconi's personal business empire, from which he launched his party in 1994, was built up dur- ing the First Republic, and he himself was closely associated with Bettino Craxi, leader of the now defunct Socialist Party. Craxi, who fled the country in 1993 to avoid prosecution for political corruption, died in self-imposed exile six years later, after having been found guilty in his absence. The legisla- tion by which a licensing system giving the Berlusconi media empire control of nearly all Italian commercial television was written while Craxi was prime minister. Perhaps the most astonishing fact is that Berlusconi himself was charged and found guilty of acts of corruption, though the extended appeals process means that he has never gone to prison, and almost certainly never will. His claims to innocence—the truth of which need not concern us here— are in any case less significant than that Berlusconi himself claims that he is the victim of persecution by politically biased judicial investigators, and spent much of his energies in the constutitional commission set up by parliament in 1996 seeking (to date unsuccessfully) to find ways of placing political curbs on the power of the judiciary to investigate corruption.[27]

The extraordinary nature of Forza Italia as a party which is in effect a wholly owned subsidiary of the Berlusconi business empire also casts doubt on its real commitment to a liberal system of impartial rules and institutions.[28] The awkward issue of the conflict of interest inherent in the majority-shareholder and chief executive of one of Italy's largest business empires becoming prime minister was never properly addressed—nor could it have been—while Berlsuconi was in office. Conflict of interest has also arisen in relation to legislation on equal political access to the media, given Berlusconi's control of such a large slice of commercial television.[29] As to the nature of Forza Italia as a political party, all observers have noted the almost complete absence until recently of a power structure, system of internal elections, or a rank and file. Its linkages with civil society, other than through the media, are therefore tenuous in the extreme.[30]

It is hardly surprising, therefore, given the controversial qualities that the coalition of the right displays, that the true extent of Italy's conversion to liberal values in the 1990s remains very much in doubt. None of the three parties seems to be an unimpeachable exponent of impartial rules of governance, equality before the law, or the defence of civil rights, and in their different ways all three seem doubtful exponents of the power of economic markets. And in so far as the territorial fragmentation of Italian political representation delivers each party only a modest share of the popular vote, making complex coalitions the rule, the conservative coalition retains within itself a highly developed propensity to renege on coalition commitments to voters.

## Conclusion

The collapse of the post-war Italian republic and the difficulties of making the transition to a new, more purposeful and more legitimate institutional order than the one which folded so ignominiously in 1992 can only be fully understood against features of Italian political culture which have very deep roots in post-unification history. When Italians today worry about the weaknesses of their regime, they worry about the absence of a cohesive national identity, about the differences in the wealth, attitudes, and social structures between different parts of the country, about the enduring fragmentation of parties, about the lack of a national consensus on the institutions, about the size and role of the state, and about the difficulties of building impartial state institutions. These concerns, even if all justified, are not necessarily all related in a way that constitutes a single systemic weakness, traceable directly back to 1861 and to the early decades of unification. Nevertheless, while all contemporary political problems certainly do not derive from some iron law of cultural determinism, there are features of national political culture in most societies which seem to endure, or at least adapt, from one historical epoch to another, and certainly if the structure of ideas which underlie a national political culture are to be understood, they have to be placed in historical context. One such example in the Italian case is constituted by the difficulties of establishing a secular liberal value system. It has interfered with features of the political system which are normally considered to be quite central to the working of liberal democracy: the articulation of clear and distinct party programmes between which voters can make judgements; the sense that there is some sort of relationship between the choices made by the electorate, and the formation of governments; and the possibility of alternation in power between government and opposition.

# Notes

1.  This interpretation has its roots in the debate between Giovanni Sartori and Giorgio Galli in the 1960s over the most appropriate model (polarized pluralism or imperfect bi-partism) for understanding Italian party politics. Despite their differences both models started from the assumption that Italian party politics was built on strong and mutually exclusive ideological sub-cultures that limited electoral competition, voter mobility, and the range of parties eligible for participation in government. See G. Sartori, *Parties and Party Systems*, (Cambridge: Cambridge University Press, 1976), and A. Prandi, and G. Galli, *Patterns of Political Participation in Italy* (New Haven, Conn.: Yale University Press, 1970). By the mid-1980s, this interpretation was increasingly untenable, and the publication in 1985 of Paolo Farneti's perceptive (albeit opaque) book on the party system dropped the assumption that party relations and voter identities were frozen in the cold war mould determined by subcultural politics. See P. Farneti, *The Italian Party System* (London: Pinter 1985).
2.  For accounts of the impact of the transition of the 1990s on party politics see S. Gundle, and S. Parker, *The New Italian Republic: From the Fall of the Berlin Wall to Berlusconi*, (London: Routledge, 1996); also 'Crisis and Transition in Italian Politics' (special issue of *West European Politics*, 20/1, (1997), ed. M. Bull, and M. Rhodes) especially the chapters by Bull and Rhodes, and D'Alimone and Bartolini; and V. Bufacchi and S. Burgess, *Italy since 1989: Events and Interpretations*, (London and Basingstoke: Macmillan, 1998).
3.  These issues are not explored here. For an introduction see *inter alia* J. Gray, *Liberalism* (Milton Keynes: Open University Press, 1986), and the more advanced M. Sandel, *Liberalism and the Limits of Justice* (Cambridge: Cambridge University Press, 1982).
4.  Those unfamiliar with the dimensions of the pre-fascist liberal state are referred to M. Clark, *Modern Italy 1871–1982* (London: Longman, 1984), and D. Mack

Smith, *Italy: A Political History* (New Haven, Conn. and London: Yale University Press, 1997).

5. Most classifications of European party systems produce a number of major *familles spirituelles* in which 'liberal and radical parties' are a consistent presence (the best known such classification is probably K. von Beyme, *Political Parties in Western Democracies* (Aldershot: Gower, 1985), but it is notable that all classificatory schemes recognize the internal diversity of this family group, and the electoral weakness it has suffered since the early part of the 20th cent. Compared to social democracy, Christian democracy, communism, and some of the new social movements, it has engendered little systematic comparative research as a party family, and over the last three decades the 'Liberal International' and the Liberal group in the European Parliament have always been far smaller than their Social Democrat and Christian Democrat Counterparts.

6. The relationship between Italian history and political theory in the works of several of these writers is analysed in R. Bellamy, *Modern Italian Social Theory* (Oxford: Blackwell, 1987), see esp. pp. 4–11. Antonio Gramsci's (Marxist) interpretation of 19th-cent. Italian history is best understood from his 'prison notebooks': see *Selections from the Prison Notebooks*, ed. and trans. Q. Hoare and G. Nowell-Smith (London: Lawrence & Wishart, 1971), esp. pp. 44–122, also J. Femia, *Gramsci's Political Thought* (Oxford: Clarendon Press, 1981). Piero Gobetti's (liberal/socialist) interpretation is best derived from P. Gobetti, *La rivoluzione liberale: Saggio sulla lotta politica in Italia*, ed. E. Perona, 5th edn.(Turin: Einaudi, 1995). Unfortunately, there is no English trans. of this work, but a recent essay by Paolo Bagnoli reviews the latest Italian edn. of Gobetti's work and the accompanying introductory essay by Paolo Flores d'Arcais: see P. Bagnoli, 'Piero Gobetti and the Liberal Revolution in Italy', *Journal of Modern Italian Studies*, 2/1 (1997), 34–44. Benedetto Croce's (liberal) interpretation is not easily understood from a single source of Croce's vast output, but the edited trans. by C. Sprigge, *Philosophy, Poetry, History* (Oxford: OUP, 1966) provides the best source along with R. Bellamy, 'Liberalism and Historicism: Bendetto Croce and the Political Role of Idealism in Italy c. 1880–1950' in A. Moulakis, (ed.) *The Promise of History* (Berlin and New York: Walter de Gruyter, 1985), 69–119.

7. See G. Parry, *Political Elites* (London: Allen & Unwin, 1969).

8. See *inter alia* Clark, *Modern Italy.*

9. Many of these issues are treated succinctly in C. Levy, *Italian Regionalism: History, Identity and Politics* (Oxford: Berg, 1996); see esp. A. Lyttleton, 'Shifting Identities: Nation, Region, and City', 33–52. The principal Italian historian to have treated these issues is R. Romanelli, *Il commando impossibile: Stato e società nell'Italia liberale* (Bologna: Il Mulino, 1988), a summary of which is found in 'Il sonno delle regioni', *Quaderni storici*, 41 (1979), 778–81.

10. Trasformismo is widely discussed in the historiography of 19th- and 20th-cent. Italian political development. For a simple introduction, see Mack Smith, *Italy*, 100–88. For an Italian treatment see P. Pombeni, *Partiti e sistemi politici nella storia contemporanea* (Bologna: Il Mulino, 1985), esp. 419–523. Recently, attention has returned to the practice in the context of the contemporary fragmentation of party politics (on which see later parts of this chapter) leading to the republication of Cilibrizzi's monumental 2-vol. political and parliamentary history of the liberal regime: S. Cilibrizzi, *Storia parlamentare, politica, e diplomatica d'Italia da Novara a Vittorio Veneto* (Rome: Tosi, 1998), esp. vol. ii.

11. See the history of the Action Party: G. De Luna, *Storia del Partito d'Azione 1942-1947* (Rome: Ed. Riuniti, 1997).

12. Despite the significance of the electoral and eventually moral failures of both these parties, there is little literature on either in English, though some basic narratives include sections on the fortunes of both parties. See N. Kogan, *A Political History of Postwar Italy from the Old to the New Centre-Left* (New York: Praeger, 1981); also F. Catalano, 'The Rebirth of the Party System 1944–48', in S. Woolf, (ed.), *The Rebirth of Italy 1943–50*, 56–94. Noberto Bobbio's systematic treatment of the development of contemporary Italian political thought also contains references to these parties: see esp. N. Bobbio, *Ideological Profile of Twentieth Century Italy* (Princeton, NJ: Princeton University Press, 1995).

13. The standard account of the sociological foundations of this is found in Prandi and Galli, *Patterns*. A perceptive commentary is available in A. Pizzorno, 'A Theoretical Framework for the Study of Political Parties', trans. in D. Pinto (ed.), *Contemporary Italian Sociology: A Reader* (Cambridge: Cambridge University Press, 1981).

14. See G. Poggi, *Catholic Action in Italy: The Sociology of a Sponsored Organisation* (Stanford, Calif.: Stanford University Press, 1967).

15. See R. Leonardi, and D. Wertman, *Italian Christian Democracy: The Politics of Dominance* (London: Macmillan, 1989), esp. 223–44; also more systematically in Italian, A. Parisi, *Democristiani* (Bologna: Il Mulino, 1979).

16. The literature on this process is now extensive. For an introduction in English see P. McCarthy, *The Crisis of the Italian State: From the Origins of the Cold War to the Fall of Berlusconi* (London: Macmillan, 1995), esp. 61–102; see also P. Ginsborg, 'Explaining Italy's Crisis', in Gundle and Parker, *New Italian Republic*, 19–39.

17. See P. Furlong, *Modern Italy: Representation and Reform* (London: Routledge, 1994), esp. 231–53.

18. The extent to which Italian public policy was untouched at the start of the 1990s by neo-liberal values is documented in almost all reports on the Italian economy during this period. A good summary is found in Padoa-Schioppa and F. Kostoris, *Italy: The Sheltered Economy. Structural Problems in the Italian Economy* (Oxford, Clarendon Press, 1993).

19. See I. Diamanti, 'The Northern League: From Regional Party to Party of Government', in Gundle and Parker, *New Italian Republic*, 113–29.

20. See Bufacchi and Burgess, *Italy since 1989*, esp. the chapter on political corruption, pp. 83–106.

21. Details of the extensive changes to Italian party politics in this period are found in R. Katz, and P. Ignazi, (eds.), *Italian Politics: The Year of the Tycoon* (Boulder, Colo.: Westview, 1996) and R. D'Alimonte, and D. Nelken, (eds.), *Italian Politics: The Centre-Left in Power* (Boulder, Colo.: Westview, 1997).

22. The main parameters of the changes to public policy are set out in G. Di Palma, S. Fabbrini, and G. Freddi, (eds.), *Condannata al successo? L'Italia nell'Europa integrata* (Bologna: Il Mulino, 2000), within which see esp., on public finances, S. Vasallo, 'La politica del bilancio: le condizioni e gli effetti della convergenza', pp. 287–324, and on regulation A. La Spina, 'Le autorità independenti: Rilevanza e istituzionalizzazione', pp. 199–244.

23. See G. Pasquino, 'The Government of Lamberto Dini', in M. Caciagli, and D. Kertzer, *Italian Politics: The Stalled Transition* (Boulder, Colo.: Westview, 1996), 137–52, and S. Fabbrini, 'From the Prodi Government to the D'Alema Government', in D. Hine, and S. Vassallo, (eds.), *Italian Politics: The Return of Politics* (Oxford: Berghahn, 2000), 121–38.

24. See D. Gambetta, and S. Warner, 'The Rhetoric of Reform Revealed (or: if you Bite the Ballot it may Bite Back)', *Journal of Modern Italian Studies*, 1/3, (1996), 357–76;

also A. Chiaromonte, 'L'effetto mancato della riforma maggioritario: Il voto strategico', *Rivista Italiana di Scienza Politica*, 26/3 (1996), 703–26.

25. This has led not only to the fragmentation of the party system just described, but also to the complete breakdown of co-ordinated parliamentary efforts at coherent institutional reform. The Bicamerale (the parliamentary commission charged with drafting a new constitutional framework) broke up in disarray in 1998, and in both the 1999 and 2000 referenda, voters so lost interest in and understanding of the process of reform that the government was unable to persuade the necessary 50 per cent of the electorate to vote in a referendum to address at least one part of the problem, by introducing a simple and necessary modification to the electoral system. See G. Pasquino, 'A Postmortem of the Bicamerale', in Hine and Vasallo, *Italian Politics*, 101–20; also L. Verzichelli, 'I gruppi parlamentari dopo il 1994: Fluidità e riaggregazioni', *Rivista Italiana di Scienza Politica*, 26/2 (1996), 391–414.

26. See M. Tarchi, and E. Poli, 'The Parties of the *Polo*: United to What End?, in Hine and Vasallo, *Italian Politics*, 65–86.

27. See C. Guarnieri, 'The Judiciary in the Italian Political Crisis', *West European Politics*, 20/1 (1997), 157–75.

28. The literature on the Berlusconi phenomenon is extensive, and much of it highly polemical. Useful sources are D. Mennitti, *Forza Italia: Radiografia di un evento* (Rome: Ideazione editrice, 1997), A. Gilioli, *Forza Italia: La storia, gli uomini, i misteri*, (Bergamo: Ferruccio Arnaldi Editore, 1994), and C. Golia, *Dentro Forza Italia*, (Venice: Marsiglio, 1997).

29. See L. Ricolfi, 'Politics and the Mass Media in Italy', *West European Politics*, 20/1 (1997), 135–56.

30. See E. Poli, 'I modelli organizzativi', in Mennitti *Forza Italia*, 79–110.

# 13

## Between Mutual Support and Misunderstanding: The British Labour Party and the SPD

### William E. Paterson

A first impression of Peter Pulzer might be of a classic Oxford don, atypically successful but with a talent for *bons mots* that places him securely in an established tradition. Closer acquaintance would soon reveal that this apparently most English of academics was born in Vienna and that some of the attributes we take to be typically Oxford would be seen by others as Viennese. Peter Pulzer's measured academic persona does not immediately suggest a past as a political activist, but one of the less well-known aspects of his spectacular career is the contrast between his distinction as an academic and his lack of success as a political activist when in the 1960s and 1970s he failed on a number of occasions to be elected to Oxford City Council in the Labour interest. Pulzer, himself, sees no contradiction since his psephological expertise allowed him to identify and stand for absolutely hopeless wards which carried no chance of election and potential damage to his academic work. Although Peter Pulzer's career as an activist ended some time in the past, he has maintained throughout his life an intense interest in social democracy. Here, again, he is in a well-established Austrian tradition which has continued from the Austrian Marxists, through Benedikt Kautsky down to contemporary Austrian political scientists like Wolfgang Müller and Anton Pelinka.

Most comparative analysis of social democracy explains its evolution in terms of broad categories like the decline of class as a voting determinant and the reduced role of ideology. There are few studies of the interaction between parties, their mutual influence, and the degree to which lessons are drawn or blocked through mutual misunderstanding. Given Pulzer's academic and personal interests, I have chosen to examine these themes in relation to the Labour Party and the German Social Democratic Party. This contribution is cast in the form of an examination of two episodes in the relations between the two parties. Both cases selected relate to instances where the line of influence was expected to run from Britain to Germany. The first study looks at the post-1945 period when the Labour Party, bathed in the prestige of the historic 1945 victory and in control of Germany's industrial heartland, was expected by a number of acute observers to transform the prospects and character of the SPD. The second case-study, the formulation and reception of the Schröder/Blair paper, is set in a period where Britain's power and influence is manifestly reduced but the New Labour government of Tony Blair enjoys considerable domestic and international standing.

The securing of democracy in Germany was perceived by the Allied governments, including the British, to depend crucially on the performance of political parties who provided the link between democratic politicians and a largely apathetic population. In this connection, the position of the SPD, especially in the early post-war years before the consolidation of the CDU/CSU, appeared absolutely crucial. It remains therefore something of a puzzle as to why the Labour Party, a member of the same political family, did not do more to meet SPD expectations in those early post-war years and why its influence was not much greater. From a number of different perspectives the initial conditions looked extremely promising. The Labour Party had just won by a landslide and was the flagship of democratic socialism in Western Europe. The Labour Party Programme of 1945 also bore the imprint of William Beveridge on the welfare state and John Maynard Keynes on the economy—figures who were widely regarded as the major European policy thinkers in these areas. Writing as Paul Sering, Richard Löwenthal observed: 'The possibilities of realising democratic socialism are located in European democracies and the British Commonwealth rather than in the Continental super states of the Soviet Union and the USA.' [1]

In contrast to the pre-war experience when there were few people in either party who knew the leading figures in the other party intimately, the enforced exile of the SPD party executive in London meant that situation had been transformed. Although Kurt Schumacher himself had never been to Britain before he became party leader, the group who gathered around him and who played a key role in the deliberations of the party executive contained a number of leading figures like Erich Ollenhauer, Fritz Heine, Willi Eichler, and Erwin Schoettle, all of whom had been in the London exile and who possessed a detailed knowledge and experience of the Labour Party. Moreover they continued to maintain their relationship with the contacts they had developed in the Labour Party after they returned to Germany. The SPD also maintained for a time a liaison office in London under Wilhelm Sander.

Experience with the SPD in exile also meant that there were more leading Labour Party figures than in previous periods who had direct and prolonged experience of the SPD. The appointment of John Hynd, who had been notable for contact with and defence of the SPD in exile, as Minister for Germany in October 1945, seemed to bode well for future relations between the parties. Two prominent members of the British administration, Austen Albu, who was sent to the Control Commission as Hynd's emissary, and Alan Flanders, also in the Control Commission, were influential Labour activists who were very sympathetic to the SPD. The SPD's estimation of Albu and Flanders was not misjudged and they continued to favour the SPD where possible in their official duties. This made them bitter critics of American policy and of General Clay in particular, as Albu noted in his diary: 'All agree Clay is a bastard'.[2] In January 1946 the new International Secretary of the Labour Party, Denis Healey, a fluent German speaker, replaced William Gillies who had been one of the SPD's most consistent and influential antagonists during the London exile.

Despite these favourable omens, the relationship between the SPD and the Labour Party during the years of Schumacher's leadership could never be described as close and mostly it could best be characterized as formal and correct. In this first section, an attempt will be made to explain why, contrary to the high expectations, the relationship functioned so imperfectly. This explanation will be largely centred on the Labour Party, although the expectations were much higher and the disappointment much greater on the part of the SPD. Hilary Balshaw concluded in her Oxford doctorate on British occupation policy in Hamburg that 'among Social Democrats there was still a lingering disappointment at the lack of British support for their claims to political leadership and programme of political reforms'. [3] The disappointment of the Hamburg SPD with Labour policy, which I shall argue was typical of the SPD as a whole, echoes the earlier disappointment of the exiled party executive in London with the Labour Party.

Invited to London by the Labour Party, the SPD Executive Committee in Exile originally entertained very high expectations. As Anthony Glees, one of Peter Pulzer's students has shown, these hopes were to be comprehensively dashed.[4] As the exile continued and the war became more bitter, the SPD became increasingly embroiled in controversy with the Labour Party about its past policies and present and future role and it was repeatedly attacked as being too nationalistic. Its position was an unenviable one, given the hostility of other exile socialist parties, of the International Secretary of the Labour Party, William Gillies, and of an internal opposition to the SPD leadership led by Walter Loeb and Curt Geyer. The SPD had a number of allies in the Labour Party, including Austen Albu, Philip Noel-Baker, John Hynd, Harold Laski, and Patrick Gordon-Walker, but they were too few and too uninfluential to prevail against the anti-SPD current and from mid-1943 official communication between the Labour Party and the SPD in exile ceased till the summer of 1945.

The Labour Party was in power for all but the last year of Schumacher's period as SPD leader, 1945–52. It had direct responsibility for the British zone in occupied Germany. The Labour victory in early summer 1945 was expected by many in the SPD, given the assumed preference by the Labour Party for the SPD to be reflected in significant support for the SPD, and its policies. Despite the oft repeated allegations by Adenauer of complicity between the Labour government and the SPD, this was the case only to a very limited degree and then only in the initial period of the occupation. The Labour Party–SPD relationship will be examined from two perspectives: first, in terms of practical support by the Labour Party and its associated organizations for the SPD in the re-establishment of liberal democracy in Germany, and secondly in terms of Labour Party support for SPD policies.

Perhaps the most surprising aspect of the relationship between the Labour Party and the SPD was the inability of the Labour Party to fulfil SPD expectations that it would offer the SPD significantly more support than other parties. It is, of course, true that a disproportionate number of SPD adherents were chosen as public officials. This can be explained less by unqualified support for the SPD as a party than the obvious fact that more SPD members were able to point to a respectable democratic record than supporters of other parties. Moreover the British zone encompassed a geographical area where social-democratic adherents were traditionally more numerous than in the less industrialized, more Catholic American and French zones. There was also, naturally enough, a degree of overlap between SPD and trade-union backgrounds and Bevin and other important Labour office-holders were more sympathetic to German trade unions than to the SPD.

Taking the period as a whole it is difficult to find examples of practical help by the Labour Party for the SPD and its members in the period 1945–52 of the kind offered for instance by the SPD to the Spanish and Portuguese parties before and after the collapse of the Franco and Salazar dictatorships in the construction of liberal democracies. A striking example of this lack of interest on the part of the Labour Party in practical steps to help the SPD is its lack of action on the question of the restitution to the SPD and trade unions of property which had been forcibly taken from them by the Nazi regime. The moral claim of the SPD and trade unions was beyond question and the Labour Party National Executive Committee had been informed of the need for action on this matter as early as 1946 and yet no legislative enactment had come into being by the time of the establishment of the Federal Republic in 1949. As a minute of the relevant committee noted: 'I am afraid however that we have not yet been successful in bringing out a Law to deal with the restitution of property now in the possession of German private individuals and firms'. [5]

The Labour government was also very unhelpful about expediting the early return to Germany of exiled members of the SPD. It is important to make one qualification here. The argument has been strongly advanced by Ulrich Reusch that the strictures generally applied to the Labour Party do not apply to the actions of John Hynd and his colleagues, Austen Albu and Alan Flanders: 'While the Attlee Labour Government itself maintained no special relationship to the SPD, Hynd, the minister for Germany did and this was not without impact on the behaviour of the British authorities in Germany. That the SPD executive, Kurt Schumacher, found this insufficient may have been justified from its perspective, but it is another story.'[6]

The principal instance of practical help that Reusch points to, however, is a set of negotiations on the early release of SPD members from POW camps.[7] These instances were necessarily fairly limited, given Hynd's short tenure in office. Hynd was only in his post from October 1945 until April 1947. The influence of Albu and Flanders, which was dependent on Hynd, was of even shorter duration. Hynd was succeeded by Frank Pakenham, an Anglo-Irish Catholic convert who had little of Hynd's enthusiasm for the SPD and who was determined to build bridges to Adenauer and the CDU.

Official contacts between the two parties on a bilateral basis were sparse and irregular. The degree to which relations in these early years displayed a victor/vanquished relationship comes out clearly in a letter from Denis Healey to John Hynd:

Our Social Democratic friends in Germany are asking whether it might be possible for Labour members of Parliamentary delegations to Germany to spend more time with German social democrats. . . . In particular they ask that they should be given an opportunity of visiting the Party head-quarters in Hanover, to get some idea of the Party organisation and of the people working in it, rather than that they should be asked simply to interview local representatives in British officers' messes. . . .'[8]

Bilateral visits by party leaders were a rarity. Schumacher visited Britain twice in December 1946 and 1948. In 1946 he met no important Labour politicians and in 1948 he quickly became ill. Attlee never returned the visit.

The lack of support by the Labour Party for SPD policies is much easier to account for than the relative lack of Labour Party support for the SPD in practical matters. The Labour Party was in power and its policies necessarily reflected what it took to be British national interests. 'A notable feature of the Labour ministers' pre-occupation was their minimal socialist content. The wish to reduce German power and to maintain Britain's world role at the head of the Commonwealth were aims which were shared by the whole ruling elite and reflected the thoroughness of the Labour leaders' identification with the "national interest", as traditionally perceived.'[9]

British policy in relation to Germany was also bound to reflect the fact that it was part of Allied policy. Moreover, the relative weakness of Britain in both financial and security terms was bound to be reflected in a more and more clearly dominant role for the United States in the framing of policies towards Germany and elsewhere. Occasionally, the British government was prepared to stand up to American pressure on policy towards Germany and, as Alan Bullock indicated in the celebrated case of the crisis over the distribution of proposed competencies between the Federation and the states in the

Parliamentary Council, Bevin defended Schumacher's position against strong pressure from the French and the Americans, especially General Clay.[10]

SPD disappointment was especially marked on the question of 'dismantling' German industrial capacity. As a social democratic party with an industrial base and a symbiotic relationship with the unions, the SPD was bound to be especially concerned with this question. This concern was heightened by Schumacher's reading of the lessons of Weimar and the need for the SPD to be seen to be identifying itself strongly with German interests. Representations by the SPD on this matter were made to the Labour Party on a number of occasions. In a report on dismantling of July 1949 to the Labour Party the SPD referred to the fact that the policy had been condemned by the trade unions in the United States, the SF10 (French Socialist Party), and the FO (French Trades Unions), but nothing had been heard from either the Labour Party or the TUC.[11] Why the SPD had not heard becomes clear in a report from Sam Watson, the influential Durham miners' leader, on discussions he had had with SPD representatives on dismantling at the Düsseldorf Party Conference of 1948: 'All the arguments one can use (and there are several) are rather naked in the presence of such members of the SPD'.[12]

In the period under consideration the European policies of the SPD and the Labour Party appear at first sight to have had a great deal in common. Both parties rejected official participation in the Socialist Movement for the United States of Europe (MSEUE) and neither party sent an official delegation to the Hague Congress (1948). In both parties a minority nevertheless joined MSEUE and took part in the Congress. Both parties were critical of nearly all the attempts at European integration which were undertaken from 1949 to 1952. Policies diverged on the relatively unimportant Council of Europe, where the Labour Party supported membership for Britain and the SPD was opposed to the associate membership that was afforded to the Federal Republic. On the much more important and far-reaching European Coal and Steel Community and the European Defence Community both parties were opposed—though in the case of the Coal and Steel Community only after an initial hesitation.

In the case of the SPD, the fundamental objections were rooted in the position of the Federal Republic and as part of a divided Germany. The SPD's objections to participation accorded a central role to the primacy of reunification and the necessity of *Gleichberechtigung* (equal rights) for the Federal Republic in any of the proposed institutions. Factors specific to Britain were reflected in Labour's belief that Britain lay at the centre of three circles: American, Commonwealth, and European and that entry into the ECSC and EDC would compromise the Atlantic and Commonwealth commitment. 'Europe would gain little and lose all if Britain's membership of the European community cost her freedom of initiative in the wider sphere. For Britain a United Europe must, like Commonwealth itself, remain essentially an open system. It cannot be a closed society, membership of which excludes active and independent association with other groupings.'[13] The absence of a wartime experience of invasion and defeat meant that the Labour Party maintained an attitude to national sovereignty which found few parallels in the socialist parties on the mainland of Europe.

There were, however, significant commonalities. Both parties were opposed to the participation of their respective states in the new institutions. Moreover, they shared a number of common objections. Their joint commitment to nationalization of heavy industry formed part of their objection to the European Coal and Steel Community. A shared conception of representative democracy lay behind their criticisms of the technocratic High Authority of the ECSC. It should also not be overlooked that the SPD objected to these institutions because of the non-participation of the social-democratic-led states of Britain and Scandinavia.

Despite these elements of commonality, the SPD found very little support or understanding for its *Europapolitik* from the Labour party during the Schumacher period. The Labour Party perceived the SPD's objections as nationalistic and was correspondingly critical. It was very hostile to the SPD's opposition to West German membership of the Council of Europe as an associate member. In a notably sharp speech in the House of Commons Bevin drew very bitter parallels with the experience of the Western powers with Germany and the League of Nations.[14]

Denis Healey, by no means unsympathetic to the SPD in general, after a visit to Bonn presented a very critical report to the International Sub-Committee of the Labour Party on the SPD opposition to the 1949 Petersberg Agreement. This agreement signalled the end of large-scale dismantling and German membership of the International Authority of the Ruhr and associate membership of the Council of Europe: 'I pointed out to the SPD when I met them that this was quite disastrous. In our view it was a good agreement both for Germany and Europe.'[15]

Disagreements about the wisdom of the SPD's policy on Europe also surfaced during a visit by Percy Knight to the Hamburg Party Conference in May 1950 where Schumacher told the Labour Party delegation that, from his perspective, a Labour defeat at the polls would not be unwelcome since it would mean that it would then have more time to give genuine help to the SPD.[16] At a meeting of socialist parties on 16–17 June 1950 to frame a response to the Schuman Plan, the SPD found itself isolated.

Labour Party criticism of the SPD's European policy as too nationalistic was as Richard Rose has pointed out, somewhat paradoxical given its own policy:

European Union was an issue in which a strong British lead might well have produced significant results. The lead was not given although statements by leaders of the Labour movement created hopes that it would be given. For more than thirty years British Socialists had urged a supranational authority to control the vested interests of the capitalist nation-states. When the Labour government came into office, it found that British workers, as well as capitalists, had a vested interest in national sovereignty. The electoral plea, 'Put the Nation first', (1950 election manifesto) had an unintended double meaning.'[17]

While both parties could be said to be pursuing a nationalist policy, the difference lay in the acceptability of the respective nationalisms. The experience of 1939–45 and the prestige derived from its 1945 victory meant that the nationalism of the Labour Party attracted very little adverse comment from other West European parties. Conversely, although the SPD had not been responsible for German aggression, any arguments advanced by it which could be represented as nationalist were quite simply unacceptable to the other West European socialist parties. It is difficult, however, when confronted with the double standards of Labour Party politicians, criticizing the SPD for not supporting German membership of the EDC while rejecting it for Britain, not to feel some sympathy for the SPD.

Why was the Labour Party able to offer so little support, either in the form of practical help (where its attitude normally corresponded to the instructions allegedly given by the British Admiralty to the Royal Navy 'to render all aid short of help to foreign nationals in distress') or on actual policies? For the Labour Party leadership, the short-lived nature of its two previous governments meant that the implementation of the 1945 programme and the transformation of Britain itself had clear priority over other goals. It quickly became clear that Labour's domestic policy could only be carried through on the basis of massive American economic support, given the parlous state of Britain's finances. This obviously meant a cultivation of the American relationship, a policy which had increasingly obvious consequences for British policy towards Germany. In policy differences between the Americans and the SPD, the Labour government was therefore normally likely to align itself with the American position. In the early period of the occupation, when Britain's dependence was less manifest and tension with the Soviet Union had not assumed its later proportions, the Labour government was inhibited from developing too close a relationship with the SPD for fear of offending the susceptibilities of the USSR. As Ulrich Reusch observed, the 'Foreign Office, including Bevin himself excluded very intensive contacts with Kurt Schumacher from spring to autumn 1946 since his unforgiving anti-communism threatened to complicate the relationship with the Soviet authorities in Germany.'[18]

A major element of the Labour Party's attitude at that time was the hostility and suspicion of key policy-makers towards Germany and an unwillingness to make a major exception of the social democrats. This was not true of John Hynd and his close colleagues Albu and Flanders, but Hynd only occupied the post of Minister for Germany for eighteen months. He remained a marginal figure outside the cabinet whose policy was constantly under attack.

For example, in a letter to Attlee in March 1946, Geoffrey De Freitas complained (inaccurately!) that 'Hynd is hardly ever in Germany and all members of the House know this'.[19] Part of Hynd's difficulties stemmed precisely from the fact that he was very often in Austria and Germany and was unable to defend himself against constant attack. More centrally, Hynd with little or no political backing from Attlee, and a small and inexperienced team of officials, was no match for Bevin and the Foreign Office in London and the self-confident military element of the British presence in Germany.

John Hynd's successor, Frank Pakenham, was well disposed towards Germans and had been much influenced, as Ruth Dudley Edwards argues, by the obvious privation of Germany.[20] Within the Labour leadership itself, attitudes towards Germany and the SPD were much more resentful. Ernest Bevin, the minister most influential in policy towards Germany, was hostile both towards Germany and the SPD.

It was widely believed in Germany during the occupation that the Labour government favoured and had strong links with the Social Democratic Party. Whatever may have been true of other ministers, this was certainly not true of Bevin. He regarded the Christian Democrats with suspicion as reactionaries (Frank Pakenham as an ardent Catholic was naturally more sympathetic) but, on the testimony of Morgan Philips, the Secretary of the Labour Party and Chairman of the Socialist International, as well as of General Robertson, Bevin was equally critical of the SPD. Towards the Austrian Social Democrats he was friendly and helpful but he regarded the German Social Democrats as having let him and other socialists down in 1914 and after the First World War. This reproach was strengthened by the strongly nationalist line taken by the socialist leader, Kurt Schumacher, in attacking the Occupying Powers.[21]

Attlee was much more reserved in expressing his opinions but interviews with his contemporaries indicate that he largely shared Bevin's views. Hugh Dalton, a prominent member of the International Sub-Committee during this whole period, was the most unforgiving and bitter of Germany's critics in an influential position in the Labour Party at this time. This is a note from his diary:

Monday 30th June 1952. To Tony's flat to meet Callaghan, Jenkins and Jay. Frank talk. I told them Germans were murderers, individuals excepted. They've killed all my friends in First War, etc. Deutschland über alles was their song and they meant it. You couldn't tie them with snips of paper like EDC. (European Defence Community). I said to the four young men, 'As soon as Germany is armed again there'll be a bell tolling in the distance for someone. The Third World War will be on the way. They'll be getting the Death Ship into position for launching."[22]

This hostility towards Germany was, in the opinion of those interviewed, generational and was held much more strongly by those who had experienced the First World War. Unfortunately for the SPD, those in the key positions during this period were very largely of that generation. By the time generational change took place Labour had lost office. The lack of sympathy for Germany and the SPD was not as marked in the Parliamentary Party as a whole. Its representatives wrote to the National Executive Committee on 11 April 1946 asking them to undertake steps to encourage interest in the Labour movement on the problems of contemporary Germany. The NEC replied that it had already taken steps to invite Schumacher and sent messages of encouragement and goodwill to the SPD.[23] It undertook no further steps and the PLP was clearly not sufficiently worried about the situation to pursue the matter further.

A final explanation for the poor relations between the Labour Party and the SPD at that time involves the Labour Party's view of the SPD leadership and Schumacher in particular. A representative view is contained in an International Sub-Committee minute of 1948. 'It's [the SPD] present leadership is poor'.[24] A Schumacher-centred explanation must be treated with caution, however. It is of course true that Schumacher's abrasive style was a major handicap in relations with other parties and that he completely underestimated the security needs of the other European states. 'If we had to define in a single word our aims with regard to Germany, security would be this word', wrote Ernest Bevin.[25] Nevertheless, as we have seen, the Labour Party–SPD difficulties predated his period as party leader. It is true that they improved after his death but that also reflected the fact that, in the previous year, the Labour Party had lost governmental power and as he had accurately, if tactlessly, predicted in 1950, loss of power would finally mean that it had more time for the SPD.

The failure of the Labour Party and the Labour government to engage deeply with the SPD certainly deprived it of potential influence on the SPD. It is, however, unlikely that, even if it had been prepared to reverse its priorities, the SPD would have been ready to undertake fundamental changes. Kurt Schumacher who dominated the SPD in these years was a conviction politician and he was convinced that his national strategy afforded the best chance of attracting that quarter of the West German population who were refugees. Although he himself was surprisingly pragmatic in relation to the Marxist assumptions that underlay much of the SPD's economic pronouncements at that time, he was convinced that a bout of programmatic discussion would weaken the SPD's chances in the vital and eagerly awaited first election. Like many traditional SPD leaders, he preferred the values of *Schulterschluss* (closing ranks).

Political scientists in seeking to explain change sometimes employ the concepts of critical moment and critical juncture.[26] A critical moment occurs when existing policies and institutions have visibly failed to produce the intended outcome and a critical juncture occurs when the perception of a critical moment precipitates a change from established patterns. It took the loss of three successive elections by the SPD, in 1949, 1953, and 1957, to turn a critical moment into a critical juncture and in a special conference at Bad

Godesberg in 1959 to drop all Marxist elements of the SPD party programme and to strike a new balance between state and market in a programme which was to become a template for social democracy more widely in Western Europe.

While the Godesberg Programme had an immediate and tangible influence on programmatic discussion in continental socialist and social democratic parties, its immediate influence on contemporary discussion in the Labour Party was miniscule. In the wake of the heavy defeat of the Labour Party in the election of 8 October 1959, Hugh Gaitskell, the party leader suggested at the party conference in the following month that Clause 4, which committed the party to public ownership, should be complemented by a new wider declaration of aims. This suggestion encountered furious opposition in a party still at that time heavily influenced by the trades unions and it was decisively rejected. Hugh Gaitskell did not mention the Bad Godesberg Programme in his speech, as it was widely seen in the Labour Party as too radical and too comprehensive an abandonment of socialist values. It was mentioned with approval by Roy Jenkins at the party conference in October 1960, but he was careful to lay his primary stress on the programmatic revision of the Swedish Social Democratic Party which continued to win elections— unlike the SPD who, like the Labour Party, had lost three in a row![27] In a contribution written in 1963 for *Socialist Commentary*, the journal of the Labour Party revisionists which was edited by Rita Hinden, an *émigré* well disposed to the SPD, Peter Pulzer argued for a more positive attitude by the Labour Party towards Germany and the SPD but tellingly did not mention Bad Godesberg.[28]

## The Schröder-Blair Paper

The failure of the Labour Party to follow the Godesberg model in any systematic sense ensured that in the three decades following Godesberg the SPD, for the first time, clearly owed more to liberalism at a programmatic level than the Labour Party. By the mid-1990s, however, the positions had been reversed. The dominance of politics in the United Kingdom by Margaret Thatcher, in particular her successive electoral victories over the Labour Party—and her even more comprehensive industrial defeat of the Labour movement—led to the replacement of traditional statist Labour values by neo-liberal values and of the Labour Party by New Labour. By the time New Labour came to power in 1997 the relative success of the UK economy, especially in the area of employment, had ensured that New Labour's economic policy in the election campaign and its subsequent policy in government displayed almost total continuity with its Conservative predecessors. The balance between state and market had been radically shifted to a point where market solutions were the preferred solutions not only for sectors which would have been anathema for social democracy but going beyond even classical liberalism. While the Labour Party had been radically transformed by the experience of confronting Thatcherism, the SPD was much less ready to abandon the market/state balance established at Bad Godesberg. Throughout the 1980s the German political system had remained centred on consensual practices and assumptions, where American neo-liberalism had had a comparatively minor impact. This of course was its attraction for the Labour Party in the Thatcher period. The CDU/CSU with its social wing and broad composition was never likely to implement Thatcherism. Despite losing four successive federal elections, the SPD's success at the *Land* level meant that there was little indication that it had arrived at a critical juncture a year before the federal election of September 1998. The SPD had been transformed in the 1980s but by adopting considerable elements of the new politics/ecological agenda rather than in the neo-liberal direction. The catalyst for change in the SPD lay less in electoral defeat by the CDU/CSU than electoral competition with the Greens and a series of adjustments to the party programme had largely been about the inclusion of an ecological dimension. Out of power in Bonn, the SPD did sufficiently well in *Länder* elections not to feel the pressures for a totally new start as experienced by the Labour Party after four defeats in Britain's then highly centralized system. Oskar Lafontaine became party chairman at the party conference in Mannheim in November 1995, when he replaced Rudolf Scharping. Lafontaine had been identified as a modernizer in the late 1980s when he talked of removing some labour-market rigidities but by 1996 he was firmly established as a defender of the status quo and the existing high level of social protection. At that time it was assumed that Lafontaine would be the next chancellor candidate for the SPD, a choice which Helmut Kohl believed would offer him the unprecedented prospect of a fifth successive electoral victory. Gerhard Schröder's convincing victory in the Lower Saxony *Land* election of March 1998 persuaded Lafontaine that Schröder had a much more realistic chance of beating Helmut Kohl and Schröder was adopted as chancellor candidate.

Schröder positioned himself as slightly distant from the SPD mainstream. In particular, he articulated a much more business-friendly approach. While it was clear that Schröder enjoyed the support of the SPD as the most promising chancellor candidate, it was much less clear that his policy ideas enjoyed a majority inside the SPD. In the months between his adoption as chancellor candidate and his eventual victory in September 1998, Schröder had a great deal of contact with the circle around Tony Blair and with Blair himself. His policy of 'Die Neue Mitte' (the new centre) showed distinct signs of borrowing from New Labour's Third Way.[29]

Oskar Lafontaine as party chairman and other members of the party leadership were prepared to allow a 'Neue Mitte' orientation to the SPD's electoral strategy, though they also stressed social justice as a theme. This strategy was successful but electoral arithmetic delivered a Red–Green government rather than the Grand Coalition, which Gerhard Schröder had seen as the appropriate vehicle for realizing more Third Way/neo-liberal market-oriented policies. Given that immediate prospects looked unpromising, Schröder attempted to put down a long-term marker by seeking an external ally in the shape of New Labour. In the weeks after the Schröder victory a Commission headed by Bodo Hombach in the Chancellor's office and Peter Mandelson was established to write a report on the future of social democracy in Europe. The status of this body was never entirely clear. Although the proposed paper was to be about the future of social democratic parties and governments, normally an issue that would be handled by a party body, the policy work was to be co-ordinated by the Chancellor's office and the Policy Unit in No. 10 and although some consultation with the respective parties was envisaged, it was not to be legitimized by approval by a party body before publication. The blurring of the lines between party and public bodies caused some tension on the UK side where public officials had to withdraw from discussions when manifestly party-political matters were being discussed. Progress on the paper was interrupted by the resignation of Peter Mandelson in December 1998. If Peter Mandelson's resignation impeded progress, the resignation of Oskar Lafontaine in early March 1999 from his position as MdB (i.e. MP), Finance Minister and party chairman removed a major obstacle. Lafontaine's resignation paved the way for Schröder to be elected party chairman in early April and deprived the left in the SPD of its most articulate and influential spokesman.

The paper entitled 'The Way Forward for Europe's Social Democrats' was launched in London on the eve of the European election. It is extremely neo-liberal/New Labour in tone and presents a striking contrast to Labour Party documents in the early 1990s where Germany and stakeholder capitalism were seen as relevant models. The relative performance on the employment question meant that by 1997 Germany was no longer seen as an economic exemplar. There are references to the need to create a 'robust and competitive market oriented economic framework', to reducing the tax burden on hard work and the enterprising classes, and for social democrats to take pride in healthy public finances. Even the section on an active labour market focuses on the need to work and reform of the social security system. In effect, the paper is very largely a description of New Labour practice and the adoption of its policy recommendations would add little that is new to the policy positions of the New Labour government. Adoption by the SPD on the other hand would require a fundamental shift in the party programme and policies. It is as yet unclear as to whether the paper can perform this Thatcher-analogue function. Chancellor Schröder, of course, possesses the benefits of incumbency but this advantage was weakened by the low standing of the government and the SPD's poor showing in the European election in June 1999 and a series of *Land* elections in early autumn 1999. It is by no means clear that the Schröder/Blair position represented a majority in the SPD. Ranged against it were the left of the party which, while weakened by the resignation of Lafontaine, remained a not inconsiderable element. The paper as it stood also represents too sharp a departure from the German model for those in the party close to the trade unions. In retrospect, the timing of its publication now seems extremely unfortunate. The SPD left had been weakened by the fact of Lafontaine's departure but the almost simultaneous publication of the government's new saving programme and the paper provided a target which could unite the left and the more trade-unionist elements. Moreover, the way in which it was developed by a small circle and then launched in London was more likely to produce a negative reaction than increase the influence of New Labour in the SPD. On 15 September 1999 Wolfgang Thierse, the chairman of the Basic Values Committee of the SPD published a substantial paper on the 'debate on the programmatic renewal of the SPD'. The paper is quite differently structured from the Schröder/Blair paper. It opens with an analysis of the challenges facing social democracy and then discusses four models: the market-oriented UK Third Way, the German consensus-oriented model, the French statist approach, and Sweden as a reformed welfare state. While the Schröder/Blair paper very largely recommended an ambitious transfer from New Labour to the SPD, the Basic Values Committee suggested very few radical changes and argued instead for the realization of social democratic policy at the European level. The Schröder/Blair paper was discussed at the Berlin SPD Party Conference in December 1999.

By the time of this conference, opinion in the SPD had begun to swing behind the Chancellor, who was confirmed as party chairman by 86 per cent of the vote. This change in the climate had different sources. In part it was due to Schröder's astute personnel changes (like making Franz Müntefering secretary general of the SPD), in part to party members' hostile reaction to Oskar Lafontaine's highly critical autobiography,[30] in part by the perceived need to pull together if the SPD were not to fall over an electoral abyss, and in part, finally, by a marked change of style on the part of the Chancellor (exemplified by his organization of a rescue for the insolvent construction company Philip Holzmann and his initially distinctly protectionist tone *vis-à-vis* the hostile bid by Vodaphone for Mannesmann). Discussion on programmatic issues was diffused by setting up a commission chaired by Schröder to produce a successor programme to the Berlin Programme of 1989. At present it is impossible to gauge how much this will bear the imprint of the Schröder/Blair paper, since no fixed date for the conclusion of the programmatic discussion has been given.

'My Party's called Liberal, but it's basically quite Socialist. With these Europeans, it's the other way around.'[31]

## Conclusion

The two cases that have been selected allow us to draw a number of conclusions. They both illustrate the obstacles in the way of any direct transfer. At the most obvious level, transfer will only occur in any profound sense when the leader of both parties engage. Despite the widely held prior expectations, especially on the German side, this was manifestly not the case in the first episode. It was also not the case in relation to the reception of the Bad Godesberg programme by the Labour Party, where the leadership regarded full-scale renewal *à la* Godesberg as too challenging. In the second case, élite concern at the leadership level was obviously present and the problem has lain rather in the absence of sufficient support for the leader in the SPD. The relationship between the Labour Party, New Labour, and the SPD is of course part of the wider story of UK–German relations. If political parties were to play a key role in the transfer of ideas and policies, then it really had to be the Labour–SPD nexus, given that, unlike the Conservatives and the CDU/CSU, they belong to the same political family. The failure of the Labour Party then and now to exercise any marked degree of influence on the SPD reflects a wider failure on the part of post-war British governments to exert any great influence on German policy debates or practice, with the possible exception of security issues where British views were mediated through NATO. This is also true of the SPD, which failed to have any marked influence on the Labour Party, apart from the the intervention of Helmut Schmidt in the 1975 referendum campaign.

These two episodes illustrate another wider aspect of the bilateral relationship, namely as Jonathan Wright has observed 'the strains have come when either side has expected too much of the other'.[32] The SPD had unrealistic expectations of the Labour Party in the immediate post-war period and New Labour overestimated Schröder's position *vis-à-vis* his party in 1998–9. If the Schröder/Blair paper was a signalling exercise to the SPD, it was extremely unwise to launch it in London, given Schröder's then weak position.

The two episodes chosen also tell us much about the role of liberal ideas on the left. In the early period the 1945 Labour government was much influenced by Britain's most outstanding liberal thinkers, Beveridge and Keynes, while the SPD—wedded to the ideas of the 1925 Heidelberg Programme—betrayed very little influence of liberalism. Even if the Labour leadership had been engaged, it is unlikely that the SPD would have been able to accept the Keynes/Beveridge policy mix, given its reluctance to abandon its programmatic heritage. The Bad Godesberg Programme of 1959 opened up the SPD to liberal influences however and there was a period in the 1970s when a cross-fertilization between the SPD and the FDP, then strongly influenced by social liberals, appeared a possibility. This was expressed in Brandt's use of the term 'Neue Mitte' in 1972. One paradox of Godesberg had been that, just at the point when the SPD embraced liberal values more fully, its most famous liberal thinker, Ralf Dahrendorf, left to join the FDP.

The current situation presents a striking contrast. In the United Kingdom, New Labour is closely allied with the Liberal Democrats, to the extent that Prime Minister Blair appears to have contemplated the inclusion of two Liberal Democrats in his cabinet. This alliance between New Labour and the Liberal Democrats presents a robust ideological platform for Third Way policies. In Germany, the rise of the Greens in the 1980s and its negative effect on the SPD's share of the vote encouraged the FDP to regard the CDU/CSU as a permanent coalition partner and to lose interest in the SPD. For its part, the SPD changed programmatically to accommodate an ecological dimension rather than liberal/neo-liberal ideas in its 1989 Berlin Programme.[33] All Western European social democratic parties are more influenced by liberal ideas than at any point in the past, but the differences that remain are profound. The relative weakness of liberal ideas in the contemporary SPD and their dominance in New Labour render the prospects of a far-reaching initiative of the Schröder/Blair variety still fairly unpromising and the prospect of further mutual misunderstanding high.

# Notes

Some of the references in the early part of this chapter rely on work done with Jim May in the mid-1970s.

1. Paul Sering and Richard Löwenthal, *Jenseits des Kapitalismus* (Bonn: Dietz, 1978), 247.
2. Austin Albu, unpublished diary, 2 Feb. 1946.
3. Hilary A. Balshaw, 'The British Occupation in Germany 1945–49 with special reference to Hamburg', D. Phil. thesis, University of Oxford, 1972, p. 339.
4. Anthony Glees, *Exile Politics During the Second World War: The German Social Democrats in Britain* (Oxford: OUP, 1982).
5. Minute 31(6), Meeting of the International Sub-Committee of the Labour Party executive, 18 Jan. 1949: Restitution of SPD and Trade Union Property.
6. Ulrich Reusch, 'Das Porträt, John Burns Hynd, 1902–1971', *Geschichte im Westen*, (1986), 153–80, 66.
7. Ulrich Reusch, 'Die Londoner Institutionen der Britischen Deutschlandpolitik, 1943–1949', *Historisches Jahrbuch*, 100 (1980), 423–4.
8. Letter from Denis Healey to John Hynd, 2 June 1946. Labour Party Archives.
9. M. Newman, 'British Socialists and the Question of European Unity 1939–49', *European Studies Review*, 10 (1980), 91.
10. Alan Bullock, *Ernest Bevin, Foreign Secretary 1945–1951*, (London: Heinemann, 1983), 690.
11. Report from the German Social Democratic Party on the dismantling of German Industry, July 1949, Labour Party Archives.

12. Mr S. Watson, 'Report on the German Social Democratic Party Congress, Düsseldorf, September 10–15, 1948', Labour Party Archives.
13. Denis Healey, 'The Labour Party and European Unity. Report for consideration of International Sub-Committee of NEC, October 26, 1949', Labour Party Archives.
14. Bullock, *Ernest Bevin*, 764.
15. International Sub-Committee minutes, Mar. 1950.
16. 'Report on the German Social Democratic Party Conference. Hamburg, 20–26 May 1950', by Mr Percy Knight, to International Sub-Committee of NEC, Labour Party Archives.
17. C. R. Rose, 'The Relationship of Socialist Principles to British Labour Foreign Policy 1945–51', D.Phil. thesis, University of Oxford, 1960.
18. Reusch, 'Das Porträt', 66–8.
19. Attlee Papers 1937–46, University College, Oxford, Box 2.
20. Ruth Dudley Edwards, *Victor Gollancz. A Biography* (London: Gollancz, 1987), 448–9.
21. Bullock, *Ernest Bevin*, 690.
22. Ben Pimlott, *The Political Diary of Hugh Dalton, 1918–20, 1945–60* (London: Weidenfeld & Nicolson, 1987), 591–2.
23. International Sub-Committee of the NEC, 12 Apr. 1946.
24. International Sub-Committee of the NEC, 'Memorandum on International Socialist Policy 1948', cited by James May and William E. Paterson, 'Die Deutschlandkonzeption der Britischen Labour Party 1945–49', in Claus Scharf and Hans - Jürgen Schröder (eds.), *Politische und Ökonomische Stabilisierung Westdeutschlands, 1945–84* (Wiesbaden: Franz Steiner, 1999)
25. Rolf Steiniger, 'Die britische Deutschlandpolitik in den Jahren 1945/6', *Aus Politik und Zeitgeschichte*, 1 (1982), 46.
26. William E. Paterson, 'Ambivalenz und Nachahmung: Grossbritannien und die Berliner Republik', *Leviathan*, Sonderheft, 19 (1999).
27. Anthony J. Nicholls, 'Zwei Wege in den Revisionismus: Die Labour Partei und die SPD in der Ära des Godesberger Programms', in Jürgen Kocka, Hans-Jürgen Puhle, and Klaus Tenfelde (eds.), *Von der Arbeiterbewegung zum modernen Sozialstaat*, (Munich: K. G. Saur, 1994).
28. Peter Pulzer, 'The Labour Party and the Germans', *Socialist Commentary*, 6 (June 1963).
29. Bodo Hombach, *Aufbruch: Die Politik der Neuen Mitte* (Munich: Econ, 1998)
30. Oskar Lafontaine, *Das Herz schlägt links* (Munich: Econ, 1999).
31. Colombian delegate at the Stockholm Centenary meeting of the Socialist International in June 1989, cited in K. Heidar, 'The Norwegian Labour Party: En attendant l'Europe' in Richard Gillespie and William E Paterson (eds.), *Rethinking Social Democracy in Western Europe* (London: Frank Cass, 1993).
32. Jonathan Wright, 'The Role of Britain in West German Foreign Policy since 1949', *German Politics*, 5/1 (1996), 39.
33. Stephen Padgett, 'The German Social Democrats: A Redefinition of Social Democracy or Bad Godesberg Mark 2', *West European Politics*, 16/1 (1993), 28–38.

# 14

# A New Government—a New Democracy?
# The Red–Green Coalition in Germany

*Max Kaase*

## Prolegomenon

With the 1989 eclipse of communist ideology and power in Central and Eastern Europe, the political order of democracy has proved to be the preferred way of organizing society, resting on the principle that in politics the pluralist interests of the people can be articulated and represented without fear of repression and that through the operation of market mechanisms citizens are furnished with economic conditions sufficient to conduct their everyday lives. On the other hand, however, liberal democracy has been subjected to ever closer internal scrutiny, and with this, alternate conceptions of how to organize a democratic polity are now more a matter of debate and controversy than ever before.

Political parties in democracies have come to be accepted as indispensable collective actors which, not least through competitive elections, mediate between government and electorate. This elevated role for political parties is, for instance, reflected in the German Basic Law, which in article 21(2) states that political parties participate (*wirken mit*) in the formation of political will. There is, however, an accumulation of empirical evidence suggesting that the capability of parties to penetrate society through linkages with social groups like churches or trade unions, and through party membership, is on the wane, at least in Western Europe.[1] If this diagnosis is correct, little consolation for this sad and serious state of affairs can be obtained from political thinkers, especially when it comes to finding realistic functional equivalents for parties or even a completely new institutional architecture for democracies where parties would no longer have an important place, or even any place at all.

Especially in Europe with its multitude of nation-states and its institutional, social, and cultural diversity, many nation-specific approaches have emerged over the last two centuries about how to cope best with the challenges originating from modernization. However, according to comparative analyses, not all institutional and procedural options for organizing a democratic polity are equally capable of solving problems such as slack economic growth, unemployment, the lack of a role for women in society, and internal strife.[2] Therefore, political science is particularly interested in the question of which type of democracy is most capable of sustaining the acceptance and support of its citizenry. Here, one focus of debate has been between parliamentary and presidential systems, with the verdict slightly in favour of the former.[3] Another controversy has been conducted over the question whether majoritarian or consociational/consensual democracies perform better.[4] These are not trivial questions, given that in the transformation societies of Central and Eastern Europe intelligent constitutional engineering was asked for, and that effective democratic government is one of the most important conditions for achieving democratic legitimacy.

Richard Katz has pointed out that 'in the party government ideal, total control of the government is turned over to a team of leaders who are entitled to exercise power by virtue of having obtained the approbation of a majority in a freely contested election'.[5] From this, three core elements of party government can be extracted: free competitive elections, homogeneous parties, and government control. As the reference by Katz to an ideal-type already signals, things are much more complex in reality. This is why Gunnar Sjoeblom speaks of the dimensions of 'partyness' of government, referring to the degree of party control over the government, 'party governmentness', referring to the degree of party penetration in social power relations, and 'partyness of society', referring to the role of parties in society.[6]

A leitmotif of Peter Pulzer's reflections on democratic government is that party government must be *responsible*, that is, that any government can be held accountable for its decisions in elections.[7] Pulzer clearly associates an accountable government with the Westminster model of Britain, for instance when he argues that responsible party government is enhanced by a unitary constitution, a unicameral legislature, and an overlap between executive and legislative functions, and that it is hampered especially by strong pressure groups.[8] At this point the impact of the electoral system must also be considered. While Pulzer is careful not to overemphasize its role in producing responsible party government, he leaves little doubt that *stable* governments are conducive to a well-operating democracy. While majority rule is not the *deus ex machina* which produces this stability by itself, Pulzer regards it as an important element, which can help to promote it. On a marginal note it is of course ironic that one pillar of the Westminster model—the electoral system of first-past-the-post—is recommended for change in the report of the

Independent Commission on the Voting System convened in 1997 by the Labour government.[9]

In his initial work on typologizing democracies, but also more recently, Arend Lijphart identifies two dimensions, each operationalized by five institutional variables, according to which democracies can be characterized with particular succinctness.[10] In a recent publication, he terms these the executives–parties dimension (epitomized by the two-party systems versus multi-party systems dichotomy) and the federal-unitary dimension.[11] Lijphart shows that the validity of this classification not only holds for his previous (1984) twenty-two, but also for a larger set of thirty-six democracies.

Though in his earlier work, he had classified Germany as 'majoritarian-federal', his own data did not fully support his classification.[12] Instead, it would have been more appropriate to place Germany into an intermediate category, since it scored much lower than, for instance, the United Kingdom and the United States on majoritarianism, that is, on the factor which is almost identical with the effective number of parties. Lijphart's 1999 analysis shows this very clearly.[13]

The typological location of Germany based on Lijphart's classification pertains to the politico-institutional realm. But the heightened emphasis on the more consensual elements in the overall political make-up of Germany also sits neatly with Katzenstein's characterization of Germany as a 'semisovereign state':

The three nodes of West Germany's policy network open the state to the influence of parties, subordinate levels of government, and interest groups. But in fusing state and society, these nodes are also conduits in the formulation and implementation of policy. Since it links tightly most of the major organised political actors, thus multiplying potential sources of veto, West Germany's semisovereign state is not well equipped to initiate bold policy change. But by its very structure, West Germany's semisovereign state is well suited to bring about steady, incremental policy change.[14]

It is against this background that the result of the German general election of 27 September 1998 and the ensuing government change will be discussed. Before this topic is approached, however, two rather persistent elements in the German political process, which also rank highly in Peter Pulzer's thinking, will be addressed: coalition governments and federalism.

## How Accountable is the German Way of Governing?

'The most important functional systems structure their communication through a binary code which under the perspective of the specific function in question demands universal validity and excludes third options . . . Regarding the political system . . . the code is defined by the concentration of power in the hands of the state . . . One can only hold or not hold positions in parliament, government and administration, and therefore politics is coded according to government and opposition . . .'[15]

In his systemic perspective, Luhmann has pointed to an element that has long been regarded as essential for a healthy democratic process: the institutionalization of the chance of a role change between government and opposition. In modern societies the struggle for government power is increasingly over finding the appropriate means to deal with a given problem successfully (valence issues) and less so over political ends (position issues). Nevertheless, there is widespread agreement that, at a given point in time, the threat of being removed (to those who control the government) and the promise of obtaining office in the future (to those out of power) are the central forces behind the behaviour of parties and politicians in a party democracy. It is, therefore, not just by chance that Samuel Huntington in his work on regime transitions tests democratic consolidation by the two-turnover test: there have to be at least two peaceful government changes through free elections before a democracy can be considered consolidated.[16]

Since democracies depend on the free acceptance by and the support of their citizens, the logic of government and opposition roles makes it probable that those citizens who adhere to any one of the present opposition parties will be more dissatisfied with the government than those who adhere to the governing parties.[17] This situation is obviously aggravated if a particular government stays in office for an extended period in time. However, the potential threat to democracy that may result is often reduced, if not neutralized, by the fact that citizens distinguish between support for the democratic system as such and support for the incumbent authorities.[18] The question nevertheless arises at what point and under which circumstances dissatisfaction with *government* is generalized to dissatisfaction with the *democratic system*. Therefore, the concept of government turnover through elections and its role in the democratic process comes to the fore again, especially in terms of generating citizen support not only for the incumbents, but also for the polity as a whole.

One controversial debate in electoral studies is whether people judge the performance of a government retrospectively or prospectively. This controversy does not need to be discussed here in any detail.[19] What is important is the assumption underlying both perspectives, namely that governments are especially held responsible for their actions in elections;[20] McDonald, Budge, and Hofferbert show that, with respect to the impact of economic conditions on the vote, the clarity of government alternatives does indeed make a big difference.[21] This, then, leads to the question of how accountability can be best secured institutionally, for in the logic of the democratic process, this is central for establishing creativity, innovation, and political control.

If accountability in politics means that decisions taken by governments and associated agencies have an unequivocal addressee, no matter whether the outcomes of those decisions are positive or negative for the citizenry, then—and even the consensualist Lijphart has to concur on this point—two-party systems are best suited to create it.[22] Yet, in the real world of contemporary democratic politics, pure two-party systems are rare. In the May 1997 general election in Britain, the epitome of the Westminster model, the two major parties, Conservative and Labour, gained but 74 per cent of the vote, though 88.6 per cent of the seats, while the Liberal Democrats obtained 16.8 per cent of the votes and 7 per cent of the seats, and the remaining, mostly regional parties, obtained 9.2 per cent of the votes and 4.4 per cent of the seats.[23]

Here Lijphart makes the obviously valid point that in this kind of a 'two-party system' a government may even be kept in office against the wishes of a majority of voters.[24] In terms of accountability, however, the argument is ill-taken; what is relevant is the fact that during and at the end of a parliamentary cycle the voters with a one-party government always know beyond any reasonable doubt which party to blame should policy outputs not be to their liking.[25]

Transferring this line of thinking to Germany, one has to keep in mind that at no time since 1949 has the Federal Republic been governed by a one-party cabinet; from 1949 on various smaller parties—notably the Free Democrats (FDP)—have teamed up with a major party, either the Christian Democrats (CDU/CSU) or the Social Democrats (SPD), the only exception being the time of the 'Great' (CDU/CSU–SPD) Coalition between 1966 and 1969. Thus, accountability as defined above has been reduced substantially throughout the history of the Federal Republic. Indeed, a standard defence of parties in coalitions has been that the 'other' party in government ought to be blamed for policy measures not being taken despite their apparent desirability or necessity.

There may even have been issues where such a claim was justified and was perceived as such by the media and the public at large. Between 1994 and 1998 the FDP tried to implement a modern immigration law, for instance, but could not overcome CDU/CSU opposition. More frequent, however, are instances when it is less clear who is to blame. This is especially true if one considers the second structural factor in the German political system that has an impact on government accountability: the German variant of co-operative federalism.

This is not the place to discuss, in detail, the multi-faceted nature of German federalism.[26] In the essential area of law-making, the German constitution distinguishes between laws for which the consent of the *Länder* is deemed necessary, and laws for which the Bundestag has unrestricted authority at least in principle.[27] This complex situation of accountability is aggravated by the fact that, according to article 77 of the Basic Law, a distinction needs to be made between the so-called *Einspruchsgesetzgebung* (a law proposed, for example, by the government and supported by the Bundestag majority, which does not require the consent of the Bundesrat, but can eventually be rejected by the Bundesrat anyway) and the *Zustimmungsgesetzgebung* (a law proposed, for example, by the government and supported by the Bundestag majority, which does require the consent of the Bundesrat majority).[28]

The required co-operation between the Bundestag and the Bundesrat is complex enough for it to be safe to assume that it is alien to the average citizen. This *Politikverflechtung* (policy networking), even more so than coalition governments, is a structural hindrance to political accountability, a problem which is accentuated by a regulation in article 77 of the Basic Law, which provides for a reconciliation committee (*Vermittlungsausschuß*) to be called into action if the Bundestag and the Bundesrat cannot agree on a given law.[29] While the reconciliation committee was not activated very frequently between 1983 and 1991, the situation can vary.[30] For the period 1972–6, as Pulzer observes, the *Vermittlungsausschuß* was more active than in all other parliamentary periods before taken together.[31] An additional aspect, though, is even more important than this variability. Recent experience corroborates the view that the *Vermittlungsausschuß* is often involved in legislation which is particularly important for the policy of the national government, as in the 1997 efforts for tax reform.

The institutional tension between the Bundestag and the Bundesrat and the specific variant of German co-operative federalism have been a matter of debate since the foundation of the Federal Republic. Though various commissions for constitutional reform have addressed this topic (the last one operating in 1992/3), they have done so with little impact, since neither the Federation nor the *Länder* have been inclined to give up established positions.

In party-political terms, the issue gained prominence in the year preceding the 1998 general election, when the conservative–liberal federal government accused the SPD and Alliance 90/Greens of blockade politics (*Blockadepolitik*) because the voting strength in the Bundesrat enabled the opposition parties to counteract legislation accepted by the government majority in the Bundestag.[32] This situation, however, had also arisen before in the 1970s with reverse roles, when an SPD–FDP majority in the Bundestag had to face a CDU/CSU majority in the Bundesrat. Since German voters—and this is in part an outcome of *Politikverflechtung*—use state elections in order to express their sentiments *vis-à-vis* the federal government, the potential blockade along party lines is a way of life in German politics. It has to be kept in mind, however, that voting in the Bundesrat also follows specific *Länder* interests in the best tradition of federalism, thereby rendering the situation even more complex for the voters than if it were just a matter of partisan strength in the two chambers. That partisan majorities in both chambers are the exception rather than the rule is exemplified by the fact that the brief period of SPD–Alliance 90/Green majorities in both the Bundestag and the Bundesrat after the 1998 general election has already been 'corrected' regarding the

Bundesrat by the outcome of six of the seven state elections after the general election (see Table 1). Only in Bremen, which had been ruled for the previous four years by a great coalition, was the SPD able to hold its ground in the 6 June 1999 election, but its federal coalition partner Alliance 90/Greens experienced a 4.1 percentage point loss, while the CDU gained 4.5 percentage points, resulting in the continuation of the SPD–CDU coalition. To complete the picture, it must finally be mentioned that in the European election on 13 June 1999 both governing parties also suffered losses (SPD −1.5 percentage points, Alliance 90/Greens −3.7 percentage points) while the CDU/CSU scored considerable gains (+9.9 percentage points).

Interestingly enough, with globalization pressures having troubled Germany since the early 1990s, German federalism has now also become a persistent topic of public debate, reflecting the need for a change from co-operative to competitive federalism. It must be admitted, however, that in these controversies the democratic notion of enhanced accountability through visibility of the division of power between the federal and the state level has at best played an implicit role; economic and fiscal considerations dominate.[33]

In sum, then, the prevalence of national coalition governments and German federalism are factors that systematically reduce the chance for unambiguous government accountability to the citizenry. Peter Pulzer weighs the impact of these two differently.[34] Regarding federalism, he argues that only *de facto* unicameralism is compatible with and conducive to responsible party government. With respect to the first consideration, it was the observed *stability* of German coalition governments which convinced him (at least in 1978) that in Germany national coalitions had been 'a good deal less ephemeral than the electoral coalitions of Sweden, Norway and the Netherlands which have also tried to combine structured electoral choice with multi-partism'.[35] However, his support for this type of 'majoritarian government' is not systematically argued. Rather, it has a distinct *ad hoc* character in that it refers especially to the fact that in German elections, coalition preferences of the parties were increasingly expected to be specified during campaigns and could therefore become an integral part of the voters' decision-making strategies.[36] It is ironic, then, that in exactly the year Pulzer's 1982 article was published, the Schmidt government was overthrown through an FDP change in coalition preference not based on an election. This event does not sit easily with Pulzer's concept of responsible coalition party government as outlined in 1978.

It must be emphasized that in political science the general role of accountability for a legitimate and at the same time innovative democratic polity is far from clear. While at least in principle, little can be argued against more accountability, the problem is that in real life accountability has a price. As Lijphart convincingly points out, accountability as conceptualized in this chapter comes in a basket with other features of the executives–parties

Table 1. *Results of state (Bundesland) and European elections since the 1998 general election (%)*

| Parties | Hesse | | | Bremen | | | European election | | | Saarland | | |
|---|---|---|---|---|---|---|---|---|---|---|---|---|
| | 1999 | 1995 | % change | 1999 | 1995 | % change | 1999 | 1994 | % change | 1999 | 1994 | % change |
| SPD[9] | 39.4 | 38.0 | +1.4 | 45.0 | 44.1 | +0.9 | 30.7 | 32.2 | −1.5 | 44.4 | 49.4 | −5.0 |
| B90/Greens | 7.2 | 11.2 | −4.0 | 9.0 | 13.1 | −4.1 | 6.4 | 10.1 | −3.7 | 3.2 | 5.5 | −2.3 |
| CDU | 43.4 | 39.2 | +4.2 | 37.1 | 32.6 | +4.5 | 48.7 | 38.8 | +9.9 | 45.5 | 38.6 | +6.9 |
| FDP | 5.1 | 7.4 | −2.3 | 2.5 | 3.4 | −0.9 | 3.0 | 4.1 | −1.1 | 2.6 | 2.1 | +0.5 |
| PDS | — | — | | 2.9 | 2.4 | +0.5 | 5.8 | 4.7 | +1.1 | 0.8 | — | +0.8 |
| Right-wing parties | 2.9 | 2.3 | +0.6 | 3.3 | 2.8 | +0.5 | 2.1 | 4.1 | −2.0 | 1.3 | 1.4 | −0.1 |
| Other parties | 2.0 | 1.9 | +0.1 | 0.2 | 1.6 | −1.4 | 3.3 | 6.0 | −2.7 | 2.2 | 3.0 | −0.8 |
| Total | 100 | 100 | — | 100 | 100 | — | 100 | 100 | — | 100 | 100 | — |
| Turn-out | 66.4 | 66.3 | +0.1 | 60.1 | 68.6 | −8.5 | 45.2 | 60.0 | −14.8 | 68.7 | 83.5 | −14.8 |

| Parties | Brandenburg | | | Thuringia | | | Saxony | | | Berlin | | |
|---|---|---|---|---|---|---|---|---|---|---|---|---|
| | 1999 | 1994 | % change | 1999 | 1994 | % change | 1999 | 1994 | % change | 1999 | 1995 | % change |
| SPD | 39.3 | 54.1 | −14.8 | 18.5 | 29.6 | −11.1 | 10.7 | 16.6 | −5.9 | 22.4 | 23.6 | −1.2 |
| B90/Greens | 1.9 | 2.9 | −1.0 | 1.9 | 4.5 | −2.6 | 2.6 | 4.1 | −1.5 | 9.9 | 13.2 | −3.3 |
| CDU | 26.6 | 18.7 | +7.9 | 51.0 | 42.6 | +8.4 | 56.9 | 58.1 | −1.2 | 40.8 | 37.4 | +3.4 |
| FDP | 1.9 | 2.2 | −0.3 | 1.1 | 3.2 | −2.1 | 1.1 | 1.7 | −0.6 | 2.2 | 2.5 | −0.3 |
| PDS | 23.3 | 18.7 | +4.6 | 21.4 | 16.6 | +4.8 | 22.2 | 16.5 | +5.7 | 17.7 | 14.6 | +3.1 |
| Right-wing parties | 6.0 | 1.1 | +4.9 | 3.9 | 1.3 | +2.6 | 2.9 | 1.3 | +1.6 | 3.5 | 2.7 | +0.8 |
| Other parties | 1.0 | 2.2 | −1.2 | 2.2 | 2.2 | 0 | 3.6 | 1.7 | +1.9 | 3.5 | 6.0 | −2.5 |
| Total | 100 | 100 | — | 100 | 100 | — | 100 | 100 | — | 100 | 100 | — |
| Turn-out | 54.4 | 56.3 | −1.9 | 59.9 | 74.8 | −14.9 | 61.1 | 58.4 | +1.7 | 65.9 | 68.6 | −2.7 |

[9] For 1995 state elections in Bremen, results for AFB (Arbeit für Bremen und Bremenhaven), a split-off from the SPD, have been added to the SPD results.

dimension, which jointly prevent or are negatively associated with the 'kinder, gentler, and more generous politics' in consensus democracies.[37] Still, evidence in favour of the accountability argument should surface when a direct government turnover from one to a differently composed coalition government results from an election—as was the case on 27 September 1998, in Germany—and not from a party realigning its previous coalition preference as with the FDP in 1969 and in 1982.

## *On the Way to the 1998 General Election*

In many studies of (West) German political culture the government change of 1969 from a CDU/CSU–SPD coalition to a social-democratic–liberal government is regarded—quite in line with Huntington's (1991) thinking on democratic consolidation in his book on *The Third Wave*—as an important step in the firm establishment of German post-war democracy. While the particular circumstances of the 1982 government turnover, which came about through the Liberals leaving the Schmidt government, in other words, not following an election, gave some reason for concern at the time, neither turnover came about as a direct consequence of the people's electoral choice. It was different in 1998, when the change of government resulted from the votes the contending parties were able to attract: after all the parties not reaching the 5 per cent clause hurdle were eliminated from the calculation of parliamentary seats as the electoral law prescribes, the SPD scored 298 seats (+46 compared to 1994), the CDU/CSU 245 seats (−49), the FDP 44 seats (−3), the Alliance 90/Greens 47 seats (−2), and the PDS 35 seats (+5). With this (small) majority of 345 seats (51.7 per cent) SPD and Alliance 90/Greens were able to form a government, as they had indicated they would during the campaign. On 20 October 1998, both parties signed an elaborate coalition agreement with the ambitious title 'Departure and Renewal—Germany's Way into the 21st Century' (*Aufbruch und Erneuerung—Deutschland's Weg ins 21. Jahrhundert*).

Up to election day the outcome of the vote was wide open. This was a different situation from the general elections of 1990 and 1994 when the CDU/CSU had also lagged behind but had recovered during the election year.[38] In 1998, after sixteen years under a Kohl government, a pervasive feeling—more sentiment than rational choice—had spread early on, suggesting that it was time for a change. According to the monthly surveys by the Mannheim-based Forschungsgruppe Wahlen (Research Group on Elections) for the Second German Television Network (ZDF), up to the day of the election the proportion who agreed with the statement that a change in government was due was never less than two-thirds of the citizens entitled to vote. This belief shows in the data presented in Figure 3, which displays the party rankings across the 1998/9 period. According to these data the CDU/CSU–FDP coalition could at no point in 1998 muster a majority over the SPD–Alliance 90/Greens opposition parties. The degree of dissatisfaction with the Kohl government surfaces even more clearly when one considers the average ratings on a +5/−5 sympathy rating scale of the government and of the various parties as displayed in Figure 2. There can be no question that the general mood of the public was in favour of 'throwing the rascals out'.

On the other hand, these figures also indicate that the government during the election year was almost capable of closing the gap with the opposition parties, a dynamic which is well-known not only in Germany, but in other democracies too. If this recovery is interpreted as ambivalence on the part of the voters, there is a lot of additional evidence to support this claim. Most telling is probably the finding from the Infratest-dimap election day exit poll that 16 per cent of the voters made up their minds on whom to vote for only on the day of the election and 10 per cent 'during the last days'.[39] Furthermore, *on average* the SPD neither had a strong advantage over the CDU/CSU in the domain of political issues nor in the domain of the two candidates for chancellorship.[40] In those fields deemed most important by the voters—reduction of unemployment, tax reform, social justice, the environment—the SPD was, however, clearly ahead of the CDU/CSU. The voter ambivalence resulting from this situation also shows in the Infratest-dimap finding that in the last two months before the election, voters were almost evenly divided on whether a SPD-led government would be better equipped to deal with the agenda of problems to be approached after the election. Thus, to summarize the situation until election day, voters were caught between the two coalition government options available to them. In the end they decided in favour of innovation, of giving a new set of élites, who had been kept on the hard benches of the opposition for sixteen years, a chance to show that they were better able to cope with the tasks ahead for Germany. It is in this sense that the vote was also a vote against Helmut Kohl, even if it would be wrong to attribute the lost election more or less exclusively to the man who had first promised not to run again in 1998 but who had then changed his mind and with this decision put his predestined successor, Wolfgang Schäuble, into an awkward position indeed.[41]

## A New Government: What has Changed?

Willy Brandt's inaugural speech as the chancellor of the SPD–FDP government in the autumn of 1969 is still remembered for a pervasive programmatic message: to dare more democracy (*mehr Demokratie wagen*). This saying reflected the spirit of the times very well, and it remained an overarching

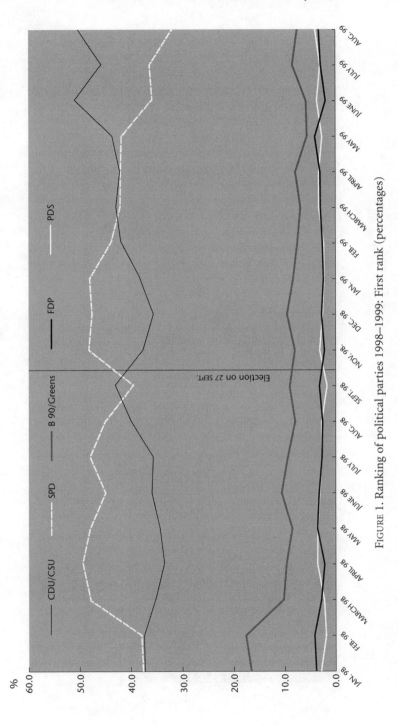

FIGURE 1. Ranking of political parties 1998–1999: First rank (percentages)

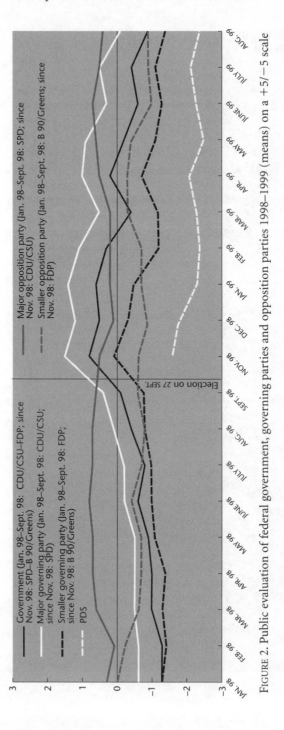

FIGURE 2. Public evaluation of federal government, governing parties and opposition parties 1998–1999 (means) on a +5/−5 scale

motto during the decade after Brandt had resigned from office because of a spy in the chancellery. While such an overarching motto could not be put forward by the new government, the SPD–Alliance 90/Green coalition treaty defined a very demanding policy programme for the 1998–2002 legislative period: economic stability, social justice, ecological modernization, reliable foreign policy, inner security, strengthening of civil rights and equality for women.

Analyses of the policy positions of the five parties represented in the new Bundestag indicate that in all major domains on the left–right dimension, the SPD in its 1998 campaign made an unprecedented move to a middle-of-the-road-position.[42] This validates the party's claim to seek the support of the 'new centre' (*Neue Mitte*), a segment of voters which has not been clearly defined in either socio-structural, ideological, or issue-related terms, and which is probably not even definable in this way. Under these circumstances, it is not surprising that the 'new centre' seems to be a particularly volatile part of the electorate. In addition, in view of the ambivalence of the voters with respect to the policy implications of an eventual government change, expectations *vis-à-vis* the new coalition must have been running high. As a look at Figures 1 and 2 can verify, there was initially a great deal of goodwill towards the Schröder government.

For detached observers, substantial ambiguities remained as to whether the coalition could really deliver the partially contradictory programme it had assigned to itself in the fifty-page coalition agreement. For one, there were structural tensions within the SPD membership between those supporting Schröder's economic modernization concept and traditional social democrats often located in the trade-union camp, who advocated their interpretation of social justice and were not willing to depart from the beloved German welfare state, campaigning instead for a redistribution of wealth through tax reform and the reduction of unemployment through state interventionist measures. The latter concept was epitomized by the new Minister of Finance, Oskar Lafontaine, and a group of hand-picked economic advisers who wanted to follow Keynesian demand concepts and sought to control international money markets. Furthermore, problems quickly surfaced with the Alliance 90/Green coalition partner, which tried to push through a new piece of immigration and citizenship legislation against the preference not only of the CDU/CSU, but also of most of the SPD supporters. In addition, it had installed a Minister for Environmental Affairs, Jürgen Trittin, who managed in no time to antagonize not only nationally, but also internationally, almost every actor he had to deal with in pushing through his environmental reform plans, especially with respect to the end of nuclear energy in Germany.

In retrospect, it is difficult to understand how in sixteen years of opposition the parties had not been able to design a reform programme in sufficient operational detail to be implemented quickly and successfully after the new government was formed. By the beginning of 1999 first signs of voter disappointment were already starting to surface, and with the surprising victory for the CDU and the FDP in the Hesse state election in February 1999, a truly spectacular decline in partisan support both for the SPD and Alliance 90/Greens got under way, despite the fact that inside and outside Germany there was widespread agreement that the new government was handling Germany's role in the Kosovo conflict extremely well. This decline, which can be directly tied to failures in policy areas claimed as being absolutely essential for the new government—citizenship law, nuclear energy, labour market, pensions and health system reform, and economic modernization—and not so much to matters of political style as the SPD argued, by early October 1999 culminated in defeat in five more state elections, three in the East and one in the West—the Saarland—and in Berlin (see Table 1), not to speak of the defeat in the September local elections in Northrhine-Westphalia, the largest German *Land*.

For a while Chancellor Schröder seemed not to suffer in public ratings from the loss of support for the government; however, by May 1999 his reputation had started to decline substantially and, quite unexpectedly, in the autumn of 1999 the Alliance 90/Green Foreign Minister Joschka Fischer was for a period the most popular German politician. The downfall of Lafontaine in the ratings and then his disappearance from the list of rated politicians reflect his decision in the spring of 1999 to resign both from his ministerial post and from his position as party leader, a decision which has left deep marks internally and externally on the SPD (for the ratings of the various politicians see Figure 3).

With this brief account of what happened politically in Germany in the first year after the government change, the question can now be addressed whether this has had an effect on the legitimacy beliefs of the electorate. A question on satisfaction with democracy is included by the Forschungsgruppe Wahlen every second month in their ZDF surveys. These data have also been recently used in an analysis of the effects of the perceived economic performance of the German government on democratic satisfaction.[43]

Three elements in Table 2 deserve special mention. The first is the way that the almost even balance of satisfaction and dissatisfaction at the beginning of 1998 changed noticeably during the campaign in the direction of the satisfaction category. This can be interpreted as a corollary of voter mobilization and reiterates observations from previous elections: campaigns—however disliked they may be—nevertheless make citizens rally behind the democratic flag. The higher satisfaction level reached in October 1998 by the time the new government took office stayed almost unchanged until mid-1999, and only afterwards did dissatisfaction with the government (see Figure 2) seem slowly to have an impact on democratic satisfaction. The change in government thus obviously had a positive effect on the appreciation of

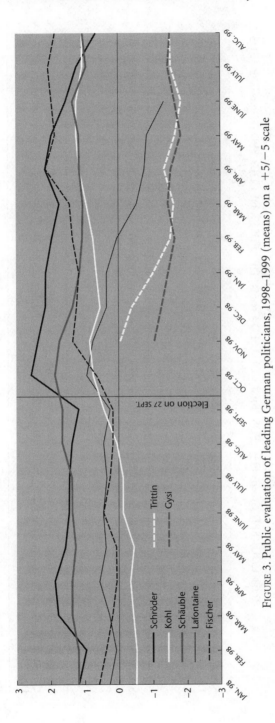

FIGURE 3. Public evaluation of leading German politicians, 1998–1999 (means) on a +5/−5 scale

Table 2. *Satisfaction with democracy in Germany 1998–1999 (%)*

**2/1998**

| Satisfaction with Democracy | Total | Voters of the | | | | |
|---|---|---|---|---|---|---|
| | | CDU/CSU | SPD | Greens | FDP | PDS |
| Satisfied | 50 | 64 | 48 | 49 | 66 | 19 |
| Dissatisfied | 47 | 34 | 50 | 48 | 34 | 81 |
| Don't know | 3 | 2 | 2 | 3 | — | — |

**4/1998**

| | Total | Voters of the | | | | |
|---|---|---|---|---|---|---|
| | | CDU/CSU | SPD | Greens | FDP | PDS |
| Satisfied | 64 | 49 | 55 | 51 | 51 | 19 |
| Dissatisfied | 33 | 47 | 39 | 45 | 45 | 81 |
| Don't know | 3 | 3 | 6 | 4 | 4 | — |

**6/1998**

| | Total | Voters of the | | | | |
|---|---|---|---|---|---|---|
| | | CDU/CSU | SPD | Greens | FDP | PDS |
| Satisfied | 54 | 70 | 49 | 60 | 73 | 24 |
| Dissatisfied | 42 | 26 | 48 | 37 | 26 | 70 |
| Don't know | 4 | 4 | 3 | 3 | 1 | 6 |

**9/1998 (38th week)**

| | Total | Voters of the | | | | |
|---|---|---|---|---|---|---|
| | | CDU/CSU | SPD | Greens | FDP | PDS |
| Satisfied | 57 | 69 | 58 | 64 | 59 | 13 |
| Dissatisfied | 40 | 27 | 41 | 35 | 39 | 87 |
| Don't know | 3 | 4 | 1 | 1 | 2 | — |

**10/1998**

| | Total | Voters of the | | | | |
|---|---|---|---|---|---|---|
| | | CDU/CSU | SPD | Greens | FDP | PDS |
| Satisfied | 62 | 63 | 73 | 55 | 51 | 36 |
| Dissatisfied | 35 | 35 | 25 | 44 | 45 | 59 |
| Don't know | 3 | 2 | 2 | 1 | 4 | 5 |

**2/1999**

| | Total | Voters of the | | | | |
|---|---|---|---|---|---|---|
| | | CDU/CSU | SPD | Greens | FDP | PDS |
| Satisfied | 61 | 62 | 66 | 68 | 82 | 27 |
| Dissatisfied | 36 | 36 | 31 | 32 | 17 | 73 |
| Don't know | 3 | 2 | 3 | 1 | 1 | — |

**4/1999**

| | Total | Voters of the | | | | |
|---|---|---|---|---|---|---|
| | | CDU/CSU | SPD | Greens | FDP | PDS |
| Satisfied | 61 | 63 | 73 | 64 | 80 | 34 |
| Dissatisfied | 35 | 33 | 25 | 32 | 20 | 66 |
| Don't know | 4 | 4 | 2 | 4 | — | — |

**6/1999**

| | Total | Voters of the | | | | |
|---|---|---|---|---|---|---|
| | | CDU/CSU | SPD | Greens | FDP | PDS |
| Satisfied | 62 | 64 | 73 | 74 | 67 | 34 |
| Dissatisfied | 36 | 34 | 26 | 25 | 32 | 63 |
| Don't know | 2 | 2 | 1 | 1 | 1 | 3 |

**9/1999**

| | Total | Voters of the | | | | |
|---|---|---|---|---|---|---|
| | | CDU/CSU | SPD | Greens | FDP | PDS |
| Satisfied | 57 | 61 | 72 | 58 | 61 | 20 |
| Dissatisfied | 40 | 36 | 27 | 38 | 31 | 77 |
| Don't know | 3 | 3 | 1 | 4 | 8 | 3 |

*Question:*  What would you say in general about German democracy: Are you rather satisfied or rather dissatisfied?
*Source:*  Monthly Politbarometer surveys conducted by the Forschungsgruppe Wahlen for the Second German Television Network (ZDF)

democracy by the German public. This corresponds to what one would expect from the reduced accountability notion discussed in this chapter. On the other hand, the signs of decline, if this development of public opinion continues, point to the fact that the beneficial impact of government change evaporates quite easily if people's expectations are not fulfilled. In this sense, a government–opposition exchange is but one—and clearly a fragile—mechanism of sustaining democratic system support.

The second point to be made is that adherents of opposition parties indeed have problems with democratic satisfaction, and it is here that the positive impact of an election campaign is most visible. In this context, it is particularly worth mentioning that PDS voters are the only ones who consistently and at a high level—only slightly and very briefly reduced immediately after the election—display a critical stance toward German democracy. Since the PDS has no strength to speak of in the 'old' *Länder*, this finding mainly reflects the partial, but lingering schism between a particular group of former GDR citizens and the rest of the citizenry in their visions of a desirable polity.[44]

Thirdly, and interestingly enough, the loss of power for the CDU/CSU and FDP has, as of autumn 1999, in terms of democratic satisfaction not left the kind of mark on their supporters one would have expected: both voter groups continue to be as satisfied, or even more so, with German democracy as the average electorate. It almost looks as though these voters have accepted the idea of government change as an important ingredient of the democratic process; if this interpretation is correct, then this would reinforce the belief that Germany has become a consolidated democracy.

Finally, for the sake of fairness, it must be mentioned that there was a substantial decline in turn-out in most of the state elections and in the European election (all in 1999 after the general election of 1998) which might be regarded as a challenge to the consolidated democracy hypothesis; however, in the view of this author this should merely be regarded as a drop of water in a good wine.

## A New Democracy?

After the electoral victory of SPD and Alliance 90/Greens, voices could be heard in the German public arena proclaiming that this would undermine the liberal-democratic traditions which had slowly grown in (West) Germany since 1949 and which had given Germany its national as well as international political identity. While such interpretations at least in part reflected explicit policy stances by the SPD and the Alliance 90/Greens as laid down in their coalition agreement, these concerns were even more based on the fact that the new government could, at least in principle, rely on a partisan distribution of votes in the Bundesrat that gave it a free hand in legislating. Table 3 represents the distribution of votes in the Bundesrat after the 27 September 1998 general election and after the Berlin state election on 10 October 1999.

While initially the SPD-controlled *Länder* were close to the constitutionally relevant two-thirds majority of forty-six votes, the new situation is one almost of impasse, and continuation of the 'great coalition' between CDU and SPD in Berlin does not change this balance. Thus the distribution of Bundesrat seats implies that practically no essential legislation can be pushed through by the federal government without some reconciliation with the policy preferences of the CDU/CSU (not considering the fact that the *Länder* may well align on certain issues along the dimension of *Länder* and not of partisan interests and that the federal government may tailor legislation so that no Bundesrat approval is necessary). In sum, whatever hopes or fears existed after the general election about a major change in the political outlook of the Federal Republic: after the state elections of 1999 they can no longer be substantiated. In addition, the next two state elections in 2000 in Schleswig-Holstein and Northrhine-Westphalia can only worsen, but not improve, the voting situation for the federal government in the Bundesrat since both *Länder* are presently governed by an SPD–Alliance 90/Green coalition.

It is clear, then, that in structural terms Peter Pulzer's argument on German federalism as a major factor impinging on the notion of responsible party government remains in force—as does the argument that this particular institutional *mélange* is not conducive to easy government accountability *vis-à-vis* the voters. By implication, co-operative federalism remains a matter for debate, and one can only agree with Anderson when he argues that 'while the

Table 3. *Distribution of votes in the Bundesrat after the general election on 27 September 1998, and after the Berlin state election on 10 October 1999*

| Partisan control of *Länder* votes | Number of Bundesrat votes | |
|---|---|---|
| | immediately after general election | after Berlin state election |
| Only CDU or CSU | 10 | 17 |
| CDU–FDP coalition | 6 | 11 |
| CDU–SPD coalition | 11 | 11 |
| SPD–FDP | 4 | 4 |
| SPD–B 90/Greens | 18 | 13 |
| SPD–PDS | 3 | 3 |
| Only SPD | 17 | 10 |
| Total | 69 | 69 |
| CDU/CSU controlled | 16 | 28 |
| Open | 11 | 11 |
| SPD controlled | 42 | 30 |

scholarly literature on the dynamics of government popularity in Western democracies is extensive, it has seldom directly addressed questions of institutional design and the role institutions play in the assignment of credit and blame'.[45] The problem of diffuse accountability is further aggravated by the penetration of a broad variety of social interests into the governmental decision-making processes, which motivated Peter Katzenstein to speak of Germany as a semi-sovereign state, and which has been frequently criticized by Peter Pulzer in his reflections on responsible party government.[46]

With regard to coalitions and responsible party government one can, at least for practical purposes, side with Peter Pulzer when he argues that German political practice has made coalitions acceptable because voters are clearly informed ahead of time—at least in general elections—which parties would form a government if they obtained the necessary electoral support. The government change of 1998 has testified to the ability of the German electorate to bring such a change about even under conditions of proportional representation. However, in accountability terms this is a situation quite different from one where voters can punish or reward one governing party directly and under a situation of utmost transparency.

There is one final consideration concerning the logic of the government–opposition mechanism in democracies as 'a form of government that involves the voters in making decisions on matters of importance to people. Being able to make decisions requires that the people be presented with a choice between viable and real alternatives.'[47] There can be no question that the functioning of this mechanism is an important factor in providing reward and blame and thereby creativity, innovation, and control for a polity. However, the recent German example discussed here suggests that the impetus for 'throwing the rascals out' can evaporate fairly quickly if the former opposition has not done its homework of formulating alternative policy options properly. Furthermore, government change is an instrument that, by the logic of the democratic electoral process, can unfold its potential only infrequently and at long intervals. It is not by chance, therefore, that in European polities the mass media and extra-parliamentary groups have made so much headway in influencing political decision-making. This is another field where institutional engineering is called for. This thought necessarily leads to a consideration of the pressures from globalization, of transnational institution-building, and of regionalization, all of which contribute to a situation where national political systems are fundamentally challenged in their legitimacy and effectiveness. Under such circumstances, the problem of accountability has to be reconceptualized in very different terms, which go beyond the bounds of this chapter.

# Notes

1. T. Poguntke, *Parteiorganisationem im Wandel: Gesellschaftliche Verankerung und organisatorische Anpassung im europaeischen Vergleich* (Wiesbaden: Westdeutscher Verlag, 2000).
2. A. Lijphart, *Patterns of Democracy: Government Forms and Performance in Thirty-Six Countries* (New Haven, Conn., and London: Yale University Press, 1999).
3. A. Lijphart (ed.), *Parliamentary versus Presidential Government* (Oxford and New York: OUP, 1992). J. J. Linz and A. Valenzuela, *The Failure of Presidential Democracy. Comparative Perspectives*, (Baltimore: Johns Hopkins University Press, 1994).
4. A. Lijphart, 'Democracies: Forms, Performance, and Constitutional Engineering', *European Journal of Political Research*, 25 (1994); Lijphart, *Patterns of Democracy*, 1–17.
5. R. S. Katz, 'Party Government and its Alternatives', in Katz (ed.), *Party Governments: European and American Experiences* (Berlin and New York: Walter de Gruyter, 1987), 4.
6. G. Sjöblom, 'The Role of Political Parties in Denmark and Sweden', in Katz (ed.), *Party Governments*, 156–7.
7. P. Pulzer, 'Responsible Party Government and Stable Coalition: The Case of the German Federal Republic', *Political Studies*, 26 (1978), 181–208; Pulzer, 'Responsible Party Government in the German Political System', in H. Döring and G. Smith (eds.), *Party Government and Political Culture in Western Germany* (London and Basingstoke: Macmillan, 1982), 9–37. Pulzer, 'Responsible Party Government: What has Changed?', in H. Döring and D. Grosser (eds.), *Großbritannien: Ein Regierungssystem in der Belastungsprobe* (Opladen: Leske + Budrich, 1987), 15–29.
8. Pulzer, 'Responsible Party Government', in Döring and Smith, *Party Government*, 10–11, 13.
9. Independent Commission on the Voting System, *The Report of the Independent Commission on the Voting System*, presented to Parliament by the Secretary of State for the Home Department by Command of Her Majesty (London: HMSO, October 1998).
10. A. Lijphart, *Democracies: Patterns of Majoritarian and Consensus Government in Twenty-One Countries* (New Haven, Conn.: Yale University Press, 1984), 211–22; Lijphart, *Patterns of Democracy*, 9–47, 243–57.
11. Lijphart., *Patterns of Democracy*, 3.
12. Lijphart, *Democracies*, 216.
13. Lijphart, *Patterns of Democracy*, 248.
14. P. J. Katzenstein, *Policy and Politics in West Germany: The Growth of a Semi-Sovereign State. Policy and Politics in Industrial States* (Philadelphia: Temple University Press, 1987), 385.
15. N. Luhmann, *Ökologische Kommunikation* (Opladen: Westdeutscher Verlag, 1986), 75–6, 169–70.
16. S. P. Huntington, *The Third Wave: Democratization in the Late Twentieth Century* (Norman, Okla.: University of Oklahoma Press, 1991), 266–7.
17. For convincing empirical evidence in favour of this claim see C. Anderson and C. A. Guillory, 'Political Institutions and Satisfaction with Democracy: A Cross-National Analysis of Consensus and Majoritarian Systems', *American Political Science Review*, 91(1997), 66–81, and D. Fuchs, G. Guidorossi, and P. Svensson, 'Support for the Democratic System', in H.-D. Klingemann and D. Fuchs (eds.), *Citizens and the State. Beliefs in Government Series*, (Oxford: OUP, 1995).

18. M. Kaase and K. Newton, Beliefs in Government. Beliefs in Government Series, 5; (Oxford: OUP, 1995).
19. For a sophisticated empirical analysis based on longitudinal data from sixteen democracies see M. D. McDonald, I. Budge and R. I. Hofferbert, *Assessing the Economic Basis of Electoral Choice—Where There is a Choice*. Mimeo (Binghamton, New York: Department of Political Science, Binghamton University, 1999).
20. C. Anderson, *Blaming the Government: Citizens and the Economy in Five European Democracies* (Armonk, NY: M. E. Sharpe, 1995).
21. McDonald et al., *Assessing Electoral Choice*.
22. Lijphart, *Patterns of Democracy*, 288–9.
23. Stewart Wood, 'The British General Election of 1997', *Electoral Studies*, 18 (1997), 147, 151.
24. Lijphart, *Patterns of Democracy*, 288.
25. This accountability assessment may become more complex, though, if there exist conditions like a strong system of pressure groups to interfere with political decision making. See Pulzer, 'Responsible Party Government', in Döring and Smith, *Party Government*, 10–13.
26. For a general analysis of this complex topic see G. Lehmbruch, *Parteienwettbewerb im Bundesstaat: Regelsysteme und Spannungslagen im Institutionengefüge der Bundesrepublik Deutschland*, 2nd, rev. edn. (Opladen and Wiesbaden: Westdeutscher Verlag, 1998); with reference to responsible party government this is also considered in Pulzer, 'Responsible Party Government and Stable Coalition', 602–6, and in Pulzer, 'Responsible Party Government', in Döring and Smith, *Party Government*, 31–2.
27. In the three parliamentary periods between 1980 and 1990 an average of about 56% of the laws were classified as requiring the approval of both parliamentary chambers; see Verwaltung des Deutschen Bundestags (ed.), *Datenhandbuch zur Geschichte des Deutschen Bundestages 1983 bis 1991* (Baden-Baden: Nomos Verlagsgesellschaft, 1994), 825.
28. For a detailed analysis of the political implications of the federalized element in the national legislative process see T. König, 'Probleme und Perspektiven der deutschen Zweikammergesetzgebung', in M. Kaase and G. Schmid (eds.), *Eine lernende Demokratie: 50 Jahre Bundesrepublik Deutschland* (WZB-Jahrbuch 1999, Berlin: edition sigma, 1999).
29. On *Politikverflechtung* see F. W. Scharpf, *Optionen des Föderalismus in Deutschland und Europa* (Frankfurt and New York: Campus, 1994); F. W. Scharpf, B. Reissert, and F. Schnabel, *Politikverflechtung: Theorie und Empirie des kooperativen Föderalismus in der Bundesrepublik* (Kronberg, Ts.: Scriptor Verlag, 1976); Lehmbruch, *Parteienwettbewerb im Bundesstaat*, 90–135.
30. Verwaltung des Deutschen Bundestags (ed.), *Datenhandbuch zur Geschichte des Deutschen Bundestages*, 858.
31. Pulzer, P., 'Responsible Party Government and Stable Coalition', 604.
32. For a detailed discussion of this problem see T. König, 'Probleme und Perspektiven'.
33. A. Ottnad and E. Linnartz, *Föderaler Wettbewerb statt Verteilungsstreit: Vorschläge zur Neugliederung der Bundesländer und zur Reform des Finanzausgleichs* (Frankfurt and New York: Campus, 1998).
34. Pulzer, 'Responsible Party Government and Stable Coalition', Pulzer, 'Responsible Party Government', Döring and Smith (eds.), *Party Government*.
35. Pulzer, 'Responsible Party Government and Stable Coalition', 607.
36. Pulzer, 'Responsible Party Government', in Döring and Smith, *Party Government* 25–8.
37. Lijphart, *Patterns of Democracy*, 293.

38. For 1994 see B. Weßels, 'Wahlpräferenzen in den Regionen: Stabilität und Veränderung im Wahljahr 1994—oder: Die "Heimkehr" der CDU/CSU-Wähler von 1990', in M. Kaase and H.-D. Klingemann (eds.), *Wahlen und Wähler: Analysen aus Anlaß der Bundestagswahl 1994* (Opladen and Wiesbaden: Westdeutscher Verlag, 1998).
39. M. Rettich and R. Schatz, *Amerikanisierung oder Die Macht der Themen* (Bonn: InnoVatio Verlag, 1998), 6.
40. Infratest dimap, *Wahlreport: Wahl zum 14. deutschen Bundestag. 27. September 1998* (Berlin: Infratest dimap. Gesellschaft für Trend und Wahlforschung, 1998), 132–52.
41. For analyses of the 1998 election see O. W. Gabriel and F. Brettschneider, 'Die Bundestagswahl 1998: Ein Plebiszit gegen Kanzler Kohl?', *Aus Politik und Zeitgeschichte*, B52/98 (18 Dec. 1998); M. Jung and D. Roth, 'Wer zu spät geht, den bestraft der Wähler: Eine Analyse der Bundestagswahl 1998', *Aus Politik und Zeitgeschichte*, B52/98 (18 Dec. 1998); Rettich and Schatz, *Amerikanisierung*; U. Feist and H.-J. Hoffmann, 'Die Bundestagswahl 1998: Wahl des Wechsels', *Zeitschrift für Parlamentsfragen* (1999 2) 214–51. F. U. Pappi, 'Die Abwahl Kohls: Hauptergebnis der Bundestagswahl 1998?', *Zeitschrift für Politik*, 46 (1999), 1–29. P. Pulzer, 'The German Federal Election of 1998', *West European Politics*, 22/3 (1999), 241–9.
42. See the essays by H.-D. Klingemann, 'Kontinuität und Veränderung des Deutschen Parteiensystems, 1949–1998', in Kaase and Schmid, *Eine lernende Demokratie: 50 Jahre Bundesrepublik Deutschland*, 125–7; and König, 'Probleme und Perspektiven', ibid. 63–85.
43. T. R. Cusack, 'Die Unzufriedenheit der deutschen Bevölkerung mit der Performanz der Regierung und des politischen Systems', ibid. 237–61.
44. This point is very succinctly made by the East German writer Monika Maron in 'Neueste Nachrichten vom Nachzügler unserer verspäteten Nation', *Frankfurter Allgemeine Zeitung*, 216 (17 Sept. 1999).
45. C. Anderson, 'The Dynamics of Public Support for Coalition Governments', *Comparative Political Studies*, 3 (1995) 350–83.
46. The most recent example of German consensus politics is the pact for employment (*Bündnis für Arbeit*) which is a revival of late 1960s concerted action and reflects a corporatist understanding of politics without considering that only the government is legitimated by the citizenry.
47. McDonald *et al.*, *Assessing Electoral Choice*, 21.

# V

## A Celebration of Genius

# 15

## Fiddlers on the Roof: Some Thoughts on a Special Relationship

### David Schoenbaum

Like the terrified horses of Picasso's *Guernica*, Chagall's fiddlers on the roof are among the most familiar and evocative icons of our time. In a century equally notable for Jewish achievement and calamity, the visibility and success of Jewish violinists from Central Europe, Russia, even Odessa alone, lead almost automatically to speculation about a special relationship between Jews and the violin. In fact, the relationship is neither new nor self-evident. But the tangle of legend, nostalgia, and truth that historians have learnt to call the master narrative, has made it seductively easy to assume that it was both.

Although the evidence is inferential and circumstantial, the relationship actually points back to the beginnings of the instrument. After the expulsion from Spain in 1492, Jewish players and Spanish instruments, among them the lute, showed up in Venice. When Venice extended its sovereignty to Cremona, Spanish Jews or their descendants showed up in Cremona too. There they became neighbours, perhaps even landlords,[1] of Andrea Amati, the first in a line of notable makers that was to extend 200 years.

In Cremona as elsewhere, Jews entered the rag trade, ran inns for itinerant co-religionists, and taught music.[2] Lute construction meanwhile served as a model for violins, whose design differed significantly from anything north or south of the Alps.[3] From then to now, the Cremonese model has remained the standard violin, and its makers have been known as luthiers. The diffusion of Cremonese instruments and Cremonese Jews began soon afterward. Jews were driven out of the city in 1597. Some may have turned up in Amsterdam, home of the largest Sephardic community north of Italy. There Ashkenazic fiddlers drifted in from Poland to play in local bordellos, and local makers produced first-rate Italian-influenced violins by the mid-seventeenth century.[4] Directly or via Antwerp, other Sephardim made their way to England, where the Inquisition was unlikely to be a problem, and the Tudors seem to have looked actively for Jewish players.[5]

At the same time, a favourable conjunction of supply and demand was transforming the style of the instrument and the course of Western music.

The walls of any Dutch museum confirm how Protestant Europe associated the northern version of the instrument with dancing masters, street musicians, and drunks. In Italy, on the other hand, the violin was associated with cardinals and princes, gentlemen collectors, and up-scale entertainments like the opera. By the end of the seventeenth century, the opera orchestra had led to a proliferation of court orchestras, composition for instruments, and demand for virtuoso performers.

The robust export market for Italian culture in all its forms turned out to be a crucial multiplier. Eighteenth-century English gentlemen paid their respects to Italian music by collecting Italian violins and violinists.[6] Twentieth-century Soviet waiters paid theirs by finding a table for a party of Italian gentlemen—in reality the touring Borodin Quartet, resourcefully addressing one another in phrases like 'Fermato poco ma presto subito'—in what might have been the only restaurant in Krasnoyarsk.[7]

The globalization of violins and violinists coincided with a revolution in music itself, as composers from Haydn to Schoenberg adapted and developed new worlds of form around violin-based ensembles, and German impresarios from Johann Peter Salomon to Hermann Wolff developed new markets for their products. The Enlightenment and the great revolutions in France and industry were multipliers too. The former favoured the *Bildungsbürger*, the educated professional and passionate amateur, who regarded music as good and true as well as beautiful, took Beethoven as seriously as Goethe and Shakespeare, played an instrument, bought concert tickets, and sent his children to music lessons.[8] The latter favoured the middle class in every sense, including a flourishing big city concert culture,[9] a rail and telegraph network that made it possible for Wolff to promote and deliver his performers across the continent, and a violin industry capable of turning out a million stringed instruments and 100,000 bows a year by the 1830s.[10]

The first Jews to feel the impact, and make a good thing of it, were in Central Europe. But the ripples and echoes moved progressively north and eastward. The effects could be seen in swift generational increments as German and Austrian, then Hungarian, Polish, Lithuanian, and Russian Jews shifted from village to city, small business to the professions, and religion to culture. By 1848 30 per cent by 1871 80 per cent of German Jews could already be classified as bourgeois. By 1858 Jews comprised 8–9 per cent of Berlin's journalists, 11–12 per cent of its doctors,[11] and what can only have been a large and growing share of its concert audience. Baptism was the ticket of admission to European culture, Heine declared in a famous epigram. To go by Jewish gymnasium attendance—30 per cent of total enrolment in Vienna, 36 per cent in Budapest, 46 per cent in German-speaking Prague, 50 per cent in German-speaking Lvov, around 1900—*Fidelio*, *Zauberflöte*, and command of the ablative absolute were more like it.

Successive generations of Mendelssohns acted out the process in Berlin. In the 1760's, Moses Mendelssohn was among the first to take Judaism to Germans and bring German culture to Jews. In the 1830s and 1840s, his grandson Felix rediscovered Bach, created the Leipzig conservatory, and composed one of the greatest of all violin concertos. Later descendants, now known as von Mendelssohn, collected instruments, including a Stradivari viola from Hill's of London, the era's leading shop, and a Stradivari violin from Carl Flesch, the era's leading pedagogue. The first, in 1892, was bought for home use in a regular amateur quartet. The second, in 1930, was bought as a favour to Flesch, after he lost his shirt in the Wall Street crash.[12]

Equally assimilated, although the family continued idiosyncratically to assert its Jewish identity long after it too had become Protestant, successive Wittgensteins did similar things in Vienna. In the 1830s, Hermann, the patriarch, took in his wife's young cousin, Joseph Joachim, to study at the Vienna Conservatory, then sent him to Leipzig to study with Mendelssohn. In 1865, Hermann's son, Karl, took off for America, arriving with nothing but the violin he continued to take along on business trips the rest of his life. Of Karl's nine children, including the philosopher, Ludwig, at least two were serious pianists, one a talented cellist, and one son 'played several instruments like a virtuoso.'[13]

Joachim's career subsumed the whole era. Between 1831, when he was born in a village on the Austrian–Hungarian border, and 1907, when he was buried in the cemetery of Berlin's Kaiser Wilhelm Memorial Church, the little Jewish boy from Hungary had become a protégé of Mendelssohn, a confidant of Clara Wieck Schumann, and a Prussian-German icon. From his London debut at 13 to his jubilee appearance sixty years later, British audiences loved him too.

In 1869 he was invited to build a Berlin conservatory in one of Berlin's most Jewish neighbourhoods.[14] In 1879 he introduced Brahms's violin concerto as its dedicatee. For over thirty years he performed the Beethoven quartets before subscribers plausibly characterized as more a congregation than an audience. During the secular holiday season on the eve of the new year 1880, he even made an audience of a congregation. A member of the state church since the 1860s, Joachim conducted a benefit concert at Berlin's Oranienburgerstrasse synagogue, second only to Budapest's Dohany utcai (Dohany Street) synagogue as Europe's most imposing. The imperial family and court were in attendance. Beethoven's Fifth was on the programme.

In 1913, Franz and Robert von Mendelssohn presented the conservatory, the House that Joachim Built, with a memorial including niche, bust, allegorical female figures, a lute, a lyre, and a pedestal. A quarter-century later in a very different Germany, the monument was—literally—deconstructed. A few weeks later, the Oranienburgerstrasse synagogue was torched.[15] German-Jewish violinist was officially declared an oxymoron.

If Joachim was a casualty in effigy, Flesch was among the casualties in real life. A grandson and great-grandson of rabbis, Flesch, like Joachim, was a product of village Hungary, where he was born in 1873. He too had begun his career at the Vienna conservatory, where the senior professor Hellmesberger had it in for Jews, the short-sighted, and talented pupils of his colleague Adolf Grün, who was also Jewish and a Joachim protégé. It was Flesch's luck that he qualified in all three categories.[16]

The Jewish connection, unsurprisingly, would pursue him all his life. In Berlin, where he spent many of his most productive years, Jewish violinists were thick on the ground. Flesch himself calculated that of sixty-three violinists listed in the standard directory of concert artists for 1927–8, thirty had Jewish antecedents.[17] Jewish names, large numbers of them from Germany's Eastern neighbours and the Austro-Hungarian successor states, are conspicuous among the applicants for his famous summer courses. More, and very distinguished, Jewish players—Wolfsthal from Vienna, Rostal from Teschen, Szeryng from Warsaw, Goldberg from Wloclawek, Ivry Gitlis from Haifa, Ida Haendel from Chelm—are conspicuous among the students who were to carry his name far into the century.

Writing in 1928, in an overview of the instrument and the profession, Flesch was struck by how many gifted Jews were drawn to the violin as compared to the piano. He had no explanation, save perhaps a weakness for the quasi-operatic possibilities of a solo voice as opposed to multiple lines. But he saw nothing genetic in this. Joachim, who was as Jewish as any 'Jewish' violinist, had played very differently, he noted.

In 1931, the year of Joachim's centennial, Flesch returned to the theme in an essay on tone production. There was no such thing as a natural aptitude for tone, he emphasized in an introductory paragraph. It was still an observable fact that historical circumstance had favoured gypsies, the French, and East European Jews. In the French case, he inferred that this had something to do with learning the instrument from Italians. In the Jewish case, he associated it with centuries of listening to cantors in the synagogue. But whatever the source, he emphasized, tone was no substitute for music, and no excuse for teachers to beg off their professional responsibilities by pleading biological inevitability.[18]

The paragraph led to an extraordinary confrontation with his colleague Gustav Havemann, himself a Joachim pupil, who kept his mentor's portrait in his studio. Before joining the conservatory faculty in 1920, Havemann had made a respectable career as an orchestra player. In a place where experiment was the order of the day, he now made his mark as a member of the November Group, an ensemble dedicated to new music. In 1928, like Flesch, he also published a book on violin technique. A year later Havemann informed Georg Schünemann, the deputy director of the conservatory, that he intended to vote Nazi, after concluding that all Weimar governments were leading to the abyss, and that Jewish influence was ruining Germany.[19] He then organized an orchestra of similarly minded players under the banner of a League for German Culture, and paid them out of his own pocket.

Flesch's innocuous paragraph apparently confirmed his worst suspicions. As 'an Aryan German in Germany', Havemann announced in an open letter to the country's leading musicians' weekly, he could not let it go unchallenged. Germans too had a sense of tone, born of centuries of listening to chorales in churches, he argued. 'You want to impose a Jewish tone on us, that our race rejects as too effete and sensual for works by our race.' Flesch's puzzled and slightly exasperated attempt at a rational reply led to a joint statement a few weeks later, in which both men affirmed that their personal relationship was as cordial as ever and stressed their commitment to devote all their strength to the service of German art and youth.[20] A little more than a year afterwards, Havemann himself became director of the conservatory, and purged the faculty, including Flesch. In 1951 the same Havemann was appointed to head the violin department at the newly created Hanns Eisler conservatory in the Soviet sector of the now-divided city.[21]

In many ways, the rendezvous of Jew and violin in Russia took a similar course. But from the beginning, there are a few significant differences. Russia's Jewish population was much larger and poorer than Central Europe's, still heavily traditional, and decades away from legal emancipation. In 1910, 615,000 Jews comprised less than 1 per cent of the population of Germany. In 1897, some four million Jews comprised 11 per cent of the population of the Pale of Settlement, the vast tract extending south and eastwards from the Baltic to the Black Sea. Two-thirds of Russian Jews earned their living in what were officially classified as industry, crafts, commerce, and insurance. Of these, a critical mass, nearly a third of the city's population in 1892, lived in Odessa, a kind of Black Sea San Francisco, where a recognizable version of the modern world was clearly visible by 1860, and even Jews went to the opera.[22] But another two-thirds of Russia's Jews lived in towns of under 10,000.[23]

Millions were drawn to Hasidism, the pietist revival and reform movement that swept Eastern Europe in the eighteenth century. Others clung to the rigorous Lithuanian scholasticism that regarded Hasidism with distaste and dismay. Still others opted for *Haskalah*, the Russian-Jewish version of the Enlightenment. A minority took the path of full assimilation. Among them was the pianist Anton Rubinstein, born Jewish in 1829. In 1831, Rubinstein and fifty members of his family joined the Orthodox Church under pressure from the official anti-Semitism of Tsar Nicholas I. In 1862, he founded the St Petersburg Conservatory, Russia's first. He then served two terms as its director, retiring from the second in 1891 in protest at the official anti-Semitism of Tsar Alexander III.[24]

In contention, even overt conflict with one another, tradition and change both contributed to the evolution of the Russian-Jewish violinist. The violin had been a familiar, even ubiquitous, Jewish folk instrument since the eighteenth century.[25] In contrast to traditional Orthodoxy, Hasidism favoured song and dance. Encroaching secularism favoured the encroachment of secular music. The enormous output of mass-produced instruments from Mirecourt, Mittenwald, and Markneukirchen only made violins more accessible. 'Look at the walls,' people said in Jewish Eastern Europe. 'As many fiddles as hang there—that's how many men.'[26]

The huge prestige of Western and specifically German culture were leveraged, in turn, by the practical example of travelling virtuosi, and the availability of conservatory places, theoretically open to any qualified 14–year-old, that led to a brave new world of social status, economic security, and empire-wide civil rights. Oppressive poverty, rising expectations, and the threshold sense of existential crisis common to ever-widening circles of Russian Jews, did the rest. By the end of the nineteenth century, the violin was a recurring motif and symbol in Yiddish fiction.[27] Chagall did not come from nowhere.

The magic even worked in New York, where the young Sol Hurok began a memorable career in artist management by linking the passion for the violin to the passion for socialist politics. How to get Jewish socialists to a party fund-raiser? Hurok proposed bringing the young Efrem Zimbalist. A recent arrival in America like Hurok and much of Brownsville, Zimbalist had been a student activist at the St Petersburg Conservatory in 1905.[28] His manager immediately saw the publicity value. Zimbalist agreed to come for $750, a third of which he then wrote over to the party. Soon afterwards, he appeared under Hurok's management at a sold-out Carnegie Hall.[29]

Among the consequences was a flourishing culture of parents, equivalent to the stage, ballet, tennis, or football parents of other times and places, but singularly focused on the violin. Little Nathan Milstein, born into an assimilated, Russian-speaking, Odessa family the last day of 1903, took up the violin because his mother thought it would be nice.[30] 'All the folks in our circle . . . used to have their children taught music,' says the narrator of Isaac Babel's 'Awakening,' speaking for many Odessa families. 'Our fathers, seeing no other escape from our lot, had thought up a lottery, building it on the bones of little children.'[31]

Leopold Auer was neither a sufficient nor a necessary condition. He was none the less a catalytic figure in all that followed. Concertmaster in Düsseldorf at 23, with a decoration from the Duke of Saxe-Meiningen, and ten years of nomadic concertizing already behind him, Auer returned from a Black Forest holiday in 1868 to find an urgent message from the St. Petersburg Conservatory, inviting him to succeed the great Henri Wieniawski, himself only 25, as professor of violin. A third assimilated Jew from village Hungary, Auer had even got his childhood religious instruction from Flesch's great-grandfather.[32] His father, a house painter, took him to Budapest at 8 to study with the concertmaster of the National Opera. Soon after, Auer made his début, performing the Mendelssohn concerto in a little Hungarian folk costume. Like his great peers, Auer too studied in Vienna. He then went to Paris, and from there to work with Joachim. With nothing in his memoirs to suggest the contrary, it can only be assumed that the Petersburg offer seemed another sensible career move.

Originally hired for three years, he was to remain another forty-six, incidentally becoming a loyal subject of the Tsar, and joining the Russian Orthodox Church. It was no coincidence that his collateral duties included command appearances at court; violin solos at the Imperial; and dutiful gigs with the Grand Duke Constantine, a dedicated amateur cellist. The outbreak of the First World War briefly left him, and protégés including the young Jascha Heifetz, stranded in Germany, where Auer ran a summer studio near Dresden. He none the less returned to Russia, and continued teaching. In the end, it took a global war, and a revolution that swept away a half-century's support systems, to make him leave St Petersburg for good.

Over his long tenure, 270 students passed through his class. Before Auer, it was generally assumed in and out of Russia that great violinists were Italian, French, Belgian, German, Austrian, or Hungarian. After him, it seemed noteworthy if they were anything but Russian Jews, even when the Russian Jews happened to come from America or Israel. Remarkable for a patriarchal age and an overwhelmingly male profession, one of the earliest figures to surface is a young woman. Born in Odessa in 1872, Sophie Jaffe first studied with Auer. She then left for Paris, where she won a first prize at the Conservatory in 1893, and left a lasting impression on her classmate, Flesch. According to Bachmann, she then 'made numerous successful tours of Germany, and upon inheriting a fortune retired from the concert stage.'[33] This was several years before the prodigious boys who were to assure Auer's place in the pedagogical pantheon had even been born. After the First World War, according to Flesch, she reappeared in Zürich as a refugee.[34] The refugee experience was a common denominator. In most other particulars, the experience of her younger, poorer, boy colleagues would be quite different.

Throughout, Auer continued to play concerts as far afield as Istanbul and London, while regularly touring the provinces. There his growing reputation led to encounters at once familiar to any touring performer and only occasionally notable for their long-term consequences. 'I was used to visits from local geniuses when I was on tour, for they menaced me in every Russian city where I stopped,' he remarked of one such meeting in 1901.[35] What distinguished the latest genius from most others was that he really showed signs of being one. The meeting would turn the pupil into an international superstar. It would thereby transform a respected teacher into an acknowledged genius too.

Mischa Elman was the grandson of a self-taught violinist, who made prayer shawls for a living, and the son of a Talmudic scholar, who sold hay by the bushel. Not yet 11, he had taken up the violin at 5, bounced in and out of school, rejected the patronage of a local countess, who offered full support in return for full assimilation, then toured the Russian backwoods to raise money for further study in Berlin or Paris. When this failed, he auditioned again for Auer. Auer immediately telegraphed Glazunov, the director of the conservatory, to get him a scholarship.

On Elman's arrival in St. Petersburg, Auer not only showed him off in high society, incidentally raising 300 rubles for him at a dinner musicale, he found a grand duke willing to put up 3000 rubles to buy him an Amati. His effort on behalf of Elman's father was at least as noteworthy. For the moment, the elder Elman was employed pro forma as butler in a private home. When Plehve, the Tsar's deeply anti-Semitic interior minister, turned down Glazunov's request for a residence permit, Auer intervened personally, organizing a private recital for Plehve and the cabinet. After three weeks of stonewalling, Plehve issued the permit.

In 1904, barely a year after starting with Auer, Elman made his début in Berlin and Vienna. Dressed in a silk sailor suit, he did the same in London in 1905, even sharing a command performance before Edward VII and the King of Spain with the singers Caruso and Nelly Melba. In 1906, he cut his first record in Paris, playing an aluminum violin into a metal horn. On his return to London, Baron Alfred Rothschild presented him with a gold watch, and set him up with a car and driver.

By now, Auer was busy with Zimbalist, who premiered with the Berlin Philharmonic in 1907 at age 17. The son of a violinist and opera conductor in Rostov, Zimbalist arrived in St Petersburg in 1904. He then walked the streets with his mother, camping out in all-night restaurants until Mrs Zimbalist secured the residence permit that would allow them to share a rented room. Then came Toscha Seidel, born in 1899, whose mother had to commute from Finland while waiting for the residence permit allowing her to live with her son. Then came 10-year-old Jascha Heifetz, son of a violinist from Vilna. In his case, the resourceful Auer solved the problem by registering Heifetz's father as his student too. Then came Milstein, 11, whose mother's permit seems only to have needed a call from Glazunov to Prince Volkonsky, the deputy minister of interior. By now it was wartime. Then came the revolution.

Soon all but Milstein were in America. Elman had already toured the United States in 1908. Zimbalist had settled there in 1911. With a guarantee of fifty concerts and $25,000, Heifetz arrived via Siberia, Japan, and San Francisco, for a legendary New York début in October 1917. Sascha Jacobsen, no Auer pupil, and perhaps not even Russian-born,[36] sold out New York's three biggest concert halls soon afterwards. In April 1918 Seidel arrived on the same boat as Auer himself. Before long, all of them seemed as much a part of the landscape as Carnegie Hall.

'I liked the sound—circa 1921—of the given names of four internationally renowned violinists then living in New York,' Ira Gershwin recalled many decades later. The conjunction of Mischa, Jascha, Toscha, Sascha, led to what 'surely must have been one of the best-known unpublished and non-commercial hits of the Twenties', he added. With his brother George at the piano, the Gershwins sang it at every party, where even the figures in the title liked it.

> We really think you ought to know
> That we were born right in the middle
> Of Darkest Russia,
> When we were three years old or so,
> We all began to play the fiddle
> In darkest Russia.
> When we began,
> Our notes were sour—
> Until a man
> (Professor Auer)
> Set out to show us, one and all,
> How we could pack them in, in Carnegie Hall.
> Temp'ramental Oriental Gentlemen are we:
> Mischa, Jascha, Toscha, Sascha—
> Fiddle-lee, diddle-lee, dee.[37]

'Darkest Russia' and 'temp'ramental Oriental' were obviously a blend of cipher and self-irony. But it was hard to miss the joke or misread the code. What was true in New York was just as true in Buffalo, where Julius Singer presented twenty-eight pupils with names including Weinberg, Rosenberg, Alpern, and Cheplovitz, at the Central YMCA in 1914, or in Toronto, where Maurice Solway, his brothers, and Russian-born father paid off an ineffectual band then grabbed their violins and continued on their own, at a family wedding in 1924. Solway went on to study with Ysaye, and make a distinguished career as a teacher, chamber, and orchestra player. A cousin played for many years in the Philadelphia Orchestra.[38]

An immigrant from somewhere near Riga, Singer had revisited Europe in 1904–5 for a heady year in Berlin, and a summer with Ottokar Sevcik, another emblematic teacher. The brochure printed on his return identifies a darkly earnest young man in tails as 'Mr. Julius Singer, Solo Violinist, And Teacher of the Celebrated Sevcik Method of Violin Playing.' Even after moving to Buffalo's more respectable west side, he maintained his east side studio, his daughter recalled, 'because that's where the Jews were.'[39] His daughter also played the violin from age 6, winning a scholarship to Juilliard at 16, where she studied with Sergei Korguyev, once Auer's assistant. Twice each term, she even appeared before Auer himself, now in his eighties. She remembered an exchange with a classmate, another gifted violinist, after passing a couple of particularly elegant ladies on Fifth Avenue. 'They can't play the Beethoven Concerto', her classmate reminded her.

Catherine Drinker Bowen, of Philadelphia's Main Line, recalled how the

class war looked from the other side of the hill. A serious amateur from a
family of serious amateurs, she had been allowed to attend Baltimore's
Peabody Conservatory, but only over her father's deep reservations. 'With us,
music is an accomplishment, not a profession', he reminded her. Bowen eventually made it to the first desk of the conservatory orchestra. But she felt
perennially disadvantaged 'compared to the pale, black-haired youths' around
her. Their style and English were 'obviously short of middle class.' But unlike
herself, she realized, they were playing for their lives.[40] Dorothy DeLay of
Medicine Lodge, Kansas, an aspiring professional, and later one of the
legendary teachers of her generation, experienced similar feelings at Juilliard
on the eve of the Second World War. The next best thing to being a Jew was to
marry one, she concluded, and did.[41]

   While the Jewish violin school flourished in America, it survived and recovered in Russia, where an *ad hoc* system of imperial subsidy and aristocratic
patronage was superseded by a rigorously centralized system of public support. The new system, which extended from school entry to the conservatory,
was designed to produce world-class violinists, just as similar tracks were
designed to produce world-class chess players,[42] and later world-class athletes.
Equally suspect as such and as class enemies, Jews continued to aim for the
conservatories, where entrance standards remained high, the student profile
remained largely unchanged, and the most important teachers continued to
be Jews. Undeterred by a decade of war and revolution, Moscow Conservatory
pianists carried off first and fourth prizes in 1927 at the First Chopin
Memorial competition in Warsaw. In 1928, the year of Stalin's victory over 'the
right', a parallel worker-peasant faculty, organized as the Russian Association
of Proletarian Musicians, took over the conservatory in a short-lived cultural
revolution. It threw out all class enemies, dispensed with examinations,
declared soloists redundant, and purged the repertory of reactionary composers, among them Tchaikovsky, Schumann, Chopin, Scriabin, Rachmaninov,
and Bach. At the Second Chopin competition in Warsaw in 1932, Soviet
pianists carried off no prizes, and even failed to qualify for the final round.[43]
The same year all proletarian art groups were abolished, and the conservatories returned to normal.

   Normality, of course, was a relative quality in the Soviet Union. As Bach,
Tchaikovsky and examinations returned to the conservatories, much of the
Soviet élite stood on the threshold of Stalin's great terror, and the other arts,
including musical composition, were subjected to a radical purge. Orchestra
players, conservatory professors, and other musicians even enjoyed a pay rise.
As before, the new course coincided with a sea change in Soviet policy. This
time the shift was to the 'right.' With the proliferation of fascism and rise of
the Nazis, policy-makers acknowledged the need for bourgeois (Western)
allies. Irrespective of social origin, performing artists practised an essentially
bourgeois art that was now seen to be good for the Soviet image.

Ironically, at the Wieniawski competition in Warsaw in 1935, contestants were pre-emptively interviewed by a Polish government official to minimize any risk that a Jew might come in first.[44] Not including first place, Jews none the less won five of nine prizes,[45] among them David Oistrakh and Boris Goldstein from the Moscow Conservatory, who finished second and fourth respectively. Flesch's pupil, the 7- or 11-year-old Ida Haendel of Chelm,[46] won first prize for Polish entrants. Two years later, at the legendary Queen Elizabeth competition in Brussels in 1937, Soviet competitors, including two women and four Jews, won five of six prizes. At the year's parade commemorating the twentieth anniversary of the October Revolution, a contingent of Moscow schoolchildren marched with a yellow streamer with red letters reading 'We want to be violinists.'[47]

There were certainly plausible incentives. The Dutch-born Henri Temianka, who finished a place behind Oistrakh at the Warsaw competition, then toured the Soviet Union at Oistrakh's initiative, was interested to see that his host lived in a three-room apartment and drove a small car. Even fourth place was worth a medal, car, and apartment, not to mention a warm smile from Stalin, to the 14–year-old Goldstein.[48] Temianka's pianist, 'an average Russian,' on the other hand, occupied one corner of a single room.[49]

While Oistrakh earned twice as much in an evening as the average worker earned in a month, conservatory professors far surpassed and good orchestra players matched the earnings of chief engineers.[50] Even the professional orchestra player or teacher could expect a pay-off in social respectability, and pride of association with one of the few areas of endeavour where the Soviet Union really did produce a world-class product. In contrast to most other vocational choices, music also provided a margin of personal expression, a buffer against or escape from the oppressiveness of public life, even an occasional chance to travel, although the family naturally stayed at home.[51] But Jews, as so often, were more equal than others.

In its way, Oistrakh's career proved to be as emblematic as Joachim's. Born in Odessa in 1908 to a singer and semi-professional instrumentalist, he made his Leningrad début in 1928. Soon afterward, he moved to Moscow, where the studied indifference of Soviet concert functionaries left him playing open-air concerts in so-called concert brigades. A first prize in the All-Ukrainian competition in 1930, followed by a film engagement in 1933, and assistant professorship at the Moscow Conservatory in 1934, helped turn things around. But Warsaw, then Brussels, was a watershed.

Seventeen years would pass before he was again allowed to play in the West, but he was now an established figure. In 1942, Oistrakh joined the Party. In 1953, he played *ex officio* in the Hall of Columns, where Stalin was lying in state. For all that, he was a friend in deed to colleagues in need like the young Borodin Quartet, and stood up for the embattled Shostakovich, just as he stood up for the Soviet Union. A quarter-century after Hurok first tried to sign him, the post-Stalinist thaw finally brought Oistrakh for a triumphal tour of the United States. A year later, the year of Suez and the Hungarian Revolution, the Ukrainian-born, American-raised and trained Isaac Stern became the first Western violinist to tour the Soviet Union, reportedly with the help of a subsidy from Hurok. 'They send us their Russian Jewish violinists, we send them our Russian Jewish violinists,' it was said in Washington.

Both artists enjoyed packed houses and ecstatic reviews. But in contrast to Stern, who was allowed virtually no contact with his audience, Oistrakh was cheered and fed from coast to coast by colleagues and old friends like Milstein and Temianka. In the warm glow of superpower *détente*, his Soviet managers even allowed him to keep about half the $100,000 Hurok paid them.[52] After a career of playing a socialized Strad from the state collection, a stunned Oistrakh let Milstein take him to Wurlitzer's to buy a Strad of his own,[53] as well as an Amati.

In 1961, Oistrakh again became an instrument of policy by other means. This time it was Vienna to coincide with the Kennedy–Khrushchev summit. But he refused to sign a statement declaring the Soviet Union not only the worker's, but the Jewish artist's homeland after the Soviet Union broke off diplomatic relations with Israel in 1967. If non-Jews had been among the signatories, he would have signed too, he insisted. His refusal none the less led to a daylight burglary that precisely targeted his awards, career memorabilia, recordings, and tapes.[54] Unlike Rostropovich, he agreed a year later to appear in Prague after the Soviet invasion.[55]

At once hilarious and appalling, Rostislav Dubinsky's memoir of the Borodin Quartet is an anthology of Jewish opportunity and humiliation. As the book begins, twenty Jewish entrants including the author are knocked out after the first round of the 1945 Moscow competition, the great Leonid Kogan after the second, and only Julian Sitkovetsky, a later Queen Elisabeth winner, is allowed to reach the finals. All were students of the equally Jewish Avram Yampolsky.

A few years later, Dubinsky's newly created quartet, with its four Jewish members, was demonstratively passed over, not only in favour of 'real' Russians, but Georgians who never auditioned, to represent the Soviet Union at a competition in Prague. Soon afterward, Jewish players were crowded out of an élite student orchestra created to represent the Soviet Union at the First International Youth Festival. At this point, two of Dubinsky's players dropped out. 'We aren't Jews anymore, but they wouldn't allow us to become Russians, and they never will', one observed.[56]

Prudently reconstructed with two non-Jewish party members, the quartet would eventually work its way to international acclaim. It was even invited, like Oistrakh, to play while Stalin's body lay in state. Yet its support for Shostakovich alone led to crisis after crisis, and for younger composers like Schnittke to endless bureaucratic resistance. After a last skirmish over a proposal to programme Schœnberg, the story ends with the author's decision 'to use my Jewish origin and get out of this shit' after thirty years.[57] In 1981, Dubinsky accepted a professorship at Indiana University.[58]

As it had for decades, America continued to raise and develop distinguished Jewish violinists. But the new Mischas and Jaschas were as likely to come from Israel with the help of Stern's America–Israel Cultural Foundation; from Russia, like the young Maxim Vengerov, led westwards after the collapse of the Soviet Union by Zakhar Bron, probably the last of the great Russian-Jewish teachers, or from East Asia or the Asian-American immigrant community, with names like Kyung-wha, Midori, even Sarah.

Like the end of the Tsars that brought a first generation of teachers to the Zionist *yishuv*, and the collapse of Central Europe that brought much of the Hebrew University and the Palestine Philharmonic to Jerusalem, the implosion of communism again enriched the West and left its marks on Israel. 'If they're not carrying a violin, they must be doctors,' Israelis said as thirty of the new immigrants created a brand-new Russian chamber orchestra in Ashdod in 1990.[59]

But Bron, a pupil of Boris Goldstein and Igor Oistrakh, seemed the likelier bridge from the age of Joachim, Auer, Flesch and the fiddler on the roof, to the age of MTV and the Internet. In 1990, Bron left for the West with four brilliantly talented pupils in tow, the majority of them Jews. 'When Auer left, that was the end of the St Petersburg school,' he told an interviewer. 'When I left the Soviet Union, that was the end of the Novosibirsk school.'[60]

Successively, even concurrently, professor in Lübeck, Rotterdam, Cologne, and Madrid, he now spends his life at 35,000 feet, *en route* to clinics and master classes from Sweden to Tokyo. A global teacher of global violinists, his current Mischas and Jaschas include a Daishin from Japan, even a Chloe from Frimley, and his students come from almost anywhere.[61] Who will replace the Viennese engineers and their children, who once sat in Joachim's congregation, or the New York socialists and their children, who once thronged to hear Zimbalist, is another question.

# Notes

1. Elia Santoro, 'Collezione civica del Commune di Cremona', in *Cremona, Liuteria e Musica in una Città del'Arte* (Cremona: Turris, 1994), 17.
2. Elia Santoro, *Violinari e Violini* (Cremona: Turris, 1989).
3. Annette Otterstedt, 'What Old Fiddles Can Teach Us,' *Galpin Society Journal* (Apr. 1999). Cf. John Dilworth, 'The Violin and Bow: Origins and Development', in *The Cambridge Companion to the Violin*, ed. Rubin Stowell (Cambridge: Cambridge University Press, 1992), 9–11.
4. John Dilworth, 'Vain, Golden Age,' *The Strad*, (Sept. 1991).

5. Peter Holman, *Four and Twenty Fiddlers* (Oxford: OUP, 1993), 82 ff., 105–6.
6. Namely, Simon McVeigh, 'Felice Giardini,' *Music and Letters,* (Oct. 1983).
7. Rostislav Dubinsky, *Stormy Applause* (New York and London: Hutchinson, 1989), 131.
8. Namely, Thomas Nipperdey, *Wie das Bürgertum die Moderne Fand* (Berlin: Siedler, 1988), 11–13.
9. Cf. William Weber, *Music and the Middle Class,* (London: Holmes & Meier, 1975); Cyril Ehrlich, *First Philharmonic* (Oxford: OUP, 1995).
10. Walter Kolneder, *Das Buch der Violine* (Zürich: Atlantis, 1972), 171 ff.
11. David Sorkin, *The Transformation of German Jewry* (New York and Oxford: OUP, 1987), 107 ff.
12. See Arthur Hill's unpublished diary, entry for 16 May 1892; Max Rostal, draft chapter, Fassung II, in Folder 'I. Fassung + Verschiedenes,' Max Rostal papers, Berlin: Hochschule der Künste.
13. Allen Janik and Stephen Toulmin, *Wittgenstein's Vienna* (New York: Simon & Schuster, 1973), 170.
14. Evyatar Friesel, *Atlas of Modern Jewish History,* (New York and Oxford: OUP, 1990), 120.
15. See Beatrix Borchard, 'Im Dienst der wahren Kunst,' in *Die Kunst hat nie ein Mensch allein besessen* (Berlin: Hockschule der Künste, 1996), 365 ff., 356–60.
16. Carl Flesch, *Erinnnerungen eines Geigers* (Freiburg and Zürich: Atlantis, 1960), 24 ff.
17. Carl Flesch, *Die Kunst des Violinspiels,* ii (Berlin: Ries & Erler, 1928), 64.
18. Carl Flesch, *Das Klangproblem im Violinspiel* (Leipzig: Peters, 1931), 5.
19. Undated memo from Havemann attached to letter of 9 March 1935, from Conservatory Director Stein to Prussian Minister of Education, Landesarchiv Berlin, rep 80, Acc 3223, Nr 163/1.
20. *Allgemeine Musikzeitung* 49, (1931,) quoted in Albrecht Dümling and Peter Girth, *Entartete Musik* (Düsseldorf: Der kleine Verlag, 1993), 84–6.
21. Personnel file, Hochschule der Musik Hanns Eisler.
22. See Steven J. Zipperstein, *The Jews of Odessa* (Stanford, Calif.: Stanford University Press, 1985), 32 and 65–6.
23. Friesel, *Atlas,* 32–3.
24. Boris Schwarz, 'Interaction between Russian and Jewish Musicians in the 19th and 20th. Century,' in Judith Cohen (ed.), *Proceedings of the World Congress on Jewish Music 1978* (Tel Aviv: Institute for the Translation of Hebrew Literature, 1982), 204 ff.
25. A. Z. Idelsohn, *Jewish Music* (New York: H. Holt, 1929), 455; Alfred Sendrey, *The Music of the Jews in the Diaspora* (Cranberry, NY, and London: T. Yosselhoff, 1970), 345.
26. Quoted in Moshe Beregovski, 'Jewish Instrumental Folk Music (1937),' in *Old Jewish Folk Music* (Philadelphia: Jewish Publication Society of America, 1982), 542.
27. The author is grateful to Ronald Robboy, a cellist in the San Diego Symphony, not only for pointing this out, but supporting it with an extensive bibliography.
28. Boris Schwarz, *Great Masters of the Violin* (New York: Simon & Schuster, 1983), 430; Leopold Auer, *My Life in Music* (New York: Frederick A. Stokes, 1923), 334.
29. Harlow Robinson, *The Last Impresario* (New York: Viking, 1994), 29–31.
30. Nathan Milstein, *From Russia to the West* (New York: Limelight Editions, 1990), 5.
31. Isaac Babel, 'Awakening,' in *The Collected Stories* (New York: Criterion, 1955), 305.
32. Flesch, *Erinnerungen eines Geigers,* 148.
33. Alberto Bachmann, *An Encyclopedia of the Violin* (New York: Da Capo, 1975), 366.
34. Flesch, *Erinnerungen eines Geigers,* 60.

35. Auer, *My Life in Music*, 320.
36. See Bachmann, *Encyclopedia of the Violin*, 366: 'Began the study of the violin at eight, and at eleven came to America with his parents'; Schwarz, *Great Masters* 507, 'Sascha Jacobsen, born around 1897, was, in fact, a native New Yorker, though his manager tried to make him into a Russian fiddler because it was the rage of the day.'
37. Ira Gershwin, *Lyrics on Several Occasions* (New York: Limelight Editions, 1997), 177–9.
38. Maurice Solway, *Recollections of a Violinist* (Oakville, NY, and London: Mosaic Press, 1984), 15–17.
39. Interview with Bernice Singer Baron, Milwaukee, Wis., 14 Aug. 1999.
40. Catherine Drinker Bowen, *Friends and Fiddlers* (Boston, Mass.: Little, Brown, 1937), 22 ff.
41. Interview with Dorothy DeLay, Aspen, Colo., 28–29 July 1998.
42. See 'The Soviet Chess Machine: Another Empire Crumbles', *The Economist* (21 Dec. 1991).
43. See Juri Jelagin, *The Taming of the Arts* (New York: Dutton, 1951), 187–90.
44. Henri Temianka, *Facing the Music*, (New York: McKay, 1973), 28.
45. Henry Roth, *Violin Virtuosos from Paganini to the Twenty-First Century* (Los Angeles, Calif.: California Classics, 1997), 142.
46. According to Ida Haendel, *Woman with Violin* (London: Gollancz, 1970), 11, the author was born in 1928. According to *The New Groves Dictionary of Music and Musicians* (London: Macmillan, 1980), viii. 20, she was born in 1924.
47. Jelagin, *Taming*, 226.
48. Dubinsky, *Stormy Applause*, 3.
49. Temianka, *Facing the Music*, 30.
50. Jelagin, *Taming*, 217.
51. Mstislav Rostropovich and Galina Vishnevskaya, *Russia, Music and Liberty* (Portland, Oreg.: Amadeus Press, 1983), 114 ff.
52. Robinson, *Last Impresario*, 346
53. Milstein, *From Russia*, 210 ff.
54. Dubinsky, *Stormy Applause*, 262–6.
55. Rostropovich, and Vishnevskaya, *Russia*, 21.
56. Dubinsky, *Stormy Applause*, 28.
57. Ibid. 291.
58. See David Rounds, 'Quartet Tradition, Russian-Style,' *The Strad* (June 1995).
59. Serge Schmemann, 'Edgy Strangers Happily Resist the Melting Pot' *New York Times*, (6 April 1998).
60. Interview with the author, Lübeck, 11 Aug. 1997.
61. Olivier Bellamy, 'Zakhar Bron, le mâitre de violon,' *Le Monde de la Musique* (June 1999). Cf. David Schoenbaum, 'Gegen den Strom,' *Frankfurter Allgemeine Zeitung* (17 October 1997).

# INDEX

*Index*